Fact & Fiction

READINGS IN AUSTRALIAN LITERATURE

Fact & Fiction

READINGS IN AUSTRALIAN LITERATURE

EDITED BY

AMIT SARWAL

REEMA SARWAL

AUTHORSPRESS

Worldwide Circulation through Authorspress Global Network
First Published in 2008
by
Authorspress
E-35/103, Jawahar Park
Laxmi Nagar, Delhi-110 092
e-mail: authorspress@yahoo.com

Fact & Fiction: Readings in Australian Literature
ISBN 978-81-7273-433-6
Total Pages: 423
Price: Rs 950/-
US$ 38

Book Design and Typeset: Amit Sarwal
Cover Design: Reema Sarwal & Amit Sarwal

Printed in India at Virgo Press, Delhi.

to
both our parents . . .
for
supporting us in every decision
and for their
unconditional love

Acknowledgements

We would like to acknowledge the support, valuable contribution and patience of our contributors in this endeavour.

We would also like to thank the Endeavour Asia Programme, Department of Education, Science and Training, Australian Government which enabled us to visit Monash University, Australia, where this project was born.

Special thanks are also due to Prof. Richard Nile, Dr. Nicholas Birns, Dr. Richard Hosking, Prof. Rae Frances, Prof. Peter Snow, Dr. Andrew Hassam, Dr. Peter Murphy, Dr. Tseen Khoo, Prof. J. V. D'Cruz, Prof. David Walker and Dr. Chandani Lokugé for their kind support, suggestions and interest in our work.

Personally, a very special thanks to Russell, Jenny, Sean, Cecilia, Peter, Clare, Rebecca, Sonia, Kama, Michael, Clo, Suboohi, Ehsan, Darius, Laila, Rakesh, Tupur and Deepa who made us feel at home in Australia.

Preface Comprehension Without Closure
Australian Studies for the Twenty-First Century?

Nicholas Birns

In late 1994, when I became Book Review Editor of *Antipodes*, I wrote to Professor Subhas Chandra Saha, a leading Indian expert on Australian literature, then, teaching at the University of Manipur, India. (Saha has since moved on to a series of evermore prominent administrative positions in Indian universities.) In writing to Saha, I concluded with a rather hortatory final sentence in which I hailed the incipient cooperation of the literary cultures of three great multicultural nations—Australia, India, and the United States heralded by the cultural cross-fertilization implied in his envisioned contribution to *Antipodes*. The point is that it was possible to say this in the 1990s. Today, the war on terror and its side effects have made the world situation so parlous as to preclude this euphoria.

Amit and Reema Sarwal's collection, *Fact & Fiction: Readings in Australian Literature*, reveals Australian literature unbound by many of its constraining truisms. Marilyne Brun's essay on Brian Castro (b. 1950), for example, jettisons the scheme of the immigrant writer intent on entering the mainstream of the new national literature by showing how Castro's writing explodes congealed notions of identity and centrality around which this formula revolves.

India-based critics have an unusual predominance, giving the volume a unique emphasis, but the range of scholars represented is international, including some of the most active and prominent emerging scholars in the field. Many of the names have crossed my desk as editor of Antipodes, and two, Jonathan Highfield and Jean-Francois Vernay have originally published their contributions to the anthology in *Antipodes*.

Often, the Indian scholars assay themes long-practiced by critics of other nationalities, but with which they necessarily have more familiarity, such as Krishna Barua's essay on the "mandala" as symbol in Patrick White (b. 1912 – d. 1990). Barua makes an intriguing link between the symbolic complementarity of flesh and spirit in White's more metaphysical mid-period novels and the bodily complementarity felt by the transgendered protagonist of *The Twyborn Affair* (1979). White is concerned with embodiment in an explicitly sexual way in his later work, and Barua threads together the queer and the visionary in a fashion, intriguingly, also achieved by Aneeta Rajendran in her essay on lesbian themes in Elizabeth Jolley (b. 1923 – d. 2007). Barua's concerns, though reach beyond the erotic to the ontological, as she argues that the fragmented protagonists of *The Vivisector* (1970) and *A Fringe of Leaves* (1976) testify to a kind of mandalic integration of which their psychic disjecta membra are the potential components.

It is good to see the oeuvre of Vijay Mishra (b. 1945) receive such sustained treatment by Gunjeet Aurora, and (considering how importunate the 1987 and 2000 coups in Fiji have been in the history of the contemporary South Pacific) it would be equally gratifying to see writers of the Indo-Fijian diaspora such as Sudesh Mishra (b. 1962) and Brij V. Lal, as well as writers who have come directly from India such as Subhash Jaireth, receive equivalent treatment in another venue. Reema Sarwal's treatment of the prominent Indo-Fijian author Satendra Nandan (b. 1939) is a good start, and the volume also features a discussion of a prominent Sri Lanka diaspora writer, Yasmine Gooneratne (b. 1935).

J. V. D'Cruz and William Steele focus on the far too neglected David Martin (b. 1915 – d. 1997), showing how this Central European Jewish emigre not only excelled in both adult's and children's fiction but also was one of the first to seriously explore Asian themes in Australian writing and, in general, to be, as an Australian writer, both international and political. Martin won the Patrick White award in 1991; he is just one of the writers whose aesthetic and moral integrity is under recognized by the marketplace. What it meant for D'Cruz and Steele, though, do more than reintroduce us to Martin; they hypothesize a model of "additive exile" where exile becomes a condition of curiosity and not just plaintive lament.

Salhia Ben-Messahel gives a rare exegesis of the Aboriginal crime writer Philip McLaren (b. 1943), showing how genre fiction can examine society from an oblique and subversive perspective. Isabelle Benigno traces the exploration of motifs of indigeneity and landscape from white writers such as Eleanor Dark (b. 1901 – d. 1985) to Aboriginal writers such as Kim Scott (b. 1957). Reema Sarwal also concludes with Scott after considering the work of Jessica Anderson (b. 1916). The positioning of white writers as paratextual adjutant to Aboriginal production, rather than either preemptive heralds or appropriating free-selectors, is an intriguing motif of both Benigno's and Sarwal's treatments. Similarly, Lisa Slater traces Stephen Muecke's (b. 1951) affirmative journeys through indigenous landscape, which promise comprehension without closure, understanding without appropriation.

Categories of genre and landscape can also acquire paratextual connotations, as, in the first instance, Carol Hetherington and Toni Johnson-Woods (frequent *Antipodes* contributors) show in their essays on Arthur Upfield (b. 1890 – d. 1964) and Kerry Greenwood (b. 1954), and, in the second instance, Malathy Anandavalli in her discussion of Tim Winton's (b. 1960) Western Australia as textual space.

Patrick West's piece on Gerald Murnane (b. 1939) follows in the especially philosophical vein of criticism on that multifarious and endlessly rewarding author, David Malouf (b. 1934), previously pioneered by Imre Salusinszky, H. W. Fawkner, and Paolo Bartoloni. But West not only adds a specific Spinozan (and, in our era, therefore apodictically Deleuzian) torque to the analysis, but makes a heuristic distinction between Malouf's deployments of a self-other distinction that ultimately derives from romantic binaries versus Murnane's examination of sheer life, what Fawkner would call "affectivity," that at once is more free and more fundamentally mysterious then a mere differentiation between self and nature. West is also a creative writer, and the skillfulness of his prose assists him in threading the reader through the difficult and abstract "plains" of Murnane's trackless tableau.

I have always felt that, as a writer, Murnane has something in common with Christopher Brennan (b. 1870 – d. 1932)—the Irish background, the sense of impalpable mysticism, the trope of the absent woman, the idiosyncratic and deep learning—and Philip Ellis's essay on Brennan's criticism shows us how it operates, much as do Murnane's essays, as both good expository writing in its own right and as an invaluable *vade mecum* to the creative oeuvre.

It is, indeed, important not to promote the novel to an overly hegemonic position in Australian literature. Australian poetry and drama are generally underrated outside Australia, as is nonfiction prose, autobiographical writing, and prose history. The latter is given scope in this book through Stephen Gaunson's article on Ned Kelly's letters and Mark McKenna's deservedly eulogistic tribute to the idealistic large-mindedness of Manning Clark (b. 1915 – d. 1991). Criticism on Australian literature also needs to become less Anglocentric in terms of ethnicity. Igor Maver's essay on the Slovene migrant Jo e ohar (b. 1945) is a good companion to the treatment of David Martin elsewhere in the volume, but much more work on migrant literature, by both Europeans and Asians, is needed, especially in likening this body of work to larger Australia and world literary-historical patterns. There are also many novelists writing today, such as Rodney Hall (b. 1935), David Ireland (b. 1927), Michael Meehan (b. 1948), and Brenda Walker (b. 1957), whose works would repay close examination. Even more, the generation of writers below forty-five such as Delia Falconer (b. 1966), James Bradley (b. 1967), Elliot Perlman (b. 1964), Tim Richards (b. 1960), Vivienne Cleven (b. 1968), and Samuel Wagan Watson (b. 1972) would repay treatment in sustained discursive critical modes that would accord more scrupulous and meditative coverage than their usual place of reception—the weekend-supplement book review—is capable of performing. These writers have, at a still relatively early stage in their careers, produced remarkable work, and it is the academic critic, not the literary journalism, who is really capable of responding to it in an meaningfully interpretive way. In other temporal direction, nineteenth-century writers such as Marcus Clarke, Henry Kendall (b. 1839 – d. 1882), and Catherine Martin (b. 1848 – d. 1937) still have not been acknowledged as full stakeholders in what the French critic Pascale Casanova has called "the world republic of letters."

Analysis of Australian literature, also should take explicitly political associations more into account. This is especially true of criticism written by scholars based outside Australia, who, in the past, have tended to emphasize rather apolitical formalist approaches. Some of this was not just a result of methodological preferences, but because of the inadequate coverage of Australia in global journalism and the slow pace by which news traveled abroad made extramural analysts unusually dependent solely on the books in their hands and unable to reap any of the benefits of understanding the cultural context of the books. Now that we have the Internet, it can function as a giant paratext, embedding and ramifying the meanings available to us in the works themselves. This is especially true now when political reverberations are felt throughout so much of Australian literature.

These political reverberations can be seen in Sharyn Pearce's commanding overview of recent Australian children's literature also leaves us with the disquieting im pression that the end that the events of 2001 may have upended our critical categories more than even most radical cultural analysts supposed. The events of 2001 also find their way into Bev Curan's particularly perceptive and intelligent essay on fear of foreign languages in David Malouf. *Remembering Babylon*, notes Curan, appeared in 1993, the year of the first attack on the World Trade Center. Much like Barua, Curan links what might seem mystical aspects of Malouf's vision "his em phasis on bird and animal speech, his search for a basically pantheistic planetary tongue" to the more material political issues of Australian monolingualism and the paranoia about migrants and indigenous people it induces.

Neoconservatives in the US often like to boast of Australia as a com ponent of "the Anglosphere." Curan's essay shows that Australia's membershi p on this sphere is neither entirely natural or entirely without repression of envisaged and feared others. India has also been claimed as part of the Anglosphere, and various establishmentarian figures in the US have gloated that English-speaking Indians working in call enters for US corporations will guarantee the future hegemony of Anglo-American capitalism on the planet. Euphoria, of whatever political stri pe, is not really a discerning posture with respect to culture, not because pessimism is wiser than optimism is not but because euphoria is so dependent on generalities and on extrapolating plausible trends that it misses the crucial nodes of detail around which texts and cultural meanings constellate. This anthology is well-placed to let us, with respect to this vista, perceive what America's greatest twentieth-century poet, Wallace Stevens, called "ghostlier demarcations, keener sounds."

Contents

Introduction
An Indian Ocean Outlook
Australian Studies in Australia and India

Richard Nile

Literary studies have been the mainstay of Australian Studies internationally. Among the earliest international literary programs, Anna Rutherford began teaching Australian Studies at the University of Aarhus in Denmark in 1968. Around the same time, Bernard Hickey founded programs in Venice which he continued from the late 1980s at the University of Lecce. Bruce Clunies-Ross introduced programs to the University of Copenhagen following his appointment there in 1971 and Richard Hosking taught the first course in Australian Literature at Jawaharlal Nehru University, New Delhi, to a handful of students from all over India in 1989. Australian Studies Centres and Chairs followed in Asia, Europe and North America.

In keeping with this trend, Indian interests in Australian Studies became especially strong in the literary field. Among the many influences, we can locate two princi pal sources. International interest in Australian literature flowed from Patrick White's Nobel Prize in the mid 1970s and some of the first work by Indian scholars of Australian Studies dates from this time. White still commands considerable respect and scholarly curiosity on the subcontinent. The second source of interest springs from a deepening intellectual concern for postcolonial studies and new literatures in English.

There are many reasons why literary studies continue to be among the most im portant international studies on Australia. Although creative in origin and imaginative in execution, literature has a very long tradition of representing peoples and places. This aspect dates back to antiquity and, through the oral traditions of story-telling, even further. Across several centuries, literature has been characterised by the primary sub-classification of nation. So much so that it is now commonplace among literary scholars and general readers alike to associate particular works with the nationalities of their authors—Shakespeare with England, Tolstoy with Russia, Kalidasa with India, and so on—and by this process for writers to be linked to their com patriots.

The process of grouping writers, like all processes of grouping, contains elements of contrivance and convenience, and there is a good deal of sli ppage in our use of contem porary critical uses of nation when applied to literature or any creative or cultural undertaking for that matter. For exam ple, the modern nation state of Britain is vastly different to the Elizabethan England of Shakespeare's time. The contem porary Indian republic is as remotely connected to the India of Kalidasa. Tolstoy's Russia, closer in time to our own, has seen at least two revolutions and many transformations since the time of Tzar when Tolsoy created his masterpieces.

In such com pany, Australian literature appears as something of a late starter. While the much imagined "great southern land" existed within the literary desires of Europeans, long before permanent European settlements were established, Indigenous Australians com posed their worlds through oral traditions, performance and symbolic paintings, among a com plex of other cultural and creative practices. Many of these practices had existed across tens of thousands of years. Most were displaced or destroyed by the coming of the Europeans. Some have been recuperated in more contem porary writing by Aboriginal Australians.

The development of an Australian literature, therefore, can be said to date from early European colonisation and, in the wake of the establishment of the first permanent European settlement of New South Wales in 1788, the arrival of successive waves of literate, primarily working class, immigrants, many of whom up to the 1850s were transported in chains. While the colonies of Australia recorded higher levels of literacy than Britain or Ireland—the two princi pal sources of migration—local publishing lagged well behind the ready-made abilities to read and write. The first convict shi ps carried printing presses but it was several years before the appropriate expertise and skills arrived on Australia's fatal shores to produce the first gazettes. And because Australia was founded as a prison, there was a high degree of government intervention in what was written, what was published and what was read.

More broadly and arguably more influentially, Australian literature would be composed within the English language. English was both colonial and the principal language of the majority of the settlers. Australia shares this linguistic feature in common with other settler societies, such as Canada, New Zealand, and the United States—though the primacy of English in the US is being challenged by the widespread use of Spanish into the twenty first century. While Spanish may yet displace English as *the* global language, English was, nonetheless, part of the cultural baggage of the early immigrant settlers and its arrival in Australia was part of the spread of the English language throughout the world. Today English is widely recognised as the world's global language. Australian English is seen as a development out of and variant of this international English.

The first writings on Australia emanated from three primary sources. One was the official—a meticulous record of the colonies and their relationships with Britain. As a place of new settlement, established under the direct auspices of the British government, the colonies of Australia generated a great deal of official writing, from convict indents, despatches and shipping records, to official orders and correspondence to and fro. The remaining two sources of writing tended to be curiosity driven. One fell within the growing discourse of scientific enlightenment as the experience of colonisation generated a great deal of curiosity-driven scientific research and social-scientific writing, from botany to history and anthropology. Into the third group we find more personally driven correspondence, sometimes containing elements of one and two above, but also including the first efforts at creative and imaginative writings, from diaries, memoirs and travelogues to more, genre-based, creative writing.

A primary readership for these three forms of writing was European and, in particular, British. However, literate exchanges between the settlers also became a part of everyday life. Governors sent edicts, officers received and gave their orders which were passed down the ranks, gaolers kept records of prisoners, sentences and stores, and official gazettes and newspapers sprang up. Scientific knowledge was similarly shared around, including important information on the seasons, climatic conditions, and soil types and, perhaps most frequently, settler impressions of the Indigenous peoples, and the new land's unusual flora and fauna. Personal letters were exchanged back and forth, stories and verse composed and read, and sketches were produced and performed. Out of these, more complex forms of creative writing developed as poetry, drama and fiction. Although there was unlikely to have been any proper consciousness of it at the time, Australia was coming into existence as a highly literate, well-read and creative community.

The settlers also shared among themselves the news they received from Home, from much anticipated letters from friends, family and loved ones, published newspapers, and creative and non-fiction writings in the form of magazines and increasingly books. Within such personal and formal cultural frames the peculiar experience of being a settler Australian began to take shape within and as literature. Accompanying these, a precious few Indigenous stories and observations of Indigenous creative practices were recorded and communicated. By the end of the nineteenth century the colonies of Australia constituted, per head of population, the largest global market for published writing in English. Australia was simultaneously the single largest export market for English-language books produced in Britain.

The term literature, when applied to formal studies, often refers to two primary aspects. In broad terms these are the creation and production of largely imaginative works and secondly the existence of such works in the material form of published items—such as plays, poetry, short fiction, and novels. A third aspect is often overlooked. The cultural historian, Raymond Williams, argued several decades ago now that the term literature derived from an early form of literacy, and that literature took its intitial bearings from the capacity to both read and write. Taking Williams as a start point, we might observe that the transformation from *literacy* to *literature* roughly coincided with the settlement and colonisation of Australia. The reading aspect of literature is often hinted at in literary studies—the reading position is after all the position of the literary critic–but only more recently has it become implicated in textual analysis and author studies which have been the primary undertakings of studies on literature.

Consequently, literary studies as Australian Studies have tended to emphasise both textual analysis and author studies as the central components of Australian literature. Two schools emerged in the twentieth century. The first viewed Australian literature as an offshoot of English literature. The second was more nationalist in orientation and spoke of the distinctiveness of the Australian experience in generating an equally distinctive Australian literature. The one looked back to Marcus Clark and charted a course through to Henry Handel Richardson in the first half of the twentieth century. The other began with *Bulletin* writers of the 1890s, in particular, Lawson, Furphy and Paterson, and charted a course through to Richardson's residentially Australian counterpart, Katharine Susannah Prichard.

These positions were politicised and reinforced during the cold war of the 1950s and 1960s so that the one highlighted aesthetics while the other spoke of nationalism. The one was consciously conservative. The other was intellectually radical. Australian literature was formally introduced into university studies in the 1960s and the different interpretations developed as arguments about canons. The first argued that Australian literature was a sub-branch of and therefore inferior to the greater achievements of English literature while the other proposed a national canon of Australian writers.

Patrick White upset the divide and complicated the arguments between the differing positions. White's Nobel Prize meant that he was unquestionably great according to the principles of the one. The problem was that he had also turned away from Europe to take up residence in Australia—to live his life as an Australian writer, unlike Richardson who died as an expatriate and, in White's own time, novelists like Martin Boyd and Christina Stead. White had the right resdiential credentials as far as the other was concerned, but he wrote in a manner that was contrary to the radical nationalist position. Patrick White's success as a world-class Australian author intensified textual analysis and author studies as the principle concerns of literary critics. Those particular aspects of literary criticism are amply present in this volume, with its focus on authors and literary themes. Yet it is also apparent that the subjectivity of the reading position is part of the equation, thus there are considerations of popular fictions, literary critics and historians.

Australian Studies began to take root within the Australian university system in the 1970s with the first programs established at the Curtin University and the University of Queensland. Its introduction coincided with an increasing intellectual interest in Australia as expressed through the disciplines—as Australian history, literature, politics, anthropology, sociology and so on. Interdisciplinary Australian Studies existed quite comfortably with these developments and with what became regrettably termed the nationalisation of the Australian curriculum, which meant, in actuality, the introduction of formerly absent Australian subject matter. The interdisciplinary nature of Australian Studies brought the field into conflict with the aspiring new field of Cultural Studies.

Cultural Studies began to appear on the academic radar around the same time as Australian Studies and while, within an Australian context, both took on similar subject matter, an intellectual skirmish ensued. Cultural Studies practitioners accused Australian Studies of being under theorised and overly nationalist in approach. Australian Studies retaliated by suggesting that in its deployment of particularly European-based and obfuscating cultural theory, Cultural Studies was foreign and imperialist. In all, it was a fairly unedifying affair. As it turned out, Cultural Studies significantly influenced the arts, humanities and social sciences across three decades to the end of the twentieth century. Across the same time frame, Australia became more and more the principal site of scholarly enquiry. In the process, the disciplines became increasingly interdisciplinary and increasingly concerned with Australian subjects.

Australian Studies takes a different bearing internationally. In place of the primacy of approach, which is the case in Australia, the subject area itself defines what is and is not Australian Studies. Non-Australian-based studies on Australia fit comfortably into the category of "Australian Studies," whether the approach is disciplinary, such as in literary studies, or interdisciplinary or, more recently, transdisciplinary, such as Cultural Studies.

While studies in Australian literature tend to predominate other disciplinary fields are also notable, particularly history. To the present volume, for instance, it may be noted that India and Australia, for example, share colonialism in common. This is manifest in many of the chapters. And by coincidence both countries share a common anniversary date. Australia celebrates Australia Day on 26 January which is also India's national day of independence. While the date is shared, there are vast differences in the commemoration of these national days on either side of the Indian Ocean. We might reasonably suppose that colonialism and nationalism, therefore, mean different things in their particular contexts. The study of history is concerned with just such comparisons, coincidences and differences.

In its contemporary manifestation, Australia is sometimes referred to a European settler society in the Asia-Pacific region. As ever, the concept of Asia is hopelessly amorphous and the Pacific comes perilously close to achieving a similar distinction. Asia accounts for something like two thirds of the world's population while the Pacific is the world's most substantial ocean and covers a third of the earth's surface.

In the land of the platypus and the echidna, Australians exhibit a liking for paradoxes while the island continent is more properly defined by three great oceans, not one. The Indian and the Pacific oceans sit west and east of the continent, with the mighty Southern Ocean channels both, across the roaring forties, to Antarctica. Yet the Indian Ocean seems to be strangely absent from Australian self perceptions. I make this observation as a West Australian, and as someone who grew up on Australia's Indian Ocean coast. Here the sun rises majestically out of the land—Australian deserts—and sets with equal grandeur into the water. The sun also rises but earlier on the east coast, two time zones away, from the ocean before burning out into the land. Observing its setting across the Indian Ocean, you look out westward to and imagine Africa and the subcontinent. Here east becomes west and west becomes east. You grow up with a significantly different geo-political bearing on the 'left coast' of Australia.

The geographical and cultural significance of the Indian Ocean rim is suggestive of other connections. On the Australian side, studies in Indian history, politics and cultures have been major academic preoccupations since the 1970s. Indeed, it might reasonably be argued that Australian academic work on Indian successfully challenged more Euro-centric but in particular British-centric influences in the social sciences and only to a lesser extent the arts and the humanities. Studies in Indian history were especially notable from the 1970s from which time onward foreign relations, politics, religion and sociology also trended towards an Indian subject matter. Early intellectual contacts, via Indian history, in particular, helped pave the way for Australian Studies in India. Today, Indian Studies on Australia cover a wide range of disciplines and approaches.

However, the pre-eminence of literary studies remains. In part, this comes from the profound Indian respect for scholarship in the creative fields and a strong impulse towards better understanding the relationships between creativity and lived experiences. Australian literary studies quite literally offer a window onto the life and characteristics of the Australians. As a consequence, the Indian focus on Australian Studies has already begun to produce some of the most important scholarship in Australian literature.

For these reasons, among many others, this present volume is most welcome. The ensemble of scholars brought together and skilfully choreographed by the editors showcase advanced scholarship on Australia with two primary intentions. The first is to cluster and promote leading scholarship on Australia by Indian and Australian scholars. The second important intention is to reach out to new generations of scholars in preparation for their studies on Australia.

These twin objectives are achieved and in the process we learn new things about Australia from both Indian and Australian perspectives. Personally, I am delighted to see this particular axis of interpretation develop, and not simply on account of my Indian Ocean outlook. Intellectually, the compass swings differently when the Australian orientation is Indian, more so than the longer established patterns of intellectual exchanges and cultural flows with Europe which are also critically important. Equally so, through shared but different experiences of colonialism, including the English language and English literatures, scholarship on new literatures in English such as Australian and Indian are enriched and significantly enhanced. The current interventions and exposes on Australia provide a reorientation for readers of English language literatures everywhere. In the process, the volume reinstates the importance of studies on literatures through deep scholarly enquiry.

J. V. D'Cruz
William Steele

Additive Exile in David Martin

The Necessary Other that Makes for Place and Home[1]

Exile of some ilk is becoming an increasingly ineluctable aspect of human experience. Even the dwindling minority who can reasonably remain in one physical location throughout life are likely to experience dislocation across time. Unfortunately, literary explorations of exile tend to present a truly unappetising picture of what awaits us: so for instance, exiles such as Judith in Blanche d'Alpuget's *Turtle Beach* (1981) show a blinkered disconnection from their new environments to go with their disjunction from home (for an extended discussion, see D'Cruz and Steele 2003). Such subtractive models of exile, however, need not and do not reflect the experiences of everyone. Exile can engender belonging rather than spell its loss, leading to multi ple homes rather than none at all and to a "foreigner's gift of em pathetic insight" (*Where a Man Belongs* 15) in stark distinction to the blindness and dismissiveness of subtractive exile. Over a long career culminating in over four decades of literary work in Australia, David Martin, himself an exile, consistently illustrated how such an additive exile may be lived.

Martin produced a body of writing which, leaving alone any other merits, is im pressive in its volume and diversity. It includes six major novels—*Tiger Bay* (1946), *The Stones of Bombay* (1950), *The Young Wife* (1962), *The Hero of Too* (1965), *The King Between* (1967), *Where a Man Belongs* (1969); short stories—*The Shoes Men Walk In* (1946) and *Foreigners* (1981); two autobiographical works, one for adults—*My Strange Friend* (1991)—and one for children—*Fox On My Door* (1987); several volumes of poetry for adults—*Battlefields and Girls* (1942), *From Life: Selected poems of David Martin* (1953), *The Poems of David Martin, 1938-1958* (1958), *The Idealist* (1968),

David Martin's Beechworth Book (1993); adolescents—*I Rhyme My Time* (1980) and children—*Spiegel the Cat* (1961) and *The Kitten Who Wouldn't Purr* (1987), and an anthology—*Eight by Eight* (1963); numerous children's novels—*Hughie* (1971), *Frank and Francesca* (1972), *The Chinese Boy* (1973), *Katie,* written with his wife, Richenda Martin (1974), *The Cabby's Daughter* (1974), *Mr. P. and His Remarkable Flight* (1975), *The Devilish Mystery of the Flying Mum* (1977), *The Man in the Red Turban* (1978), *The Mermaid Attack* (1978), *Peppino* (1983), *The Girl Who Didn't Know Kelly,* illustrated by his son, Jan Martin (1985), *Clowning Sim* (1988); shorter fiction—*Gary* (1972); verse—*Rob the Robber* (1954); plays—*The Shepherd and the Hunter* (1946), *Birth of a Miner* (unpublished, performed in 1949); travel pieces—*On the Road to Sydney* (1970); and psycho-social works on film—*Psychological Effects of the "Western" Film,* co-authored with F. E. Emery (1957) and television—*Television Tension Programmes* (1963). Following the author's death in 1997, this work is enduring something of a dip in popularity; much of his published work is not easy to locate, and a major, extended study of Martin's contribution to Australian literature and life is yet to be written. This may, in part, be because this contribution is characterised by such great diversity on the one hand and by a conspicuous lack of showiness on the other, making its particular overarching merits both harder to define and easier to overlook. We would like to suggest that this is a great pity. Knowledge, experience and an extraordinary openheartedness and empathy[2] combine consistently in Martin's work to point to ways in which all of us in our various experiences of exile can belong to each other and to the places where we find ourselves, whether in Australia or elsewhere. It is humane and constructive yet not hectoring, and it illustrates and respects difference while recognising and addressing the Australian difficulty of accommodating it.

Born in 1915 as Ludwig Detsinyi and arriving in Australia in 1949, Martin has described himself as "a Hungarian, a German, to some extent a Jew, and besides a number of other things, an Australian" (*On the Road to Sydney* 1). This is a most emblematic formulation; nothing relevant is excluded nor subordinated to anything else, yet neither is everything blended into a mush. And, just as the Self cannot hive off parts of itself and maintain its health, so is the Self incomplete without the Other that makes it what it is and links it to where it is.

While a hybrid, fed by many strands in his own rich experiences, David Martin's reality, in the terminology of Estava and Prakash (2004), "is necessarily experienced from [his] own horizon of intelligibility" (11). More specifically, we might see Martin, in Sudesh Mishra's (2005) terminology, as a "classical exile" acutely "able to differentiate between the states of banishment and belonging," not a "modern exile [. . .] deprived of such certitudes" (100). He does not, vapidly or imperialistically, imply any claim to be equally at home everywhere. What he does do, though, is recognise that every place is someone's home and that self and other, human and animal, figure and landscape all cohere to build it.

Not long after his arrival in Australia, in 1950, Martin was already exploring such themes in *The Stones of Bombay* (1950). This is the story of Babu Rao and his son Shankar, refugees from Karachi arriving in Bombay following partition. (1950, by the way, is a very early date for an Australian novel about South Asia, the existence of which has largely gone unnoticed in this country, until recently a significant blind spot in Australia's foreign relations.) The novel is, more or less, an account of their new landscape opening up for Shankar and his father through those with whom they interact. Initially, they are confined to the harbour area, a restriction enforced both literally and symbolically by a policeman who confiscates Shankar's shoes while "gripping his lathi [truncheon] and dealing the air a playful blow" (*The Stones of Bombay* 17). But this act provokes neither from the narrator nor from Shankar the kind of response we tend to get from Western commentators: outraged condemnation of Asian police states and/ or corrupt bureaucracies compared with the liberal and transparent efficiency of, say, an Australian government department.[3] Shankar's father merely reminds his son that he can get other sandals. And, later on, the shoes are furtively returned by the policeman, who has discovered they are the incorrect size: "What big feet you have, you fellows!" (*The Stones of Bombay* 39).

Both the lack of condemnation and the lack of comparison are important in the recounting of this apparently trivial incident. Implicit in the former is a recognition on the part of both parties that the other has its place. As Ashis Nandy (2002) has demonstrated in work on intercommunal relations in Cochin (or Kochi, Kerala, India) and elsewhere, for different communities to coexist harmoniously it is not necessary for them to love each other, no more than it is necessary (or even desirable) for footballers to love the opposing team. However, just as without the opposing team there can be no football, so Ashis Nandy shows that without its diverse communities the story of Cochin cannot be told and neither can its map be drawn. The communities need each other for Cochin to fall into place (157-209). Likewise, in Martin's Bombay, policemen and refugees accept each other as part of the landscape and the story; they do not seek to airbrush the other out. As we shall see, Martin recommends a similar inclusivity in Australia.

It is probably trite to observe that an exile's sense of loss is compounded by a certain habitual comparison. Sydneysiders can hardly find themselves marooned in Melbourne without noticing that the Yarra is no Sydney Harbour. Such comparisons not only confront the exile with a constant vision of loss, they also exclude from the presence of a new landscape and people. As Martin Buber's work (1958) suggests, one can be in relation, or not, to a tree or to a person (and to God): either way, "Every *It* is bounded by others; *It* exists only through being bounded by others [. . .]. *Thou* has no bounds. When *Thou* is spoken, the speaker [. . .] takes his stand in relation" (4; see also, D'Cruz, 1979: 51-59). Without such an openness to relation, the way of "It" typically becomes the colonising response to exile, one which takes power over the Other by denying it singleness and particularity, assimilating it instead into a paradigm based on the Self's experience and thereby rendering the Other into both a mere resource and an abject failure. But this path, in the end, makes exile-victims of all parties, denying them those meetings beyond measure and comparison, those meetings which, according to Buber, assure you of your solidarity with the world.

Martin's travel sketch *The Road to Sydney* (1970) illustrates very directly both the subtractive misery of an exile beset by comparison and differentiation, and the additive fulfilment of entering into unmediated relation with the Other. Martin tells us that he hitchhiked from Melbourne to Sydney as a kind of psychotherapeutic self-investigation after an extended stay in Europe (latterly Asolo, Italy) in the late 1960s. Upon returning in January, he is depressed initially by "the dreary suburbs of Perth" and then finds himself in crisis as he passes through Port Pirie, which he describes as "certainly not another

Asolo, which is not its fault" (*The Road to Sydney* 1)—a characteristically generous Martin "limiter" even in his moments of comparison! However, a giant papier-mâché Father Christmas attached to the town silo proves too much to bear. He pleads to his wife "Richenda, I really can't take it any more. Let's go back to Europe, to Italy [. . .] anywhere! Do we have to go on living in a country where they tie Father Christmases to the roofs of silos?" (*The Road to Sydney* 1). Not atypically, his distress is caused by an aspect of the built environment, that is, on the interface between landscape and people. And this distress at the physical environment puts him out of relation to the people–Martin may be an Australian, but in this case the country is not named and, unusually for Martin, its people are "they," not "we." The difficulty and distress are elaborated on as Martin undertakes his journey. Early on, as he approaches Seymour, he describes Australian towns in general:

> Having mostly been founded within a few years of each other they all look much alike, save possibly to those who live in them. Their houses seem screwed into the soil rather than to have grown from it, and a good handyman could probably remove them without getting up a sweat. (*The Road to Sydney* 17)

What underlies this temporariness, the prefabricated air, the divorce from landscape? The recognition that those who live in the towns might see things differently hints that lack of relation could be the culprit. As Martin puts it later on (in Benalla):

> As we deny and preach against the cult of love, so our houses deny the background against which they rise [. . .]. The sense of harmony we lack is a lack of will, the will to know ourselves as denizens of the continent we occupy. Thus we have become more colonial than we were at the beginning, a curious historical phenomenon. (*The Road to Sydney* 43)

A denizen is not a coloniser—for that status the occupation to which Martin refers is sufficient. A denizen is one who belongs to the country and, interestingly, it is a term applicable to animals and plants as well as people. To want to belong in this sense, we have to want to enter into relation with our country, to allow it and its prior denizens to admit us into belonging. We need to eschew the power that comes from manipulatively ordering, comparing and excising—or stand forever outside in an exile of double loss. We have lost whatever homes we had and, without openness to relation, we lose all hope of being at home where we find ourselves now.

What is needed here in the exile, Martin suggests, is not a sharp and surgical eye, it is an open and clear vision. Openness implies no lack of particularity—indeed quite the reverse. It is the openness to appreciate the vision of the Other as a total and coherent thing, not bounded by our experience of it, and, for that, relation with the Other is necessary. This we can exemplify by Martin's resonating with the exact yet fresh landscape paintings of Lorna Chick which he sees in Benalla Art Gallery, particularly "Olinda Grove," with a shed bearing the name "Worringa Turkeys" in "uncompromisingly exact lettering" on its roof (*The Road to Sydney* 45). How easily, without relational vision, this could be ridiculed along the lines of the Father Christmas on the silo roof! However, instead, "This heartfelt concentration on minutiae becomes a total vision, a seeing of the reality which the sophisticated seer always and paradoxically misses" (*The Road to Sydney* 45). In this way, consistently, Martin relates with those who relate with the local—and always *peopled*—landscape. Approvingly, Martin notes: "[. . .] in some places the instinct for the local resists discouragement" (*The Road to Sydney* 45). The use of "heartfelt" (in Martin's reference to Miss Chick's painting) is not coincidental. It is in such humble relation that the exile can add a second home rather than subjugate a secondary one. Martin laments the absence of photos on old Chinese headstones in Australian cemeteries, as the photos he sees on the Italian graves say something to him (*The Road to Sydney* 53-54). It is striking (and also interestingly Buberian) that Martin wants the face to speak to him, not disembodied words. Not only does Martin relate to places through people, the very physical nature of his relating to people is not unakin to, in the best sense, treating them as landscapes.

Comparison and pre-knowledge may be in the end inevitable in some measure, yet they block relation. As Martin puts it in Violet Town, "This is my time to unlearn comparisons, because they hide the one truth that matters—Violet Town has a proud history" (*The Road to Sydney* 35-36). Or in Albury: "Verona is Verona and Albury is Albury" (*The Road to Sydney* 78). With the capacity to relate to one set of particulars, one can relate to another, but without "relating" each to the other—as then, paradoxically, one would step outside relation and start to compare and control. At this non-categorising and non-judgemental point, we enter the realm of the I-Thou mode of relating. Martin's *The King Between* (1966) is about "Lhaodia," which may fairly safely be equated with Laos (Lhaodia is a plausible Romanised rendition of the Chinese name for Laos), in the Cold War, where the US and China face each other off. But their respective ambassadors plus the US ambassador's wife refuse to accept the dictum that an ambassador is one who typically lies abroad for the good of his country and actually include the interests of the Lhaodian people to the chagrin of their respective intelligence and other state agencies, that is, against the wishes of their own governments, almost. They come to care for the people of the country they are supposed to "undermine." To pursue one's own interest is to the advantage of each separately, to work inclusively for Lhaodia is to serve a higher cause—or, as in Ashis Nandy's phrase, "the true antonyms are always the exclusive part versus the inclusive whole" (1983: 99).

One of Martin's fullest accounts of the inclusion and addition that could perhaps ennoble (or at least facilitate) exile, and the excisions that can cripple it, is to be found in his comic novel *The Hero of Too* (1965). Here we find a portrait of rural Australia in which all need the Other geographically, historically, socially and psychologically, yet none in the town of Tooramit ("Too") can accept that fact, possibly arising out of what Ashis Nandy has described as "Australia's ambivalence towards itself" (2003:3). It takes outsiders, somewhat adrift in Too, to catalyse the town into some recognition of its necessary relations. These outsiders, a young teacher from the city and the daughter of an English doctor, arrive in Tooramit in 1950, coinciding with its 75th anniversary celebrations.

For its wheat to thrive, Protestant Tooramit, on the plain, needs the water from its hated Other, Catholic Boobyalla in the Quandong mountains (leaving aside that each needs the other for footy). The social classes, locked in mutual contempt, need each other and turn out to be relations. These relationships are uncovered, among other things, by smashing the town's sacred yet narrow myth of the most salient episode in its story, the "Affair at the Bridge" in which a suitably dauntless Boobyallan bushranger, Dick Grogan, and his masked offsider come into an affray with the grandfather of the present shire President. But Grogan is not dauntless; he is retiring and harried, and an effeminate bisexual to boot. With characteristic generosity, Martin notes of the two parts of Grogan's sexuality that "it simply so happened that his heart was big enough to encom pass the two" (*The Hero of Too* 241). His masked offsider turns out to be the local Chinese herbalist, Lam, living on the margins of the town near the part-Aboriginal Snowy who, strikingly, has perfect hearing but is unable to speak. And it also turns out that the shire President's grand*mother*, Maggie Bollman, had a much more significant role in the Grogan episode than did his grandfather Sam.

1965 is a very early date for a book like *The Hero of Too.* Martin pinpointed exactly that Australia's story of its own past was predicated on exclusions. These key exclusions relate to ethnicity, class, religion and masculinism, and all of them are aired in Too. Truth, class and religion interlinked were perhaps fairly obvious dividers in the 1960s, but Martin's analysis (see also D'Cruz and Steele, 2003: 85) of these exclusions reads as if written much later:

> This [division of class, size and sect] was the foundation of the conflict [between Tooramit and Boobyalla], but there was more to it. The Walloons do not hate the Flemings because they are pious and speak Flemish, but because they are dirty and superstitious. The Flemings, again, hate the Walloons not because they speak French and have factories and coal mines but because they are superstitious, dirty and treacherous. By the same token, Boobyallians hate Tooramitians [. . .] chiefly because they are bad sports and foul fiends on the football field. Tooramitians [. . .] say that Boobies [. . .] are coarse brutes and savages whose chief idea of sport is breaking other people's bones. There is truth in both these charges [. . .]. (*The Hero of Too* 114)

As for the ethnic and masculinist exclusions in Australia, merely noticing their existence as problematic was unusual in the 1960s. Indeed, Martin's em pathetic accounts of female desire (Maggie Bollman) and growing up gay (Grogan) might be unusual at any time. And Martin didn't just *notice* ethnic exclusion—focussing on the Chinese and on Aborigines—concerns developed further in *The Chinese Boy* (1973) and *Hughie* (1971) respectively, as he zeroed in on the most salient ones in Australia. Writing back the Indian, such as in the novel *The Man in the Red Turban* (1978), or especially the Chinese into the Australian story is a recurrent concern of Martin and of his characters (such as Steve in *The Hero of Too*), for "they too helped to build Australia," as the "Afterword" to *The Chinese Boy* points out. And this writing back, as with all Martin's writing, is founded on learning from being in relation with his subjects: *The*

Chinese Boy is dedicated to "The Honourable Committee and Members of the See Yap Society, Melbourne, with Sincere Respect."

Martin is no apologist for Australia, whether in *The Hero of Too* or elsewhere. He depicts a society in which all components are marooned in their separate exiles, unable to see that the Other is a necessary part of the story if home and place are to be built. Even a beauty contest becomes an intolerable referendum between the classes as well as an exercise in comparing the inherently incomparable (and, as Martin might observe, that would apply to all people and places); the locals could not dream of the outcome preferred by a recently arrived Hungarian character, namely, that both contestants "could have worn the crown together, a dual monarchy and a genuinely Hungarian solution" (*The Hero of Too* 291). The implication in much of Martin's work is that "the foreigner's gift of empathetic insight" (15), noted by an Anglo-Australian character in *Where a Man Belongs* (1969), might draw attention to the need to include both, rather than to choose; it is a confident concrete fictional rendition of Ashis Nandy's general insight, noted earlier, that "the true antonyms are always the exclusive part versus the inclusive whole" (1983: 99) rather than one exclusive part versus the other.

Lam, on the town's margins, makes a threefold contribution to the local Tooramit/Boobyalla story: he is bushranger, herbalist and keeper of the joss who, in his will, generously bequeaths the joss house to the local community. But, although his herbalism is handy enough, his bushranging is unthinkable. And the selfsame local lawyer who, at his funeral, states that "We shall make your beautiful house a memorial to you and your brothers. Nothing will be changed, nothing shall be lost" (*The Hero of Too* 357), has ignored Lam in his lifetime and stolen the joss to impress his lady-friend as Lam lay dying. Australia, it appears, can accept the relic but not the person.

In *The Hero of Too*, as elsewhere in his work, Martin is concerned with the people who live "ahistorical lives," as Nandy (2003) puts it, typically those at the bottom of the social pile (shire presidents and the like, in *The Hero of Too* as elsewhere, tend to denigrate myth and rely on "objective" historical accounts). Martin is essentially smashing the Anglo-masculinist myth and creating a new one, one that clarifies the necessity of the Other even if that necessity can never be historically verified. No one will ever know that Lam was Grogan's masked comrade; the evidence has been destroyed. But the point is it must be *imagined*, just as bisexual bushrangers must be imagined. The additive spirit must come first; the inclusive history can then follow, should it be deemed to matter (for a discussion of the com peting paradigms of myth and history, see Nandy, 2003: 83-109).

This broad elevation of the mythic spirit[4] is to be found again, with enhancements, in *The Mermaid Attack* (1978), which depicts the near-drowning fantasy experience of a young Australian girl who joins the Waterworld, a commune of merfolk who name her Usra. Together, they help both whales injured by Russian harpoons and porpoises turned into tools of high-tech warfare by Americans who abuse their innate trustfulness and intelligence. It needs to be said that *The Mermaid Attack* is no literary monument, but a melodramatic and sometimes rather trite children's novel written at a time by which its author was increasingly turning to non-fiction. Its im portance, rather, rests in its clarification of the relational spirit infusing all of David Martin's work. Typically for him, the commune are a diverse lot; as the Egyptian mermaid Rhodis explains to Usra, "we always like to be at least four, I mean from four different countries and four different times" (*The Mermaid Attack* 7). The other two members are merboys from Italy and Japan respectively, and they are aided by the "ageless and immortal" Frenchman Captain Nemo, a "Perpetual Honorary Citizen" of the Waterworld (*The Mermaid Attack* 21-22). This assortment, however, does not betoken any vapid universalism in which the world is strained of local particulars and all becomes one. On the contrary, the characters retain and love their original homes; as the Japanese merboy Tamotsu tells Usra, he lived "in a village of the Inland Sea [. . .] one of the most beautiful spots on earth" (*The Mermaid Attack* 47), as one's home so often is. Similarly, though the eponymous *Man in the Red Turban* is happy in Australia, he returns in the end to his home in India. This does not make him a failed migrant, but merely betokens that his ties to his home in India are retained unbroken, notwithstanding his success in making a home in Australia.

If there is in David Martin's work relatively little of that sense of loss which Nandy (2004) sees as marking out the Western modernist, the reason might be that, somewhat despite himself, Martin is neither particularly modernist nor particularly Western. As a "classical exile," he is more of what Nandy has termed a "critical traditionalist." His characters retain and cherish their origins, and that spirit is broadly approved, though without necessary approval of the traditions themselves—for example, practices varying from wife-beating among Greek Australians—*The Young Wife* (1962)—to rabbit-shooting among Anglo-Australians—*The Hero of Too*—are presented squarely and without any sense that they are hallowed by virtue of customary acceptance. As the scrolls alongside Lam's joss proclaim in *The Hero of Too* "all the red-hearted heroes must die, but even in heaven they shall think of home" (68). The trick for the exile is recognition that every place is someone's home, and thus among the most beautiful spots on earth. Perceiving that relationship, Martin and his exiles can resonate with it precisely because they have not abandoned their homes; and, once we feel our place of exile to be a home, then we can count and know ourselves among its denizens, human and otherwise. This outlook is not Pollyanna-ish; Martin does not shirk from making it clear that a welcoming host makes it easier for the newcomer to feel at home than does a begrudging, resentful or downright hostile one.[5] However, it remains in the exile's power to perceive a place as a home, even if one in which she or he is not presently welcomed. Overwhelmingly, his work promotes and reflects the possibility of solving intercultural problems through each party perceiving and respecting the other's rootedness in their home. As Nandy (2004) points out, "there has to be some degree of robust optimism—and an engagement with the future that transcends history but shuns millennialism—to power the grassroots theories of critical traditionalism today" (7-8).

The Mermaid Attack, with its focus on partnership with and assistance to animals, does not delineate strictly between humanity and its other tenants-in-common of this world. Rather, the position taken is that, as Captain Nemo puts it, "everybdy must eat [. . .]. [b]ut [. . .] all who live owe a debt to all that lives and wants to live!" (*The Mermaid Attack* 25) Or, when Rhodis puts "something" in Usra's hand, Martin stresses "But it was no object [. . .]. It was a baby turtle" (*The Mermaid Attack* 29). This outlook is not well accommodated by modern democratic thought; the "one vote, one value" concept is not extended readily to animal (or child) suffrage. On the contrary, it echoes traditional, now often submerged, relational patterns in which, for instance, small farmers might kill their animals in the end, but they will also know them by name. Interestingly, given Martin's Indian experience, these patterns are not just generally traditional, but have some specifically Indian overtones. In a recent novel *Light of Lights* (2003), Lata Pimplaskar, a US writer of Indian origin, describes the vicissitudes of the love between a Christian missionary (Tony) and a young Hindu in India. Tony approaches his Indian supervising priest, Father Paul, for advice, and begins by asking if he is disturbing him. Father Paul replies:

> "You westerners are very mannerly. By now you know we people just drop in on you. You see, we live with all kinds of disturbances. Besides people, everyone else drops in on us, flies, goats, cows." (*Light of Lights* 134)

Just as Martin stresses that a turtle is "no object," so India's hierarchical social system, while it might differentiate endlessly between humans, can also see something not unakin to personhood in a fly. On the other hand, the very stress on human equality in the modern West, including the Australian state, can serve to exclude more comprehensively from consideration animals, plants, and rising generations, none of them voters. In addressing the sharpening environmental crisis facing the world and Australia in particular, we have much to learn from such a traditional, relational attitude to nature.

In *The Road to Sydney* (1970), Martin visits a property called "Landscape" (14). "Apt name, but strange," he muses. Unbounded space alienates David Martin (*The Road to Sydney* 358). Here Steve reflects on the Chinese that "Someone was needed to tell their story. It should not be left to the rain and the rocks" (*The Road to Sydney* 358). Yet landscape, bounded and peopled, need not be strange if we belong to each other and to it. Working-class Lacy makes love to upper-crust George in an abandoned, half-open timber-cutter's shelter with grass inside, a bark-slab roof and a felled trunk near the entrance. "She knew this place, she had been there before. Her mind, emptied of thought, absorbed its peace" (*The Hero of Too* 188). Similarly, as a child, Grogan had sought refuge in a cave, and, "receiving the tormented boy, it had offered him hospitality against the rain and a friendship that demanded nothing [. . .] it was his cave that called him back" (*The Hero of Too* 273). This is a landscape in which people are in relation with nature, not in observation of it.

Can Australia's more established exiles accept the gift of belonging to each other, and to the landscape, which the more recently arrived and the land itself point towards? The question is left open, but the direction is clearly indicated. A certain kind of relationship between people, both individually and in groups, is crucial to this; and a not dissimilar relationship needs to pertain between people and other creatures. Each needs to be so much a part of the other's life and identity that their absence would be bewildering and unthinkable. Such a "necessary Other" transmutes strange space into inhabited place, and builds home for both parties by making the experience of each an authentic and essential part of that place. The question is, then, why such relationships arise in some cases of exile but not others. Martin's work strongly suggests the importance of two humble habits: listening with preconceptions and mistrust suspended, and getting on with the business of living with others in all its manifestations of concreteness and abstraction. Typically, it will be the more concrete modes of relating that will be marginalised in a country such as Australia. (for a further discussion of notions of the concrete and the abstract, see D'Cruz and Steele, 2003: Chapter 4). At a time of national reductionism where negotiation increasingly consists of laying down the law to "outsiders within," these lessons of Martin's oeuvre are more pertinent than ever. David Martin's voice is not central to Australia's view of its own literary history,[6] nor does it emerge from an Anglo-Australian psyche (for an earlier assessment of Martin by the present authors, see D'Cruz and Steele 2004), yet this *is* a quintessential Australian voice, ie, a voice we might all wish to describe as the Australian of our imagination, warm, open and welcoming, but it is one that only reaches us from the many peripheries of life in modern Australia.

Endnotes

[1] This essay was originally published in *Landscapes of Exile*, ed., Anna Haebich and Baden Offord (London: Peter Lang, 2007).

[2] This openheartedness manifests itself, among other things, in a conspicuous lack of irony in the author's style. Irony comes in many guises, but all could

probably be said to be characterised by a certain authorial disengagement and distance from characters and/or narratives, and often by a rather evasive and underhand poking of fun. Martin does not go in for this, though humour is abundantly present in his work.

[3] This was all, it seems, remarkably similar to Martin's first visit to India, by ship, through Bombay—landing the day after Mahatma Gandhi had been assassinated, the city was under hartal (cessation of work as an expression of protest) at the time, and he was only able to move through customs by the favour of the port medical officer and via the offices of a policeman leaning on his lathi (truncheon) (*My Strange Friend* 193).

[4] Martin's reach for myths to explain important aspects of one's environment is not a mode of thinking and writing common in Australia, outside of our Indigenous or the more concrete or more "ahistorical" of its peoples. Similarly, rare accounts of bohemian life in Australia (Kirkpatrick 1992), or of syncretic spiritualism (Roe 1986), or of the occult (Drury and Tillett 1982; Richmond 2004), are muted expressions of "aberrant" thinking that attempt to make sense of oneself and one's environment i.e. knowledge not sanctioned by rationalistic elites serving cultural majorities, and are little if at all reflected in general accounts of Australian life and history. For instance, despite what Hilary Carey (2003) refers to as Alfred Deakin's (the Australian Prime Minister in 1903) "preoccupation with spiritualism, Swedenborgianism and eastern religions as representative of those Victorian thinkers who sought out alternatives to both conventional denominational Christianity and the Darwinian materialism" (75), David Walker (1999) noted that historian J. A. La Nauze's (1965) influential two-volume biography of Deakin "clearly considered Deakin's religious interests and his fascination with India subjects best passed over as briskly as possible" (20-21). Fortunately for Deakin and for us, Al Gabay's (1992) account has authoritatively restored the religious component to the Deakin narrative, though such findings have yet to find its line and shade meaningfully integrated in the mosaic of lived experiences that makes up a more complete Australian portrait.

[5] See, for instance, the stories in *Foreigners* (1981), particularly "Jesus in the Market" (44-52), in which the grandmother of a young boy of Spanish heritage (Alváro Jesus Piñeiro) is humiliated in a Camberwell supermarket. As she "reached over to finger the sausages [. . .] and picked up a little barrel of pickled onions [. . .]," the store supervisor admonished him: "will you please tell her not to handle these articles [. . .]. Because of hygiene." "He was not in a forbearing mood. He followed them to the cold meat section [. . .]" asking her slowly and loudly, "Would you like any of this?" Flustered, she nodded. The supervisor "himself jotted the price on the package and disdainfully dropped it into her bag" (49-50).

[6] While Martin is particularly out of favour currently, he was even in his heyday of fame still seen as a marginal figure—im portant, sometimes crucial even, but not *central.* It would seem that nothing non-Anglo could possibly be seen as central. The last line about the author on the dust cover of the first edition of *The Hero of Too* (1965) states that "his work is as well regarded in Britain as in Australia—though one of the latter's [unnamed] best critics describes him as 'the most im probable Australian writer who ever existed.' "

Works Cited

Buber, Martin. *I and Thou.* Trans. R. G. Smith. 2nd ed. New York: Charles Scribner's Sons, 1958.

Carey, Hilary M. "Australian Religious Culture from Federation to the New Pluralism." *Legacies of White Australia: Race, Culture and Nation.* Ed. Laksiri Jayasuriya, David Walker, and Jan Gothard. Crawley, WA: U of Western Australia P, 2003.

d'Alpuget, Blanche. *Turtle Beach.* Ringwood, Victoria: Penguin, 1981.

D'Cruz, J. V. "Martin Buber: Education in the Renewal of Culture." *Perceptions of Excellence: Studies in Educational Theory.* Ed. J. V. D'Cruz and Wilma Hannah. Melbourne: Polding, 1979. 49-73.

D'Cruz, J. V., and William Steele. "Doing Cultural Pluralism in Australia, Against the Tide: An Interim Response to our Reviewers." *Cultural Ambivalence, Cultural Politics.* Ed. S. Perera. Spec. issue of *Borderlands e-journal* 3.3 (2004). <http://www.borderlandsejournal.adelaide.edu.au/vol3no3_2004/dcruzsteele_doing.htm>.

——. *Australia's Ambivalence Towards Asia: Politics, Neo/post-colonialism, and Fact/Fiction.* 2nd ed. Clayton, Victoria: Monash Asia Institute, Monash UP, 2003.

Drury, Neville, and Gregory Tillett. *Other Temples Other Gods: The Occult in Australia.* Lane Cove, NSW: Hodder & Stoughton, 1982.

Estava, Gustavo, and Madhu Suri Prakash. "A Dialogue with Ashis Nandy." Introduction. *Bonfire of Creeds: The Essential Ashis Nandy.* Ashis Nandy. New Delhi: Oxford UP, 2004. 1-16.

Gabay, Al. *The Mystic Life of Alfred Deakin.* Cambridge: Cambridge UP, 1992.

Haebich, Anna, and Baden Offord, eds. *Landscapes of Exile.* London: Peter Lang, 2007.

Kirkpatrick, Peter. *The Sea Coast of Bohemia: Literary Life in Sydney's Roaring Twenties.* St. Lucia: U of Queensland P, 1992.

La Nauze, J. A. *Alfred Deakin: A Biography.* Melbourne: Melbourne UP, 1965.

Martin, David. *David Martin's Beechworth Book.* Melbourne: David Lovell, 1993.

——. *My Strange Friend.* Chi ppendale, NSW: Pan Macmillan, 1991.

——. *Clowning Sim.* Melbourne: Collins Dove, 1988.

——. *The Kitten Who Wouldn't Purr.* Melbourne: Macmillan, 1987.

——. *Fox On My Door.* Melbourne: Collins Dove, 1987.

——. *The Girl Who Didn't Know Kelly.* Melbourne: Hutchinson, 1985.

——. *Peppino.* Melbourne: Hutchinson, 1983.

——. *Foreigners.* Adelaide: Rigby, 1981.

——. *I Rhyme My Time.* Brisbane: Jacaranda, 1980.

——. *The Mermaid Attack.* Melbourne: Outback, 1978.

——. *The Man in the Red Turban.* Melbourne: Hutchinson, 1978.

——. *The Devilish Mystery of the Flying Mum.* Melbourne: Thomas Nelson, 1977.

——. *Mister P and His Remarkable Flight.* Sydney: Hodder & Stoughton, 1975.

——. *The Cabby's Daughter.* Sydney: Hodder & Stoughton, 1974.

——. *The Chinese Boy.* Sydney: Hodder & Stoughton, 1973.

——. *Gary.* Melbourne: Cassell, 1972.

——. *Frank and Francesca.* Melbourne: Thomas Nelson, 1972.

——. *Hughie.* Melbourne: Macmillan, 1971.

——. *On the Road to Sydney.* Melbourne: Thomas Nelson, 1970.

——. *Where a Man Belongs.* Melbourne: Cassell, 1969.

——. *The Idealist.* Brisbane: Jacaranda, 1968.

——. *The King Between.* London: Cassell, 1966.

——. *The Hero of Too.* Melbourne: Cassell, 1965.

——. *Television Tension Programmes.* Melbourne: Australian Control Board, 1963.

——, ed. *Eight by Eight.* Brisbane: Jacaranda, 1963.

——. *The Young Wife.* London: Macmillan, 1962.

——. *Spiegel the Cat.* Melbourne: Cheshire, 1961.

——. *The Poems of David Martin, 1938-58.* Sydney: Edwards & Shaw, 1958.

——. *Rob the Robber.* Melbourne: J. Waters, 1954.

——. *From Life: Selected Poems of David Martin.* Sydney: Current Book Distributors, 1953.

——. *The Stones of Bombay.* London: Allan Wingate, 1950.

——. *The Shepherd and the Hunter.* London: Allan Wingate, 1946.

——. *The Shoes Men Walk In.* London: Pilot, 1946.

——. *Tiger Bay.* London: Martin & Reid, 1946.

——. *Battlfields and Girls.* Glasgow: William MacLellan, 1942.

Martin, David, and F. E. Emery. *Psychological Effects of the Western Film.* Melbourne: Department of Audiovisual Aids, Melbourne UP, 1957.

Martin, David, and Richenda Martin. *Katie.* Sydney: Hodder & Stoughton, 1974.

Mishra, Sudesh. "Exile." *The Future of Knowledge and Culture: A Dictionary for the 21st Century.* Ed. Vinay Lal and Ashis Nandy. New Delhi: Penguin-Viking, 2005. 100

Nandy, Ashis. "Modernity and the Sense of Loss." Draft paper. 25 May 2004. 25 November 2006 <http://www.fize.de/pdf/f.ize_sense_of_loss.pdf>.

——. "History's Forgotten Doubles." *The Romance of the State: And the Fate of Dissent in the Tropics.* Ed. Ashis Nandy. New Delhi: Oxford UP, 2003. 83-109.

——. "Time Travel to a Possible Self: Searching for the Alternative Cosmopolitanism of Cochin." *Time Warps: Silent and Invasive*

Pasts in Indian Politics and Religion. Ed. Ashis Nandy. London: Hurst & Co., 2002. 157-209.

——. *The Intimate Enemy: Loss and Recovery of Self Under Colonialism.* Delhi: Oxford UP, 1983.

Pimplaskar, Lata. *Light of Lights.* London: Athena, 2003.

Richmond, Keith. *Progradior and the Beast: Frank Bennett and Alister Crowley.* London: Neptune, 2004.

Roe, Jill. *Beyond Belief: Theosophy in Australia 1879-1939.* Kensington, NSW: New South Wales UP, 1986.

Walker, David. *Anxious Nation: Australia and the Rise of Asia 1850-1939.* St. Lucia: U of Queensland P, 1999.

Jean-Francois Vernay

FICTIONAL REALITY STRIKES BACK
C. J. KOCH'S NOVELS FROM FICTION TO FRICTION[1]

Call it a truism or not, it has repeatedly been acknowledged by scholars and writers that a set borderline between fiction and non-fiction can hardly be established, particularly since the eighteenth century when the novel started mimicking the real world. This blurred distinction, which has climaxed in the postmodern contention that history and fiction are interchangeable, is still a disruptive factor causing friction between fiction writers and the critics.

As Tasmanian-born novelist Christopher J. Koch (b. 1932) has recently released *The Many-Coloured Land* (2002), a non-fiction book on Ireland, it may be fruitful to assess the influence of reality in his fiction, as such interaction has often been the butt of his detractors. Christopher Koch's novels—may they be realist, *à clef* or historical—dangerously coexist with the real to such an extent that they spin the reader in search for identification into a web of illusions. In an attempt to separate the wheat from the chaff, I take a closer look at the aforementioned genres in Koch's corpus and clear up the misunderstandings, misconceptions, and confusion which launched heated debates and perhaps gave Koch a reputation of a "writer standing against the tide" (Marr 7).

If most of Koch's novels are steeped into realism, *The Boys in the Island* (1959) singles itself out as an exception. Even though most place names (St. Kilda Road, Little Collins Street, Brunswick, Port Phillip Bay, Melbourne, Fitzroy Street, Port Melbourne, or Bourke Street) in this first novel actually exist, it is convincingly unsubstantial evidence for the reader to sense realism which would be clearly at odds with the euphoric-dysphoric alternating moods pervading *The Boys in the Island* and Koch's stylistic turns regarded as the hallmark of his poetic style.

One of the foremost misconceptions about Koch's writings is their being pigeonholed as naturalist novels. Properly speaking, "naturalism"

> should be used to describe works of literature which use realistic methods and subjects to convey a philosophical form of naturalism, that is, a belief that everything is part of nature, and can be explained by natural and material causes—and not by supernatural, spiritual or paranormal causes. (Cuddon 416)

By principle, Koch cannot be taken as a follower of that literary school in so far as many of the naturalist tenets are at variance with his writing. By these tenets, I mean this inclination to use Manichean patterns in contradistinction to Koch's extensive use of interactive antonymic dualities, ambivalence, and syncretism; this depiction of mediocre characters and setting while Koch's are just ordinary so that his readership can easily project itself in the described situations; and this rejection of grandeur along with the people in the cast of main characters whereas Koch does not focus on masses but on individuals who yearn for grand ideals or dream of the impossible, even though they are doomed to failure. The hotchpotch of criteria jointly drawn from the realist and naturalist streaks may have contributed to the confusion in the novelist's mind torn between these two classical literary schools, as can be witnessed through a series of interviews from 1985 to 1995:

> I see it as an important function of the novel: to portray the society in which the novelist lives. I am a naturalist in my methods, but that doesn't mean I see the novel simply as explaining the nature of society. *I believe in naturalism as a method, not as an end.* (Interview, 1985: 25; my emphasis)

When Koch claims his subscription to naturalist writing ("I believe in naturalism as a method") all the while ruling out its function ("not as an end"), namely the philosophy of naturalism which stands for the clear-cut distinctions between both trends, are we not invited to read his words as a periphrastic definition of realism? A decade later he blurts out: "I don't like to depart from reality too much. I am not interested in naturalism" (Koch qtd. in Chenery 10). These words testify to Koch's rallying to the realist movement which he opposes to naturalism, a quite unusual counterpoise, since the literati has always more or less welded together realism and its historical offspring naturalism. However, in his following assertion (1995), we notice that these twin notions are closely associated in his mind since both his formulas—"I don't like to depart from reality too much" and "I'm not interested in stepping outside the bounds of naturalism" (Koch, Interview: 9)—are almost synonymous.[2] Are we to ascribe these offbeat ideological stances to Koch's theoretical confusion of literary schools (which I personally doubt) or to journalistic misprint/misunderstanding of Koch's words?

There is obviously a realist streak in Koch's corpus which runs through his last five novels, even though he refuses to admit it and dismisses most literary influences:

> I am not a realist, a naturalist, or any other kind of "ist" [. . .]. What I do is to write novels that are essentially in the mainstream tradition, and which try to depict life and the human spirit, in many aspects. However since the advent of "magical realism"—a mode I detest—*any* novel not written in that mode is called "realistic." This is because magical realism is simply upgraded surrealism—a method which in my view never produced anything of importance. Neither, in my opinion, has magical realism—simply because it fails to depict life or the spirit at any level that is truthful, or with which readers can engage. It's essentially trivial, and its fate will be the same as the artefacts of the other avant-garde movements of the 20th century: to die the death of minor art. As to Marxist realism—which is already dead—I detest it. It too distorts life and diminishes it: as all work does that's written to a prescription. I don't write to prescriptions. (Koch, Personal interview: 2002)

With good grounds to be suspicious about realism, the novelist alludes here to another myth which begs to be blown up. Undeniably, there is no such thing as the existence of a monolithic conception of realism from which derive other forms like naturalism, magical realism, surrealism, social realism, humdrum realism, to name a few. To do justice to each proponent, these trends must all be viewed individually. If Koch draws part of his inspiration from realism, he is by no means a social realist, not to mention a naturalist, a magical realist or anything else for that matter!

According to Koch, in *The Doubleman* (1985), the novel is an imperfect form, "a form that tries to push the whole of life into a box" (vii). Borrowing from *realis* (Latin for "real," from which derives the word coinage realism), the realist novelist is—to put it grossly—a top-flight journalist who collects information from life and his readings. Taking a keen interest in people, his works cover exhaustive routes: from anonymity to fame like Robert O'Brien's switch from clerk work to successful journalism—*Across the Sea Wall* (1965), from inexperience to experience as witnessed at the outcome of Guy Hamilton's journey through Asia—*The Year of Living Dangerously* (1978), from childhood to death as spanned by the hagiographic account of Mike Langford's life—*Highways to a War* (1995), and from failure to victory as exemplified by Robert Devereux who frees himself out of servitude—*Out of Ireland* (1999). Language, while mirroring reality, remains the privileged tool of that mimetic enterprise which lures the reader into some enticing realistic fallacy. Platonic *mimesis* is in fact a re-presentation, i.e. a new presentation of reality (implying transposition) shown in another context (viz., recontextualisation through transformation) thereby conjuring an imaginary construct, a fictional reality. Thus, during the writing process, authors have the choice between a reconstruction of reality (fleshing out from the actual world), the construction of their reality (elaborating on pure fancy), or a subtle admixture of these two as in Christopher Koch's novels.

Koch's "reality effects," to use Roland Barthes' terminology, authenticate the contents of the novelist's narratives. To fit the requirements of the realist tradition, the account must originate from the discovery of primary sources which, because they purport to belong to the reader's reality, give credence to the story. Naturally, the readers are told that they owe the existence of *Highways to a War* and *Out of Ireland* to the legacy Mike bequeathed to his long-life friend Raymond (*Highways to a War* 14, 58). In a similar way, editor Raymond Barton reveals in a mock-preface that Mike's diaries "lay hidden for one hundred and twenty-five years, on a hop farm in southern Tasmania" (*Out of Ireland* vii), not to mention the personal letters inserted in *Out of Ireland* which "came from the same period as the diaries" (*Highways to a War* 60), and were discovered in the secret drawer of an antique writing slope. The authentification is double since the reader is constantly reminded in *Out of Ireland* through an editor's note that the letters "survived [. . .] in the secret drawer of [Devereux's] writing slope" (*Out of Ireland* 48) which are now in Ray's possession (*Out of Ireland* 76, 274, 509). What is more, in an attempt to add verisimilitude to his fiction, Raymond accounts for the genuineness of his epilogue by "a wonderful find: a long and detailed letter by Robert Devereux, sent from California following his escape, and addressed to his fellow exile in Van Diemen's Land, Thomas O'Neill" (*Out of Ireland* ix-x). What could be taken as further evidence, Koch—like most realists who painstakingly collect information on their topics of interest—has gone as far as to quote his various sources in his traditional Author's Note (*Out of Ireland* 705) so as to validate the accuracy of his knowledge. Further devices root the reader in an artificial reality: some are visual such as the references to paratextual iconography (as in Koch's latest novel featuring geographical and topographical maps of former Tasmania; see *Out of Ireland* 702-703), while others are narrative like oral mimicry constructed through the use of reported speech (*Across the Sea Wall*, *The Year of Living Dangerously*, *Highways to a War*, and *Out of Ireland*), accent transcription, and different linguistic registers—as exemplified by John Langford's agrammatical speech which betrays his precarious education: "I know, Robert, it *don't* smell like roses" (*Out of Ireland* 375). In short, realism is not a slice of reality but a literary rendering of reality as the artist does not plagiarise the real but shapes it. Given that realism boils down to a matter of construction (using echo and analogy networks, precise chronologies along with historical and/or geographical framework, cultural foundations, *inter alia*), Christopher Koch's building methods fittingly suit the realists' whose overstructured novels challenge social disorder. C. J. Koch has made no mystery about his interest in architectonics: "[. . .] I like to think that writing a novel is like architecture. You have to structure well. You have to get the foundations right" (Interview, 1997: 133).

Characters, places and timelines all contribute to the realist streak in *Across the Sea Wall*, *The Year of Living Dangerously*, *Highways to a War*, and *Out of Ireland*. Many of Koch's characters—while remaining fictional—are borrowed from actual people whose names are either inserted in the novel (as in the case of Robert Devereux who takes his name and background from the author's great-great uncle) or altered (like Monsieur Lenoir in *Out of Ireland*, a pseudonym for Monsieur William Legrand, a nineteenth century Hobart bookshop owner). Paradoxically enough, in order to achieve a convincing lifelike and likely character such as Mike Langford, for the character to have the thickness of reality in fiction, Koch feels the need to merge two or three real human beings to create such an illusion:

> I would say that [Langford is] based very much on Neil as a personality and in [. . .] his myth. [. . .] [Langford's] life in the book is very much invented. That's why it takes such a long time to write a novel, if you're serious about invention. He's also based on Tim Page, one of the most daring photographers among the British in the Vietnam War, and a little bit on Errol Flynn's son, Sean Flynn, who was a combat photographer. (Interview, 1995: 8)

Similarly, central to Koch's minute poetic descriptions, the *topoï*—when not made up—are modelled on pre-existing places (the Wayang Bar in *The Year of Living Dangerously* is a faithful description of the Ramayana Bar within Hotel Indonesia, and the hop farm in *Highways to a War* is based on the one that was run by the author's uncle and cousins in the 1940-50s). Genuine place-names also partake from a reality effect which, beyond the addition of local colour, offers recognisable landmarks to the readers. As for timelines, all of Koch's novels—save *Across the Sea Wall* and *Highways to a War*, two analeptic accounts developing on a reminiscent mode—follow a linear plot mimicking the succession of events. While the matching of spatiotemporal bearings in the linguistic and extralinguistic fields can act as a safeguard for diffluent imaginations, it chiefly encourages the reader's projection in his world of fiction(s) by creating an emotional attachment, an effect which the *roman à clef* also achieves by conjuring the spitting image of real human beings. And we know how important the key concept of identification is for Koch:

> But when the rocks of reality and consistent personality are lost altogether, then why should we care, and why should we believe? We lose interest, we can't identify; it's a private game, a minor entertainment. (*Crossing the Gap* 163)

It is commonly accepted that authors are at ease with writing about their immediate experiences—may it stem from their familial, educational, or social background. Koch, who readily admits, "[. . .] I would never write about a place or any background that I didn't know, and I don't believe one can write well about things one doesn't know" (Interview, 1985: 18), is no exception. The *roman à clef* is a literary work in which actual people are presented under an alias. In Koch's first three novels, the mathematically-orientated reader will guess that Francis Cullen and Robert O'Brien are both born in 1932, like Koch himself, while Cook's surname is an anglicised version of its German counterpart Koch. More generally, all six novels could each be perceived as a *roman à clef*, in so far as Koch's characters traditionally take from his family, friends or relatives. The modelling of Shane Noonan (a figure which only appears in the 1974 version of *The Boys in the Islands*) on Anthony Wren—Koch's schoolmate who died an untimely death in the 1950s—launched the first controversy in Koch's literary career. This literary vampirisation on life sparked off friction between the novelist and the critics and obliged Koch to clear up the misunderstanding by means of what could be termed as a right of reply:

> Shane Noonan is of course not Tony Wren—however much he may have drawn life from him. A novelist has to keep pointing out that his characters are not exact portraits of real people. I am not in the business of writing autobiography or biography, and I have never drawn a character exactly from the life. Of course they are based on real people in some way—if they were not, they would be types, merely: bloodless cut-outs. But other, imaginary characteristics are added—and usually my characters are an amalgam of two or three people. A small example of the fictional character supplanting the real one: Father Campion remembers Tony Wren as having the sandy hair I gave Shane Noonan. In fact, he had striking red hair, inherited from his late mother, an Irish Davern. (Koch qtd. in Campion 41)

Interestingly enough, such a response revives the heated fact/fiction debate from which attempts made to draw a clear-cut borderline between fancy and reality in Koch's work. However, in 1980, Christopher Koch unfortunately overlooked one crucial aspect of the issue. In spite of two subsequent biographies told by homodiegetic narrators—Richard Miller's account of his youth and adulthood in *The Doubleman* and Robert Devereux's diary entries spanning three years of servitude in *Out of Ireland*—Koch, in this above-quoted excerpt, implicitly opposes fiction to (auto)biographies which he would probably classify as non-fiction ("I am not in the business of writing autobiography or biography"). Why should transcriptions of life fragments and life itself be amalgamated? If, as Xavier Pons (2001) wisely puts it, "All writers of fiction are necessarily ventriloquists, who put words into the mouths of imaginary characters, creating the illusion that their dummies are actual human beings" (61), the reciprocity of this formula is all the more apposite: *putting words into the mouths of imaginary characters, as ventriloquists would, logically turns authors into writers of fiction.* What is implied here is that no matter how much resemblance a character has to a human being, the latter can still be distinguished by speech. A literary representation of Tony Wren is not Tony Wren in so far as Christopher Koch could not have possibly given a faithful transcription of Tony's words. Thus, the literary representation of that young man singles him out, thanks to his *sui generis* speech content.

To add fuel to this fact/fiction debate, I must add it takes more that a few borrowed elements from life to fall into the pitfalls of unoriginality. Of course, stating that *Across the Sea Wall* is a work of pure fancy would fall short of mendacity. Any Koch reader familiar with the novelist's biography would recognise in James Baden the portrait of Robert Brian, a friend of Koch with whom he visited India in 1955 guided by a Sikh Mohindra Singh (renamed Sunder Singh in the novel). Such examples, which can be found at least by the hundreds in Australian literature, pale into insignificance when it comes to judging a novelist's craft; and yet they put into question the possibility, if not utopian dream, of *ex-nihilo* creation. The intrusion of the real into fiction (from the writer's viewpoint) or the eruption of fiction in the real (from the reader's viewpoint) naturally leads us to focus on the value of history within the story.

Christopher Koch is particularly fond of historical novels[3] which he sees as "true fictions," in other words: fictions with *realis* overtones. The lustre of historicity which enriches these narratives is not only due to the use of an essentially past tense which tips out the story in a historical perspective but also to the mentioning of reality-based events along with actual facts (as a token of truth, Koch often quotes his sources in an author's note while thanking the various specialists who contributed to the building of verisimilitude in his accounts) and to the staging of historical figures such as President Sukarno, combat-cameraman Neil Davis and political exile John Mitchel (respectively under the guise of mythic Michael Langford, and convict Robert Devereux) which, all in all, remain quite fictitious. The authors' notes of the historical diptych speak for themselves:

> The late Neil Davis, my fellow-Tasmanian and schoolmate at Hobart High, who covered combat for a decade in Indochina, and was killed covering a minor Thai coup in 1985, may be seen by those who knew him as the model for Mike Langford. In this they will be partly right—but only partly. Mike Langford's legend is similar to Davis's, and Mike carries the nickname that was once Neil's: "the Lucky One." But as is usually the case with characters in novels, Langford is a composite: *mostly invented*, and inspired as well by other war photographers [. . .]. And despite his Tasmanian origins, Langford's family background is *entirely different* from Davis's. So too are all his personal relationships, the crucial events of his life, and his eventual fate. All are essentially fictions. (*Highways to a War* ix; my emphasis)

> [Robert Devereux] was inspired in many ways by John Mitchel, and shares a good many of Mitchel's ideas and features of character. But his origins and background are *quite different.* He shares his name and ancestry with a great-great uncle of mine of the same period, an Anglo-Irish gentleman who never came to Van Diemen's Land, but emigrated instead to America, and of whom no more was heard. The events taking Devereux to Bermuda, and the facts of his circumstances there, are very similar to those experienced by Mitchel—but the people Devereux encounters on the "Medway" are *fictitious.* And once he reaches Van Diemen's Land, his circumstances and his fate become entirely different from Mitchel's. His character also changes, becoming somewhat different from that of the figure who was my starting-point. All the other characters in the novel (except for the invisible Governor of Van Diemen's Land), are *invented*, with no historical models. (*Out of Ireland* 704-5; my emphasis)

Unsurprisingly, even though historical details are of utmost importance since they contribute to reading fluency,[4] the fictional dimension remains central to Koch's novels,[5] the skilful craft of which is reflected in microconstructions, as exemplified by the selection of historical facts which, far from being gratuitous, aims at heightening a sense of tragedy.[6]

A bird's eye view of the novelist's literary output will help the reader notice Koch's marked inclination for friction should we refer to Devereux's power struggle with the colonial administration, to the military upheavals in his Asian novels, to Miller's Faustian conflict, or to Francis Cullen's and Robert O'Brien's rebellious natures at odds with society's conformism. What the reader retains from these situations of conflict is their ability to generate greater empathy on the reader's part whose heart bleeds all the more when it comes to tragedies. Besides, friction with the literary critique enhances the realistic overtones of Koch's fiction all the more as it clubs together the factual/fictional dimensions merging in a so-called "faction genre" ("Faction" is a portmanteau word which is the combination of "fact" and "fiction." It first came to designate some fictionalised form of journalism. Curiously enough, applied to literature, it indicates quite the opposite: namely the departing of novels from fiction to espouse facts from reality). In other words, Christopher Koch has been accused of presenting accounts based on actual events and written in a fictional style. Such allegations are bound to soil the author's reputation by challenging his creation skills; hence the controversy following the publication of *Highways to a War.* Journalist Luke Slattery and Evan McHugh (1996) redundantly exposed Koch's alleged outrageous borrowings from Tim Bowden's *One Crowded Hour* (1987) relating Neil Davis' biography (for a quasi-exhaustive list of these analogies, see Jillet 1995; Slattery and McHugh 1996; Koch 1996). The biggest issue focussed around the parallel drawn between the following excerpts:

> It was now eleven-thirty, and the sun was growing hot. The streets were still very quiet, and out of the Palace it was quieter still. The big wrought-iron gates in front were locked as usual, and we drove down a side street to the service entrance, where journalists had always entered in the past. This gate was open, and there was no sign of the guards who used to be posted there. We walked into the grounds and around to the front of the long white building with its flight of marble steps going up to the entrance.

> Here we found an even bigger quiet than the one in the city. (*Highways to a War* 417)

To be compared with Tim Bowden's book which reads:

> At 11.30 on the morning of 30 April 1975, Neil Davis waited in the grounds of Independence Palace in Saigon to film a moment of history. The sun was high and hot. The relentless roar of Saigon's chaotic traffic—an unholy mélange of battered and ancient Peugeot taxis, buzzing Hondas and motorised cyclos making kamikaze dashes under the wheels of heavy military traffics—was stilled. An unfamiliar calm hung over the central district. All looting had stopped.
>
> About forty or fifty South Vietnamese soldiers, their weapons piled, were sitting and lounging in the shade of some trees, waiting to surrender. Behind them, the circular lawns and ceremonial driveway led the eye to the impressive tier of marble steps in front of the main entrance to Independence Palace. (Bowden 335)

This accusation turns out to be redundant and to no avail since Koch denies all accusations of plagiarism by quoting his sources in his prefatory note:

> There is one exception: although even here, I'm afraid, fiction has played fast and loose with fact. On the day after the fall of Saigon, Mike Langford waits inside the grounds of the Presidential Palace as Neil Davis did, to find himself filming the arrival of the first North Vietnamese tank through the gates. But Mike is taking still pictures, not shooting film, no real-life equivalent of Jim Feng was there at all, and the personal circumstances underlying this sequence are also fictitious. (*Highways to a War* ix)

And yet, such warning did not deter the journalist from drawing comparisons between both books to insinuate that Koch's novel is but a poor imitation of a life account drawn on reality. While this implicit statement clearly irritates the incriminated novelist[7] and ironically reinforces realistic fallacy; such friction gives considerable weight to fiction(s) to such an extent that Koch feels the urge to use his right of reply, stressing his achieving an original work:

> This is the story of a man who goes to Asia without a job, and is led into photographic war coverage by an old ASIS agent who prevails on him to supply him with information from the field. This man at the end, will lead Langford to his doom in Cambodia when he seeks to rescue Ly Keang. It is also the story of a

> photographer who decides to step outside his role and to take up a cause—literally to put down the camera and take up the gun on behalf of the free Khmer. None of the cameramen I knew or read about did any of these things. This is the story I invented. (Koch, 1996: 22)

Amidst the seven prominent characters of *Highways to a War*, four of them (Dmitri Volkov, Harvey Drummond, Claudine Phan, and Ly Keang) are the result of complete fabrication. The other three find their counterparts in reality (Mike Langford is reminiscent of Neil Davis, Jim Feng takes from Joe Lee, while Raymond Barton is probably mimicking Tim Bowden's function as biographer). Such method, as Koch rightfully states, is part and parcel of novel-building: "having begun with facts, and elements taken from real people, the novelist then invents, and a story is born. Unless this magic takes place, you do not have a novel" (Koch, 1996: 22).

It is noteworthy to mention that the more knowledgeable the reader is, the more efficient realistic fallacy becomes. Should Neil Jillet and Don Anderson fail to know about Australian life, they would not have reproachfully pointed out that "a Launceston newspaper that could only be *The Examiner* is called *The Courier*" or that "there is not, nor was not, a Catholic Church in Kellett Street" (Jillet 9; see also Anderson 1985) in Sydney. But they are not the only ones to have fallen in the pitfalls of fictional illusion. Despite the worldwide success of *The Year of Living Dangerously* (it was made into a movie in 1982 and performed on stage by the Black Swan Company at the Perth Festival in 1999), its Peter Weir screen adaptation has been censored by Indonesian authorities for the plot reflected a disturbing and unflattering reality. As time heals all wounds, the film was finally released on 8 November 2000, thirty years after Sukarno's death, two years following the end of Suharto's dictatorship. If Christopher Koch does not novelise facts, he uses them as props in his fiction so as to present his provocatively resembling vision/version of reality. Such fictional representation challenges reality and benefits from its friction-packed feedbacks which, by overlapping the fact/fiction borderlines, spin a wider web of illusions. Such is the power of "illusionists," to take up Guy de Maupassant's apt nickname for realist novelists. Fictional reality strikes back in the reader's world, with a vengeance!

ENDNOTES

[1] For a more detailed analysis of this and other themes in Koch's work, see Jean-François Vernay, *Water from the Moon: Illusion and Reality in the Works of Australian Novelist Christopher Koch* (New York: Cambria, 2007).

[2] Koch declares: "[. . .] I'm not interested in stepping outside the bounds of naturalism. I see no great future for non-naturalist novels [. . .]. Originality, in other words, is the material and execution. It's not in adopting any particular tricks" (Interview, 1995: 9).

[3] Indeed, half of his opus is dedicated to historical novels, namely: *The Year of Living Dangerously* whose title is borrowed from President Sukarno's historical quote when he christened year 1965; *Highways to a War* whose working title was "Van Diemen's Land," Tasmania's historical name until 1856; and *Out of Ireland* which draws from John Mitchel's historical diaries.

[4] "In regard to the situation with the US embassy with the arrival of the helicopters, you can't even have a wrong helicopter in that situation. Dozens of people will notice it. [. . .] I make a difference between background and background material, and fiction, and I give a lot of time and trouble to creating a fictitious story" (Koch qtd. in Slattery and McHugh 25).

[5] See for instance Koch passing comments on *Highways to a War*: "[. . .] since it's essentially a historical novel. You have got to get the chronologies and the events and the whole society right. At the same time, I believe it's vital not to let yourself be diverted by factual detail from the main story, which has to remain fiction" (Interview, 1997: 67). See also: "The conflicts in Vietnam and Cambodia form the background here for a work of fiction [. . .]. Only the historical events are true" (*Highways to a War* viii).

[6] "It seems to me that history—recent history, often as recorded by journalists—can be heightened, so that it takes on some of the overtones of tragic drama. This I've attempted to do. No facts are included in my account of Saigon's fall simply as facts. They are selected to build the music of tragedy" (Koch, 1996: 22).

[7] "If someone is trying to say this is an unoriginal piece of work or a fictionalisation of *One Crowded Hour*, they will find that it's a totally different personal story that goes on" (Koch qtd. in Slattery and McHugh 25).

Works Cited

Anderson, Don. "C. J. Koch's Lonely Novel of a Betrayed, Isolated Character." *National Times* 26 April-2 May 1985: 32

Bowden, Tim. *One Crowded Hour.* Sydney: William Collins, 1987.

Campion, Edmund. "Two Memories of Tony Wren." *Quadrant* 24 (December 1980): 38-41.

Chenery, Susan. "Highways Back into Asia." *Sydney Morning Herald* 1 July 1995: (Spectrum) 10A.

Cuddon, J. A. "Naturalism." A *Dictionary of Literary Terms.* London: Penguin, 1991. 416.

Jillet, Neil. "The War between Fact and Fiction." *Age* 23 July 1995: (Agenda) 9.

Koch, C. J. Personal interview. 23 April 2002.

——. *The Many-Coloured Land: A Return to Ireland.* Sydney: Pan Macmillan, 2002.

——. *Out of Ireland.* 1999. Sydney: Vintage, 2000.

——. Interview. By Adrian Mitchell. *Australian Literary Studies* 18.1 (1997): 67-72.

——. "Fact vs. Fiction: Author Strikes Back." *The Weekend Australian* 13-14 July 1996: 22.

——. *Highways to a War.* Ringwood, Victoria: Minerva, 1995.

——. Interview. By Helen Daniel. *Australian Book Review* 173 (August 1995): 7-9.

——. *Crossing the Gap: A Novelist's Essays.* London: Chatto & Windus, 1987.

——. "C. J. Koch in Conversation with Michael Hulse: In London." By Michael Hulse. *Quadrant* 29.6 (June 1985): 17-25.

——. T*he Doubleman.* 1985. Ringwood, Victoria: Minerva, 1996.

——. T*he Year of Living Dangerously.* 1978. Ringwood, Victoria: Minerva, 1996.

——. *Across the Sea Wall.* 1965. Sydney: Angus & Robertson, 1982.

——. *The Boys in the Island.* 1959. Sydney: Sirius, 1987.

Marr, David. "Beyond the Brave." *Sydney Morning Herald* 9 October 1999: (Spectrum) 7.

Pons, Xavier. "The Novelist as Ventriloquist: Autobiography and Fiction in Peter Carey's *True History of the Kelly Gang*." *Commonwealth* 24.1 (Autumn 2001): 61-72.

Slattery, Luke, and Evan McHugh. "Fact vs. Fiction." *The Weekend Australian* 6-7 July 1996: 25.

The Year of Living Dangerously. Dir. Peter Weir. Prod. Jim McElroy. MGM, 1982.

The Year of Living Dangerously. Adap. Dickon Oxenburgh. Dir. Andrew Ross. Prod. Black Swan Company. Perth Festival - Playhouse, Perth. February 1999.

Vernay, Jean-François. *Water from the Moon: Illusion and Reality in the Works of Australian Novelist Christopher Koch*. New York: Cambria, 2007.

Colonisation, Convicts, and National Convictions

C. J. Koch's *Out of Ireland* and Kate Grenville's *The Secret River*

Dunya Lindsey

> There is another complication in the imagined dialogue between Us and Them. White Australia has a strongly underdog culture, one that grew directly out of the experiences of transportation, exile. So even if the convicts raped and murdered blacks (which they certainly did) they also left for succeeding white generations a keen nose for injustice.
>
> The peculiar history of Sydney has left us with two sets of underdogs in the cultural dynamic. Judging our ancestors' behaviour with our ancestors' values, we find their behaviour abhorrent. (Carey 56)

The writer here is Peter Carey (b. 1943), probably the novelist who has been most influential on the way in which recent Australian fiction treats its national narratives, and his comments here indicate the double consciousness that informs not only his own fiction but also the novels of many of his contemporaries modern Australia as the product of the inextricable relationship between convict settlement and indigenous dispossession. Likewise, Hodge and Mishra (1990) have argued that

> Australia was founded on a double guilt: the dispossession of the Aboriginal people and the excessive punishment of large numbers of British and Irish people, mainly from the poorer classes, for crimes against the property of the ruling class. (116)

The notion of the convict implicit here and in Carey's comments is not the criminals documented by historians, such as A. G. L. Shaw (1966). Rather he is the victim of an hierarchical, unjust and corrupt Old World: he is Gray's "village-Hampden"—most prominently portrayed in Robert Hughes's widely-read *The Fatal Shore* (1987: 159), and Russel Ward's (1958) prototype of Australian mateship, egalitarianism and anti-authoritarianism (51, 81). This powerful popular conception has been influential in the way they are represented in antipodean fiction, as in works by Christopher Koch (b. 1932) and Kate Grenville (b. 1950). The convict is a central symbolic figure in Australian literature: rejected by and rejecting the colonial center, this representation of the convict figure ("Us") presents this cohort of the first white settlers as the victims of imperial injustice rather than perpetrators of dispossession.

It is not surprising, therefore, that recent fiction focuses on the prisoners rather than the gaolers. The convict becomes an acceptable originary settler of the newly-acquired land. But necessarily invoked alongside the convict are the indigenous Australians ("Them") who are displaced, both literally and symbolically, and whether featuring as characters or not in the literature, the dispossessed indigenous Australians are the dialectical counterpart of the convict settler. This article will consider the way this relationship is depicted in Christopher Koch's *Out of Ireland* (2000) and Kate Grenville's *The Secret River* (2005).

Commentators have long observed the connection between historical novels and nationalism. Susan Lever (1998) has noted that the bicentenary celebrations of white colonisation produced historical "national or monumental narratives" by many of Australia's leading novelists and "returned to rather traditional grounds for the discussion of Australian life: the convict, the pioneer, the bushranger, the Australian prisoner of war" (327). Storytelling itself is intimately connected to the idea of nationhood; as Benedict Anderson (1983) notes, the rise of the nation (or "imagined community") coincided with the rise of the novel and newspapers and the means to represent the nation to the populace (24-25). Within this, historical representation is crucial: Lowenthal (1985) remarks, "Awareness of history likewise enhances communal and national identity, legitimating a people in their own eyes" (44). This is so especially of Australia: Brenton Doecke (1995) has observed that reflecting "on this status of historical fiction in Australian literary history" involves, among other things, tackling "the role of nationalist values in Australian writings" (50). If the rise of the novel roughly coincided with idea of nationhood (and, for that matter, white settlement of Australia), then the historical novel coincided with its fruition. The connection seems central to the genre, as critics have identified, particularly in relation to the English historical novel. For Georg Lukács (1962), Walter Scott's patriotism was "vital for the creation of a real historical novel" and in Lukács's model, history is evolutionary and historical novels need to bring

> the past to life as the prehistory of the present, in giving poetic life to those historical, social and human forces which, in the course of a long evolution, have made our present-day life what it is and as we experience it. (57)

Avrom Fleishman (1971) has observed that Scott's "myth of the Norman yoke" has influenced the model of the English historical novel and notes a legacy of "racial emotions, political ideas, and plain nonsense [. . .] that has still not subsided" (27-28). Embedded in the genre of the historical novel, then, are assumptions about what constitutes a nation and the nature of its formation: that history moves teleologically, and that the nation shares an experience of struggle, a racial identity and a political philosophy.

In this sense, the Australian convict, as popularly depicted, is a perfect candidate for the narrative of nation-building and the progenitor of modern Australia: the shared Anglo-Celtic ancestry (this hyphenation has in Australian discourse elided any implicit difference between these groups), the egalitarian philosophy, and above all the hardship and determination required for surviving transportation and then cultivation in the newly-acquired land.

But the nationalist narrative evident in the genre of historical fiction has been complicated in recent times by the deconstruction of grand narratives and historical writing, and also by recent debates in the public sphere. In Australia, public debate about the colonization of the continent has complicated this narrative of the rise of the nation from its modest penal origins. In particular, the 1988 bicentennial celebration of white settlement, the Mabo decision in 1992 by the High Court of Australia which established native land title, and especially the recent "history wars," which disputes the degree and means of the displacement of indigenous Australians from the continent, highlight the mythologizing implicit in any single historical narrative. Furthermore, as Linda Hutcheon (1988) explains,

> [. . .] recent critical readings of both history and fiction have focused more on what the two modes of writing share than on how they differ. They have both been seen to derive their force more from verisimilitude than from any objective truth; they are both identified as linguistic constructs, highly conventionalised in their narratives forms, and not at all transparent either in terms of language or structure; and they appear to be equally intertextual, deploying the texts of the past within their own complex textuality. (105)

As A. S. Byatt (2000) has remarked "The renaissance of the historical novel has coincided with a complex self-consciousness about the writing of history itself" (9). If, in fact, as a result of this self-consciousness "fiction has stepped in to satisfy society's need for a simpler, plot-driven past" (Hsu-Ming 129-130), in Australia it is a fiction that is also self-consciously literary in its constructions of the past. A heightened self-consciousness about the making of Australian history has meant that recent Australian novels have thus not only recorded a version of the past firmly situated in the colonial period, but have also examined the way that past is represented. Carey's "underdog" culture, which he links to the judgment of the white settlers by their descendents, indicates a crucial trope in Australian historical fictions: that while convicts remain mythologized as nation-builders, a critical self-reflexivity and implicit evaluation about this mythologizing is becoming increasingly apparent—though there are earlier examples of this self-reflexivity, among which are Thomas Keneally's *The Chant of Jimmie Blacksmith* (1972) and Robert Drewe's *The Savage Crows* (1976).

Christopher Koch's *Out of Ireland* exploits the intertextual relationship invoked by the *Irish* convict as the archetypal exile. Exile is a critical component in the depiction of convictism in Australian fictions of the past and has become central to the mythos of the righteous convict, especially in Australian depictions of the Irish convict. The exilic status of the convict again stresses his victimhood, having been forcibly removed from his home to the antipodes and taken, in the words of Koch's protagonist, the Young Irelander Robert Devereux, "away from all that was civilized, known and loved" (*Out of Ireland* 29). Central to the exilic narrative is the concept of the "homeland," invoking as it does ownership and familiarity of the land a depiction that correspondingly involves the colonization of the continent and the effect of this on indigenous Australians. Emphasis on the exilic status of the convict or settler allows the positioning of this character as a victim in the process of colonization, the reluctant nation-builder. Edward Said (1978) has remarked that "White settlers in Africa, parts of Asia and Australia may once have been exiles, but as pioneers and nation-builders, they lost the label 'exile' " (181). Nevertheless, the fictional convict is customarily depicted as the exile of the Old World, and when it is an Irish convict who is the exile, fiction taps into the ubiquitous trope of the Irish exile outlined in innumerable and already-written ballads and poems.

Koch's protagonist, Robert Devereux as an Irish political transportee, demonstrates the invocation of a com plex web of associations that affects the novel's depiction of his convictism and response to the penal colony. Jennifer Rutherford (2001) points out, writing about Tim Winton's *The Riders* (1994), that the Australian protagonist's Irish identification invokes "the primordial and organic belonging of Irish Catholics to the land and in the heroic anti-colonial rebel tradition":

> In this conceit Europe and England must be figured as colonial oppressors "of Australia" and the Irish rebel tradition re-enacted long after its ecli pse in Ireland, in order to occlude the central fact that Australians were not victims of colonisation but colonisers. As victims of dispossession, of famine, of the crown, "and of a contem porary Eurocentrism—they are positioned elsewhere than at the scene of the crime." (161)

Koch's Irish rebel Robert Devereux is a literal embodiment of this tradition and has become the victim of "British tyranny's agents and gaolers" (*Out of Ireland* 5) for having fought English colonization and thus become "a man without moorings: a man without a home or citizenshi p" (*Out of Ireland* 28). In Devereux's conception, Tasmania is a reflection of an ancient Ireland prior to colonization by the British, idealized and made representative by the Young Ireland movement in their nationalist struggle for autonomy: the Quoin in Van Diemen's Land, reminds him of "the fairy hills of Ireland" (*Out of Ireland* 283). In response to Devereux's reflection, his fellow political exile observes that "No doubt the unknown nature spirits of Van Diemen's Land were familiar to the vanished blacks—of whom, he tells me, the settlers of Bothwell lived in fear until quite recently" (*Out of Ireland* 283). Similarly, when the convicts take shelter in a shepherd's hut they invoke the lost Eire: feasting on hearty mutton chops and brandy, they sit on rudimentary chairs, one of which is dubbed "Carter's throne," sing the anthem of their movement, *Rósín Dubh* (*Out of Ireland* 292-293), discuss their thwarted revolt (*Out of Ireland* 293-298) and listen to the stories of their host:

> As we'd eaten, the old shepherd had told us tales of his early days here, when any unexplained sound outside could mean the arrival or marauding Aborigines, and when an isolated stockman like himself lived in fear of being speared at his door. (*Out of Ireland* 292)

Colonization of Van Diemen's Land is thus depicted as a kind of reclamation by the colonized Irish, while the actual indigenous inhabitants become menacing figures that threaten this repossession. In another incident, however, Devereux escorts Kathleen on a walk "to exchange final kisses" in a "gloomy" gully:

> Something has once happened here, I thought: something grim and sad. Perhaps the vanished Aboriginal people had used it for their ceremonies; or more likely, some of them had been slain here by the valley's first settlers. (*Out of Ireland* 454-455)

Kathleen also finds the place ominous: "It's a place where ghosts might be," she says, and she hears "queer voices" at night, which Devereux dismisses as nocturnal animals (*Out of Ireland* 455). Yet the function of the invocation of the first inhabitants and their dispossession and possible murder is to provide a setting for the misunderstandings regarding religion and social status between the educated Protestant gentleman convict and the poor Catholic serving-girl. Andreas Gaile (2002) has observed, that in Van Diemen's Land, Devereux and the other Young Ireland transportees

> use their imported myths and narratives as a matrix that helps them come to terms with the alien surroundings and make sense of the place [. . .]. The rebels conquer and appropriate to their understanding a place far "away from all that was civilized, known and loved." (152-153)

Ultimately, however, the conquest and appropriation to which Gaile refers is at the expense of the original inhabitants of the land.

The marginalisation of indigenous dispossession is mitigated, to some extent, however, by both the focus of the novel and Koch's deployment of paratextual and narrative devices that serve to mimic historical writing and highlight its fictionality. The novel contains an "Author's Note" supplying a detailed bibliography of sources for his novel (*Out of Ireland* 705), but also details how his fictional character Robert Devereux differs from his historical model, John Mitchel, and adds:

> If I am seen to have taken a liberty in drawing on the real Young Irelanders to create my imaginary creatures, I can only ask indulgence, and point out that this sort of liberty is a time-honoured tradition in the novel. (*Out of Ireland* 704)

The presence of such notes around the narrative lends the text historical legitimacy and also reinforces its fictionality. Likewise, the use of a first person narration in a journal form, while lending an immediacy found in archival scraps through the utilisation of historical sources and period diction and language, also serves to destabilize the narrative as authoritative or monumental.

Similarly, the narrative strategies in Kate Grenville's *The Secret River* serve to disrupt the monumentalism of the transportation and settler story. The novel is narrated from the perspective of William Thornhill, and his encounters with the Darug people on the Hawksbury River are clearly representative only of his im pressions; the narrative in this sense cannot be considered a totalising (or "true") view of the interactions. Though Thornhill is nearly illiterate, his can scrawl his name (*The Secret River* 34-35), and his signature marks the text as his own: this is *his* story of colonisation rather than *the* story. Yet it is his name that intertextually points to his role as dispossessor of the Darug tribe, both literally and symbolically. His name is not unique, it is "*as common as dirt*," as his sister taunts (*The Secret River* 11). His response is to shout "*William Thornhills will fill up the whole world*" (*The Secret River* 11), referring to his status as the future nation-builder and echoing the defiant cry of Shakespeare's Caliban. The allusion here is significant: Caliban has been frequently described as representative of the colonial subject and Thornhill's appropriation here positions himself as colonised, oppressed and reviled, displacing the indigenous Australians who will later be driven from their land or murdered so that he might colonise the territory.

Laurie Hergenhan (1983) has noted:

> The sense of the dead hand of the past is confronted in heightened form in convict fiction; here, versions of an Australian dream can arise, but only to be dispelled. Behind these tensions lie the conflicts of colonialism and independence, of the metropolis and the anti podes. (8)

The tension between the metropolitan centre and the anti podes is initially evident in the novel through the thoroughly popular conception of Thornhill as the disenfranchised im perial subject. He is born into squalid poverty in 18th century London, so hungry that he eats bedbugs (*The Secret River* 11-12), so poor that he helps his tubercular father collect excrement from the streets of Southwark in the winter to sell to the morocco works (*The Secret River* 13-14) and the mother steals to buy bread (*The Secret River* 14). Orphaned at thirteen, he works on the wharfs where he learns to steal brandy, then is apprenticed to his sweetheart's waterman father in the waterman trade, where he learns the realities of the English class system, "up to his thighs in water one day, holding the boat up to the ram p, so his fares could get in without wetting their feet" (*The Secret River* 29) he hears a customer tell his com panion "*Be cautious, my love*, he said. *Don't expose your leg to the boatman!*" (*The Secret River* 30). Thornhill's London is a Hogarthian[1] world of grime, poverty and drink and his criminal trajectory is an inversion of Hogarth's twelve steel plate narrative engravings, *Industry and Idleness* (1747). Though he is as diligent and hardworking as the engraving's industrious apprentice, and likewise dutifully marries the master's daughter, it is not enough. Thornhill fails, not through fecklessness, but through bad luck: his wife's parents die, leaving only debt and unemployment. The couple begin thieving, unable to survive on his income and, when he caught smuggling, he is not hanged as is the idle apprentice, but transported to Australia. Grenville's convict is thus the victim of the inequities of the Old World and, in the opening paragraph of the novel Grenville references the most prominent exponent of this view of Australian convicts, Robert Hughes's *The Fatal Shore*. Where Grenville writes "There was no need of lock, of door, of wall: this was a prison whose bars were ten thousand miles of water" (*The Secret River* 3), Hughes declares, "An unexplored continent would become a jail. The space around it, the very air and sea, the whole transparent labyrinth of the South Pacific, would become a wall 14,000 miles thick" (*The Fatal Shore* 1). There are other illusions—the gentry incident dramatises an engraving in the Guildhall Library (*Searching for the Secret River* 63)—as well as verbatim and modified uses of historical documents, and the result is a web of intertextual references to the popular myth of convictism as a condition of being more sinned against than sinning.

This self-reflexivity in the novel is evident in the (guilty) convicts' memorisation of their last defence before facing trial: "*I am as innocent as the child unborn*" (*The Secret River* 61). This mantra not only points to the popular conception of transported convicts, but is also indicative of the thematisation of representation and storytelling within the novel. Thornhill, too, memorises this defence, but in his first attempt to tell his story he is overwhelmed by "the power of words" (*The Secret River* 63) and he forgets his story: "he called out desperately, *I am as innocent as the child unborn*, but the words had not meaning after so much rehearsal" and the judge isn't listening (*The Secret River* 65). Sentenced to be hanged, he is

> without his story, stripped naked of his tale of injured innocence, stripped of everything but the knowledge that his moment of hope had been and gone, and left him now with nothing ahead but death. (*The Secret River* 66)

Though his sentence is commuted to transportation, this remains a moment of figurative death recurring in the narrative (*The Secret River* 4), the moment when Thornhill was unable to tell his story, to speak authoritatively, is a condition that haunts him in the colony. In the first meeting between Thornhill and the Darug people, Thornhill listens to an elder trying to communicate with him:

> *You ain't making no sense to me, mate,* he said. *Not a blinking word.* A thought made him laugh, and that made him bold. *You might as well bloody bark, mate,* he said, feeling his cheeks bunch up with the fun of it.
>
> The old man's face did not show any appreciation of the joke [. . .]. When he spoke again it cut across Thornhill's honour like water on a flame. He made a chopping action with the side of his hand [. . .]. (*The Secret River* 144)

Thornhill is patronizing; in a faintly pathetic imitation of the English gentry he calls a man who is clearly a commanding figure "*good lad*" (*The Secret River* 143) and "*old boy*" (*The Secret River* 144). Though we do not know what he is saying, it is the elder who is authoritative here: "the old man cut across his words as if they were of no more im portance than the rattle of wind in a tree" (*The Secret River* 143). When Thornhill claims his territory, "*My place now*" (*The Secret River* 144), the man is not im pressed and the eventually interaction ends with Thornhill slapping the man, which sounds like "slow ironic applause" (*The Secret River* 146). The man leaves in disgust.

While Thornhill is given speech and the ability to narrate his life, he does not remain in control of it—it is physical force, a massacre prefigured in the slaps of this first meeting, in which he eventually gains dominance over the Darug people, and thus over his own story. He and his fellow-settlers concoct a tale to explain the slaughter:

> They would need to have their own story ready. Yes, they had gone to have a parley-voo with the blacks. Yes, they had shown them their guns. They had even fired over their heads. The blacks were not stupid. They had got the hint. They had dispersed.
>
> If there was any doubt cast on the story, the very absence of the blacks could be brought forward as evidence of its truth. (*The Secret River* 301)

This is the version of events that reverses earlier interactions: in the past he had been ignored, had not taken a gun (*The Secret River* 191) and the

Darug people had remained. After the massacre, Thornhill gains ownership of his story: his dominance is expressed, like the Biblical Adam, through the power of naming—his land is now called Thornhill's Point (320) and the creek nearby Thornhill's Creek (*The Secret River* 313)—and he remakes his history:

> This story had William Thornhill not born in dirty Bermondsey but in clean Kent, by the chalk cliffs. Had not been caught greasy with fear at Three Cranes Wharf, sweating over pieces of timber belonging to Mathhias Prime Lucas, but by the excise men on some pebbly beach with a boatload of French brandy. Had not swung for it, because on the outward trip he had worked for the King, carry English spies into France.
>
> It was a well-made story, every corner of its construction neatly finished [. . .]. (*The Secret River* 321)

Thornhill the thief becomes Thornhill the smuggler and patriot, his story becomes the stuff of romantic adventure taken from a fellow-colonialist Loveday, who has similarly updated the story to another romantic cliché, "involving a young girl, a cruel father and a false accusation" (*The Secret River* 321). Fleishman (1971) notes that

> The historical novel is pre-eminently suited to telling how individual lives were shaped at specific moments of history, and how this shaping reveals the character of those historical periods. (10)

In Thornhill, Grenville takes this a step further—not only is he both representative of and shaped by colonisation of Australia but the brutal act which finally assures control of the land enables him to relate his own story. The fact that this story is taken from another, and probably fiction, only reinforces the fictionality of national historical narratives.

In contrast, the stories of the indigenous people in *The Secret River* are only gleaned through inference. Grenville was wary of appropriating the point of view of the Darug people: "I'd always known I wasn't going to try to enter the consciousness of the Aboriginal characters. I didn't know or understand enough, and felt I never would" (*Searching for the Secret River* 193). The result is an ambivalent representation of the Darug people: largely unvoiced, though ever present. The indigenous people in the novel, though not silent—Thornhill hears them talk and laugh without understanding their speech—are given almost no direct speech by an indigenous Australian in the novel, the author having decided to eliminate all the dialogue: "It might have been historically accurate to have the Aboriginal characters speaking broken English, but it made them less sympathetic, more caricatured" (*Searching for the Secret River* 198). The result is a literal portrayal of the way in which the indigenous people have no voice among the settlers.

The few instances of indigenous direct speech seem similarly disempowering—in English (the language of the coloniser), futile or supplicant, as in the case of Scabby Bill, a scarred, drunk "shameless black man" who haunts Sydney Cove begging "*Missus, Missus*" for some crusts of bread (*The Secret River* 91). The first instance is in a prologue entitled "Strangers," when Thornhill ventures outside his Sydney hut one night and encounters an indigenous Australian:

> [Thornhill] took a threatening step forward [. . .]. *Be off!* Empty though it was, he raised his hand against the man.
>
> The mouth of the black man began to move itself around sounds [. . .]. In the fluid rush of speech Thornhill suddenly heard words. *Be off*, the man was shouting. *Be off!* It was his own tone exactly.
>
> This was a kind of madness, as if a dog were to bark in English. (*The Secret River* 6)

There is a disturbing objectification of the man speaking to Thornhill here: this is present not only in the man's mimicry and the bestiality of the Johnsonian allusion (which, as we have seen, is repeated elsewhere), but in the complete lack of agency attributed to the indigenous man: it is "the mouth" that "move[s] itself around sounds," rather than the man forming the words. This seems to deny agency to the nameless man, as does the fact this man, like all indigenous figures in the novel is not identified by his name (only those given to them by the Thornhills). What the man's mimicry does, however, is to de-naturalize both the narrative position and the gaze of Thornhill. Read in terms of Homi Bhabha's (2004) concept of "mimicry," this moment destablizes the colonial authority of Thornhill: "The *menace* of mimicry is its *double* vision which in disclosing the ambivalence of colonial discourse also disrupts its authority" (Bhabha 126). His own words are estranged, and the

> repetition of *partial presence*, which is the basis of mimicry, articulates those disturbances of cultural, racial and historical difference that menace the narcissistic demand of colonial authority. (Bhabha 126)

Thornhill's order, based on his status as the white colonizer, becomes, in the mimicry of the colonized, no more than as if "a dog were to bark in

English." Coming as it does prior to the chronological story of Thornhill's life, transportation and settlement on the Hawksbury River and interaction with the Darug people, this moment of "mimicry" destabilizes Thornhill's colonial authority thereafter. The very power he gains through having the speaking position is destabilized through the man's repetition. In fact, after the man speaks, Thornhill cannot: "His own words had all dried up" (*The Secret River* 6), yet it is after this moment that the narrative of his life begins. Further, his dominant position is further undermined by a later encounter on the Hawksbury with a young man which provides a textual mimicry, mirroring the earlier encounter almost exactly: "The man spoke loud and hard [. . .]. In any language, anywhere, that movement of the had said, *Go away.* Even a dog could understand *Go away* when he saw it" (*The Secret River* 147). Ultimately, then, Thornhill's narrative is undermined: though he eventually regains his power to tell the story of his life (and claims land) through brute force, the words he might use for this have already lost their authority. Grenville's novel, then, problematises the very nature of historical writing and complicates the position from which we make our national fictions.

The history of Australian literature is also in many ways the literature of Australian history: antipodean fiction constantly invokes, appropriates and positions the past as a central concern of the imaginative life of its national fictions. Peter Pierce (1992) has asked:

> Is the yearning for "origin," the search for roots, the establishment of provenance, a keen business in the historical fiction of a post-colonial culture such as Australia? More contentiously still, which narratives of the past, or rather whose stories, have writers preferred? (305)

The penal past, the European foundational settlement of the continent as a convict colony, remains the commonly invoked moment of origin in Australian fiction, and the convict the ubiquitous progenitor of the nation-to-be. Laurie Hergenhan noted in 1983 that

> It may be that for a long time the convicts displaced the Aborigines as a focus for the doubts and fears about white settlement in the Australian continent; that convicts, not Aborigines, provided a guilty past. (2)

The novels of Grenville and Koch of almost twenty years later show both how much and how little Australian fiction has shifted from this position. If Koch's Irish exiles invoke the popular conception of convict victimology and thus displace indigenous dispossession to a footnote of Irish history, in Grenville's novel the displacement of indigenous Australians from the land is the central focus of the narrative, despite invoking another iteration of convict disenfranchisement. Furthermore, both novels embody an ambivalence about the way in which national stories are made and told: intertextuality, subjective narration and subtle invocations of prior representations of the convict past implicitly challenge the monumentalism of the national convict mythology. Far from being "protected by the soft glow of 'history,' " as Drusilla Modjeska (2002: 8) termed it, these Australian historical novels are confronting crucial assumptions on which contemporary Australian national narratives of identity are formed, and in examining the colonisation of Australia, a subject that has serious and ongoing consequences for contemporary indigenous Australians.

Endnote

[1] Sir William Thornhill was the name of Hogarth's father-in-law. Thanks to Prof. Clive Probyn for noting this.

Works Cited

Anderson, Benedict. *Imagined Communities: Reflections on the Origin and Spread of Nationalism.* 1983. London: Verso, 1991.

Bhabha, Homi. *The Location of Culture.* Oxford: Routledge, 2004.

Byatt, A. S. *On Histories and Stories: Selected Essays.* London: Chatto & Windus, 2000.

Carey, Peter. *30 Days in Sydney: A Wildly Distorted Account.* London: Bloomsbury, 2001.

Doecke, Brenton. "Challenging History Making: Realism, Revolution and Utopia in *The Timeless Land.*" *Australian Literary Studies* 17.1 (May 1995): 49-57.

Drewe, Robert. *The Savage Crows.* Sydney: Collins, 1976.

Fleishman, Avrom. *The English Historical Novel: Walter Scott to Virginia Woolf.* Baltimore and London: The Johns Hopkins P, 1971.

Gaile, Andreas. " 'Going Double': Exploring Contradictions of Australianness in Christopher Koch's *Out of Ireland.*" *Antipodes* 16.2 (June 2002): 151-156.

Grenville, Kate. *Searching for the Secret River.* Melbourne: Text, 2006.

——. *The Secret River.* Melbourne: Text, 2005.

Hergenhan, Laurie. *Unnatural Lives: Studies in Australian Fiction about the Convicts, from James Tucker to Patrick White.* St. Lucia: U of Queensland P, 1983.

Hodge, Bob, and Vijay Mishra. *Dark Side of the Dream: Australian Literature and the Postcolonial Mind.* North Sydney: Allen & Unwin, 1990.

Hogarth, William. *Industry and Idleness.* 12 plates. 1747. 7 March 2007 <http://www.tate.org.uk/britain/exhibitions/hogarth/modernmorals/industryidleness.shtm>.

Hsu-Ming, Teo. "Future Fusions and a Taste for the Past: Literature, History and the Imagination of Australianness." *Australian Historical Studies* 33.118 (2002): 127-39.

Hughes, Robert. *The Fatal Shore: A History of the Transportation of Convicts to Australia, 1787-1868.* 1987. London: Vintage, 2003.

Hutcheon, Linda. *A Poetics of Postmodernism: History, Theory, Fiction.* New York and London: Routledge, 1988.

Keneally, Thomas. The Chant of Jimmie Blacksmith. 1972. Ringwood, Victoria: Penguin Books, 1976.

Koch, Christopher J. *Out of Ireland.* Sydney: Vintage, 2000.

Lever, Susan. "Fiction: Innovation and Ideology." *The Oxford Literary History of Australia.* Ed. Bruce Bennett, Jennifer Strauss and Chris Wallace-Crabbe. Melbourne: Oxford UP, 1998: 308-331.

Lowenthal, David. *The Past is a Foreign Country.* Cambridge: Cambridge UP, 1985.

Lukács, Georg. *The Historical Novel.* Trans. Hannah Mitchell and Stanley Mitchell. 1962. Harmondsworth: Penguin, 1981.

Modjeska, Drusilla. "Give Me the Real Thing." *Sydney Morning Herald* 31 August 2002: (Spectrum) 8.

Pierce, Peter. "Preying on the Past: Contexts for Some Recent Neo-Historical Fiction." *Australian Literary Studies* 15.4 (October 1992): 304-312.

Rutherford , Jennifer. "The Colonising Victim: Tim Winton's Irish Conceit." *Flight from Certainty: The Dilemma of Identity and Exile.* Ed. Anne Luyat and Francine Tolron. Amsterdam: Rodopi, 2001. 151-163.

Said, Edward W. *Reflections on Exile and Other Literary and Cultural Essays.* London: Granta, 2001.

Scheckter, John. *The Australian Novel 1930-1980: A Thematic Introduction.* Vol. 8. *Studies of World Literature in English.* Gen. Ed. Norman R. Cary. New York: Peter Lang, 1998.

Shaw, A. G. L. *Convicts and the Colonies.* London: Faber & Faber, 1966.

Ward, Russel. *The Australia Legend.* Melbourne: Oxford UP, 1958.

Winton, Tim. *The Riders.* Chi ppendale, NSW: Pan Macmillan, 1994.

The Core of Reality
"Mandala" as a Leitmotif in Patrick White's Fiction

Krishna Barua

Patrick White (b. 1912 – d. 1990), the 1973 Nobel Laureate from Australia, was undoubtedly one of the most powerful novelists of the 20th century. There are those who unreservedly praise him for the versatility and energy of his writing, and those who denounce his works as pretentious and peri phrastic jugglery, dealing with abnormal men and women only. The phrase "difficult novels of a difficult man" has come to stay. In his own words, he has been regarded as "an intruder, a breaker of rules, a threat to the tradition of Australian Literature" (*Flaws in the Glass* 139). Initially rebuffed by readers, White has survived and weathered the years of abuse and his status today is undisputed.

The purpose of this paper is to determine "the core of reality" (Mcgregor 219) in Patrick White's novels, and observe a clear statement of the syntax of ideas based on a close study of the consciousness White's characters who are constantly on a quest to discover to one concentric mandalic wholeness. I attem pt to trace Patrick White's use of mandalic arrangements not only in the structuring of the novels but also to illustrate the two different modes of perceiving reality—conscious reason and intellect against natural intuition. Further, I examine the exact relationshi ps of Patrick White's texts to the concise and com pendious delineation of the profoundly eloquent Shri Yantra geometrical device in Hindu and Buddhist traditions.

Mandalas are arrangements or patterns, which give expression to the infinite possibilities of the human subconscious. In Hindu and Buddhist religious philosophies, a mandala is supposed to aid concentration by restricting psychic vision to the center which leads to the essence, the point—the "Bindu" of spiritual and psychic integration:

> The mandala (a geometric structure based upon the squaring of a circle around a unifying centre [. . .]): the desire for spiritual unity

> and psychic integration. [. . .] [In] its classic form mandala juxtaposes the triangle, the square, and the circle with their numerical equivalents of three, four and seven. (Guerin et al. 151)

Whereas the "mandala" in Tibetan Art has an appeal beyond their original liturgical role. To psychologists, they are universal images that reflect

> [. . .] fundamental human instincts, while, for many, they attract through their blend of order and harmony and their multi ple levels of mystery, as well as their expression of a range of profound emotional and intellectual meanings. The word "mandala" derives from the words for "essence" and "container" and so is akin to the defination of a "stupa" as a container of religious essence. Mandalas functioned as an aid to meditation but were also commissioned, in typical Buddhist fashion, as a prayer for the welfare of others.they also represent the cosmos, in a diagram that gave order to the vast universe, including the central element as the "world mountain" where the aspirant is to find his or her own place and realize reintegration with the vast powers of nature and the gods. (Fisher 82)

Even in Javanese Art, there is domination of one Buddhist monument erected around 800 AD:

> To many it is a three dimensional mandala, to others it is a funery monument; a place of meditation, the support leads one from the mundane world through exam ples of exem plary behaviour, ever upwards, to the realm of the celestial Buddhas and finally to the ultimate goal: a single, large but em pty stupa. The sense of earthly reality is gradually replaced by more abstract images—there is transportation by powerful mystical forces a remarkable evocation of earthly and divine world. (Fisher 82)

As in the Buddhist view, the centre of the universe is a mountain, Meru, from the top of which rise the various levels of the heavens.

> This towering mountain is surrounded by seven circular, cocentric chains of mountains, each separated by one of the seven oceans. Painted mandalas provided a two dimensional medium for illustrating aspects of this Buddhist vision, and the concept was addressed in the largest monument in the Buddhist world, The Borbudar in Java, embodying many of the same elements. (Fisher 82)

The structuring of the novels and the relentless pursuit of what White preferred to call "the razor blade truth" (*Flaws in the Glass*

155) conforms precisely to the mandalic representations and the ambiguity of Truth in Hindu and Buddhist philosophy. The "mandala," with its intricate linear com position is conceived and designed as a support to meditation, more precisely to a concentrated visualization and intimate inner experience of the polar play and logic-shattering paradox of eternity and time. Here one does not fail to perceive the progression of the cyclical design or the mandalic pattern, which forms the ideal motif of life in Patrick White's creative perception. The awareness of pure being that the protagonists try to achieve, as well its skilful presentation is thus inherent in the basic structure. We see therefore, in the use of allusions and parallels in the novels, subtle sensibilities framed by the mystic ideas of the East which lead to "a sort of psycho-expressionism where fragments of the real and the unreal, the actual and the imagined, fuse together in a state of psychic trance" (Shepherd 30).

The theme of mandalic wholeness in White's fiction is suggested in his first novel, *Happy Valley* (1939) itself. The theme of suffering, pain and sacrifice as being necessary for the purification of the soul, and spiritual insight, is laid down in the epigraph taken from Mahatma Gandhi:

> It is im possible to do away with the law of suffering, which is the one indispensable condition of our being. Progress is to be measured by the amount of suffering undergone [. . .] the purer the suffering the greater is the progress. (*Happy Valley* Epigraph)

Moreover, White has portrayed the immensity and timelessness of the universe where man is the minutest of atoms. Yet his despair and futility create living values by affirming life and feeling the pulse of existence. Oliver's belief that "There is a mystery of unity about the world" (*Happy Valley* 166), antici pates the structure of White's later novels. In *The Living and the Dead* (1941), White presents the rootlessness inherent in a decaying urban society, indifferent to love or a sense of values, where the inhabitants are muffled and trapped by ennui and unconcern. Then there is the imagery of Chinese boxes "one inside the other, leading to an infinity of boxes, to an infinity of purpose" (*The Living and the Dead* 357).

White's third novel, *The Aunt's Story* (1962) is a moving tale of the vicissitudes of a shy and forlorn girl, Theodora Goodman, in her search for love and meaning in life. It begins with her childhood and ends with her confinement in middle age in a lunatic asylum. She is the first of White's illuminati or elect paving the way for Laura in *Voss* (1957), Mary Hare in *Riders in the Chariot* (1961) and Rhoda Courtney in *The Vivisector* (1970).

One of the epigraphs to *The Aunt's Story* reads, "When your life is more real, to me you are mad." Theodora approaches reality by complete dissolution of self. The loneliness of an individual in the ceaseless quest for the true self, "the solitary spirit utterly stripped" (Herring and Wilkes 136), is the dominant issue in *The Aunts Story.*

It was to overcome "the exaltation of the average" ("The Prodigal Son" 118), that Patrick White had conceived of *The Tree of Man* (1955), which was an attempt to portray, "every possible aspect of life through the lives of an ordinary man and woman and at the same time [. . .] to discover the extraordinary behind the ordinary" ("The Prodigal Son" 118). It is the story of a pioneering farmer, Stan Parker, who with his wife Amy comes and settles on a small isolated part of virgin wilderness near Sydney. The assertion of an indomitable will to strike roots, despite formidable odds, which assail life endlessly, signifies suffering in various forms. Primarily it is a question of choice, conviction and a desire to grasp the essence of one's own being. The suffering of the Parkers is essential for them to penetrate through the layers of superficialities, to arrive at the "core of reality as opposed to the merely superficial" (Mcgregor 219) of the true self.

Within this simple framework of a family unit, there is an intricate and involved design through which Patrick White explicates his vision. Stan's quest for permanence is illustrated by his life and career marked by the pattern of the mandalic structure of four distinct stages of innocence, experience, suffering and reconciliation.

The Parker family in *The Tree of Man* (1967), thus becomes the pivot where conflicts start as a bond, or as alienation and severance of ties. The mandala motif is apparent in the novel, when in the contentment of married bliss, the Parkers stand together inside the mandala formed by the mulberry tree; and again in the midst of the uncertainty after Amy's betrayal and his son's delinquincy, Stan feels the warmth and mandalic wholeness of Con's milk bar and contrasts it with his own dismembered one. This state of Stan's disenchantment is necessary for his insight, which makes him accept it as an experience to be undergone. The juxtaposition of Amy and Stan, the children, the years of "mud and metal" (*The Tree of Man* 199) and the gradual break up of familial ties—the triangles formed by their individual conflicts and release into fantasy—all indicate "the inner unconscious drama of the soul, an inner drama which is mirrored in the events of nature" (Tacey 34). Stan's final illumination reflects the mandalic symbolism where man places in the centre of himself the recondite princi ple of life, the divine seed, and the mysterious essence, the light that burns within him and which spreads out and is diffused. As Stan sat with Amy in the garden, "and all was circumference to the centre, and beyond that the world of other circles" (*The Tree of Man* 474), it was like "the centre of the cold and golden bowl of winter [. . .]. It was as if from his heart the trees radiated with the movements of life" (*The Tree of Man* 474).

At this point Stan points with a stick at a gob of spittle to a visiting evangelist–"That is God" (*The Tree of Man* 476). This was the pureness of Being, the same continuous mandalic circular perfection of existence. Stan em phasizes his final awareness of the joy and thrill of life: "I believe, in the cracks in the path [. . .] on which ants were massing, struggling up over an escarpment. But struggling. Like the painful sun in the icy sky, whirling and whirling. But struggling. But joyful" (*The Tree of Man* 477).

This masterly structural design becomes meaningful with the observation in Zen calligraphic motif about "The brushed circle–the enso–which means enlightenment, the present, com pletion. Just as one Zen philosophical tenet would be nowness. Or space. Sometimes you need a mark to point out space" (Tanahashi & Schneider 18).

Voss (1959), one of White's major works, is about a German explorer, who sets out on an expedition to the Australian island with a select band of followers. Almost every member of the expedition is motivated by an individual search, and in the process of self-realisation, they are burnt by suffering and pain. They realise that redem ption comes only after long struggle. As Voss tells one of his fellow explorers, "To make yourself it is also necessary to destroy yourself" (*Voss* 34). Laura, with whom Voss shares a near psychic relationshi p, also em phasizes "true knowledge only comes of death by torture in the country of the mind." (*Voss* 446). As Voss goes through the harsh agonies of the wilderness, he becomes aware of an im personal Fate, which makes man a fragile victim, a prisoner of his physical body. For Voss enlightenment comes only when his pride is humbled, and suffering blunts the ego.

Riders in the Chariot(1961) is an expressively mythopoetic work, based on Jewish Merkabah and Christian mysticism. The motif here is presented mainly through four characters, drawn from different backgrounds, and belonging to diverse nationalities. They are brought together against a common suburban Australian setting, White's fictive Sarsaparilla. These series of encounters between characters bring about a psycho-spiritual change, stri pping away the outward masks until the true inner depths are revealed.

Allied to this is the conflict of active opposites, the good and the evil; the evil inherent in a conformist modern society, or in war torn Europe, or in the unknown depths of man, but always creating in William Walsh's words, a "conflict of values" (Walsh 34). In uniting the four "elect" does Patrick White possibly suggest that intellect, artistic imagination, earthly goodness and pure instinct (which the four characters represent), reflect the perfect consciousness or do they represent "the sides of a soul of a giant Everyman, which is seen here as a divine quaternity"(Mackenzie 17).

In his next novel, *The Solid Mandala* (1966), White explores what may be called the ambiguity of existence on the basis of the story of two persons living one life, the twins Waldo and Arthur Brown. There is also the novelist's pervading use of Buddhist Mandala symbolism to bring out the indestructibility of the human spirit and myriad connections between mind and matter inviting challenging discourses on consciousness. Arthur's unique perception of reality leads him to celebrate "the world of light or silences" (*The Solid Mandala* 265), revealing the joy of the essential religious spirit where existence becomes a prayer, contrasted with the sterile drought in the mindscape of Waldo. Whoever meets him is drawn to him for his childlike transparency and open nature and his amazing world of faith and spontaneous warmth. This singular instinct makes him live the live the lives of others as his own. He loves to play with his four marbles, which are but transfigurations of the "mandala," and which helps him in understanding the various strands of reality better in his search for a totality of vision. His mandala dance before his neighbour, Mrs. Poulter, symbolises the theme of his life "his life, or dance was always prayerful" (*The Solid Mandala* 225). His mysticism is another way of viewing reality, which would reveal the world of "the inner man to the world of the outward man—man's microcosmic quality. The mystical experience has revealed the cosmos with man, the whole immense universe" (Berdyaev 273). Arthur feels that Waldo and he were but a translation of a would-be transvestite. He believes that it is the mystery of their basic metaphysical roots, a profound rather than superficial union that so intrigues him. This throws light on Nicholas Berdyeav's observation that "androgynity is the ultimate union of male and female in a higher God-like being, the ultimate conquest of decadence and strife, the restoration in man of the image and likeness of God" (Berdyaev 207). In this light Arthur impulsively tells Waldo that it would be better to be Tiresias, changing into a woman for a short time than the hermophrodite Adam.Thelma Herring finds in this tale "a device for dramatizing the concept of the antithetical self" (Herring 274). This is a portrayal, not of a struggle between good and evil, or between virtue and vice, but of an opposition between the luminous mystical consciousness and the psyche together with the subconscious which, in Hindu philosophy, is called "Maya." All experience is a conflict between the intuition of this "maya" and the conscious being. Thus the incommunicable mystery of man which is the constancy of the centre, the all unifying vision of the "mandalic" Truth, can be arrived at through the blunderings of a maze of experiences. Arthur's ultimate understanding reflects the teaching of Zen Buddhism which asks not to negate, but to constantly live and move in the Great Affirmationm of Life. If Zen emphasises anything at all in terms of a "philosophy" it would be "nowness"—the "present moment, the present mind" (Tamahashi and Schneider 15).

We can explain the "mandalic" symbolism thus:

> Man places in the centre of himself the recondite principle of life, the divine seed, and the mysterious essence. He has the vague intuition of a light that burns within him and which spreads out and is diffused. In this light his whole personality is concentrated and it develops around that light. (Tucci 26)

Patrick White in his early novels highlights the drama of conflicting human situations through a spiritual viewpoint against the banal surface of Australian urbanity, and argues it out as the dominant theme of his work. Even later in his career, when he wrote *The Vivisector*, his aim was chiefly to analyze the fragmented process of the vivisective perception of the artist, Hurtle Duffield, both in his encounters with Sydney—the "Zeitgeist" of Australian cultural Bohemia, as well as with its fringe dwellers. Sydney in this novel reflected the dark arenas of the human spirit and the innumerable afflictions of tragedies, which remain untraced, serving as a platform to transmute the artist's metaphysical experiences into concrete terms. Into the primary theme of art as a quest for identity is interwoven the novel's recurrent reaction to stimuli, the "Dreck" (German for mud) which exists with the "sauberkeit" (clean), and the relevance of the ugly and the transient with the beautiful and the eternal.

With *A Fringe of Leaves* (1976), Patrick White shifted the centre of the stage to Mrs. Ellen Roxburgh, who suffers a shi pwreck and subsequently loses her child and is captured by aborigines. The whole narrative is a record of her growth, suffering and final possible redem ption. The metaphysics of suffering, the question of resilience, survival and endurance is treated with varied em phasis. The penal settlement and the life of the convicts form an integral aspect of this novel. The archetypal themes of White about the condition of exile and the renunciation of identity show that Ellen Roxburgh, in grappling with what is the core of an evolving self, is equally forged in life's crucibles.

The Eye of the Storm (1973) opens with Elizabeth Hunter in her deathbed and as the narrative flows through flashback and recollections, it reveals a searching analysis of her life and situation. White has presented in her an inner crisis of sensibility. There is the suggestion that each man or woman discovers his or her innermost core of reality in his or her own way and in due time, and that there is in this regard no learning from others. The significance of the title justifies this reading. In the author's own words,

> It [the title] is in one sense the still center of an actual cyclone and in another the state of peace and spiritual awareness which Mrs. Hunter reaches on the island and again before her death. (Bjorksten 104)

This is the ultimate significance of the Buddha figure, there is only one essence, Buddhahood, enlightenment itself, the indescribable state or essence that is realized and attained when all the products and effects of "maya"—ignorance have been transcended.

> This is the sheer "Such-ness" or "that-ness" beyond differentiating qualifications, definable limitations and characteristics. This is tatha-ta, literally, "the state" (-ta) of being "so" (tatha). "Tatha" means "yes it is, so be it, amen." It is the everyday whole-hearted affirmative. Hence the term tatha-ta, "suchness" represents the utterly positive aspect of nirvana-enlightenment, the only real state or essence, not to be undone or dissolved. (Zimmer 145)

In White's last novel, *The Twyborn Affair* (1979), there is an attempt to delve deep into the ambiguous nature of all existence through the conflicting experiences of an androgynous protagonist, Eddie Twyborn. Eddie's quest for permanence under the veil of separate identities, namely, Eddie/Eudoxia/Eadith presents the ambivalent self in its experiences of a journey through what may be called the underworld of life, therby clearing the psychic debris in the realization of the integrated self. His quest is for the primordial being, a projection of man's unconscious wholeness, implying the union of man and woman in one integral *Being*. The question of consciousness, self and identity is left open for fresh possibilities, "The Real E has not yet been discovered, and perhaps never will be" (*The Twyborn Affair* 79).

A creative exploration of a baffling subject, *The Twyborn Affair* offers opportunities to assess Patrick White's mastery over the portrayal of a uniquely authentic picture of a person under stress struggling with his own ambivalent perception of life. White (1989) had confessed

> [. . .] everything I write has to be dredged up from the unconscious—which is what makes it an exhausting and perhaps finally, destructive process. I suppose all my characters are fragments of my own somewhat fragmented character. ("Why Bother with Patrick White")

This has relevance to the Shri Tantra, which, in its abstract linear design has nine triangles, interpenetrating, five pointing downward, four upward.

> Thus, the upward pointing triangle, the *Vahni,* denote the male essence of the god, and the downward pointing triangle, The *Shakti,* the female essence of his consort. The nine signify the primitive revelation of the Absolute as it differentiates into graduated polarities, the creative activity of the cosmic male and

> female energies on successive stages of evolution. Most important is that the absolute cannot be represented: for it is beyond form and spaces to be visualized as a vanishing point or dot "the drop," *bindu*, amidst the interplay of all the triangles. This *Bindu* is the power point, the invisible, elusive centre from which the entire diagram expands. The *Shri Yantra* symbolizes Life, both universal life and individual, as an interaction of cooperating opposites, signify the continuous process of creation, a dynamism in the eternal procreative moment exhibited in a static pattern of geometrical repose. This is the archetypal *Hieros Gamos*, or "mystical marriage" represented in an abstract diagram–a key to the secret of the phenomenal mirage of the world. (Zimmer 147)

It becomes amply clear to any perceptive reader that in treating the subtle edges of experience and the nature of reality as a whole, White could fuse the confessional with a harmonious philosophy and an all pervading psychological art with the energy of creative fiction, a multiple view of human experience. In the process, in novel after novel, he has presented what may be called "the crystallization of a mode of experience which is the act of literary creation" (Murry 52). White admitted that at times Truth to him "was the property of silence–the silence filling the space between words" (*Flaws in the Glass* 182). He wanted to convey the immensity of space, within and without, giving a fresh cosmic dimension to the eternal Truth, as envisaged in the Upanishads, that consciousness is infinite and absolute. White's primary concern in all his novels is a kind of vivisection, which unravels the elemental self from the tangle of consciousness through a repeated process of self-discovery, bringing on moments of rare felicity. All his novels in their unified entirety encompass the fluctuating moments of experience in relation to man and men, environment and nature. The paradigm changes are but the offshoots of the self, changeable, moment by moment, situation by situation.relationship to relationship, inevitably leading to the search for the centre, the "mandalic" whole. More precisely, to a concentrated visualization and intimate inner experience of the stages of consciousness that lead inward from the everyday polar play of ignorance––"avidya"—to the logic shattering paradox of eternity and time to the realization of the Universal Self (*Brahman-Atman*)–the "mandalic" kernal of man's existence. Transcendence resides not beyond but within, where the basic psyche merges with the soul and consciousness in celebration of what can be appropriately called "the mystery of Unity" ("The Prodigal Son" 118).

Works Cited

"Why Bother with Patrick White." 2001. 14 December 2006 <http/ abc.net.au/arts/white/opinions/white.html>.

Barnard, Marjorie. "The Four Novels of Patrick White." *Meanjin* 15.2 (1956): 156-170.

Berdyaev, Nicolas. *The Meaning of the Creative Act.* New York: Collier, 1962.

Bjorksten, Ingmar. *Patrick White: A General Introduction*. Trans. Stanley Gerson. St. Lucia: U of Queensland P, 1976.

Fisher, Robert. *Buddhist Art and Architecture.* London: Thames & Hudson, 1993.

Guerin, Wilfred L., et al. *A Handbook of Critical Approaches to Literature.* 3rd ed. New York: Oxford UP, 1999.

Herring, Thelma. "Self and Shadow: The Quest for Totality in *The Solid Mandala.*" *Ten Essays on Patrick White.* Ed. G. A. Wilkes. Sydney: Angus & Robertson, 1970. 72-80.

Herring, Thelma, and G. A. Wilkes. "A Conversation with Patrick White." *Southerly* 33.2 (1973): 133-141.

Mcgregor, Craig. "An Interview with Patrick White." *In the Making.* Ed. Craig Mcgregor. Melbourne: Nelson, 1969. 216-219.

Mackenzie, Manfred. "Patrick White's later Novels: A Generic Reading." *Southern Review* 1. 3 (1965): 5-17.

Murry, J. Middleton. *The Problem of Style.* London: Oxford UP, 1952

Shepherd, Ron. "An Indian Story: 'The Twitching Colonel.' " *Patrick White: A Critical Symposium.* Ed. Ron Shepherd and Kirpal Singh, Adelaide: Centre for Research in the New Literatures in English, 1978. 28-33.

Tanahashi, Kazaaki, and T. David Schneider. *Essential Zen.* New York: Harper Collins, 1994.

Tacey, David. " 'It's Happening Inside': The Individual and Changing Consciousness in White's Fiction." *Patrick White: A Critical Symposium.* Ed. Ron Shepherd and Kirpal Singh. Adelaide: Centre for Research in the New Literatures in English, 1978. 34-40.

Tucci, Guissepe. *The Theory and Practice of the Mandala.* London: Rider & Co., 1961.

Walsh, William. *Patrick White's Fiction.* Sydney: George Allen & Unwin, 1977.

White, Patrick. *Flaws in the Glass: A Self Portrait.* London: Jonathan Cape, 1981.

——. *The Twyborn Affair.* 1979. London: Penguin, 1981.

——. *A Fringe of Leaves.* 1976. London: Vintage, 1997.

——. *The Eye of the Storm.* 1973. London: Vintage, 1995.

——. *The Vivisector.* 1970. London: Vintage, 1994.

——. *The Solid Mandala.* London: Penguin, 1966.

——. *The Aunt's Story.* 1962. London: Vintage, 1994.

——. *Riders in the Chariot.* 1961. London: Vintage, 1996.

——. "The Prodigal Son." 1958. *The Writer in the Modern World: An Anthology of Twentieth Century Prose.* Ed. Harry Payne Heseltine and Stanley Tick. Melbourne: Cheshire & Cheshire, 1962. 115-118.

——. *Voss.* London: Eyre & Spottiswoode, 1957.

——. *The Tree of Man.* 1955. London: Penguin, 1967.

——. *The Living and the Dead.* London: Penguin, 1941.

——. *Happy Valley.* London: George G. Harrap & Co. Ltd., 1939.

Zimmer, Heinrich, and J. Campbell, eds. *Myths and Symbols in Indian Art and Civilization.* Princeton: Princeton UP, 1990.

"A World the Shape of an Eye"
Gerald Murnane's *The Plains* and Benedictus de Spinoza

Patrick West

The fiction of Gerald Murnane (b. 1939) interests me in large part because it engages with some of the philosophical concerns of Benedictus de Spinoza (b. 1632 – d. 1677), being inflected by them in ways that should complicate our understanding of his novels and short stories. This paper will introduce the similarities between the themes of *The Plains* (1982) and several of Spinoza's ideas, with particular reference to the productive concept of the "common notions" explored by Gilles Deleuze (b. 1925 – d. 1995) in his work on Spinoza (see Deleuze 1988 and 1992). However, Deleuze also allows us to articulate Murnane's difference from other Australian writers in a more general way; the emphasis on "innocence," "positivity" and Life that Deleuze finds in Spinoza is also at work in *The Plains.* With this in mind, I point out the concern with "vision" that Spinoza and Murnane share, as well as distinguishing the latter's work, briefly, from that of a writer with whom he is sometimes compared—David Malouf (b. 1934). At a fundamental level, both Spinoza and Murnane are in search of the same thing—ultimate perspective, perfect vision, community. (The connections among these things will become apparent shortly.) While on this occasion I will only discuss *The Plains*, it should be noted that Spinoza's influence can also be discerned clearly in other works of Murnane, most notably in the short story "Land Deal" (1980) and in the novels *Tamarisk Row* (1974) and *Inland* (1988).

There is no conscious engagement with Spinoza's philosophy by Murnane, who would certainly not consider himself a twenty-first century Spinozist, and may not even have read his work. Spinoza is rather a "fluctuating influence" on *The Plains*; he inhabits it strangely and unpredictably. The degree to which Spinoza's concepts take Murnane's text unawares is finally matched, however, by that to which *The Plains* allows us to rethink the philosopher's thought. In this novel, there is rich material for a reciprocal evaluation of Murnane's writing and the philosophy of Spinoza, although I formally prosecute only the first of these projects here. In simple terms, I want to put the case for Spinoza's importance to readers of Murnane's fiction, and also express some of the pleasures to be gained by reading this Australian writer alongside the best loved of Deleuze's philosophical "heroes." To date, most studies have either praised Murnane from a deconstructive viewpoint, or critiqued him as within the Romantic tradition. By contrast, *The Plains* gives us new possibilities for thinking about community and the relations between men and women. There is a sort of practical pleasure in reading this text, one equivalent to Deleuze's view of philosophy as a toolkit for living.

The Plains is a novel that *asks* to be described at a philosophical level, rather than through the more common devices of character development or plot. While in places it is a very funny text, most of our pleasure as readers is a direct result of the many speculations on being and consciousness that occupy the minds of all those who live on the plains and try to interpret them. This text involves thinking and speculation as a sort of infinite "opening up" to the world. Here is the first similarity with Spinoza. In his major study *Expressionism in Philosophy: Spinoza* (1992), Deleuze borrows a fertile phrase to describe his subject's intellectual milieu: it is characterised, he writes, by "an innocent way of setting out in one's thinking from infinity" (28). Deleuze takes this phrase from Merleau-Ponty's *Les Philosophes célèbres* (1956: 136). The best example of this tendency, he proposes, is Spinoza; but what does this phrase mean? I do not think of "innocence" in this case as a childlike exploration of the world unhindered by "adult" morality. While this notion does capture a little of the flavour of *The Plains* (and indeed of Murnane's fiction in general) it is not a reading of "innocence" that pins down Murnane's philosophical connection to Spinoza. "Innocence" in *The Plains* implies instead the concept of "positivity" that Deleuze attaches to it in his appreciation of Spinoza.

What I sense above all in Murnane—and this sets his fiction apart from most other Australian writers—is an engagement with what Deleuze simply calls Life: that is, the "positivity" of not attending to what restricts us, pulls us under, hurts us. Life as a series of encounters with all its possibilities. "Actually, there is only one term, Life, that encompasses thought," writes Deleuze "but conversely this term is encompassed only by thought. Not that life is *in* thinking, but only the thinker has a potent life, free of guilt and hatred; and only life explains the thinker" (1988: 14). Here is Deleuze at greater length on this topic:

> In his whole way of living and of thinking, Spinoza projects an image of the positive, affirmative life, which stands in opposition to the semblances that men are content with. Not only are they content with the latter, they feel a hatred of life, they are ashamed of it; a humanity bent on self-destruction, multi plying the cults of death, bringing about the union of the tyrant and the slave, the priest, the judge, and the soldier, always busy running life into the ground, mutilating it, killing it outright or by degrees, overlaying it or suffocating it with laws, properties, duties, em pires—this is what Spinoza diagnoses in the world, this betrayal of the universe and of mankind [. . .]. In the reproach that Hegel will make to Spinoza, that he ignored the negative and its power, lies the glory and *innocence* of Spinoza, his own discovery. In a world consumed by the negative, he has enough confidence in life, in the power of life, to challenge death, the murderous appetite of men, the rules of good and evil, of the just and the un-just. Enough confidence in life to denounce all the phantoms of the negative. (1988: 12-13; my em phasis)

Specifically, *The Plains* does not exacerbate the detrimental effects of "negativity" by drawing on the latter's power in order to make something "new" (for exam ple, a fresh constitution of the subject). Such a procedure must inevitably contradict the philosophy of Life, because it relies on subjugating one expression of Life in order to construct another, with both actually suffering harm. To this extent, Murnane's fiction should be distinguished from that of David Malouf, who frequently em ploys the inchoate force of the Other (Woman, or the non-Western figure, for instance) as the crucible from which to produce an ideal version of the Self (Man, a Western figure). Malouf frequently incites "negativity" in order to produce what can only be a com promised "positivity" in texts like *An Imaginary Life* (1979) and, more recently, his 1993 historical novel *Remembering Babylon* (for a review of this work with a similar case to my own, see Otto 1993). Murnane, by contrast, does not reproduce this sort of thinking, which is drawn from Romanticism and the Hegelian dialectical tradition. Instead, the film-maker in *The Plains* is attracted to the possibilities of Life, and furthermore he understands the passage towards this best of all philosophies as dependant on the perfection of his vision—the perfect film, or the achievement of ultimate perspective. In this respect, Murnane's text refers constantly to mirrors, lenses and glass:

> I heard of a scheme for building a system of indoor aquaria and stocking each tank with fish of one species only but arranging the whole so that viewers might see, through numerous thicknesses of pellucid glass and intervals of faintly clouded water and images of clouded water in faintly clouded glass, multi-form patterns of two colours that mattered. (*The Plains* 42)

And there are "goldsmiths, with eyes made monstrous by lenses gri pped under their brows" (*The Plains* 44). More specifically, there is a concern with perspective in *The Plains*: "[. . .] the presence of the plains filled the silent room while I myself tried to see them from the position that was the ideal centre [. . .]" (*The Plains* 123). Here, therefore, we have another similarity with Spinoza, whose parergal em ployment was as a grinder of lenses, a fact that Deleuze lingers over in this passage:

> The geometric method, the profession of polishing lenses, and the life of Spinoza should be understood as constituting a whole [. . .]. He [refers] to the third eye, which enables one to see life beyond all false appearances, passions, and deaths. The virtues—humility, poverty, chastity, frugality——are required for this kind of vision, no longer as virtues that mutilate life, but as powers that penetrate it and become one with it. Spinoza did not believe in hope or even in courage; he believed only in joy, and in vision. He let others live, provided that others let him live. He wanted only to inspire, to waken, to reveal. The purpose of [. . .] the third eye is not to command or even to convince, but only to shape the glass or polish the lens for this inspired free vision. (1988: 14)

Let me qualify and refine this connection between Deleuze's reading of Spinoza and *The Plains* before going on. Murnane is far from naively joyful. His novel is actually quite sensitive to the restrictions on the possibilities of human life, which are fundamentally to do with language. All the supposed film-maker ever does is write ream upon ream of notes for the film, "The Interior," which he never begins to shoot; and there is a constant sense of the foreboding presence of speech and writing in the text. Language is figured as something that proliferates and engulfs, with adverse effects; and nowhere more so than in the library where the narrator spends much of his time:

> The countless volumes of this library are close-set with so much speculative prose, so many chapters after chapters appear in parentheses, such glosses and footnotes surround the thin trickles of actual text that I fear to discover in some unexceptional essay by a plainsman of no great reputation a tentative paragraph describing a man not unlike myself speculating endlessly about the plains but never setting foot on them. (*The Plains* 101)

The Plains in addition, however—and this is its primary impulse—suggests a way of going beyond the linguistic excesses that also troubled Spinoza, and which challenged him, furthermore, to transcend them too. Spinoza was born less than twenty years after the death, in 1616, of William Shakespeare, the playwright who represents more than any other figure the pre-eminently *linguistic* character of seventeenth-century Europe. While Spinoza does not refer to Shakespeare, one can sense his presence in the philosopher's distrust of language as a way of engaging with the basic truth of the world. Language, for Spinoza (as a philosopher rather than a poet) was the least reliable element of the lowest level of knowledge.

Up to this point, I have argued for a similarity between Murnane and Spinoza that, taken by itself, is perhaps too general to be useful; it lies in Life, "positivity," and "an innocent way of setting out in one's thinking from infinity" (1992: 28).This comparison can be established more concretely by means of Spinoza's concept of the "common notions." Some terms to be introduced in what follows have a specific meaning in Spinoza's philosophy. By "bodies," first of all, Spinoza expands and inflects our contemporary comprehension of human body—not only is it a complex entity matched by other non-human bodies on the same plane of existence, but the body for Spinoza is the key to a human's life. (He is writing, of course, before the modern idea of the discrete subject set apart from the rest of the universe, and defined by the mind—in short, Man as "invented.") At this level, too, Murnane engages with Spinoza. In *The Plains*, the idea of the subject uncannily resembles Spinoza's early modern perspective on it:

> [. . .] no thinker has seriously entertained the possibility that the state of a man at some moment in his life may be illuminated by a study of the same man at some moment said, for convenience, to have preceded the moment in question. For all their preoccupation with childhood and youth, plains-men have never considered, except as illustrations of self-evident falsehoods, the theory that the flaws in a man result from some primal mishap, or its corollaries, that a man's life is a decline from a state of original satisfaction and that our joys and pleasures are only a compromise between our wants and our circumstances. (*The Plains* 84-85)

In this passage, Murnane captures the major consequence of the version of the subject proposed by Spinoza, which is that as bodies in flux with all other bodies—being affected by them—we lack an essential or fixed nature. We are defined by external encounters. "For it comes about at times," writes Spinoza "that a man suffers such changes that it is difficult to say he is the same [man] [. . .]" (Part IV, Proposition 39, Note 167). Interestingly, however, Spinoza would probably not see as a "self-evident falsehood" the last sentiment of this passage about the delimited nature of our joys and pleasures. This is a good example of Murnane's text critiquing Spinoza's philosophy, rather than the other way round (*The Plains* 85). It would be a valuable project to think about how, from quite similar initial premises, Murnane and Spinoza come to opposed conclusions in this respect. However, such a task goes beyond the scope of the present paper.

A "Common notion" is what two or more bodies (and, on a secondary stratum, the minds associated with those bodies) have in common. When it encounters another body with which it agrees, a body is able to increase its power twice over: first, by virtue of the agreement itself; and second, through the "common notion" it is therefore able to form with that body. All bodies enjoy a certain relation of motion and rest (what Spinoza labels extension). A body increases its power when its relation of motion and rest agrees with the relation of the body it encounters, and when it becomes active through the better understanding of that agreement, which is the part of the "common notion." On the other hand, a body loses power when its relation of motion and rest does not agree with that of another body it encounters—in the extreme case, this leads to death. All the bodies involved in an agreeable or good encounter necessarily benefit from it, because increase in power relies, in the end, on the "coming together" of every body. To this extent, there is a theory of sociability and community entwined with Spinoza's concept of the "common notions." Such an increase in power (agreement plus the "common notion," leading towards action) can also be called composition, and its opposite, decomposition. Ultimate decomposition is death, but the acme of composition is the same as "the intellectual love of God" (Spinoza: Part V). It is this that Deleuze calls "inspired free vision" (1992: 14). Or Life itself.

The practical face of composition is *activity*. The more active we are able to be, the nearer we approach to perfect vision; and we can increase our capacity to act by maximizing both the number of good encounters we have, and the sensitivity of our body to the effects of these encounters. (This second requirement is the most difficult to fulfil; as the obscure trigger for the recognition of a "common notion" it is not easily explained and I will leave it here for subsequent consideration.) How are we able to heed this first demand then? Spinoza points out that all bodies, despite their possible lack of agreement on a specific level, nevertheless have extension (motion and rest) in common on the universal level. This allows us to judge which encounters will be favourable to us, and which will not, because the universal "common notion" adds to our knowledge of the nature of all bodies. It has a very practical function, akin to the biological (not abstract or mathematical) nature of all the "common notions." Spinoza's universe is therefore not only atomic (capable of producing an infinite number of encounters, random or planned), but unified (practically so) through the universal "common notion." How does all this come together in *The Plains*? It appears to set the scene, at least, for the emergence of good encounters and, eventually, for the irruption of "inspired free vision" (1992: 14).

Murnane's text is also characterized by atomism and unity. Take these lines for exam ple: "He saw the countless objects in his home as a few visible points on some invisible graph of stupendous com plexity" (*The Plains* 21), and "They lie far apart, but I can see them as a constellation if I wish" (*The Plains* 49). Besides many passages like this one, however, there is one long section in *The Plains* where seven figures, designated only as 1st Landowner, 2nd Landowner etc., stand around a bar talking while the film-maker listens (*The Plains* 46-62). There is a form of unity here to the extent that there is no differentiation through proper names (indeed, there are none in the text whatsoever), but there is also atomism as an effect of the numbers used to designate the speakers. (In addition, there is an interesting coincidence here between Spinoza's famous device "God or nature" (Part IV) and the absence of proper names in *The Plains.* It is almost as if the specificity of God, as the model of proper names which deny unity, is dissolved by Spinoza into the basic unity and remarkable atomism of his version of nature. Just as the Landowners partici pate in both these things.) The following passage is also characterized by its interplay of unity and atomism:

> I thought at first that they were talking only of women. But then I distinguished three quite separate conversations, each advancing steadily. Sometimes one or other topic occupied them all, but usually each man divided his attention among the three debates, leaning across the man beside him or leaving his stool for a moment to engage some opponent along the bar. (*The Plains* 47-48)

The topic is initially seen as unified, before the film-maker perceives it as atomic. The Landowners themselves, meanwhile, switch back and forth between the unity of common speculation on one of the three topics, and what might be described as a multi ple or atomic approach. I understand this as akin to Spinoza's philosophical system, in which universal unity allows one to judge the outcome of the atomic connections (good or bad encounters) that are also foregrounded as active.

There is, in addition, significance in the reference to women in this passage. Women in *The Plains* are fundamentally associated with the body. However, this is not a conservative move on Murnane's part, as some theoretical traditions that deny the com plexity of the body would have it. The idea that the "common notions" are fundamentally to do with bodies produces women as key actors on the plains in the escape from language towards "the intellectual love of God," perfect vision, community (Spinoza: Part V). As part of the unity and atomism of *The Plains*, women are central to its project. Deleuze was fascinated by a utopian sentence of Spinoza's: "We do not know what the body can do [. . .]" (1988: 17). The following line from *The Plains*, one of the Landowners speaking, sensationally approximates this sentiment: "But do we know what our own bodies are leading us towards?" (*The Plains* 50). Murnane's answer (at least the answer his fiction might give) would, I believe, mirror Deleuze's: towards new sorts of communities, ones based on a "common notion." "It is no longer a matter of utilizations or captures, but of sociabilities and communities," writes Deleuze (1988: 126).

Furthermore, as with Spinoza, bodies in *The Plains* do not only *encounter* other bodies (the strongest im plication in the Landowner's question), they are also figured as more and more sensitive to the effects of their encounters: "I com posed my face to register a variety of powerful emotions" (*The Plains* 10). To this extent, Murnane's text hints at a solution to the problem I passed over in the above: how to think about the obscure trigger required for the recognition of a "common notion"? Murnane adds to our appreciation of Spinoza, as much as the other way around (although, as I have already commented, I am only concerned with the second of these projects here).

Recalling another of Spinoza's concepts—parallelism—it is here as if mind or intellect (the speculations of the Landowners) do not have to dominate over the body nor, which would be the same thing really, does the body have to subjugate the mind: in both cases the same structure of "negativity" would obtain. The mind does not subjugate the body, because *The Plains* insists on the (bodily) possibility of the "common notions," and the body does not have power over the mind, because the "common notions" are determined to be inclusive, communitarian. Deleuze calls parallelism "a correspondence between autonomous or independent series" (1992: 107). Murnane's text escapes the Romantic trap that denies Life, therefore, not by deconstructing the Hegelian oppositions with which it works (a post-structuralist or deconstructive project), but by adopting a model from the seventeenth century, in which the body and the mind finally proceed together, on what might be called the "plain" of Life. (I am not convinced by either Sue Gillett's (1990) approach, which reads Murnane as working inside Romanticism, nor by Imre Salusinszky's (1989 and 1993), which argues that Murnane deconstructs this (and other) traditions.) The body, with all it can do, might lead the mind, but it is not above it. Deleuze encourages the Spinozist to "engage in a comparison of powers that leads us to discover more in the body than we know, and hence more in the mind than we are conscious of" (1988: 90).

By the end of the novel, it is clear that the film-maker will not make the film he has been planning for so long. There is nevertheless a proleptic vision of *The Interior* as itself only an aspect of another film, which implies that we may already be closer to the ideal of perfect vision and community than we know: "I had sometimes thought of *The Interior* as a few scenes from a much longer film that could only be seen from a vantage point that I knew nothing of" (*The Plains* 66). If the film-maker's goal is only a stage on the way to somewhere else, how many stages might we, by the last page of the book, already have traversed? This is how I would like to think about *The Plains* in the end; although the question must still fascinate any reader: Is ultimate perspective possible? This was the challenge Spinoza set his contemporaries, and it continues to call to us from *The Plains* of contemporary Australian literature.

Works Cited

Deleuze, Gilles. *Spinoza: Practical Philosophy.* Trans. Robert Hurley. San Francisco: City Lights, 1988. Trans. of *Spinoza: Philosophie Pratique.* Paris: Universitaires de France, 1970.

——. *Expressionism in Philosophy: Spinoza.* Trans. Martin Joughin. New York: Zone, 1992. Trans. of *Spinoza et le Problème de L'expression.* Paris: Minuit, 1968.

Gillett, Sue. "Loving and Hating the *Inland* Reader: Postmodern Ploys or Romantic Reaction?" *A Sense of Audience: Essays in Post-Colonial Literatures.* Ed. William McGaw. Spec. issue of *Span* 30 (April 1990): 59-68.

Malouf, David. *Remembering Babylon.* 1993. London: Vintage-Random, 1994.

——. *An Imaginary Life.* London: Chatto, 1979.

Merleau-Ponty, Maurice. *Les Philosophes célèbres.* Paris: Lucien Mazenod, 1956.

Murnane, Gerald. *Inland.* 1988. Sydney: Pan-Picador, 1989.

——. *The Plains.* 1982. Ringwood, Victoria: Penguin, 1984.

——. "Land Deal." *Velvet Waters.* 1980. Ringwood, Victoria: McPhee-Penguin, 1990. 55-60.

——. *Tamarisk Row.* 1974. London: Sirius-Angus, 1983.

Otto, Peter. "Forgetting Colonialism." Rev. of *Remembering Babylon*, by David Malouf. *Meanjin* 52.3 (Spring 1993): 545-58.

Salusinszky, Imre. *Gerald Murnane.* Ed. Chris Wallace-Crabbe. Melbourne: Oxford UP, 1993.

——. Murnane, Husserl, Derrida: The Scene of Writing." *Australian Literary Studies* 14.2 (October 1989): 188-198.

Spinoza. *Ethics and Treatise on the Correction of the Intellect.* Trans. Andrew Boyle and G. H. R. Parkinson. 1677. London: Dent, 1993.

Apparitions of Desire
Homo-Eros in Elizabeth Jolley's Fiction

Aneeta Rajendran

Australian fiction in its early years did not, by and large, have very strong female fictional presences, and it was only from the 1970s onwards that the feminine managed to make herself heard, but even so, in the meanwhile, Australia almost destroyed, with lack of encouragement, one of its most comprehensive fictional intelligences—Elizabeth Jolley (b. 1923 – d. 2007), who migrated to Australia from Britain in 1959 suffered as many as thirty-nine rejections of one manuscript in one year. By the end of the 1990s, writers as diverse as Beverley Farmer (b. 1941), Elizabeth Riley (b. 1946), Finola Moorhead (b. 1947) and Susan Hawthorne (b. 1951) had tried their hand at writing the lesbian from Down Under, but even so, the most challenging oeuvre still remains Jolley's. Her first book was published only in 1973,[1] when she was already 53, but she had begun writing in her twenties, and much of the work that got published in the 1970s draws upon these early writings, which makes her even more of a trailblazer, given her enforced literary solitariness. Critical acclaim came still later, and sustained critical enquiry even later, with the result that most major works on Australian history did not mention Jolley except in passing even when discussing important Australian women novelists of the 1980s, in which decade Jolley published almost a dozen works.[2] However, in retrospect, it is now more than evident, to both the critical and the general public, that Elizabeth Jolley's is a literary talent that ranks in the premier scale of Australian writers. Jolley's writing will reward sustained inquiry, given the depth and focus of her engagement with life.

A number of Jolley's works use the same characters, in different literary skins, with the result that the reader feels that she is caught in the web of a rather grand design here, but it is a felicitous design. For Jolley's protagonists, being impossible outsiders to their worlds, come equipped with a fine sense of the ridiculous, a consequence probably of their location as observers to their own lives, even within their own narratives. Her compassion for her characters is unfailing—their inadequacies, their inability to cope with the pinched misery of their small lives, all register memorably in the mind of the reader because Jolley, with the sureness of touch possessed only by major writers in any language, is able to depict them with tenderness, with empathy, even as her sharp comic touch never misses the ridiculousness of the characters' stratagems.

Jolley's superlative comic genius is almost perverse in the range of the life-altering littlenesses she is capable of depicting. Meanwhile, the protagonists who embark upon these stratagems teeter perennially on the brink of exile—they never can belong, and often do not wish to belong. Self-reflexive humour is often the only survival strategy at their disposal, the only garment they are able to pack as they flee in the dark from their chimaeras now become real. In novel after novel, Jolley calculatedly creates an atmosphere of psychological uncertainty and disorientation by repeating, like strains of music, words, phrases, characters that bear uncanny similarities to other characters, events retold in a slightly different way each new time. And in novel after novel, the authorial voice and the voice of the various narrators reveals a fine awareness, anchored in their knowledge of human absurdity, of the vicissitudes of being human, female, and often, bisexual or lesbian. I am going to examine below three novels, *My Father's Moon* (1989), *Cabin Fever* (1990) and *The Georges' Wife* (1993), as illustrative of some of Jolley's central fictional concerns—woman as seeker, woman as mother, woman as daughter, woman as lover of women, woman as wife and mistress of a man, and finally, the woman as unfulfilled seeker, but as careful writer and archiver of her own life-experiences, and in this sense, successful, besides being a light unto future generations, though the protagonist herself is completely unable to value her contribution positively.

While they are separate works in themselves, these three novels may also be read as companion pieces in a fictionalized autobiography. Vera Wright, Jolley's fictional alter-ego, is sometimes a runaway, sometimes an exile sent to Botany Bay for life, sometimes a mother, sometimes a daughter, often in love with a woman and sometimes with a man. By way of random imagery and constantly altering time frames, Jolley's narrator recreates her life: from her days in boarding school, her youth in an army hospital during World War II, her complex relationships with her parents and friends, her love-affair with the ambivalent and distant Dr. Metcalf, her experiences of social stigma and loneliness brought on by her status as an unwed mother in the years following the War, her attempts at providing her daughter a decent life by working at a variety of live-in jobs; her next affair with the much older Mr. George, and subsequent marriage to him in Australia, where she resettles, to the present time of writing, presumably in Australia, alone to all outward appearance. Through all of the novels runs a series of repetitions, of characters with resemblances to one another, bits of music, snatches of song, events whose ramifications are yet to fully emerge. An almost phantasmagoric sense of déjà vu is created and kept up throughout the trilogy, with very few explanations that will finally "solve" the disquieting questions earlier renditions of the same episode have raised. In breaking the mould of the traditional narrative—both that of the novel and the fictionalized autobiography, in refusing to "solve the puzzle" by showing the ghosts melt in sunlight, Jolley forces the reader to enter the design. Once in, much like the fly in the web, we are left with no choice but to inspect closely the ambiguities of human desire, as manifested in the characters' often fraught lives.

The fictional universe of the trilogy is a predominantly gynocentric one: their connecting thread is the presence of the various women (or their apparitions) who have had crucial, life-altering effects on Vera. Sometimes it is a mother—Vera's real mother, or positive mother surrogates like Gertrude and the Rice Widow, or apparitional, ardently-desired surrogates like staff-nurse Ramsden—that constitutes the link; at other times, it is various disaffecting and disabusing loves, like Lois and Magda, who reappear on Vera's fictional terrain. The figure of the mother, whether biological and surrogate, is an almost overpowering one in the "daughter's" negotiation of life, threatening, as it were, to strangle the daughter with the umbilicus itself. This perceived unconcern of the mother produces an anxiety so abject in Vera that she is extremely susceptible to young women like Lois and Magda whose difference from the "mothering" women is both positive and negative—on the one hand, they cannot strangle Vera; but on the other hand, they lack a nourishing placenta. Instead, they suck Vera's soul out, but Vera, almost always, makes herself available for abuse. Elizabeth Jolley's exploration of relationships between women is thus extremely aware of the fineness of the line between what is "lesbian" and what might be designated as "normal" female bonding. At the same time, Jolley reveals an equally fine appreciation of the sadnesses of lesbian love, instead of focusing, in Utopian fashion, upon only its joys. But given the period—the decades after the Second World War, when much of the narrative was written, and given the absence of the explicitly sexual from the page, how do these novels make their border crossings between the homosocial, the homosexual and the homoerotic? I shall examine how exile functions as a crucial metaphor for erotic unhappiness and sexual silencing. Exile, self-chosen or imposed, is a crucial strategy employed by both author and writer-protagonist in their re-structuring of eros in this trilogy.

Which begs the question: what exactly is a lesbian novel? Should we look exclusively for acts of sexual consummation? Or would primary erotic affinities, preferably between characters who are not biologically related do? Or should we also stipulate that the author should be lesbian? And what if she's had children, and husbands? Would she still be a lesbian writer, this putative author of lesbian fiction? Lesbian fiction has always been marked by this enforced amorphousness of definition. Bonnie Zimmerman (1981) offers a helpful set of guidelines for membership: first, the writer must identify herself with the lesbian community, second, there must be a central lesbian character and third, the work must be read by lesbians as an affirmation of lesbian existence. Elizabeth Jolley does almost none of these things: though critics have remarked that the two overpowering themes in her fiction are "lesbianism and motherhood," Jolley herself has been very recalcitrant on the subject, though almost all her works draw very closely upon autobiographical sources. And never in her novels is any character identifiable solely as a lesbian—in fact, her characters actively resist any attempt to collapse their selfhoods with their sexual identities or proclivities. However, it is in the reading that the proof of this pudding lies—Jolley's fiction is actively "lesbian" in its re-triangulation of the laws of eros that decree that women's primary erotic affinities and loyalties should be male-centered. And, above all, Jolley's work also portrays the lesbian as an older woman—a rare and shocking (!) sight in most lesbian literary landscapes. All too often, the reader is forced to be content with the Utopian lesbian novel's very dubious equivalent of "and they lived happily ever after," when we are certain that this elision is merely a strategy to safeguard the reader against disillusionment in a hetero-patriarchal universe that is also ageist.

Traditional ideas of the "lesbian," as much as newer queer ideas, help in the interpretation of Jolley's works. Catharine Stimpson's (1982) definition of "lesbian" as "a woman who finds other women erotically attractive and gratifying" confines itself to the "flesh," which "distinguishes it from gestures of political sympathy for homosexuals and from affectionate friendships which women enjoy with each other" (301). Lesbianism, then, is "a commitment of skin, blood, breast and bone," (301) for Stimpson, while Adrienne Rich (1986) prefers "the term *lesbian continuum* to include a range—through each woman's life and throughout history—of woman-identified experience; not simply the fact that a woman has had or consciously desired genital experience with another woman" (qtd. in Zimmerman 121). While this is a very inclusive definition, it risks eliding specificities that pertain to the sexual. Lillian Faderman's (1981) definition of lesbian to describe "a relationship in which two women's strongest emotions and affections are directed toward each other" might prove most useful (qtd. in Zimmerman 122). Faderman does not make sexual contact a defining factor, but instead prioritises intimacy: "By preference, the two women spend most of their time together and share most aspects of their life with each other" (qtd. in Zimmerman 122).

Vera, with no apparent contradiction in her own perception of things, does not find the categories and roles of mother and lesbian exclusive. The figure of the lesbian, whether it be in the sense of the woman who carnally desires other women, or in the sense of the woman who has homosocial, but not necessarily sexual relationships with other women, is central to Elizabeth Jolley's fiction. Vera's life-story is an illustration of how female homosociality and homosexuality are part of a very porous if not seamlessly joined continuum between the affectional and the sexual. There is no very clear demarcation of the "lesbian" to other forms of female interaction, such as mother–daughter bonds, sisterly ones, and so on.

Eve Kosofsky Sedgwick, in *Between Men* (1985), posits that male homosocial bonding, with the triangle of man–man–woman at its core, is the prime means by which patriarchal society maintains its heterosexual stranglehold over other sexualities. Setting Sedgwick's argument between women in *My Father's Moon*, *Cabin Fever* and *The Georges' Wife*, one can see how this triangular formation can be counterplotted to achieve the subversive aims of the lesbian fiction, where men are between women: here, the male erotic triangulation, that, according to Sedgwick is the precondition for female desire, is either conspicuous by its absence, or crumbling under assault. Terry Castle's *The Apparitional Lesbian* (1993) holds that the ghostly figure of the lesbian character often re-shapes fictional eros in implicit, often covert, subversive ways that make it impossible to view heteronormativity as either omnipotent, or universally satisfying. As Castle (1999) puts it, what is achieved is the decanonisation of "the canonical structure of desire itself" (83). Conventional erotic geometry is mercilessly side-stepped with these new coordinates, but is this a stable configuration? Will it hold? The lesbian novel seems to treat of the reconfigured, re-triangulated erotic triangle in two distinct ways. There is the euphoric, or Utopian view of this new system of codification, and there is the Dystopian version, the dying fall, the narrative of the femme damnée.

The energies of the "euphoric" lesbian novel are, as Terry Castle notes, primarily comic and visionary. Such novels can thus be called novels of liberation, and cling, even when the possibilities look increasingly grim, to the hope of euphoric resolution, often successfully replacing the male–male–female triangle with the female–female–male one, through community, sorority and stable female bonding. The narrative of damnation shows the collapse, often under its own contradictions, of the female–female–male triangle; when equilibrium is restored, the erring women are once again back in the fold of the magnanimous or malevolent, as the case may be, male wing.

The almost entirely gynocentric worlds of hospital and maternity home posit a very plausible dissolution or non-existence of male homosociality: the male presence is tenuous, if not altogether non-existent, and would make possible at least a shortlived euphoric celebration. However, Vera suffers so much joylessness in each such female compartment–lack of food in one boarding school, post-partum depression and emotional deprivation in another–that it is obvious that Jolley does not see the euphoric consolation as a viable one, given that it can be kept alive only in environments that the male is artificially excluded from. In all, the trilogy is pessimistic about the threat of homosexuality *as such* to happiness. All lesbian relationships, consummated or unconsummated, are ultimately ruptured by the constrictions society places on women. Jolley is unflinching in her analysis of the disaffection, unhappiness, tendencies towards suicide, and self-hatred, to name only a few "taboo" subjects, all of which exist within lesbian culture.

The balance thus, hangs in favour of the narrative of damnation. Vera creates for herself a mythology of darkness, a world in which she moves through dreams and shadows, and this shadow world of her love for another woman is always in direct contrast to the other world, of sunlight and flowers, in which she loves men, men like Mr. George and Dr. Metcalf. Vera does rebel, paradoxically, both by the acting out of the devalued female role and the total or partial rejection of her sex-role stereotype, but in the end, capitulates, never seeing the Rice Widow, or replying to her letters, after a visit, when "No one in the world (including Mr. George), knows where we are" (*The Georges Wife* 169), that looks like an assertion of absolute independence.

Vera's withdrawal from the Rice Widow is the juncture at which the narrative of damnation takes over the narrative of escape, though this is counterbalanced with Vera's, and by extension, Jolley's gentle ridicule of the lesbian novel's tendency to end euphorically: "I am certain that a confrontation of recognition, a reunion, with exclamations and animated conversation, on a train would be like the hoped for ending of a particular kind of novel. I mean, how can anyone's life, in reality, at the present time, contain the fulfillment of expectation and the happy ending of a romantic fiction" (*Cabin Fever* 237). There will be no such utopian vision of happiness or fruition, of desire fulfilled, and hope realised. At the time of Jolley's writing these novels, which predates their publication by a couple of decades, this kind of happy ending might not have been a feasible one, one more indication of Jolley's effort at realistic representation of the lesbian.

This resignation to heterosexual unhappiness in the place of what may have been homo-erotic/lesbian fulfillment, places the novels within the gird of what, according to Catharine Stimpson, have, traditionally, been the two repetitive patterns discernible in lesbian fiction. These are the dying fall, a narrative of damnation, of the lesbian's suffering as a lonely outcast attracted to a psychological lower caste; and the enabling escape, a narrative of the reversal of such descending trajectories, of the lesbian's rebellion against social stigma and self-contempt (Warhol 301-302). Jolley's trilogy, in spite of the quietness of its rendition of the protagonist's deep unhappiness, despite her movement from relatively lower-middle-class nurse to well-off doctor, is in essence a narrative of the

problem of identifying or defining the lesbian text. Silenced by a homophobic and misogynistic society, writers who write about lesbian desire have been forced to adopt coded and obscure language, and internal censorship. Vera, and by extension, Jolley, decides to censor herself by giving up the notion of "speaking" her desire, a strategy that might reflect the early date of the conception and writing of these books, since lesbian silence is, now, itself gradually becoming a thing of the past, especially in the First World. Vera prefers to revert, instead, to the older language of symbol, buying a violin case, though ironically, no violin, to impress Vera with this display of her love of music, so as to avoid the near-total humiliation she fears if "outed," should Vera not return her love. The trilogy thus becomes one long plaint of unhappiness, partly self-created, and partly socially prescribed, the timidity of their expressions of love marking the time of their coming into the world.

My Father's Moon, *Cabin Fever* and *The Georges' Wife* are all scarred and fissured by the slant telling of the truth, and marked by images of self-abnegation, diminution, sadness, and the wish for death. Writing the lesbian into existence in the days before Stonewall, before the Feminist and Gay movements, writers had to use codes and strategies for survival, and the silences in the text are an indication of the actual state of the society, or the historical moment, in the first half of the last century that Vera, the literal "writer" of the story, inhabits. Vera inhabits the "Well of Loneliness" that Radclyffe Hall (1928) warned of. Vera's experience of isolation is an overpowering one, despite the gynocentrism of the nursing-hospital setting. Vera's story, and by extension, Jolley's texts, are shaped by the simple fact of their having been written without the knowledge of the experiences of others, and with little or no hope of support from a woman's and/or lesbian writing community. The only place where lesbian relationships are acceptable in this post-war England setting is in the nightmare atmosphere of Fairfields. But there again, there are hints of promiscuity and emotional disaffection which leave Vera unenthused and desirous of escape. There is no "network" of lesbian foremothers, no other system of sanctioned homosocial bonding to help Vera tide over her crises. The desperations of having to be dependent on men, of the never-acknowledged fear of the potential exclusion attendant on the "outing" of a lesbian identity, of the marginality of lesbian existence on the periphery of patriarchy trigger off the elliptical style of her narration. The act of writing is also associated with silence, and further complicated by the inadequacy of language.

My Father's Moon, *Cabin Fever* and *The Georges' Wife* are tactfully reticent about what lesbians do with one another, and of course about what they do in bed, though occasionally, a coyly explicit statement may break through: for instance, Vera says "Lois is fond in bed introducing me to previously unimagined experiments and sweetness" (*Cabin Fever* 222). But the Lois episode is one solitary oasis in a desert of erotic silence. Beyond this, one has to be content with that staple of lesbian fiction, the archetypal lesbian kiss, which Jolley treats with typical restraint, neither denying nor wholly revealing lesbian eroticism: "The kiss the widow gives me [. . .] is not a cool-li pped brushing of a powdered cheek crum pling against mine. It is a com pelling kiss, masterful and tender at the same time" (*The Georges Wife* 105). The kiss, of course, has vast metonymic possibilities, while, simultaneously, its exact signification is left deliberately opaque.

However, it is not the erotic silences that are most disturbing, but the psychic ones—Vera attem pts to walk off a balcony in *My Father's Moon*, when she is pregnant, and is only just prevented by her father. The im possibility of reconciling lesbian love with motherhood produces a constant state of anxiety and tension for the protagonist. The motif of the missing mother is an im portant structural and thematic link that joins all the three novels. Where the protagonist is desirous of being mothered, she is forced to mother her children before she can find a suitable mother surrogate. Non-sexual bonding is a very im portant part of the novel, though Vera's bonds with her own mother are full of grief, anger and frustration. But Vera suicidally spurns a number of surrogate mothers: Gertrude, the first in the series, is the symbol of maternal plenitude itself, as opposed to her less demonstrative, real mother. Gertrude is turned down for the flashy and inconstant Magda, who betrays Vera by deserting her, along with her husband, Dr. Metcalf, whose child Vera is pregnant with. Vera's affair with Dr. Metcalf, the father of her child, is so shadowily represented that one wonders if he is not really an excuse for immaculate conception of a sort, an excuse invented because Vera is really drawn to women, who cannot "father a child"—Ramsden and Gertrude are in the wings then. The circumstances and even the veracity of Dr. Metcalf's supposed death are kept shrouded in mystery, with the result that he begins to seem, in retrospect, less an actual person than a wraith Vera invents to exorcise herself of her forbidden love for staff-nurse Ramsden, Gertrude and Magda. Gertrude, like Ramsden, stays on Vera's mind, with her letters to Vera, like those from the Rice Widow, her last lover, taking on a talismanic function: Gertrude is the mother incarnate, nature herself, who alone can resuscitate Vera. But Vera has severed her connections with her metaphorical parent, and thus, the resurrection is always deferred. Gertrude too dies, her death symptomatic of the lesbian narrative of damnation, where thwarted desire manifests itself as death.

However, some form of resurrection is at hand, in the form of the Rice Widow, who appears only in the last book, *The Georges' Wife*, where hers is the overpowering presence. This book begins and ends with her, and she alone of all characters, male or female, is able to give Vera, now presumably in her thirties, both emotional succour and mental stimulation. The Rice Widow, who is not given any other moniker throughout, nicknames Vera as "Migrant"—and Vera has indeed now become a migrant, not only in that she has come to Australia, but in that she travels between being the nurse of the man she has married, a man who constantly demands attention, and being the Rice-Widow's companion on their escapades together.

The primary source of tension between the lovers is that of the strain between their little world and the larger world of society and family that fears them. The world of the ship, where the pair first meet, is a restricted, hermetically sealed one, but this does not stop, metaphorically, the blue waters of the oceans in which it sails, from rushing in. The two of them are with each other a great deal, and Vera feels "closed in and safe" (*The Georges Wife* 118) when they are together in the widow's cabin, where she begs to be allowed to stay. Mr. George does not like their friendship, but the widow refuses to be dissuaded, saying, tersely, that "a man, like an illness, can separate people, can break a friendship [. . .]" (*The Georges Wife* 116), the implication being that the women's relationship is, on the other hand, not possessive in the way a heterosexual one might be. This does express a revolutionary model of sexuality which in its structure, its content, and its practice defies the fundamental principles and assumptions of patriarchal culture, such as the assumption that women will direct their emotional energy to one man, and to their children from this relationship. Whenever the widow appears, there is an affirmation of the value of femaleness, women's bodies, women's sexuality, distinctly unlike the Vera in the company of anyone else in the novel.

But towards the end of *The Georges' Wife*, one realises that the widow is the destination, the Holy Grail, of Vera's quest and that Vera will once again not stay the full distance. The Rice Widow's house, like Vera's mother's, "stands open to the spring, to all the seasons" (*The Georges Wife* 165) and here, for the first and for the last time, Vera is able to feel at one with nature. But the widow's rice farm, in the middle of huge plains, remains only a mirage in the desert of Vera's life. Though the house is calming and open, it is also exposed—"and when darkness falls it is a black impenetrable darkness and it comes quickly with a cold wind as in a desert" (*The Georges Wife* 164). The house is a place of unnatural enclosure, despite its location in the open fields stretching out to the horizon, "It is just the same here as it was on the ship, isn't it?" (*The Georges Wife* 166), asks the widow, and so it is. It is a private world, where neither routine pursues them, nor Mr. George's presence, as it had done on the real ship. But most idylls, even of refound Edens, must end.

"The suppression of the homosexual component of human sexuality, and by corollary, the oppression of homosexuals, is [. . .] a product of the same system whose rules and relations oppress women," writes Gayle Rubin (qtd. in Sedgwick, 1991: 465). Because such a system defines women's subject positions and social standing through their relationships with men, with male-female relationships being given priority over female-female ones, male-female relations may occasion the disruption or destruction of female-female relations. But again, it is also the widow who tells Vera of the need to have her relationship with Mr. George recognised, socially, because "the whole world [. . .] is for couples" (*The Georges Wife* 135).

It is, also, however, the widow who mothers Vera, initiating her into a number of cultural observances and protocols, passing on vital information about female survival, though it is almost certain that Vera, as the successful daughter, will outgrow her need to be "mothered." That the line of succession of this "mothering" is tenuous, and therefore, not a biologically determined one is evident when Vera realises she has no one to pass the legacy on to, because her daughters are at a distance, literally and figuratively. Vera, despite the widow's repeated entreaties, terminates the relationship through withdrawal. The widow, unable to bear her loneliness, goes to Europe, where she dies in a bus accident. This death finds Vera inheriting her money, but Vera is unable to use the money to find herself happiness, now that her real mentor has died, leaving her alone, irrevocably this time, for ever. The tragedy of Vera's breaking-off from the Rice Widow is evident when she is left with no one to whom she can, in turn, mother, though, paradoxically, she has chosen to leave her for the apparently satisfying heterosexual prerogatives of wifehood and succumbing to the lure of the institution of the family, of the "family" of two parents and their offspring, though she has had bitter experiences with the pettiness of this arrangement. Even though the lesbian may have children whom she loves, she must reject the patriarchal family, which the stigma against her helps to maintain, if she is to attain self-fulfillment as well. This tension between the role of the mother, which the lesbian may desire, and the traditional family structure, in which women are subordinate, is characteristic of lesbian writing. As Catharine Stimpson puts it, man may have both paternity and power, but a woman must too often choose between maternity and comparative powerlessness (Warhol 308). Jolley's novels explore this paradox through Vera's need to both become part of a similar structure, and to break out of its bounds.

The three novels are dialogised in that they undermine ideological unity, whether of the patriarchal or feminist, liberal or conservative sort. Vera's naïveté forces into the open the unspoken repressions of the marginalised by the dominant, thus making them vulnerable to interpretation, contradiction and dialogue. This takes place in a continuous manner in the trilogy, with each moment of absolute and paralysing seriousness being matched by a corresponding comic moment, with the interplay of the two moods throughout placing the content in perspective. But despite her acerbic comments, wry humor and mordant wit, the play of speech which is traditionally allowed the male fool is denied the uncomprehending woman. Vera's desire to walk off the edge of the corridor into the abyss is a cry for help, a cry for her terrible isolation to be recognised by those around her. Instead of being a form of rebellion, this attempt at suicide is that point of no confronting those whom cultural conditioning has deprived of the very means of protest or self-affirmation. Vera's very silence is the insistent voice of the beleaguered female, the cry for help from the one whom patriarchal social structures will not recognise at all as an entity. It turns out, then, that all silence has a meaning. The trilogy, in dealing with lesbian themes and relationships, concerns itself with the trauma of unrequited longing, a longing of almost cosmic totality because the love object is denied not by circumstance or chance, but by necessity. Silence becomes the passport into the territory of the dominant world. Such silence signifies a subterranean belief in the magical power of language: if the lesbian were to name herself, her utterance might carry a taint from speaker to listener, from mouth to ear. Vera's silence is also a shrewd refusal to provoke punitive powers—be they of family or society. *My Father's Moon*, *Cabin Fever* and *The Georges' Wife* are lesbian novels that redraw hetero-patriarchal topographies of desire even as they follow the protagonist's life-path from girlhood through menopause and ageing. The protagonist captures her sense of being unhappily exiled from any possibility of love and tenderness both by hetero-patriarchal expectations and the conventional structure of family. But other, disquieting silences in the text point to Vera's own choices, which reveal the extent of her own absorption, internalization, and finally, acceptance of these expectations, judging herself as having failed using these as her measure. Vera's personality functions throughout the text as a metaphor for the sad success of the interpellation of the subject into the hegemonic heteronormative sexual ideology, and thence, into conformity and mandatory unhappiness.

The figure of the woman-seeker is an extremely rare one in early Australian fiction. The male explorer figures in almost every work, ranging through the bush, but the woman was expected to be safely, if claustrophobically, confined to the home, where, however, instead of security, privation and danger greeted her at every turn. Jolley's fictional landscape is characterized by the flat, horizontal bush-landscapes of this early fiction, but the incongruous figure in this landscape is that of the women—like the Rice Widow or the de-registered obstetrician of Palomino—riding their horses authoritatively and autonomously through spaces that are theirs to explore and to cherish—conquest is not a metaphor that would sit well with these women challengers.

The shifting topographies in the trilogy, from Vera's youth in the claustrophobic coal mining English Badlands to the almost endless horizontal bush-scapes of Australia alert the reader to the metaphoric significance space and exile have in these novels. While Vera's final home suggests an infinitude of possibility in how large a swathe of the world the eye can take in, there is a hint of inhospitability—a world with no other denizens but herself and the Rice Widow does not appeal to Vera. Australia thus becomes both a landscape of escape and a landscape of exile—Vera is cut away, by infinite space, from other modes of companionship here—her daughters, her mother, Mr. George. A coming home—to the Rice Widow—then, is paradoxically, a remaining in exile. Was this a pilgrimage made to false gods then? Is nothing to greet the weary reader, and the writer, when they come home? Was all spiritual sustenance false? Can we not kick off our scallop-shell and sandal shoon, as Byron would have said? Perhaps, only if we resign ourselves to Vera's inability to take at face value any Utopian resolution. But weary as the reader is, cut to the soul by Vera's anguish, we ourselves are unable to accept as honest any Utopian ending. While Australia offers a space, a freedom unthinkable in the crammed old world because of sheer lack of population, the lived-in familiarity of the old home is not something that can be surrendered without an acute sense of deprivation. But in the "lesbian novel," these literary journeys are often a mirror and a metaphor of the journey of coming out. But in this trilogy, Vera doesn't come out, not to herself, to those she loves. Vera will remain a secret traveler, making multiple journeys between the mother's civilization, in the old, stifling world of Europe and England, between what seems to be the daughters' sterile America, and the huge, but empty Australia where the only voices that resonate are those of the dead Rice Widow, whom Vera willingly abandoned, and thus, failed. Vera fails the Rice Widow in seeking to relinquish her role as woman-traveller, in seeking fixity, and she atones for this by accepting exile once again, as a quiet old woman, constantly seeking apparitions.

This lone ranger's identity, however, cannot be boiled down to her presumable lesbianism or bisexuality—Jolley's fiction is challenging in its very precise refusal to collapse a politics of identity with a politics of sexual identity. Her characters refuse neat pigeonholes, forcing the reader to reckon with what this authorial ambivalence might mean for the "political," "lesbian" novel. At the same time, one has to admit that their lack of neat alignment with the concerns of the overtly political sexual tract means that their disturbing fictional possibilities are larger—these novels force the reader to acknowledge that the convenience of two sexualities—homo and hetero—might really be an impediment in one's search for truths about oneself, which, to my mind, is as important a contribution, if not the greater, to art as the novel of special pleading. Her characters continue to inhabit a quiet, tormented corner of the reader's mind, defining the world, whatever its reigning ideology, in colours that are precise and capture its wit, its pathos, its desperation, with a precise, empathetic, compassionate humour that is redemptive even as the characters themselves are held spellbound by their own inability to seek grace.

Endnotes

[1] Some of her other works of the 1970s are *Five Acre Virgin and Other Stories* (1976), *The Travelling Entertainer and Other Stories* (1979).
[2] Her work, in the decade of the 1980s includes: *Palomino* (1980), *The Newspaper of Claremont Street* (1981), *Miss Peabody's Inheritance* (1983), *Mr. Scobie's Riddle* (1983), *Woman in a Lampshade* (1983), *Milk and Honey (novel)* (1984), *Foxybaby* (1985), *The Well* (1986) and *The Sugar Mother* (1988). Jolley continued to write into 2006, with *Learning to Dance* (2006) being her final publication, along the lines of *Central Mischief* (1992) both of which are her reflections on writing, and her own life as a writer. Besides these, Jolley also has to her name a collection of radio plays *Off the Air* (1995) and a collection of short stories *Fellow Passengers* (1997), in addition to novels like the *Diary of a Weekend Farmer* (1993), *The Orchard Thieves* (1995), *Lovesong* (1997), *An Accommodating Spouse* (1999) and *An Innocent Gentleman* (2001).

Works Cited

Bennett, Bruce, and Jennifer Strauss, eds. *The Oxford Literary History of Australia.* Melbourne: Oxford UP, 1998.

Castle, Terry. "Sylvia Townsend Warner and the Counterplot of Lesbian Fiction." *Literary Theories: A Reader and Guide.* Ed. Julian Wolfreys. Edinburgh: Edinburgh UP, 1999. 72-83.

——. *The Apparitional Lesbian: Female Homosexuality and Modern Culture.* New York: Columbia UP, 1993.

Daniel, Helen. "Elizabeth Jolley: Variations on a Theme." *Westerly* 31.2 (June 1986): 50-63.

Dhawan, R. K., and David Kerr, eds. *Australian Literature Today.* New Delhi: Indian Society for Commonwealth Studies, 1993.

Faderman, Lillian. *Surpassing the Love of Men: Romantic Friendship and Love Between Women From the Renaissance to the Present.* New York: Morrow, 1981.

Fahrie Edelson, Pyllis, ed. *Australian Literature: An Anthology of Writing from the Land Down Under.* New York: Ballantine, 1993.

Felski, Rita, and Zöe Sofia, eds. *Australian Feminisms.* Spec. Issue of *Cultural Studies* 10.3 (October) 1996.

Goodwin, Ken. *A History of Australian Literature.* London: Macmillan, 1986.

Hall, Radclyffe. *The Well of Loneliness.* London: Jonathan Cape, 1928.

Jolley, Elizabeth. *Learning to Dance:* Elizabeth Jolley: Her Life and Work. Camberwell, Victoria: Viking, 2006.

——. *An Innocent Gentleman.* Ringwood, Victoria: Viking, 2001.

——. *An Accommodating Spouse.* Ringwood, Victoria: Viking, 1999.

——. *Fellow Passengers.* Ringwood, Victoria: Penguin, 1997.

——. *Lovesong.* Ringwood, Victoria: Penguin, 1997.

——. *Off the Air:* Nine Plays for Radio. Ringwood, Victoria: Penguin, 1995.

——. *The Orchard Thieves.* Ringwood, Victoria: Viking, 1995.

——. *The Georges Wife.* Ringwood, Victoria: Penguin, 1994.

——. *Diary of a Weekend Farmer.* South Fremantle, WA: Fremantle Arts Centre P, 1993.

——. *Central Mischief:* Elizabeth Jolley on Writing, Her Past and Herself. Ringwood, Victoria: Viking, 1992.

——. *Cabin Fever.* New York: Harper Perennial, 1992.

——. *My Father's Moon.* Ringwood, Victoria: Viking, 1989.

——. *The Sugar Mother.* Fremantle, WA: Fremantle Arts Centre P, 1988.

——. *The Well.* Ringwood, Victoria: Viking, 1986.

——. *Foxybaby.* St. Lucia: U of Queensland P, 1985.

——. *Milk and Honey: A Novel.* Fremantle, WA: Fremantle Arts Centre P, 1984.

——. *Miss Peabody's Inheritance.* St. Lucia: U of Queensland P, 1983.

——. *Mr. Scobie's Riddle.* Ringwood, Victoria: Penguin, 1983.

——. *Woman in a Lampshade.* Ringwood, Victoria: Penguin, 1983.

——. *The Newspaper of Claremont Street: A Novel.* Fremantle, WA: Fremantle Arts Centre P, 1981.

——. *Palomino.* Collingwood, Victoria: Outback, 1980.

——. *The Travelling Entertainer and Other Stories.* Fremantle, WA: Fremantle Arts Centre P, 1979.

——. *Five Acre Virgin and Other Stories.* Fremantle, WA: Fremantle Arts Centre P, 1976.

K. Radha. "Humor in Elizabeth Jolley's *My Father's Moon.*" *Australian Poetry and Fiction.* Ed. R. K. Dhawan. New Delhi: Prestige, 1997. 101-106.

McLaren, John. *Australian Literature: A Historical Introduction.* Melbourne: Longman Cheshire, 1989.

Modjeska, Drusilla. "Extra to Life." *Australian Book Review* 200 (May 1998): 45-46.

Nettelbeck, Amanda. Rev. of *Cabin Fever,* by Elizabeth Jolley. *Westerly* 36.3 (September 1991): 114-115.

Ramamurthi, Lalitha. "Treading the Common Ground: Collective Consciousness in Women's Autobiography." *Samyukta* 1.1 (January 2001): 7-17.

Rich, Adrienne. "Compulsory Heterosexuality and Lesbian Existence." *Signs* 5.4 (1980): 631-660.

Riemer, A. P. "Displaced Persons: Some Preoccupations in Elizabeth Jolley's Fiction." *Westerly* 31.2 (June 1986): 64-79.

Sedgwick, Eve Kosofsky. "Introduction from *Between Men.*" *Feminisms: An Anthology of Literary Theory and Criticism.* Ed. Robyn R. Warhol and Diane Price Herndl. New Brunswick, New Jersey: Rutgers UP, 1991. 463-477.

——. *Between Men: English Literature and Male Homosexual Desire.* New York: Columbia UP, 1985.

Stimpson, Catharine. "Zero Degree Deviancy: The Lesbian Novel in English." *Feminisms: An Anthology of Literary Theory and Criticism.* Ed. Robyn R. Warhol and Diane Price Herndl. New Brunswick, New Jersey: Rutgers UP, 1991. 301-315.

Vanden Driesen, Cynthia, and Adrian Mitchell, eds. *New Directions in Australian Studies.* New Delhi: Prestige, 2000.

Warhol, Robyn R., and Diane Price Herndl, eds. *Feminisms: An Anthology of Literary Theory and Criticism.* New Brunswick, New Jersey: Rutgers UP, 1991.

Wilde, W. H., Joy Hooton, and Barry Andrews, eds. *The Oxford Companion to Australian Literature.* Melbourne: Oxford UP, 1994.

Williams, Bruce. "Three Short Story Writers: Peter Cowan, Elizabeth Jolley, Justina Williams." *Westerly* 25.2 (June 1980): 104-107.

Wolfreys, Julian, ed. *Literary Theories: A Reader and Guide.* Edinburgh: Edinburgh UP, 1999.

Zimmerman, Bonnie. "What has Never Been: An Overview of Lesbian Feminist Literary Criticism." *Feminisms: An Anthology of Literary Theory and Criticism.* Ed. Robyn R. Warhol and Diane Price Herndl. New Brunswick, New Jersey: Rutgers UP, 1991. 117-137.

When the Fact Becomes Fiction
Ned Kelly, His Letters and Those Films

Stephen Gaunson

> I will not take innocent life if justice is given [. . .]. I was outlawed without cause, and cannot be no worse [. . .] had I robbed, plundered, ravished and murdered everything I met my character could not be painted blacker than it is at present, but thank God my conscience is as clear as the snow in Peru. (Kelly, "The Cameron Letter": 1878)

> Kelly left his voice for us in his Jerilderie Letter. These 120 year old pages contain his DNA, and for a writer it is a thrilling moment, when you realise you can raise your character from the dead and finally have him speak a more complicated truth than our easy understanding has allowed [. . .].(Carey, *True History of the Kelly Gang:* Back Cover)

Ned Kelly's monolithic ubiquity began well before the bushranger hanged in the gallows at the Melbourne Gaol on the 11th November 1880. During his period of outlawry (1878-1880), Kelly supplied his evolving tradition a number of momentous relics. Further than his ironclad armour suit, he created two culturally significant manifestos: "The Cameron Letter" (1878) and "Jerilderie Letter" (1879) (for more on Kelly's oral folklore, see Seal 2002). Today these letters are an essential and expected ingredient in the modern Kelly narrative, regularly employed by commentators (Keneally 1969; Carey 2000; McDermott 2001; Jones 2002; Seal 2002; Castles 2005) to portray the outlaw as either a "noble robber" or "disturbed cop killer." Written by Ned Kelly when he was the world's most wanted felon, with an unprecedented amount (reward) on his head (£2000), the letters form as the closest (known) artefacts available to uncover his complex and contradictory personality.

Despite *The Argus* newspaper celebrating in 1880 the death of Kelly and close to "organised bushranging in Australia," not even Kelly could have foreseen the cultural impact his legacy would inspire over the coming eras. Through a series of Kelly feature films appearing at regular intervals over the last century (1906-2006), these works—along with the various books, plays, illustrations and music—have become significant tools in educating new audiences about the outlaw's historical narrative and letters.

The Censored Bushranger

The extraordinary success of the original 1906 Kelly film (*The Story of the Kelly Gang*) that portrayed Ned as a sympathetic hero—along with its 1911 re-release—instigated an influx of films romanticising real-life Australian bushrangers on the silver screen. Bushranging films were so popular with local audiences during the early 1900s; this cycle of celluloid still marks an anomalous boom in the Australian film industry. The historically significant twenty-one month period (1910-1912) created more than 81 narrative films (for more on Australia's early bushranging films, see Routt 2003). As a consequence to the films celebration of "real-life" criminals and the negative representation of the Australian police force, this boom, according to Bertrand (1978), was only short lived (110). By the conclusion of 1912, most Australian states refused to screen bushranging films.

The stringent censorship rules that demanded the films portray bushrangers in an "unfavourable manner," also heavily dictated the sort of cinematic representation allowed for Ned Kelly. Immortalised as a literate and gallant egalitarian national hero, in books such as *The Complete Inner History of the Kelly Gang and their Pursuers* (1969), *Australian Son* (2005), paintings by Sidney Nolan (1946-1947), and comics like *Kelly Gang Rides* (1940). Films on Ned Kelly produced during this period, present a much more ominous depiction of the outlaw. In *The Kelly Gang* (1920), director Harry Southwell cuts from a poignant scene of Constable Thomas Lonigan with his wife and young child, to the "ruthless" Ned in the following scene, killing the "noble" Constable in the Victorian Wombat Ranges.

Ina Bertrand (2003) believes these sorts of moralised scenes in the film were the reason it passed through the censors and publicly screened around the country. The next two Kelly films, also directed by Harry Southwell, *When the Kellys were Out* (1920) and *When the Kellys Rode* (1934), did not escape a censorshi p ban. The following film, *The Glenrowan Affair* (1951), appeared shortly after the removal of restrictions on bushranging films, and did take advantage of portraying Ned Kelly as an Aussie bush hero. Directed by Harry Southwell's student and co-collaborator Rupert Kathner, the film continues Southwell's visualisation of Ned Kelly as a stern and masculine Australian bush rogue, who is much older than the actual age of the historical outlaw. Kelly was only in his mid to late twenties when he died (although most agree that Ned Kelly was twenty-five, Alex Castles in *Ned Kelly's Last Days* (2005) has evidence to suggest Ned Kelly died at the age of twenty-nine). Kathner cast brutish (and middle-aged) ex-Australian rules footballer (AFL) Bob Chitty in the role of the outlaw, who became famous after receiving the nickname Captain Blood during his partici pation in one of the most violent grand final football matches ever witnessed, Chitty personified the brutish stern and strong representation of Ned Kelly during this era of films.

The striking feature of these early films is their central themes of anti-individuality and anti-intellectuality. Ned Kelly is an ocker, spontaneous, and vengeful bushranger, who by the narrative's end subsequently becomes redem ptive for his wicked criminal actions. To conclude, in *When the Kellys were Out* (1923), Ned Kelly declares his remorse: "And such is the inevitable fate of all who rebel against the righteous and mighty forces of law and order."

The closure of Kelly films by Harry Southwell and Rupert Kathner, and the abolishment to the censorshi p of bushranging films produced an entirely new cycle of cinema on Ned Kelly. A regular feature of the modern cinematic Ned Kelly—Tony Richardson's *Ned Kelly* (1970) and Gregor Jordan's *Ned Kelly* (2003)—is the inclusion of Kelly's letters. A notable reason why these letters were not a significant part of the earlier films is due to their lack of exposure. Now representing some of Australia's most momentous and insightful historical literature ever produced, apart from the heavily edited exerts that featured in *The Age* in 1878, the letters initially remained relatively unknown, uncirculated and unattainable.

It was not until J. J. Kenneally's concentration on the "Cameron Letter" in 1929 and Max Brown's concern with the Jerilderie

Letter in 1956 that the broader tradition began to seriously consider the importance of these cultural relics. Now residing as part of the ongoing Kelly Culture exhibition in Melbourne's Victorian State Library, the Jerilderie Letter attracts thousands of people every year to witness the authentic script of the outlaw's text. Although a duplicated copy sits in Canberra's National Gallery, the location of the actual "Cameron Letter" remains a point of contention for "Kellyologists."

Employing the literature as proof towards the outlaw's political foresight, compassion and literacy, *Ned Kelly* (1970; 2003) morphs the anti-intellectual ocker Australian male, into a sophisticated, intellectual and international contemporary dandy-boy. Despite the letters discussing similar events and grievances, contrary to what many Kellyologists attempt to argue (McDermott 2001), their content is not identical. By directors Richardson and Jordan each employing a different letter into their cinematic narratives—Cameron in the 1970 version and Jerilderie in the 2003 version—the central differences in the films depiction of Ned Kelly relates directly to the discrepancies of the letters. The naive bushranger from Cameron's *Ned Kelly* (1970) transcends into a vengeful outlaw in Jerilderie *Ned Kelly* (2003).

Literary Ned

Opposed to the earlier films produced when Ned Kelly was still remembered as a topical event, the 1970 and 2003 version form as essential educational texts for a young generation of Australian's; who do not recognise Ned Kelly further than artist Sidney Nolan's seminal imagery. *Ned Kelly* (1970; 2003) assembles within a wider cycle of modern texts (Drewe 1991; Carey 2000) that attempt to place the letters within the broader historical story.

On 26th October 1878, the Kelly gang—consisting of Ned Kelly, Dan Kelly and two anonymous accomplices, later identified as Steve Hart and Joe Byrne—killed Sergeant Kennedy and Constables Scanlon and Lonigan at the Stringybark Creek in the Victorian Wombat Ranges. Following the death of the police officers, the print media discussed Ned Kelly as a "cold-blooded killer." Conservative anti-Kelly Melbourne newspaper *The Argus*, termed him an "unscrupulous ruffians" (28th October 1878), accusing him of " 'mutilating' Sergeant Kennedy's dead carcass" at Stringybark Creek (1st November 1878).

After reading in *The Age* newspaper about Donald Cameron's (MLA) parliamentary interrogation of Premier Graham Berry—"the conduct of certain members of the police force as having led to the Mansfield (Stringybark) murders is scandalous"—Kelly mistakenly considered the politician as a much-needed alliance.

Stating his side to the events leading up to and surrounding the Stringybark Creek murders, Kelly dictated to Joe Byrne an open letter addressed to Donald Cameron. Signing the paper, "A Forced Outlaw," the 3,500-word document presents Ned Kelly's frustration and anger to a situation he argues was avoidable. Completed as a rough scrawl, the letter's prose, described by Ian Jones (2002) as "vivid, undisciplined and in part bombastic" (162), lacks the poetic lyricism that would become evident in his following Jerilderie Letter. Intended as a verbal speech for Cameron to deliver in parliament, Kelly opens his text casually addressing his familiarity and admiration for his reader:

> Dear Sir, Take no offence if I take the opportunity of writing a few lines to you, wherein I wish to state a few remarks concerning the case of Trooper Fitzpatrick against Mrs. Kelly, W. Skillion and W. Williamson, and to state the facts of the case to you. ("The Cameron Letter" 1878)

On December 10, 1878, the Kelly Gang invaded a station property at Faithfull's Creek with two objectives: to rob the Euroa National Bank and have Ned's letter forwarded to Donald Cameron. Despite the successful completion of these tasks, the document failed to gain the support Kelly had anticipated. Cameron, who had only intended to mock the government for their handling of the outlaw's capture, immediately distanced himself from any support for the gang's "deplorable" criminal exploits. The letter's heavily edited extract printed in the normally liberal *The Age*, merely confirmed Kelly's callous killing of the "heroic" police officers. Omitting Ned's argument of self-defence, the words read as a confessional declaration from a madman:

> As soon as I shot Lonigan he jumped up and staggered some distance from the logs with his hands raised and then fell. He surrendered, but too late. I asked McIntyre who was in the tent. He replied, "No one." I advanced and took possession of their two revolvers and fowling piece, which I loaded with bullets instead of shot. ("The Cameron Letter" 1878)

Infuriated by the published edit of the "Cameron Letter," Ned Kelly set out another plan. This time he would redraft the letter, rob a bank in the isolated town of Jerilderie and before departing, oversee the printing of his (unedited) document in their local paper. The new text, which again Joe Byrne scribed, was significantly more substantial, totalling 8,300 words. Concentrating on the similar events discussed in the "Cameron Letter," it presents a more com plete picture. Kelly also does not make the same mistake of assuming that his audience is supportive of his broader cause.

Written only two months' after the "Cameron Letter," Ned presents more intensity, hostility, and political ambition in this text. Evidenced through his poetic prose, Kelly wrote the Jerilderie Letter with a conscious awareness of its future historical significance. Displaying his intelligence and com prehension of the English language, the standard reading by pro-Kellyologists (Jones 2002; Brown 2005) is that it plainly establishes Ned's personal grievances, Irish patriotism and political motivation towards his dream of a republic of north-eastern Victoria.

On the 8th February 1879, the Kelly Gang arrived in Jerilderie and "Bailed Up" the local police station. During the proceeding bank robbery on the 10th February 1879, Ned proudly read the hostages exerts from his letter. Unable to locate the town's newspaper editor, Samuel Gill, Kelly left the document in the care of the bank's teller, Edward Living who promised to have it printed in the next edition of the *Jerilderie Herald.* Again, the outlaw's desires remained unfulfilled. On their arrival, the local police confiscated the letter. Whether the letter was Kelly's declaration of self-defence or his intention to kill more police remains a dubious issue that Kellyologists have continued to debate:

> I give fair warning to all those who has reason to fear me to sell out and give P10 out of every hundred towards the widow and orphan fund and do not attem pt to reside in Victoria but as short a time as possible after reading this notice, neglect this and abide by the consequences, which shall be worse than the rust in the wheat in Victoria or the truth of a dry season to the grasshoppers in New South Wales I do not wish to give the order full force without giving timely warning. but I am a widow's son outlawed and my orders must be obeyed. ("Jerilderie Letter" 1879)

Cinematic Ned

In the 1970 cinematic version, Tony Richardson's Kelly is an optimist whose general threats appear more like a defiant warning (with a snarling tone) than a terrorising list of demands. Heavily influenced by Sidney Nolan's baroque post-World War II painting series, which portrayed Ned as a martyr, Richardson's film presents Ned Kelly as young, and adolescent. Overlooking his original choice of Albert Finney, whom Richardson had previously directed in *The Entertainer* (1960) and *Tom Jones* (1963), he cast the scrawny and un-athletic frontman of The Rolling Stones, Mick Jagger in the title role (McFarlane, 1997: 478). Aged twenty-seven during the filming, for the first time on a movie screen Ned Kelly literally looks his age.

Replacing the Aussie bush slur for an appropriate Irish accent, Jagger's internationalised Ned proudly displays his patriotism and heritage for the emerald island. Mick's languid delivery of his dialogue—criticised by many as "poor acting"—directly borrows from Kelly's prose in the "Cameron Letter" (Hills 1970; Rick 1970; Roxon 1970). Similar to Ned Kelly's inexperience and lack of preparation for his role as an Australian bushranging outlaw, Mick Jagger, stripped of his typical glam-rock stage persona, creates the "Cameron Letter" with a measured sombre passiveness. In a scene set in the Victorian wombat ranges, Ned Kelly quietly sits at a timbre plank calmly producing his historical manifesto:

> What would people say if they saw a strapping big lump of an Irishman shepherding sheep for fifteen bob a week or tailing turkeys in Tallarook ranges for a smile from Julia or even begging his tucker, they would say he ought to be ashamed of himself and tar-and-feather him [. . .]. (*Ned Kelly*)

Opposed to the "Cameron Letter"—planned as a prewritten parliamentary speech for Donald Cameron—Ned always intended the Jerilderie Letter as a significant work of literature. Materialising as one of the countries most important autobiographic documents, it sits alongside other momentous historical works of literature, such as Raffaello Carboni's *The Eureka Stockade* (1855). Appearing as the chief Kelly literary document, the Jerilderie Letter portrays a fierce Ned who is no longer in search for a peaceful resolution. Demonstrated by Heath Ledger's hostile and politically charged performance as the outlaw in Jordan's 2003 film, Kelly is isolated from those around him, because he is closest of all to violence. Continuing from Richardson's film with Ned as an Irish immigrant, contrarily this version illustrates him as robust and tough. Despite the savaging critical attacks, the film was well received and most agreed that Ledger made a fine Kelly. Ledger's efforts awarded him an AFI (Australian Film Institute) and IF (Inside Film) nomination for Best Lead Actor in an Australian Motion Picture.

For anti-Kelly commentators, the Jerilderie Letter illustrates nothing more than a clear omission of guilt for the bushranger's callous killing of the police officers at Stringybark Creek. In the post-9/11 landscape, there has been a new curiosity in the contents of Kelly's letters, and his relationshi p with the modern social terrorist. At a debate arguing whether "Ned Kelly is an inappropriate hero for Australia?" Police Commissioner Christine Nixon, representing the affirmative, concentrated on Ned's "terrorist-like-behaviour." Ned Kelly, she contested, was merely endeavouring to "kill as many policemen as he possible could" (Nixon et al. 2006). In a recent book (2001)—including the com plete Jerilderie Letter—Alex McDermott's Preface, titled "The Apocalyptic Chant of Edward Kelly," describes the Jerilderie Letter as Kelly's declaration for terrorism:

> The Jerilderie Letter gives the im pression of a man ready to explode [. . .] this builds, and builds, until by the closing passages the letter had become a lethal thing. It shoots to kill. It occupies an imagined universe where there will be no hostages exchanged, and no survivors [. . .]. (xxvii)

Alex Castles considers Kelly's words as the ramblings from a mad lunatic, who enjoyed professing his murder of Victorian police officers. According to Castles, during Ned Kelly's trial, his counsel for defence, Henry Bindon, refused to include the letters as vital evidence: Bindon perceived the letters as a disturbing admission of guilt (191). Discussed by Tim Groves and William D. Routt (2003), Jordan's Kelly who makes demands like a terrorist, and targets prominent political figures like a terrorist, is not really a terrorist at all: the only group Ned successful terrorises is the police (27). Groves and Routt claim that Ned Kelly more accurately falls within Eric Hobsbawm's (1969) framework of the "social bandit" (50), who through his noble chivalry, becomes more of a celebrated hero, than a feared terrorist in his rural community (Hobsbawm 43).

In *Ned Kelly* (1970; 2003), Ned eludes capture because of the local support his community provide him for becoming their sacrificial lamb. Aaron Sherritt's Judas-like treachery firmly casts Kelly in the role of his region's messiah. The festive celebration that features singing, dancing and drinking in the finale at the Glenrowan Inn, illustrates Ned's general wealth of support. Unlike the bushrangers in Rolf Boldrewood's seminal novel *Robbery under Arms* (1888), who enter criminality to mimic their Western American cowboy heroes, Ned's persecutor's of injustice—the Victorian Police—force his career as an outlaw.

Ned's rage however, is not the relentless hounding from the constabulary. Kelly becomes irate when the broader populace misinterpret his noble chivalry as an opportunistic act of common criminality. In the middle of robbing the Bank of New South Wales in the 2003 film version, Ned demands Steve Hart (Phil Barantini) give one of the hostage's (Jim Russell) their watch back. After this hostage refers to the gang as "a bunch of common criminals," Kelly steps from behind the bank's counter to address the group in a passionate and poetic monologue:

> If we act like common thieves that's just what they'll call us. Ladies and Gentlemen, I must ask you to sit tight and listen to what I have to say. My mother is rotting in a prison cell because of the lies of a policeman named Fitzpatrick [. . .]. So if I could beg your patience, this is my statement to the Premier of Victoria, Graham Berry, and you here are my witnesses. Joe, take out your pen and paper, please. (*Ned Kelly*)

Richardson's and Jordan's *Ned Kelly* (1970; 2003) does not support the popular anti-Kelly chorus of "Ned as Terrorist." Employing an overtly sympathetic reading of the letters, they narrate Ned as a tragic hero whose sole political ambition is to form a Republic of North-Eastern Victoria. His writing projected onto the silver screen does not describe the mad ramblings of a lunatic who has lost touch with his own reality; as the writing of notorious hitman Mark "Chopper" Read exemplifies in the film *Chopper* (2000). Ned Kelly's demands are logical, rational and sane. When he robs, he robs only to benefit his broader community. Removed from other criminal bushranger rogues, the letters describe a sympathetic figure who continues the nation's serge towards federation, with the same political gusto as other historical social activists, such as Peter Lalor in Harry Watt's *The Eureka Stockade* (1949).

A significant reason why Ned Kelly remains as such an intriguing figure more than 125 years after his death is due to the amount of questions his actions during his period of outlawry generated. In an attempt to answer such questions—and concurrently supply a new chapter to the rewriting of Ned's history—Kellyologists endeavour to pursue the solitary source capable of providing some concrete answers: Ned's literary manifestos. With the recent release of Carole Wilkinson's book, *True Tales: Ned Kelly's Jerilderie Letter* (2007), on the Jerilderie Letter produced primarily for school children, the outlaw's literature remains an essential tool to educate new generations about his narrative, and affirm a case of him as either a cop killer or political activist.

Works Cited

Bertrand, Ina. "New Histories of the Kelly Gang: Gregor Jordan's Ned Kelly." *Senses of Cinema* (2003). 24 February 2007 <http://www.sensesofcinema.com/contents/03/26/ned_kelly.html.>.

——. *Film Censorship in Australia.* St. Lucia: U of Queensland P, 1978.

Boldrewood, Rolf. *Robbery Under Arms: A Story of Life and Adventure in the Bush and in the Goldfields of Australia.* 1888. Sydney: Angus & Robertson, 1990.

Brown, M. *Australian Son.* Melbourne: Network Creative Services, 2005.

Carboni, Raffaello. *The Eureka Stockade.* 1855. Melbourne: Melbourne UP, 1993.

Carey, Peter. *True History of the Kelly Gang.* St. Lucia: U of Queensland P, 2000.

Castles, Alex. C. *Ned Kelly's Last Days.* Crows Nest, NSW: Allen & Unwin, 2005.

Chopper. Dir. Andrew Dominik. Prod. Michele Bennett and Michael Gudinski. Beyond Films, 2000.

Doolan, Lucky. *Kelly Gang Rides.* Melbourne: L. Clapperton, 1940

Drewe, R. *Our Sunshine.* London: Penguin, 1991.

Groves, T., and W. D. Routt. "The Terrorist And The Collaborator." *Mia* 109 (2003): 22-31.

Hills, B. "Bombs Rock Glenrowan as Mick Jagger's Ned Goes Fizz." *The Age* 29 July 1970: 1.

Hobsbawm, E. J. *The Bandit as Symbol.* London: Weidenfeld & Nicolson, 1969.

Jones, Ian. *Ned Kelly: A Short Life.* Melbourne: Lothian, 2002.

Kelly, Edward. "The Jerilderie Letter." 1879. The State Library of Victorian. 28 February 2007 <http://www.slv.vic.gov.au/collections/treasures/jerilderieletter/index.html>.

——. "The Cameron Letter." 1878. *Ned Kelly's World.* 28 February 2007 <http://www.nedkellysworld.com.au/archives/ned_kelly_1.doc>.

Kenneally, J. J. *The Complete Inner History of the Kelly Gang and Their Pursuers.* 8th Edition. Moe, Victoria: The Kelly Gang Publishing Company Pty. Ltd., 1969.

Mcdermott, A. *The Jerilderie Letter.* Melbourne: Text, 2001.

Mcfarlane, B. *An Autobiography of British Cinema.* Auckland: Random House, 1997.

Ned Kelly. Dir. Tony Richardson. Prod. Neil Hartley. United Artists Corp., 1970.

Ned Kelly. Dir. Gregor Jordan. Prod. Nelson Woss, Lynda House, Debra Hayward, and Liza Chasin. Focus Features UIP, 2003.

Nixon, C., B. Jones, I. Jones, K. Bedford, J. Burnside, K. R. Mcmenomy, and J. Mcquilton. "Ned Kelly: An Inappropriate Hero For Australia?" *The Great Debate.* Beechworth: Indigo Shire Council, 2006.

Nolan, Sidney. "The Kelly Paintings." Velasquez Gallery, Melbourne. 1946-47. National Gallery of Australia, Canberra. 2007.

Rick. "Ned Kelly." *Variety* 17 June 1970: 16.

Routt, W. D. "Bush Westerns?—The Lost Genre." Lecture. Australian Centre for the Moving Image, Melbourne. 3 February 2003. 24 February 2007 <http://www.routt.net/Bill/BushWesterns.htm >.

Roxon, L. "Pop Star Fizzes as Ned Kelly." (Sydney) *Sun-Herald* 21 June 1970: 21.

Seal, G. *Tell 'em I Died Game.* Melbourne: Hyland House, 2002.

The Eureka Stockade. Dir. Harry Watt. Prod. Leslie Norman. General Film, 1949.

The Glenrowan Affair. Dir. and Prod. Rupert Kathner. BEF Film, 1951.

The Kelly Gang. Dir. and Prod. Harry Southwell. 1920.

The Story of the Kelly Gang. The. Dir. Charles Tait. Prod. W. A. Gibson, Millard Johnson, John Tait, and Nevin Tait. 1906.

When the Kellys were Out. Dir. and Prod. Harry Southwell. Ironoutlaw CD, 1923.

When the Kellys Rode. Dir. Harry Southwell. Prod. British Empire Films. Imperial Feature Films, 1934.

Wilkinson, Carole, ed. *True Tales: Ned Kelly's Jerilderie Letter.* Fitzroy, Victoria: Black Dog, 2007.

EXTINCTION, RESISTANCE AND REBIRTH

REPRESENTATION OF ABORIGINALITY IN *THE TIMELESS LAND*, *THE CHANT OF JIMMIE BLACKSMITH* AND *BENANG*

Isabelle Benigno

Aboriginal identity was first constructed in opposition to White identity, based on the perspective of colonial expansion—the prejudice that Aborigines were an inferior race. As Edward Said has argued in *Orientalism* (1978), the colonized were trapped within a discursive regime which resulted in the colonizers representing Aboriginal people as the remnants of the Stone Age doomed to extinction. This notion of so-called inferiority served not only to legitimise colonial domination but also to allow the exploitation of the Aborigines and their land.

In the first part of her trilogy, *The Timeless Land* (1941), Eleanor Dark (b. 1901 - d. 1985), a white novelist focuses her attention on the conditions that led to the dispossession of the Aboriginal land by the European colonists. It was declared *terra nullius* (land belonging to no one) since it was not properly occupied and used according to the colonisers. Under English law, Aboriginal land was thus considered as a waste land, allowing and justifying the occupation of Australia and the denial of Aboriginal rights.

In the first chapters of her novel, Eleanor Dark relates how Captain Arthur Phillip, after landing in Port Jackson, immediately takes possession of the land by drawing a circle in the sand:

> The white men's leader rising had summoned his people about him, and drawn round them in the sand a vast circle which he had given the Blacks to understand they must not cross. (*The Timeless Land* 87)

By rejecting them at the periphery, the Aboriginal people were not only dispossessed but also discriminated against because of their otherness. There arose as well the issue of the relationships that the colonisers should establish with the Aboriginals.

At first, Captain Arthur Phillip treats them with friendliness, exchanging gifts. He is determined to set up relations based on mutual trust as he needs to learn as much as possible about the surroundings to provide subsistence to his companions and the convicts. As friendliness doesn't give the results he expects, Captain Arthur Phillip kidnaps Aboriginals who realize the duplicity of the European "visitors." Arabanoo is the first Aboriginal captured:

> The heavy thing about his wrist [. . .] which he had soon discovered was obviously intended to keep him in captivity. It was no use trying to understand people who mixed friendliness with treachery. (*The Timeless Land* 173)

Eleanor Dark highlights the devastating impact of the dispossession of their land on the Aboriginals. Captain Arthur Phillip is made to realise the White man's misrepresentation of the land and its people. The episode in the novel of Phillip's attack by one of Bennelong's companions is particularly relevant and worth quoting:

> Something had disturbed the harmony? Or had there ever been any harmony? What happens in the end? Which wins, man or the earth? From some storehouse of memory, words flung up to his consciousness. The earth says to the earth: all will be ours [. . .]. There was a dignity not to be hidden or overlaid by antics [. . .] and the thought of destroying it stirred not only regret in him, but actual fear. (*The Timeless Land* 316-320)

What Europeans ignored, was the special relationship that Aboriginal people had established with their land, a link deeply rooted in their spiritual beliefs. This relationship had been denied by early colonizers who had come with preconceived ideas about what constituted spirituality largely based on the separation between natural and cultural, material and spiritual worlds. In contrast, The Dreaming (Aboriginal creative epoch) persistently emphasises the embedding of the spiritual existence into the material world: "In traditional Aboriginal thought, there is no nature without culture" (Sutton 18). According to the Dreaming, Aboriginal people are part of a whole which was formed by the Spirits Beings as they traveled across the Australian continent. The landscape isn't just a geographical entity. It also bears the marks of the Ancestral Beings in its rocks, mountains, trees, plants and other environmental phenomena. In other words, the landscape is sacred and Aboriginal people consider themselves as the custodians of the earth, aware of the spiritual forces surrounding them. As White men neglected the land, the law and the people, imposing a logic of exploitation, they couldn't but fail to understand Aboriginal people. Comforted by theories such as Social Darwinism which assumed that earlier forms of social organizations would give the way to more developed ones, the early colonizers condemned Aborigines to extinction.

Despite her will to rehabilitate Aboriginals and their culture (Eleanor Dark was undoubtedly influenced by the works of the famous Australian anthropologist Professor A. P. Elkin), she nevertheless wrote in the preface (2002) of *The Timeless Land*: "The race is nearly gone, and with it will go something which the 'civilized' world has scorned too easily" (xxviii). Eleanor Dark was a woman of her time. In the 1940s/1950s, a majority of White Australians was convinced that Aborigines were "a doomed race."

The main preoccupation of the Australian authorities from the 1920s to the 1970s was to deal effectively with the question of miscegenation. Indeed, not only did colonisation produce a colonial discourse on racial difference but also on cross-breeding. Considering that miscegenation took an active part in the evolution of Aboriginality, it is relevant to compare how White and Black novelists tackle this issue.

For Thomas Keneally (b. 1935), a white novelist whose *The Chant of Jimmie Blacksmith* was published in 1972, the assimilation policy wasn't the adequate response to the question of miscegenation. Its failure was predictable. Assimilation wasn't a new idea since the protection policy had already aimed at assimilating the Aboriginal children. In 1951, at the Native Welfare Conference, assimilation was defined in the following terms: "It is expected that all persons of Aboriginal blood or mixed blood in Australia will live like White Australians do [. . .]. Assimilation does not mean the suppression of the Aboriginal culture but rather that, for generation after generation, cultural adjustment will take place" (Broome 171).

In fact, Aboriginaes had to deny their culture and to "pass" into the White community. The assimilation policy introduced distinctions within Aboriginal society. Even when they tried to conform to White people's expectations, they were not rewarded for their efforts. For instance, Jimmie Blacksmith pays a heavy price for assimilation. Encouraged by a couple of White missionaries, Jimmie commits cultural suicide, much to the disapproval of his maternal uncle. First, Jimmie gets married, following Mrs. Neville's recommendations: "If you could ever find a nice girl off a farm to marry, your children would only be quarter caste then, and your grandchildren one eight-caste, scarcely black at all" (*The Chant of Jimmie Blacksmith* 7). He also accepts various jobs in order to get money and buy property. Jimmie is spends the rest of his life trying to fulfill White ambitions, but he also loses the battle on account of his Aboriginal upbringing and also his incapacity to overcome White racism. As his last employer (Mr. Newby) brutally reminds him:

> It doesn't matter how many times yer descendants bed down, they'll never get anything that don't have the tarbrush in it. And it'll always spoil'em that little bit of something else. (*The Chant of Jimmie Blacksmith* 61)

After this episode, Jimmie declares war on the whites and becomes Jimmie the savage. According to Thomas Keneally, Jimmie's savagery results from white people's contempt and racism. There is no place in Australian society for "mixed-bloods." The responsibility for Jimmie's failure to assimilate is not individual but collective.

Thomas Keneally uses the story of Jimmie Blacksmith to illustrate the fact that assimilation policy was condemned to failure and could only lead to the destruction of Aboriginal culture. Yet, Keneally's novel does not put into question the binary opposition between "full-bloods" and "mixed-bloods." His opinion is close to a certain colonial discourse in Australia which since the 19th century had established that the only "real" Aborigines were "pure bloods" whereas "mixed-bloods" were not Aboriginal at all. For readers of the 21st century, such an assumption is no longer acceptable since Keneally's definition of Aboriginality has been officially replaced in the 1970s by a broader one, including "mixed-bloods." Being Aboriginal has nothing to do with the percentage of blood running in your veins, as Aboriginal novelists have persistently emphasised.

In Kim Scott's (b. 1957) novels, for instance, Aboriginality is first and foremost a matter of belonging. Harley, the narrator of *Benang* (1997) is determined to put up a fierce resistance to his grand-father's project to create "the first-White-man-born." To resist, you have to be angry and this anger expresses itself in two significant episodes in the novel.

First, Harley dismantles his grand-father's house, hence symbolically deconstructing by the act of writing, the eugenic discourse of his grand-father, Ern Solomon Scat. Secondly, Harley carves words into his grand-father's flesh:

> It used to please me, when my grand-father and I lived in a crumbling house to carve words into his skin. My blade drew letters with a fine White line, but in an instant all precision would be lost in gushing blood. I bandaged his wounds to conceal what I wrote and, bathing them, considered how they grew, how they altered and elaborated on what I intended. (*Benang* 286)

By carving words, Harley shapes his grand-father, using the same method as Ern but inverting the process. This is an act of pure resistance as Harley refuses to accept his grand-father's genocidal engineering vision. Once he has destroyed it, he can engage on the path towards personal reconciliation that he can only achieve through a sense of belonging.

Harley, like other characters in the novel (his uncle Jack and his father as well), realizes that his link with the earth stems from a spiritual communion with it. He is convinced that his spiritual connection with a specific territory is inalienable. When he visits Dubitj Creek with his children, he follows the tracks that his ancestors left when they traveled across this landscape thousands of years ago:

> We came to a line across the granite where the lichen had not grown and, our feet choosing the way, we followed it. There was no real reason. No, I am too offhand. There is no reason. Lichen does not grow on that thin strip of granite, because it is the path where, again and again and again, our people walked across the granite. (*Benang* 452)

The use of past and present tenses in the same sentence refers to the Aboriginal perception of time. Indeed, the Dreaming conveys a cyclic conception of time as each Aborigine can experience the present reality of the Dreaming. Famous Australian anthropologist and historian Professor W. H. Stanner (1968) refers to it as the "everywhen." As Harley reaches the end of his journey, his feeling of the lack of groundness that he experienced at the beginning of the novel gradually disappears: "This seems too simple, I know, but this is true. I felt at peace and as if belonging" (*Benang* 451). By re-affirming his belonging to his people and place, Harley also shows that Aboriginality has nothing to do with genetics: "Now it may be for me to put a name to myself, to who or what I am. Call me of whatever you will of these; Wadjari, Mirning, Runaways, Southern people, Shell people, Nyungar [. . .]. Call it what you will. I say Nyoongar" (*Benang* 455).

The novel *Benang* (the title means tomorrow) conveys a message of hope in the future. Kim Scott suggests that there is a tomorrow for his people and his culture as the titles of the last two chapters of the novel stress: "not beginning" and "continuing." The stories of *Benang*'s characters will continue as long as Aborigines will live through nature. Their spiritual bond to it cannot be destroyed no matter how hard white people have tried to do so:

> I offer these words, especially, to those of you I embarrass, and who turn away from the shame of seeing me, or perhaps it is because your eyes smart as the wind blows the smoke a little toward you, and you hear something like a million million many-sized hearts beating, and the whispering of waves, leaves, grass [. . .].We are still here, Benang. (*Benang* 495)

The end of the sentence with the "hearts beating" echoes "the strong pulse of countless hearts beating" (*Benang* 7) in the first chapter of the novel. Harley has come full circle. Harley's story is one of return since he has found himself on this chaotic and painful journey: "We are here, Benang" (*Benang* 495).

This is a very powerful ending since Harley is referring to present (we are) and to future (Benang or tomorrow) in the same sentence. Although there have been moments of discouragement, Harley/Scott is determined to rehabilitate a sense of belonging which lies at the core of contemporary representations of Aboriginality. Yet, as Jan Teagle Kapetas (1999) has argued:

> *Benang* is much more than social history, it's a wonderfully poetic novel, a lyrical layered text, full of terrible truths quietly sung. Whispering almost. A novel in which the landscape and the sea and Nyoongar and settler families appear and disappear and re-appear again, restless as unquiet ghosts. (191-196)

It is true that in *Benang*, Scott is aware of how to recapture characters' representations and empower them. The novel allows him to deconstruct the white people's history and aboriginalize through what critic and writer Mudrooroo (1997) calls "maban reality." The latter is very close to Latin-American magic realism. According to Mudrooroo, "maban reality" could be characterized by "a firm grounding in the reality of the earth or country, together with an acceptance of the supernatural as part of everyday reality" (97). Mudrooroo advocates the use of "maban reality" to enable Aboriginal writers to present history from an Indigenous point of view rather than from a colonialist one.

In *Benang*, Kim Scott reverts to some sort of supernatural as Harley is floating through the house. At one time, Harley's lack of weightlessness presses him against the ceiling which is described as "a whiteness which was surface only, with no depth and very little variation" (*Benang* 11). At other times, Harley becomes an inanimate object: "On washing days I discovered the pleasure of letting myself flap absently on the line [. . .]. I was successfully assimilated to the laundry, washing machine, a used car" (*Benang* 33). Harley's inability to stay grounded is of course linked with his feelings of being a stranger to himself. When he looks into the mirror, Harley doesn't see his own reflected image but what his grand-father wants him to be "the first-White-man-born." Once he has managed to retrieve his sense of belonging, he no longer experiences the unpleasant feeling of being carried away.

As already pointed out, Harley recaptures his sense of belonging by resisting his grand-father's genocidal vision. This act of resistance is embodied in the novel by the recurring metaphor of the tree, a natural element firmly grounded in the reality of the earth:

> Grandad wrote: Cut down the tree. Burn it, dig out its roots. He might also have written: displace, disperse, dismiss [. . .]. My friends, you recognize the language [. . .]. I trimmed the branches which grew close to the window. I was pleased to see Grandad's grateful smile when he peered through the window frame and saw no hint of tree. I was even more pleased to see his reaction when I carried him outside, and he realized I had trimmed only those limbs which could be seen from the window, and left others intact. The tree still lived, it would grow again. (*Benang* 108)

Ern Solomon Scat's genocidal vision of breeding out the black skin colour parallels his method to cut the tree. In both cases, Ern is determined to cut Harley's Aboriginal roots. However, he fails to impose his view. Indeed, Harley refuses to cut the branches of his genealogical history, symbolically expressing his will to preserve his cultural heritage. The metaphor of the tree embodies growth but also rebirth, hence conveying a message of hope.

This is precisely what Mudrooroo is urging Aboriginal writers to do. According to him, "the writers of Indigenality" as he calls them, shouldn't dwell on the negative aspects of Aboriginality, best exemplified by the work of Aboriginal writer, Archie Weller. His collection of short-stories, *Going Home* (1986), is highly criticized by Mudrooroo for Weller's depiction of communities dominated by drugs, alcohol and stealing: "There is little that any community would wish to identify with or accept" (145). It can't be denied that Weller's characters are struggling against a very negative image of themselves, an image that the whites have instilled in their minds. Perry Dogler, one of the main characters of the short-story titled "Saturday Night Sunday Morning" considers himself as a cast-off: "Yet he will be rid of the empty bottles and discarded rubbish that litter his life" (*Going Home* 50). More explicitly, the narrator of "Fish and Chips" uses the powerful metaphor of decay to talk about his people's everyday life: "Perhaps that's why we surround ourselves with old rubbish when we die" (*Going Home* 135). Mudrooroo advocates an emphasis on the positive values of Aboriginality

> [. . .] reflecting oral traditions in which everything can be resolved or reflecting that simply because the story is being related means that the narrator, who is usually part of the action or at least a relative, has won through and survived. (147).

In *Benang*, Harley the narrator "has won through" after a very difficult journey. Scott's style is based on simplicity and sobriety, never tending to lapse into melodrama even when he talks of the sexual abuse of children or torture. Some may reproach him for lacking virulence. In fact, Scott makes the reader feel the horror rather than realise it, thus creating empathy between the reader and the characters. Scott has found a good balance between thinking and feeling. The reader is engaged in the character's journey to personal reconciliation. Both readers and characters are investigating the past. This is a major difference with works such as Archie Weller's collection of short-stories where the reader is just a spectator of the decay of Aboriginal communities. Postcolonialism challenges the colonial ways of knowing: it is no longer considered as a neutral activity. In a postcolonial context, the reader plays an essential part. Scott acknowledges the role of the reader which is a means to challenge colonial points of view. His novels are an invitation to enter into the stories of his characters in order to open white people's eyes. Aboriginal identity is indeed, definitely linked to white people's identity.

Although support to the Aboriginal cause has been demonstrated in recent years by the whites, Prime Minister John Howard has obstinately refused so far to apologise for the appalling treatment inflicted to the Aborigines since colonisation. This refusal shows that the fight for the rehabilitation of Aboriginal identity is far from being over. Aborigines are too often considered as second-rate citizens as it is stressed over and over in Scott's novels or those by Alexis Wright (b. 1950). These Aboriginal writers never lose sight of the socio-economical difficulties their fellows confront. They consider these difficulties neither as "tem porary aberrations" nor as "naive realistic situations" to quote Mudrooroo's words but they can be overcome provided Aborigines keep on fighting for their individual and collective survival as well. "We have survived," "We are still here" as Harley is hammering out. It means that despite white misconceptions of Aboriginality, Aboriginal people have never forgotten their identity. Alongside white representations, Aboriginal discourses have successfully challenged the im posed representations. As Michael Dodson (2003) has summed up:

> When we talk about an Aboriginality based on the past of our peoples, we are not talking about fabricating an identity based on a past we have rediscovered or dug up ; rather, we, the Aboriginal peoples, are already the retelling of the past [. . .]. Aboriginalities of today are regenerations and transformations of the spirit of the past; we re-create Aboriginality in the context of all our experiences, including our pre-colonial practices, our oppression and our political struggles. (40)

There are roots that make Aboriginal people what they are. Thanks to these roots, Aborigines have managed to cope with violence and oppression. They have also shown that re-birth is a never-ending possibility.

Works Cited

Ashcroft, Bill, Gareth Griffiths, and Helen Tiffin, eds. *The Post-colonial Studies Reader.* New York: Routledge, 1995.

Bourke, Colin, Eleanor Bourke, and Bill Edwards, eds. *Aboriginal Australia: An Introductory Reader in Aboriginal Studies.* St. Lucia: U of Queensland P, 1998.

Broome, R. *Aboriginals Australians: Black Response to White Dominance, 1788-1980.* Sydney: Allen & Unwin, 1982.

Dark, Eleanor. *The Timeless Land.* 1941. Sydney: Angus & Robertson, 2002.

Dodson, Michael. "The End in the Beginning: Re(de)finding Aboriginality." *Blacklines: Contemporary Critical Writing by Indigenous Australians.* Ed. Michele Grossman. Melbourne: Melbourne UP, 2003. 25-42.

Hodge, Bob, and Vijay Mishra. *Dark Side of the Dream: Australian Literature and the Post-colonial Mind.* Sydney: Allen & Unwin, 1990.

Keneally, Thomas. *The Chant of Jimmie Blacksmith.* Sydney: Angus & Robertson, 1972.

Mudrooroo, Narogin [Colin Johnson]. *The Indigenous Literature of Australia.* Melbourne: Hyland House, 1997.

Said, Edward. *Orientalism.* London: Routledge, 1978.

Scott, Kim. *Benang: From the Heart.* Fremantle, WA: Fremantle Arts Centre P, 1997.

Stanner, W. H. "After the Dreaming." *Boyer Lectures.* ABC Radio National. November-December 1968.

Weller, Archie. *Going Home: Stories.* Sydney: Allen & Unwin, 1986.

Alessandra Senzani

Experimenting with Aboriginality in Theatre
Jack Davis's *The Dreamers*

Aboriginal theatre—fully written, directed and acted by Aborigines—first came onto the Australian national publishing scene in the late 70s and early 80s, an outgrowth of the emerging Aboriginal literature of the 60s and 70s. This seemingly late start should not be surprising, since as Jack Davis (b. 1917 – d. 2000) has argued in "Aboriginal Writing" (1985):

> [. . .] our people were still battling to survive. One fact to bear on this is that three years after the first publication of an Aboriginal author, twenty-seven Aborigines were massacred in the Kimberley, for the spearing of a white man. (13)

Given the still harsh conditions Aborigines were forced to endure, it is in fact surprising that Aborigines were already able to produce their own poetry and soon enough their own dramas. Both forms were understood as tools to gain visibility on the nation's political and cultural stage.

The first theatre piece was performed in Sydney in 1971; it was Kevin Gilbert's *The Cherry Pickers,* which was soon followed by other performances, notably Bob Maza's sketches in 1972/73. However, the first Aboriginal drama to be published will have to wait until 1978 when *The Cakeman* by Robert Merritt—already performed in 1975—was finally printed. In the mid-70s, many other Aboriginal plays were brought on stage: in 1975 the two one-act dramas by Jack Davis—"The Biter Bit" and *The Dreamers*, in 1976 Gerry Bostock's—*Here Comes the Nigger*, and in 1979 for the Sesquicentenary Celebrations—*Kullark* by Davis, which was also acclaimed as the best show of the year's celebrations (Shoemaker, "Aboriginal Drama": 28). In 1982, Davis presented the two-act version of *The Dreamers* at the Perth Festival and since then

Aboriginal theatre companies have multiplied and flourished. Yet, their publication has followed a more tortuous path with most dramas waiting ten years before finding a publisher. For this reason, Adam Shoemaker in the early 80s argued that "Aboriginal drama must be one of the least known and most poorly-published areas of Black Australian artistic endeavour," especially if compared to the vivacity of its stage scene ("Aboriginal Drama" 28).

One of the reasons for such negligence in recognizing Aboriginal theatre in its beginnings was Western criticism's blind eye towards Aboriginal authors' mingling of cultural conventions and their effective use of symbolic elements. Aboriginal theatre was often dismissed under the constraining labels of "realist" and "naturalist," which ignored the authors' original (re)elaboration of Western forms aimed at challenging white ideology (for such an example, see Kaine-Jones 433). Unacknowledged was also the rich intertextuality with which Aboriginal authors weave their dramas, so as to evoke multiple stories, myths and facts, thereby (re)constructing an Aboriginal aesthetic. What unites most Aboriginal dramatists is indeed their reliance on traditional stories, so as to foster an Aboriginal identity, an attempt to inflect white forms and language with Aboriginal meanings and performance styles.[1] The result is what Christopher Balme (1997) terms a "syncretic theatre" (150), which fuses different beliefs and practices in a new synthetic and hybrid whole. Such a definition inserts Aboriginal theatre into a common tradition for writers living on the margins, who, as Ella Shohat and Robert Stam argue in their seminal *Unthinking Eurocentrism* (1994), are

> confronted with the "theatrical" challenge of moving, as it were, among the diverse performative modes of sharply contrasting cultural and ideological worlds. (42)

What needs to be always reiterated when speaking and celebrating the syncretism and hybridity found in Aboriginal texts, however, is the history of oppression and dispossession that lies behind such forms. As Shohat and Stam clearly put it, "syncretism is [. . .] a sublimated form of historical pain" (43) that always already functions as a reminder of the abuses and atrocities of the colonial enterprise. Possibly in response to the contradictory and co-optable usage of terms like syncretism in postcolonial studies, Mudrooroo (1989) prefers to refer to such a contamination of discourses, beliefs and conventions with the terms "symbolic realism" or "Aboriginal realism," which "expands European realism by taking in certain supernatural aspects, characters and situations found in Aboriginal storytelling" ("Towards a New Black Theatre" 17). Mudrooroo goes so far as arguing for an "Aboriginal reality" which greatly differs from Western concepts "in that it is an expanded reality akin to the Dreaming life" where there is not a clear-cut distinction between the categories of "the real" and of "the symbolic" as defined in Western criticism.

This paper offers an analysis of Davis's theatre that recognizes the "polysemic nature" of his dramas as Mudrooroo emphasizes in his introduction to Davis's last play in his *First Born Trilogy*: *Barungin/Smell the Wind* (1988). Davis's unique contribution to Australian theatre results from his setting in dialogue Aboriginal and Western conventions in order to achieve a mutual illumination. His polysemic theatre oscillates among multiple languages, belief systems, temporalities, and spaces, in other words the multiple heritages that inform his identity and literary work. Davis tells of a childhood spent mainly with white Australian kids, German and French immigrants. It was only later in life and thanks to his *Nyoongah* (a word that today describes Aborigines from South-Western Australia) stepfather[2] that he could fill the gaps of his Aboriginal education (Gibbs 51). As many children of marriages among whites and Aborigines, the young Davis was sent to the Moore River Settlement, one of those institutions where so-called "half-caste" children, forcibly removed from their families, were trained to become workers for white Australians.[3] The goal of such abusing practices was to break communal, familial, tribal, and territorial bonds, in the hope that, as David Horton (1994) explains, "Aboriginality could be isolated, controlled and, in the case of the children, trained out" (715). Ironically, it was in this place constructed to "bleach" Aboriginal cultures that Davis learned back his origins and acquired an Aboriginal, political and literary consciousness.

Davis's literary works thus constitute a political practice, an intervention into Australian politics that demands recognition for Aborigines' rights and voice.[4] Yet, such an overt political and cultural commitment should not lead us to dismiss Davis's *oeuvres* as just "protest literature." From the start, Aboriginal writers and critics have been aware of the risks of being ghettoized, denied a place onto the Australian literary stage. For this reason, they have soon called forth resonances between their indigenous forms and European heritages, conscious of the need to translate their aesthetic into parameters to which white critics and readers could relate. Thus, Bostock (1985) emphasized the political nature of Greek theatre, in order to counter a dismissal of Aboriginal drama as just a political statement and to support instead an understanding of the aesthetics of drama that does not do away with its politics (63).

Aboriginal theatre speaks to white Australians, to the Others who have marginalized Aborigines in their own land, in the attempt to demand recognition; in the theatre white spectators are finally forced into the role of onlookers, while Aboriginal dramatists and actors control the scene. Nonetheless, Aboriginal theatre does not marginalize its own people, but tries instead to create a polyphonic performance that responds to the traditions, meanings and needs of an Aboriginal audience. As Mudrooroo argues in *Writing from the Fringe* (1990), Aboriginal plays "provide an opportunity for fringe-dwellers to see themselves for the first time holding centre stage, talking back to the white man" (120). For this reason, most Aboriginal dramatists draw on traditional stories so as to foster an Aboriginal identity; simultaneously, however, they try to speak of contemporary Aboriginal life and to connect with other marginal literatures and peoples, in order to reclaim a visibility in the world literary arena.

This paper aims at illustrating how Davis balances these two goals in his play, *The Dreamers* (1982), the first drama written for his *First Born Trilogy*, although chronologically it comes second after *No Sugar* (1986). Davis speaks here of the contemporary metropolitan experience of Aborigines, simultaneously celebrating their survival and denouncing their marginalization. The play is set on the fringes of Perth in the 70s and tells the story of an Aboriginal family struggling with alcoholism, joblessness, criminality and disorientation. Davis does not attempt to romanticize this harsh reality; on the contrary, he opts for showing the poverty and the self-destructive attitude of some members of the family, while also conveying the Aboriginal humor and those values that he wants to be reinforced and preserved.

The Dreamers was first performed in 1973 in Bunbury, WA and then in 1975 at the Black Theatre in Sydney (on the same occasion, Davis also presented "The Biter Bit," a play that was never published). This one-act version was then extended in 1982 for the Festival of Perth (Shoemaker, "Aboriginal Creative Writing": 122). In these early versions, the action spun over one day, from dawn to sunset; the main themes, however, were already fully developed and only deepened in the two 1982 added acts "*Beeruk*—Summer" and "*Moorga*—Winter," which also enriched the drama with added songs, dances, and poems. Between the early and late versions of the play, there is a difference in tone, in that the former is more openly political, while the latter is more self-reflexive and it establishes a connection between Aboriginal Australians and other groups on the margins around the world. As Davis himself explains in "An Interview" with Adam Shoemaker (1982):

> *The Dreamers* in 1973 was more or less political—it had political overtones, especially in terms of local government. But this one is more or less a psychological play which deals with part-Aboriginal people, Aboriginal people in an urban setting, but still it applies to any ethnic group throughout the world today. It could happen in Germany; it could happen in Canada; and it not only applies to Aboriginal people or Indian people or Eskimo people; it happens to non-Aboriginal people also. We all suffer from the same thing. (112)

Davis insists on the psychological aspects of marginalization and colonization he wanted to portray in what he describes "a very cruel play," which speaks to racial and ethnic minorities in different countries, evoking Franz Fanon's (1961) analysis of the effects of colonization on the psyche of the "Wretched of the Earth." While establishing sodalities with other minorities and invoking their voices in support of the Aboriginal experience, Davis still focuses his piece on specifically Australian Aboriginal tribal stories. He wants indeed to "detail the sheer persistence of *Nyoongah* culture—the presence of the oral tradition, the *Nyoongah* language, and the presence of the past" (Tompkins 8). He thus succeeds in creating a drama that can resonate globally, while being strongly emplaced in the Australian land.

What localizes most the drama is Davis's reliance on traditional Aboriginal stories he learned from Aboriginal elders who were the source of inspiration for the drama. In particular, *The*

Dreamers grows out of a poem Davis wrote in honor of an Aboriginal elder he met in the Moore River Settlement, Worru, a dreamer as the title suggests, where "dream" should be understood in the Aboriginal sense derived from the Dreaming—the poem finds his place in the drama as an epitaph read by the nephew in honor of the character Worru). *The Dreamers* draws inspiration especially from a late encounter between Worru and Davis. Fifteen years after having left Moore River, Davis met the aged Worru in urban Perth: hardly any traces of the old warrior had remained in the body of the alcoholic pauper; his tribal knowledge had evaporated with the vapors of the alcohol and city that eventually killed him. Worru was the first person to introduce Davis to his Aboriginal heritage, thus the sight of his sunken body left the author embittered and saddened.[5]

As this anecdote suggests, Davis strongly relies on his own real life experiences for his writings; such insistence on personal stories points to his will of shaping *The Dreamers* as a drama that could tell of suffered abuses, of silenced (hi)stories, but especially of the ways and myths that the Aborigines Davis encountered taught him. For this reason, Davis repeatedly mentions nostalgia as the overwhelming feeling shaping the drama (qtd. in Shoemaker, "An Interview": 114). To convey nostalgia to its audience, *The Dreamers* plays on different temporalities, by inserting elements such as dances and song performances out of a past now gone, as well as re-enactments that interrupt the performance of the present and reiterate the significance and actuality of the past. When the curtains reveal the stage, for instance, the audience looks at an Aboriginal traditional tribal scene, which puts the emphasis on the past from the outset; the spectator could indeed be led to expect a drama set in tribal times, a misleading impression however, as the refrain in the poem performed after the first scene clarifies:

Now we who were there

who were young,

are now old and live in suburbia,

and my longing is an echo

a re-occurring dream,

coming back along the track

from where the campfires used to gleam. (*The Dreamers* 74)

The drama wants to talk about contemporary Aboriginal life, about marginalization in the metropolis of white Australia; the Aboriginal past has become only a longing embodied in the character of Worru, whose disease and demise symbolize the loss of Aboriginal cultures and the need to (re)construct an Aboriginal history and identity. The first act starts with uncle/grandpa Worru coming back from the hospital and immediately starting drinking and smoking again, two practices that help him forget and wander back in past memories. The rare moments he is able to tell a story, he mainly instructs his grandchildren, Meena and Shance, about the old times, tribal myths (as in the *moodgah tree* story, see *The Dreamers* 85-86), the *Nyoongah* language, the Moore River lifestyle, and the adventures and misfortunes of his deceased friends.

Despite these moments of lucidity, he is doomed as we learn early on; already in the fourth scene we recognize the signs of the ultimate fall, when Worru attempts to teach a tribal dance to his nephew Peter, who, to Worru's dismay, prefers instead white disco music. Crushed under the alcohol's weakness, however, Worru cannot bring the performance to an end and a tribal dancer has to take it over, moving on the notes of a tribal didgeridoo, while the characters and the audience sit still (*The Dreamers* 86). The dancer is Worru's alter-ego in the drama; he visualizes his past as a fighter and hunter and thus reinforces by contrast his physical and psychological demise; the dance performance intervenes into the metropolitan drama to contaminate it with Aboriginal meanings and forms.

Indeed, the "Aboriginalization" of white aesthetics in Davis's dramas owes much to the insertion of traditional styles of performance within his contemporary storylines; dances, mimic, gestures, and body-painting contribute to offer a glimpse of the rich rituals of the Aboriginal peoples before colonization. These elements enrich the semiotic of the overall play, which intersects different kinds of texts in a Barthesian sense, in that body language and painting are understood as independent meaningful communication systems. Not surprisingly given Worru's centrality in the drama and his role in it, it is his character that presents the most visible examples of Aboriginal mimic, gestures and oral traditions. As in traditional Aboriginal orality, Worru tells his stories not just through words, but also through his body language and gestures; kinaesthetic and paralinguistic signs are an integral part of his storytelling act, as shown in the next passage and its detailed stage directions:

> Yeah, but 'e was bad man, Billy Kimberley. Some of them trackers was real *warrah*, you know when them *yorgas* was sent to work for *wetjalas*. [*Miming a pregnant woman*] And sometimes they would come back *bootjari*, and when them *koolangarahs* was born, them trackers, Billy Kimberley and Bluey too, [*miming choking*] they would *woort beerny* them babies an' bury them in the pine plantation, night time. (*The Dreamers* 94)

In this scene, Worru employs bodily gestures to accompany *Nyoongah* words, which are not comprehensible to every character in the play and viewer in the audience. Beyond offering a comprehensible sign translation, however, the gestures, as mentioned above, also distinguish a good from a bad storyteller. In *The Dreamers*, Worru is the only character who masters this antique craft and Davis shows its fragility, which risks to disappear and be silenced by the ethylic sleep that will lead to Worru's death.

Beyond drawing attention to traditional body language, Davis inserts in his drama numerous dancing scenes. As Helen Tiffin (1995) argues, dance is typical of post-colonial theater thanks to its "function to recuperate postcolonial subjectivity because movement helps constitute the individual in society" (342). This applies particularly to Aboriginal theatre, in which dance serves as a reminder of traditional ceremonial dances, of corroborees that affirm the individual's identity and belonging within the group by performing culturally codified rituals (342).[6] In dramatic terms, the insertion of dance scenes contributes to the dynamism of the play, disrupting the linear narrative and the borders of the dramatic genre. As Tiffin argues, "what dance 'does' then is draw attention to the constructedness of dramatic representation, which suggests that it can function as an alienating device in Brechtian sense" (341). The dance breaks the realistic frame and introduces a new dimension, shifting "the play out of an essentially realistic mode and into Aboriginal reality" (Mudrooroo, 1990: 124). Moreover, we can argue that the tribal dance challenges Western forms and genres producing moving bodies that break the fourth wall and look down from the stage onto the white onlookers. In *The Dreamers*, for instance, the dancer moves "from a non-localizable past" (Balme 159) and establishes a direct relationship with the audience and sings back to them.

The dancer appears in every key moment leading to Worru's demise; at the end of the second act, for instance, when Worru comes back from the hospital, the dancer—performing dressed as featherfoot, the spirit of death—anticipates his imminent death. Beyond such foretelling function, his song also accuses the white men of committing genocide; interestingly Davis chooses to voice such strong accusations in the *Nyoongah* language, offering no translation and thus leaving the white spectator reassured in his/her ignorance.[7] From the tone of the music and the mimic of the dancer, the white viewer can only infer that life is gradually taking his last gasps. The white audience is here spared the outraged cry against the murderers of the Aboriginal peoples, although a similar accusation is voiced earlier in the drama in perfectly comprehensible English:

> The *Wetjala*'s a lion, he eats. Aw, he eats, he eats everything: land, trees, rivers, forests, even people, 'specially people. I 'member the old grandfather Kooroop used to say: 'Don't trust the *Wetjala*, he's a real *widartji*. He'll kill you for sport and eat your brains and kidney fat. (*The Dreamers* 121)

Yet, even this explicit accusation is undermined by the fact that it is Eli, the petty criminal and alcoholic who utters it. We see him come and go from state prison, complaining and reproaching his own peoples as often as the whites. It thus seems that Davis purposely refrains from openly accusing the whites, leaving up to the audience to make up his/her own mind about the current situation of Aborigines. Some critics like Elizabeth Webby (1993) argue, for instance, that "a white audience can cry for Worru without necessarily feeling any blame. Worru has surely killed himself by his inability to keep off the grog" (71). Such a reading would support dominant Australian discourses that ascribe the marginalization of

Aborigines to their own lack of responsibility and to their alcoholism. However, I would argue that Davis does instead clearly show that alcoholism, joblessness, and criminality are rather the products of a process of outright marginalization and oppression. As Peter cries out in the play, Aborigines are impotent in the predominantly white Australian society:

> Look, *Nyoongah* buy their grog from the *Wetjalas*, they break the law and they git jugged by *Wetjalas*. The lawyer's white, the cops are white, the magistrate's white, the warden's white: the whole box and dice is white. Put a *Nyoongah* against all of them. I tell you we ain't got a bloody chance. (*The Dreamers* 83)

Nostalgia, regret and anger are thus the most powerful emotions moved by this play, which purposefully focuses on all Aboriginal issues and sentiments. Indeed, there is only one white character in the whole drama, Darren, a young white friend of Worru's grandchildren.[8] Being the only white character, Darren's brief appearances acquire a greater significance in the overall economy of the play. He first enters the scene while Worru is telling a story about the evil spirits inhabiting Moore River settlement:

> Warrah Place, Mogumber, awright daytime, but *gnank weerdiny*, couldn't walk around, stay near the fire. [*Shuddering*] Too many *tjennuks, moorlies*, an', an' *widartjies*. [*Gesturing North*] They come from that way. They was real bad. Round face, an' they was white, jus' like *Wetjalas*, an' they 'ad red eyes, an' red 'air, 'an them scream, an' shout, sing out in the night time, in the pine plantation, jus' like *koolongahs*. [Shane pushes Darren through the door and throws the ball to him. Darren falls and yells as he catches it. Worru and Dolly get an enormous fright]. (*The Dreamers* 94)

The parallelism between the evil spirits' story and the sudden appearance of Darren, a white screaming kid with red hair, is too strong to be ignored and, as Webby argues, constitutes "another moment where the tribal past seems to be re-enacted in the present" (70). The tone of the scene is humorous; yet, if we contextualize this joking parallelism with the other veiled accusations mentioned above, we can see how Davis is trying to reach his white audience on different levels, trying to make them come to his own conclusion in an indirect manner. Darren's character is not simply associated with evil spirits, but also with a certain white curiosity for the Aboriginal Other, a portrayal that conveys the ambivalence in the relationships between the two groups and the double-edged curiosity of the whites, which can result on the one hand in an opportunity for a cross-cultural encounter and, on the other, in a projection of Western beliefs and constructions of difference onto the Other.

Darren's curiosity for the *Nyoongah* language and culture also reinforces by contrast Worru's grandchildren growing disaffection with their Aboriginal heritage. Meena's and Shane's knowledge of *Nyoongah* language is limited to the two extremes of *Wetjala* for white and *Nyoongah* for Aborigine. With his trilogy, Davis wants to portray this gradual erosion of Aboriginal ways and the risk of cultural oblivion represented in the polarization of the grandchildren's world in black and white, hence forgetting the many Aboriginal contributions to dominant Australian culture, which is always already hybrid. Moreover, through these two characters, Davis introduces us to the ironies and paradoxes of Aboriginal children who are schooled in white institutions and are thus required to anthropologize their own people, as when Meena interrogates her grandfather in order to fulfill her "ten-page assignment on Aborigines" (*The Dreamers* 103). In these instances, Davis uses humor both to represent a characteristically self-disparaging attitude in Aboriginal cultures and to draw attention to the anthropological dominant discourses that have contributed to the Aborigines' containment and oppression.

Humor is another constant marker of Davis's dramas, a tool he uses to both offer a relief from the tragic events he is depicting and to raise awareness on stereotypes and prejudices against the Aboriginal peoples. Davis has often argued that Aborigines "have learnt to keep themselves alive by laughing" (qtd. Shoemaker, "Aboriginal Creative Writing": 123), which might be a reason why humor is so often employed in Aboriginal literature. A white critic of Aboriginal literature who has however widely worked and published with Aboriginal authors, Shoemaker, argues for instance in "Aboriginal Drama" (1982), that:

> the most salient distinguishing characteristic of Aboriginal drama is the ability to perceive the humorous in the face of the figurative cyclone [. . .]. None of the plays written by Black Australians over the past eleven years could be termed a comedy; thus, humour acts as a respite form, or breathing space within, the seriousness of that which surrounds it. (28)

In the attempt to define the peculiar forms of Aboriginal humor, Shoemaker extrapolates its main themes and targets: it is mainly verbal and non-situational; it is often sex-related and it frequently targets religion, alcoholism, game of chance, and the know-it-all attitude ascribed to many whites or "white-thinking Aboriginals" ("Aboriginal Drama" 28). Furthermore, as emphasized by Mudrooroo, theatre often reproduces the typical Aboriginal self-deprecating humor (1990: 128), which Davis also sees as a salient feature of Aboriginal identity and that Shoemaker interprets as an "ability to invoke stereotypes in order to laugh at themselves" ("Aboriginal Drama" 32).[9] In *The Dreamers*, we find many such cases in the interaction between Dolly and her husband Roy, where she uses disparaging and self-disparaging humor to shake her husband's resignation, as when she reproaches him for not looking for a job:

> Dolly: Why don't you go down the Road Board? They'd put you on. Cousin William got a job there [. . .]. They've even got a *Nyoongah* bloke drivin' the garbage truck
>
> Meena: [*entering neat and tidy, school bag in hand*] Mum, that isn't a *Nyoongah* driving the garbage truck, 'es an Indian bloke.
>
> Dolly: What of it, still coloured, ain't he?
>
> Roy: Lot of difference, he ain't a *Nyoongah* an that's good enough for me. (*The Dreamers* 76-77)

The use of "even" here wants to show that Aborigines have often internalized the demeaning portrayals that whites have drawn of them; yet, we also perceive that there is a certain ironic self-awareness in such a use. Indeed, as the dialogue develops, we see that Aborigines are lumped together with all "colored people," drawing attention to the similarities among stereotypes used to put down minorities. Roy's intervention to reject the association of Aborigines and other perceived black minorities is not only an ironic and conscious invocation of stereotypes so as to dodge work, but also an indirect and serious reminder that Aborigines are pushed to the extreme margins of Australian society.

As shown in the above examples, humor in Aboriginal drama thus both contributes to capture the audience, offering relief from the harsh realities it often represents, and to avoid victimizing discourses, reinforcing instead the political and cultural criticism of

Australian dominant society. As Shoemaker argues, "the socio-political messages which underlie so much this form of theatre are actually enhanced by this method" ("Aboriginal Drama" 32). Davis uses humor to target both white dominant discourses and the risk for Aborigines to let these define their people and cultures. In *The Dreamers*, we are often made aware of such risks through the character of Meena and her schooling in white institutions. When we hear Meena instruct her Aboriginal grandfather on the origins of his peoples, it is hard to miss the irony and the veiled accusations against white institutions, which dismiss Aboriginal knowledge and train young Aborigines in exclusively white paradigms:

> Meena: [*imperiously*] As a matter of fact there's very little difference. They are much like aborigines because that's where we come from, India. We came across the land bridge, then the sea came behind us and Australia was iso [. . .] isolated and the only animal we brought with us was the dingo.
>
> Dolly: All right, Miss *Wetjala*, git' goin' to school. (*The Dreamers* 77)

Meena's show of knowledge is soon interrupted by her mother who ironically dismisses her as "Miss White," also reminding us of her increasing assimilation to the white ways. The two grandchildren's loss of contact with their Aboriginal past and culture reaches its ultimate conclusion in Barungin, where the adult Meena and Shane have completely torn any link to their Aboriginal past and have not passed on any Aboriginal knowledge to their children.[10] However, in this very last drama, Davis also offers a possibility of hope with the character of Robert (Jamie),[11] a young Aborigine who knows and respects his origins; he is proud of his ancestors' Aboriginal past and, while working in the Australian dominant white society and for white people, he reclaims the right to live out his Aboriginality and beliefs.[12]

An important part of such a strategy of (re)claiming the Aboriginal past and actualize it in the metropolitan present is to maintain a linguistic knowledge of Aboriginal languages, to sing them constantly back into existence and infiltrate some of their signs into English, if not turning English into an Aboriginal language as linguists like Jay Arthur have argued. Davis's original style owes much to his linguistic experimentation; leaving behind Standard English, white by definition, Davis inflects it with Aboriginal accents and meanings. All characters speak one form of Aboriginal English, depending on the region they are coming from, and they often mix in few words in an Aboriginal language.[13] *Nyoongah* expressions in Davis's plays establish a communication barrier between Aboriginal actors and author on the one hand and the white audience on the other. As mentioned above, Davis often plays with this invisible border, addressing Aboriginal and white audiences through different channels. According to Bob Hodge and Vijay Mishra (1991), Davis tries here "to combine signifiers of difference (dramatic declarations of Aboriginality) with layers of camouflage to sustain ambiguous relationshi p of Aborigines to the rest of the Australian community" (208). In *The Dreamers*, Worru represents the main sign of difference, the memory of a past that most white Australians want to repress; for this reason, in the drama he constantly switches between Aboriginal English and *Nyoongah* language, so as to sing back into life the past that white modernity wants to erase. Despite the many *Nyoongah* words, the author argues that there are no major com prehension hurdles in his dramas because gestures, mimics and dances come to the help of the white viewer and introduce him to the Aboriginal meanings that Davis wants the audience to guess and infer, rather then fully understand. He wants to encourage a form of timid and respectful curiosity for the ways of an Othered culture, accepting a certain degree of opacity. He cites as a model for his approach to language the literature of Black Americans in the United States who have bent American English to express their own meanings.[14]

The interweaving of Aboriginal and Western languages, stories and performance styles together with the many intertextual references with a global resonance prevents Davis's plays to be received passively. They demand an active partici pation from the audience, both physical and intellectual, in that we as viewers are forced reflectively bridge the gaps among the multi ple texts and languages we are exposed to.[15] For this reason, many Western critics like Maurie Scott (1997) find in Davis's plays "the strong influence of epic theatricalism—epic in sweep and scope, and often in formal Brechtian terms" (138). This might be interpreted as one more way to contain an Aboriginal cultural expression into known Western categories. However, I would argue that the comparison with Brecht is useful if we take it as an attempt to translate the objectives and experimentation of Aboriginal theatre in a language familiar to Western audiences, while still acknowledging the specificity of Davis's Aboriginality and voice—a similar strategy as Bostock's references to classical Greek theatre. We should understand these Brechtian echoes as a resonance among authors who each in his own way have tried to disrupt and reconstruct a political theatre able to raise consciousness. Indeed, Davis's plays are the result of a continuous experimentation that characterizes most Aboriginal authors, who are attempting to connect different traditions and worlds in order to express their life in the interstices and to bend an imposed language and narrative to their own meanings. In his plays, Davis has succeeded in freeing himself of the Western cage and in creating Aboriginal spaces inbetween white discourses. An Aboriginality that rises from the Australian land and resonates globally with the voices of those other(ed) cultures inhabiting the interstices.

Endnotes

[1] For this reason, it is thus useful to briefly mention the traditional Aboriginal dramatic performances, which resurface in contemporary dramas as echoes and ghosts of a past too often suppressed. Aboriginal dramatic performances are usually divided into three main forms. First, we can find the re-enactment of Aboriginal foundation myths through dances, songs and body-painting; this form is highly ritualistic and literally aims at re-enacting the rituals and myths inherited from the Dreaming. Secondly, there is the performance of myths for pure entertainment, where secret aspects of the ritual are not displayed. Finally, we have performances that do not draw on the Dreaming but on everyday life. In this last case, songs and dances are recognized as men-made—in traditional performances it was usually just men - and not inherited from the ancestors (Balme 151). The difference among these three forms is not so much in terms of content, but rather in the manner of representation, which distinguishes the sacred performances, only aimed at initiated members of the group, from the dances and songs aimed at simply entertaining and thus often performed in prose in front of the whole community (Balme 151).

[2] Davis describes Bert Bennel as "a traditionally oriented *Nyoongah*, born when there where still Aborigines in the district able to pass on the bush

knowledge and language of what are now lost generations. He had an old-world charm, the quiet confidence that results from an understanding of, and a peace with, the cosmos" (qtd. in Chesson 48).

[3] The Moore River Settlement was built in 1917 by the government of Western Australia 140 km north of Perth (Horton 714). Initially, the settlement was meant for those Aborigines who lived in camps at the margins of the major metropolitan cities. Yet, just a year after its institution, authorities started sending kids of mixed marriages as well, who were forcibly removed from their families in order to form them as future housekeepers for rich white families (Horton 715). In all Davis's dramas, we can find links back to the Moore River Settlement, this goes for his very first theatre piece, *Kullark,* as well as for the entire *First Born Trilogy,* in which only one drama, *No Sugar* (1985), is actually set on the reserve, but where all plays present characters who have lived in the reserve—the other two being *The Dreamers* (1982) and *Barungin/Smell the Wind* (1988).

[4] Davis's poetry and dramas constitute only part of his multi-level engagement in the cultural and political future of Aborigines in Australia. On the day of his death—the 18th of March 2000—Anne Buggins in her article "Author Gave Aborigines a Voice" on the *The West Australian Saturday* remembered the great writer as: "Aboriginal poet, playwright, actor and activist Jack Davis, who died yesterday, won widespread acclaim for his ground-breaking plays about Aboriginal history and his unremitting fight for justice for his people" (13). The fact that a major national newspaper honours Davis's death with a whole article on his work and achievements signals his stature within Australian society at large; unfortunately, we can easily argue that his reputation is exceptional, since most Aboriginal authors are still too often ignored by the national press and literary establishment. Davis is one of the very few Aboriginal writers to be included in the *Oxford Companion of Australian Literature* (1995) together with the poetess Oodgeroo Noonuccal. They have certainly been the pioneers of Aboriginal literature and in the front lines of the struggle to gain more rights, voice and agency within Australian society, offering a model for many young Aborigines. Davis was indeed director and editor of the Aboriginal journal *Identity,* contributing to the publication of many Aboriginal writers who could find in the journal the only outlet for their work.

[5] However, the fictional Worru draws also on other encounters that Davis had in the reserve; in his biography, Davis mentions other three Aboriginal elders who have informed his construction of the character of Worru. First, Skipper, an old blind Aborigine from the North Kimberleys lost in the old times; Secondly, Winarn, an elder from the North who spent most of his life in the Australian outback and was forced to go to Moore River after he burnt his arm and was thus considered useless as worker. In the

drama, Davis actually explicitly refers to him when mentioning all those who died in the settlement. Winarn offered Davis a model of a successful and talented Aboriginal storyteller who "was able to hold an audience until the embers of the campfire had faded into ash" (Davis qtd. in Chesson 37). Thirdly, Jack Henry, the tribal wise man who was responsible for defining the rules of the Aboriginal community and one of the few Aborigines who could still recall a time when contacts with the European colonizers were rare and the Aborigines were still masters in their own land: "an old man of such antiquity that it would have been impossible to guess his age. There was nostalgia in his speech, typical of men of great age in any society" (Davis qtd. in Chesson 39). Jack Henry's nostalgia was utterly embittered and angered by the loss of what he considered the golden age. Given the symbolic significance of these men in the construction of Davis's personality, it is understandable that the author himself performed the role of Worru in *The Dreamers.*

[6] This link to the pre-colonial past is reinforced by the use of body-painting, which "far more than a decorative function: it contains its own sign-system. In traditional culture body-painting is an essential component of rites of passage and rituals" (Balme 158).

[7] The script does include the translation instead: "The White man is evil, evil! / My people are dead / Dead, dead, dead / The white man kill my people / Kill, kill, kill / Kill (*The Dreamers* 137).

[8] *The Dreamers* is one of the few plays with an all black cast, since most authors prefer to include white characters and thereby explicitly pinpoint those responsible for the Aborigines' marginalization and oppression.

[9] Another typical form of humor in conversations among Aborigines is to tell stories of relatives or friends who have ridiculed themselves because of their clumsiness in the white world. These stories usually take the form of fully blown sketches, to which Davis refers as examples of Aboriginal theatricality because they are usually performed with extensive use of bodily language and gestures. It is Worru in *The Dreamers* who usually presents the audience with these oral anecdotes and performances:

> Well, they was gitten old fellas, them two, Cornell and Milbart, they was stayin' in Wagin an' they wanted to git to Katanning show, see? And they was *wayarning* of the train, real *wayarning.* [*Laughing*] Anyways, they got in a railway carriage and that train was goin' *keert kooliny, keert kooliny* round them bends and them corners. An'—an'—they was . . . they was . . . [*He coughs and splutters.*] . . . sitting close together, like. [*He laughs again and claps his hands*] Anyway, they went around one corner and

> Cornell got real fright and he shouted '*choo*' and he pushed Milbart like that. [*He pushes Peter almost off his seat*] And he said, he said, '*Wart arny yit*,' Milbart, git ober in de udder corner an' help me balance this thing before it bloody tips over. (85)

[10] When the *First Born Trilogy* is represented within one day, the drama *No Sugar* is performed before *The Dreamers*. In *No Sugar*, Davis tells of the forced removal of Aborigines from their lands and communities to work for white people in reserves. The performance of the second act of the trilogy before the first is not aimed at simply respecting the chronology of the story, but also at reinforcing the responsibility of colonization and white settlers for the current state of Aboriginal affairs and cultures.

[11] In interviews, Davis refers to this character, which is also present in *The Dreamers*, with the name of Jamie. Probably, in the first version of the drama, Davis had retained the name Jamie, the conscientious and proud son in *Kullark*. The name, however, was later changed to Robert in *The Dreamers* and consequently in *Barungin* as well.

[12] As Davis explains:

> Jamie has the answer. Jamie is the 1982 urban Aboriginal. He's got a good job, he's a smart-looking guy, he's got a nice suit and everything and he's got a job as a carpenter. He comes down to visit the relations and, because he's a young smart-aleck, he's telling them what to do—what they shouldn't do—and he's the modern Aboriginal. And, he's a very important part of the play. (qtd. in Shoemaker, "An Interview": 114)

[13] Given the orality of the genre aimed to be performed, Davis is particularly aware of the need to reproduce varieties that are really spoken by Aborigines so that the audience can actually relate to them. His scripts present very detailed and precise phonetic transcriptions of Aboriginal English pronunciation patterns as well as of Aboriginal languages (Gibbs 17).

[14] As Davis explains in *Aboriginal Writing Today* (1985):

> they write according to their speech patterns; they write according to their behavioural patterns and the're world famous. And I think that once we can become established as novel writers, we'll be able to use our own speech patterns, and behavioural patterns more so. (16)

[15] Davis's play with multiple temporalities, languages, genres, and styles in *The Dreamers* is even stronger in *Kullark*, a drama that plays over three historical periods: from the times of colonization, to the years in Moore River Settlement and the 1980s. Davis mingles here even more discourses

by inserting in the drama Aboriginal oral stories and also official records by white colonizers such as Neville's speeches and Stirling's diaries. In *No Sugar,* instead, Davis plays with space and disorientation by having three different stages and forcing the audience to move around together with the actors from the scenes in Northam and those in Moore River. The spectators are thus forced to join in this migration, "so sharing in the physical disruption of the Millimurru family" (Webby 74).

Works Cited

Arthur, Jay Mary. *Aboriginal English: A Cultural Study.* Melbourne: Oxford UP, 1996.

Ashcroft, Bill, Gareth Griffiths, and Helen Tiffin, eds. *The Post-colonial Studies Reader.* London: Routledge, 1995.

Balme, Christopher. "Reading the Signs: A Semiotic Perspective on Aboriginal Theatre." *Aratjara: Aboriginal Culture and Literature in Australia.* Ed. Dieter Riemenschneider and Geoffrey V. Davis. Amsterdam: Rodopi, 1997. 149-164.

Berndt, Robert M. "The Aboriginal Heritage." *Kullark/The Dreamers.* By Jack Davis. Sydney: Currency, 1982. xiii-xxi.

Berndt, Robert M., and Catherine H. Berndt. *The World of the First Australians: Aboriginal Traditional Past and Present.* Sydney: Rigby, 1964.

Bostock, Gerry. "Black Theatre." *Aboriginal Writing Today.* Ed. Jack Davis and Bob Hodge. Canberra: Australian Institute of Aboriginal Studies, 1985. 63-73.

——. *Here Comes the Nigger. Meanjin* 36.4 (Spring 1977): 479-493.

Chesson, Keith. *Jack Davis: A Life Story.* Melbourne: Dent, 1988.

Davis, Jack, and Bob Hodge, eds. *Aboriginal Writing Today.* Canberra: Australian Institute of Aboriginal Studies, 1985.

Davis, Jack. *A Boy's Life.* Broome, WA: Magabala, 1991.

——. *Barungin/Smell the Wind.* Sydney: Currency, 1988.

——. "The Life and Work of Jack Davis." *Us Fellas: An Anthology of Aboriginal Writing.* Ed. Colleen Glass and Archie Weller. Perth: Artlook, 1987. 176-191.

——. *No Sugar.* Sydney: Currency, 1986.

——. "Aboriginal Writing: A Personal View." *Aboriginal Writing Today.* Ed. Jack Davis and Bob Hodge. Canberra: Australian Institute of Aboriginal Studies, 1985. 13-19.

——. *Kullark/The Dreamers.* 1979. Sydney: Currency, 1982.

——. *The First-Born and Other Poems.* Sydney: Angus & Robertson, 1970.

Fanon, Franz. *The Wretched of the Earth.* 1961. New York: Grove, 2004.

Gibbs, Genevieve. *Educating Readers: Aboriginal English in Aboriginal Literature.* PhD thesis. U of Western Australia, Perth. 1998.

Gilbert, Kevin. "Black Policies." *Aboriginal Writing Today.* Ed. Jack Davis and Bob Hodge. Canberra: Australian Institute of Aboriginal Studies, 1985. 35-41.

——. *The Cherry Pickers.* 1971. Canberra: Burrambinga, 1988.

Glissant, Edouard. *Poetica del Diverso.* Roma: Meltemi, 1998.

Hodge, Bob, and Vijay Mishra. *The Dark Side of the Dream: Australian Literature and the Postcolonial Mind.* Sydney: Allen & Unwin, 1991.

Horton, David, ed. *The Encyclopedia of Aboriginal Australia.* Canberra: Aboriginal Studies, 1994.

Kaine-Jones, Karen. "Contemporary Aboriginal Drama." *Southerly* 48 (1988): 432-444.

Maza, Bob. Jack Charles is Up and Fighting. Dir. Dot Thopmson with assistance from George Whaley. Prod. Nindethana Theatre. Guild Theatre, U of Melbourne. 1972.

Merritt, Robert. *The Cake Man.* 1975. Sydney: Currency, 1978.

Narogin, Mudrooroo. *Writing from the Fringe: A Study of Modern Aboriginal Literature.* Melbourne: Hyland House, 1990.

——. "Towards a New Black Theatre." *New Theatre Australia* (March-April 1989): 16-17.

——. "Black Reality." Introduction. *Barungin/Smell the Wind.* By Jack Davis. Sydney: Currency, 1988. vii-ix.

Noonuccal, Oodgeroo. *My People.* 1970. Brisbane: Jacaranda, 1981.

Scott, Maurie. "Reinventing Cultures: The Politics of Cultural Reformation as Reflected in Contemporary Aboriginal Performing Arts." *Aratjara: Aboriginal Culture and Literature in Australia.* Ed. Dieter Riemenschneider and Geoffrey V. Davis. Amsterdam: Rodopi, 1997. 129-143.

Shoemaker, Adam. "Aboriginal Creative Writing: A Survey to 1981." *Aboriginal History* 6.2 (1982): 11-129.

——. "Aboriginal Drama: A New Voice in Australian Theatre." *Aspects of Australian Culture.* Ed. J. Daaler and M. Fryar. Adelaide: Abel Tasman, 1982. 28-33.

——. "An Interview with Jack Davis." *Westerly* 27.4 (December 1982): 111-116.

Shohat, Ella, and Robert Stam. *Unthinking Eurocentrism: Multiculturalism and the Media.* New York: Routledge, 1994.

Tiffin, Helen. "Post-Colonial Literature and Counter-Discourse." *The Post-colonial Studies Reader.* Ed. Bill Ashcroft, Gareth Griffiths, and Helen Tiffin. London: Routledge, 1995. 95-98.

Tompkins, Joanne. "History/History/Histories: Resisting the Binary in Aboriginal Drama." *Kunapipi* 15.1 (1993): 6-15.

Webby, Elizabeth. "The First-Born Trilogy: *The Dreamers* (1982), *No Sugar* (1985), *Barungin/Smell the Wind* (1989)." *Modern Australian Plays.* Sydney: Sydney UP, 1993. 65-79.

Wilde, William H., Joy Hooton, and Barry Andrews. *Oxford Companion of Australian Literature.* 2nd Ed. Melbourne: Oxford UP, 1995.

Salhia Ben-Messahel

Exploration of Indigenous Fate in Terra Incognita
Philip McLaren's *Scream Black Murder*

Australian crime fiction is a genre that allows marginal characters to address the public, subverting standard beliefs about Australian society and the history of European settlement, exposing the dilemma of a nation looking to the future and wondering about its post-colonial identity and its European heritage. Born in 1943 in Redfern, a multicultural suburb of Sydney with a large Australian Aboriginal community, Philip McLaren is an Australian-Indigenous author who was awarded an Australian Arts Fellowship in 1995 for his literary skills and contribution. He twice won the David Unaipon Award, in 1992 for his novel *Sweet Water–Stolen Land*, a historical thriller set in the 19th century, and in 1996 for *Scream Black Murder*, a crime-thriller set in modern Sydney.

McLaren's writing associates the crime genre to a historical voyage at the heart of Australian history. His stories explore the fate of indigenous characters in Australia, the "Terra Nullius" of European settlement which gradually surfaces as a "Terra Incognita," through the realm of mystery and fiction. *Scream Black Murder* addresses questions through a post-colonial perspective in that issues are related to the past, which sets an otherness or alterity into the present, that such present is neither punctual nor synchronous, and that the validity of historical time is always questionable.

McLaren says that his interest is to address history through the spectrum of fiction:

> I began writing initially to tell about my people, perceiving a lack of material in the area of Indigenous subject matter and a Euro-bias in published material that was available. I didn't want to approach my first book academically, as an historian might. After careful consideration and several false starts, I chose the technique employed

> by James A. Michener. Michener created fictional characters and had them walk through real history. That was the approach I took in my first novel *Sweet Water–Stolen Land.* I have experimented with many writing techniques throughout my four published works. (Personal interview 2004)

Scream Black Murder writes back to the Australian history of European settlement and challenges European approach to the country, to indigenous Australia, reminding the reader that the colony was set up in the 18th century to civilize indigenous Australians and expand Great-Britain's possessions and power, that the arrival of convicts and settlers led to the killings, genocide, acculturation, and hybridisation of black Australians.

In *Scream Black Murder* the central characters, Gary Leslie and Lisa Fuller, are confronted to their own cultural identity and to the dark secrets, or white lies, lying under the foundations of the nation. The plot tackles racial and sexual tension, allowing indigenous culture to divert colonial culture and thus, become central to the history of a serial killer. The police hunt for a white Australian maniac, Peter Simpson, who is raping and killing Aboriginal women, relies on Gary Leslie and Lisa Fuller, of the Sydney's newly formed Aboriginal homicide squad. Gary and Lisa evolve as "ethnic" heroes against "the all-white police force" (*Scream Black Murder* 58). They are asked to join the new squad, which was formed to respond to the blame laid against the white Australian police regarding the treatment of indigenous people and the number of deaths in custody. The apparent traditional police investigation becomes an instrument for sociological knowledge, showing a malaise in the urban and modern world, giving voice to Australia's latent discrimination.

The story examines the ramifications of colonisation on modern Australia by addressing the past in a language that encodes the experience of the colonised subject and uncovers socio-political reality. When asked whether his stories tackle cultural issues as a means to examine the pitfalls of national consciousness, McLaren responded positively saying: "Yes, that is deliberate. There is a glut of material of social examination published on the other side of the ledger" (Personal interview 2004).

In *Scream Black Murder*, history becomes textual; it is defined through its discontinuities and continuities, through differences between successive "epistemes" (the term used by Michel Foucault to relate to discursive formations). The story explores the crosscurrents that occur when ancient indigenous culture and the dominant Anglo-Celtic society collide. The plot works as a counter-narrative, criss-crossing the Australian continent by petitioning the past, writing that Australia has always been peopled, that it was never an em pty and unoccupied land. Homi Bhabha in his *The Location of Culture* (1994) suggests that counter-narratives of the nation continually evoke and erase its totalizing boundaries, whether they are actual and conceptual, that they in fact disturb the ideological manoeuvres through which "imagined communities" are given essentialist identities. Bhabha insists that the political unity of the nations rely on a displacement providing a space from which to address the minority, the marginal and the emergent (1994: 149). Such an approach to the text operates in McLaren's novel in that a connection between the present and the "pastness" of the past is set up in a subversive manner, showing that the history of the nation encapsulates the narratives of other people, the indigenous people and their sites of cultural differences, and that such history is a fragmented whole, a rhizomic structure.

The dishevelled form constructs the embedded narrative but also serves the purpose of the oral form of story-telling. McLaren addresses the reader, in the introduction to the novel, to express concern on major historical events that include the practice of taking Aboriginal children away from their families between 1909 and 1969 under the Aboriginal Protection Act, and stories that happened to some of his relatives. Autobiographic details and personal commitment support underlying themes that explore Aboriginal issues, from the state of Aboriginal health care in northern Queensland to racism, black deaths in custody and the devastating legacy of the Aboriginal Protection Act. Major issues that were raised at the end of the 20th century—a period marked by Australia's controversial bicentennial celebrations in 1988, the *Bringing Them Home* report about the Stolen Generations and established between 1994 and 1997, the failed referendum for an Australian Republic in 1999, and the centenary of Federation in 2001.

The text demonstrates that history and literature are inseparable, that fiction is a subversive genre—a genre that rests upon a central prologue harking back to the David Gundy murder in 1989. The prologue focuses on the true and tragic event story of Gundy, a man of mixed Aboriginal and Italian descent, who was killed by the police when they illegally raided his home looking for another man, and who has joined the long list of black Australians killed by some zealous and racist police officers. Such a prologue is central to expose social and racial injustice as part of metafiction. *Scream Black Murder* is indeed didactic, uncovering a historical sub-text and transforming reality into a highly suspect concept. The intertwining of fiction and reality creates the hybridity of the colonized indigenous and of the post-colonial subject, namely the non-indigenous. When Gary Leslie is looking for clues around Sydney Harbour, one of Australia's major cultural and historical landmarks, he is being thrust into the history of Australia's settlement, questioning the colonial appreciation of Australia as a Terra Nullius:

> Gary looked across the harbour from the busy ferry terminal at Circular Quay as he ate hot chips from a paper bucket [. . .]. He wondered what the harbour had been like before 1788 and imagined what life had been for his ancestors on coastal Australia before the British landed here.
>
> Aboriginal people claim they've always occupied this land and never migrated here, as some academics theorise. They reverse the logic of the popular concept: if people could walk south over the so-called land bridge which joined Australia to Asia, then surely they could also have walked north, after all the most ancient evidence of human habitation has been found on this continent. (*Scream Black Murder* 84)

The character's thought suggests Paul Carter's concept of "spatial history," a concept which is developed in his *The Road to Botany Bay* (1987), and that examines place "as a palimpsest on which successive inscriptions form the complex experience of place, which is itself historical" (Ashcroft 155).

Place is not only geographic as it encapsulates personal history and the development of the plot. Place is an extension of the persona, a mirror of the soul, a psychological and spiritual entity, the site of a collective split memory.

A series of climaxes and mini climaxes run in boomerang fashion throughout the plot, delving into the past and in the characters' thought, building up mystery and tension but disrupting the reader's expectations as well as the logical sequence of events usually found in crime-fiction. Thus, on the surface, suspense develops with the pace and excitement of crime stories, starting with the final issue of the crime and moving backward to the cause of the crime—which is in fact the beginning of the case—but rather than developing as a puzzle the plot relies on a series of changing patterns and twists disclosing fragments of reality. The identity of the killer is indeed revealed in a very brisk and unexpected manner, owing to a former accident in another state allowing DNA identification. The brotherly connection between Danny, the dying friend of Evelyn (the victim-to-be), and Lisa (the indigenous police-officer) is told in a blunt and unexpected manner just after Lisa is reconciled with her mother (*Scream Black Murder* 170).

The novel looks at the different experiences contrapuntally, making up a set of intertwined and overlapping narrations playing up on one another. It invites the reader into the mind of the killer, a deranged man, allowing the bad character to have a voice and to embody a kind of consciousness about issues such as the Americanisation of Australia (*Scream Black Murder* 33) and the Eurocentric control of space, or the evil effect of tourism in Surfer's Paradise, in the state of Queensland: "The whole place is like Kings Cross and Disneyland rolled up in one" (*Scream Black Murder* 109).

The direct address of the killer acts as a counter-discourse to the main action, and allows him to intrude in the development of suspense and to deconstruct mystery. Simpson justifies his own crimes and confesses the abuse he suffered as a child. He is also able to comment on cultural and social issues, expressing a populist vision about Australia and Australians alike. The fragmented narrative form alternates the third-person and first-person narratives to identify the killer from the beginning but does not ironically prevent questionings about whether the man will be caught or not.

The killer's stream of consciousness encapsulates a discursive dialogue between the past and the present, and becomes central to the appreciation of the horror of the crime and Australian history. McLaren's novel displaces the detective genre to become a thesis novel, drawing people's attention on the shortcomings of Australian society, advocating social beliefs, and purporting the idea "that the other is never outside or beyond us, that it emerges forcefully within cultural discourse" (Bhabha, 1990: 4). Parallels between the killer and the two detectives, all of them bearing childhood scars, show that the disalienation of black Australians and the alienation of white Australians converge to become a central theme. Yet, indigenous and non-indigenous Australians also converge to represent the two poles of a world, two poles in a perpetual conflict, two poles that design a Manichean aesthetics of a post-colonial society in which indigenous Australians are enslaved by their social, cultural and political inferiority, while non-indigenous Australians are enslaved by their superiority and colonial legacies.

The text rewrites a history of cultural encounters through the colonized ones and the colonial subject. The killer exterminates indigenous women as a consequence of his childhood trauma, picking his victims, raping them and killing them. He needs to have black women under his command to obtain revenge for the imago that obsesses him: the frightened and abused harmless child who was abased before the (white) overlord, namely the father and his mate (*Scream Black Murder* 110). The psychological portrait of Peter Simpson shows that he deals with indigenous people as a colon, that he is a colonizer at the centre of an empire: the empire of domination, hatred and fear. Simpson re-enacts the imperial gesture of possessing the other by taking control of the female body like the colonizers before him trespassed on the body of land: "she was just one more dead. I didn't think it mattered. I still don't. She was black" (*Scream Black Murder* 18).

Despite his initial power, Simpson is finally and ironically caught when Lisa bites into his penis and, thus, performs the symbolic act of taking revenge for all Aboriginal female victims, who had to perform fellatio on him before he pulled the trigger on them, and indirectly for all the indigenous women who used to be raped by white settlers in the colonizing process.

The psychological study of the killer and the examination of cultural encounters extend to the depiction of an indigenous community, and to the existing cultural gap between the haves and the haves-not. Various contrasts highlight the cultural fragmentation caused by colonization and current policies but they also remind the reader that indigenous Australians originate from different groups, that each of them belongs to a distinctive social group or kin category, that indigenous Australia is spread all over the island-continent, and that it is diverse.

Gary Leslie and Lisa Fuller are Koori (Aborigines of southern New South Wales and Victoria) detectives while Evelyn, "the black beauty" who becomes the killer's fatal mistake (*Scream Black Murder* 118-120) comes from Yirrkala, a small community in Arnhem Land (the Northern Territory; it is inhabited by local Aborigines and cannot be entered by non-Aborigines unless they are granted permission), which managed to keep its language and land rights. Evelyn has retained her Aboriginal heritage while Lisa and Gary are ignorant of the ways and customs of Aboriginal people (*Scream Black Murder* 131-132). Gary has donned a white mask of culture and privilege, having been educated in an all-white school and having married a white Australian of Irish descent. His life-story reflects the irony of the colonial paradigm——a wasp education that intermingles with his original indigeneity. Lisa's world mainly revolves around her Aboriginal but unfaithful husband, the archetypal ocker (this term is currently used for a boorish or aggressive white-Australian applies here to the indigenous character), and around her dream of going native, back to her ancestral roots. Her desire is expressed in her attraction for the bush (*Scream Black Murder* 102) because she is "the earth person, the conservator, the nurturer" (*Scream Black Murder* 112).

The three indigenous characters' personal stories connect and develop the police investigation as much as they become active partici pants in the dialectic between truth and fiction. Their indigeneity emerges as a field of intersubjectivity through memory, dialogue with the past, imagination, representation and interpretation, so that the text discloses cultural "revelation" but also cultural "silences." In Redfern, an Aboriginal woman stands as the elder of a clan, being treated with respect, calming down her angry mob and willing to cooperate with the Koori detectives:

> "Stop!" a thin white-haired woman called from her second story veranda. As if her words contained some magic, the group stepped back and quietened. "Harry, Joe come over here. You police, you come too."(*Scream Black Murder* 41-42)

The passage highlights the im portance of kinshi p, indicating that the female character is able to bridge the past and present and to provide some guidance to the younger generation for the future, regardless of gender roles.

The encounter of the two indigenous detectives with the Redfern and Queensland indigenous communities creates the reality of the "Other" and illustrates Gayatri C. Spivak's deconstructive moment of post-coloniality considering that the effect of colonization on indigenous Australians is disastrous but that out of such a disaster, the indigenous people proceed to develop a dynamic and vibrant culture that is now disrupting the imperial model of White Australia, and European cultures. Such encounter exposes the effects of colonization as much as it alludes to a developing culture, the marginal and hybrid culture of the colonized native, which is so active that it invariably affects Australia's European and non-European cultures:

> "This is Aboriginal land. Piss off!" A tall overweight man called to them, waving his arms.
>
> "And we're fucking Aboriginal!" Gary said as he opened the door of the car and leaped to his full height. Lisa quickly followed.
>
> "We're investigating the murders of the Kooris found here last week," Lisa said.
>
> The men ignored her and went directly to Gary. The tall one pushed his finger into Gary's chest. "We know what you are. Piss off!" (*Scream Black Murder* 41)

Language is an element of power, a device which is used to express differing cultural differences; it is a self-contained independent system which generates its own meaning and demonstrates that:

> The aim of cultural difference is to rearticulate the sum of knowledge from the perspective of the signifying position of the minority that resists totalisation—the repetition that will not return as the same, the minus-in-origin that results in political and discursive strategies where adding *to* does not add up but serves to disturb the calculation of power and knowledge, producing other spaces of subaltern signification. (Bhabha, 1994: 162)

In the confrontation scene between the two detectives and the indigenous group, the tall man's attitude is one of recrimination toward the past, encompassing displacement and social fragmentation, emphasizing the social otherness of liminal subjects. Thus, the detectives' difficulty at being accepted by their Aboriginal "brethren" derives from a social and political rather than cultural tension. Lisa and Gary have to negotiate between two worlds, between their indigenous cultural heritage and non-indigenous background. The fact that Lisa was forced to adopt a culture different from her original family is evidence of a dislocation, separation but, above all, acculturation:

> As an Aboriginal and a female raised in a strictly European, male-dominated society she recognised numerous obstacles placed in front of her from an early age but as she grew older she became more determined to overcome these obstacles and all prejudices against her. She clung dearly to her Aboriginality and, because she knew nothing of her family or clan, she felt robbed of the vital cultural connection to her language and land. (*Scream Black Murder* 10).

Like the murderer, the investigators momentarily reflect on their lives and their difficult past. The characters' stream of consciousness is scattered through the text like a vista onto another space, providing a vision from above and showing that:

> It is in the emergence of the interstices—the overlap and displacement of domains of difference—that the intersubjective and collective experience of *nationness*, community interest, or cultural values is negotiated. (Bhabha, 1994: 2)

As the plot develops, Lisa remembers her past when as a child she was taken to a remote part of Australia and educated in a repressive orphanage run by abusive adults, who claimed that she was an illiterate person, being "like so many of her race [. . .] unable to learn" (*Scream Black Murder* 104). Lisa's memory resurfaces like flotsam and jetsam, a happy childhood interrupted by a government policy towards indigenous people, namely the White Australia policy, and the haunting image of the mother who appears as a ghostly figure to warn and protect her child like an ancestral being (*Scream Black Murder* 140, 155) but also to buy back political injustice. Lisa, who wishes to connect with the land and the spiritual environment, is haunted by the image of her mother calling from "the white void" (*Scream Black Murder* 155). Lisa's dream comprises an underlying meaning that has moral, social, and political significance. Her dreaming develops as an allegory, the allegory that calls, in the words of Edouard Glissant, a "prophetic vision of the past"—a past that dissolves into the present so that the future remains an open question, and so that mystery is all the more significant as it also serves the purpose of crime-writing and the writing of the history of the people and the country—and above all of the greatest crime in Australian history which is colonization. Glissant's (1989) statement about history, colonization, the denial of the indigenous populations and writing, applies to McLaren's work and calls for "*a prophetic vision of the past*":

> The past to which we are subjected, which has not yet emerged as history for us, is, however, obsessively present. The duty of the writer is to explore this obsession, to show its relevance in a continuous fashion to the immediate present. This exploration is therefore related neither to a schematic chronology nor to a nostalgic lament. It leads to the identification of a painful notion of time and is full projection forward into the future [. . .]. (Glissant 64)

Lisa's personal story unleashes the negative aspects of the Aboriginal Protection Act of 1909 while Gary has to confront the past, being the only black in a white school and having to best his adversaries at sports to be accepted by the white mainstream. Both characters are "graspable only in the passage between telling/told between "here" and "somewhere else," considering that "in this double scene the very condition of cultural knowledge is the alienation of the subject" (Bhabha, 1990: 301).

Cross-cultural tensions surface through the investigation of the two indigenous detectives, who need to outperform their white colleagues as a condition of acceptance and who, in fact, are subjected to racism and hypocrisy:

> They knew they could not expect a lot of co-operation from the detectives in their section. The whole department felt threatened. They were already tarnished as racists by the media. Success by the Aboriginal unit at their expense wasn't something they wanted to assist. (*Scream Black Murder* 6)

White colleagues associate the appointment of Lisa and Gary to an Australian affirmative action scheme rather than to their own skills and intelligence:

> The much-publicised Aboriginal recruits, Gary and Lisa, had to run the gauntlet to reach their partitioned area, situated next to the toilets at the rear of the building [. . .]. The new recruits were unpopular with government bureaucrats because they were politically forced onto them. Their careers balanced precariously on a blade's edge, they needed t find the killer quickly. (*Scream Black Murder* 32)

Racist taunts are at times openly stated, terms such as "Abos," the derogatory word for Aborigines, or "fucking blacks," used by the Police Commissioner in full view of the State Minister for Police, are as violent and strong as those used by the white killer. A similar racist approach is observed in the state of Queensland where an unlawful law applies to indigenous people considering that the police put more efforts in investigating on white people's deaths rather than on the deaths of indigenous people (*Scream Black Murder* 135, 144).

The narrative subtly associates the thoughts of both killer and detectives to denounce the hypocrisy and injustice of the authorities that are eager to solve the case when the body of a white woman is found (*Scream Black Murder* 90-93). The cynicism of the police behaviour is counterbalanced by the statement of the killer who, ironically, feels compassion for Lisa and Gary:

> It's because she was white. They kicked the Abo cops off the case, although no-one is saying so. I feel sorry for them, they're not on TV anymore. (*Scream Black Murder* 93)

Lisa and Gary's attitude in front of an unfair justice system stems from resistance rather than rebellion. Their behaviour and determination to catch Simpson by all means, demonstrate that:

> Resistance [. . .] need not *necessarily* mean rejection of dominant culture, [. . .] the most effective post-colonial resistance has always been the wresting, from imperial hands, of some measure of political control over such things as language, writing and various kinds of cultural discourse, the entry into the "scene" of colonization to reveal frictions of cultural difference, to actually make use of aspects of the colonizing culture so as to generate transformative cultural production. In this way the colonized subject "interpolates" the dominant discourse, [. . .]. (Ashcroft 47)

.Gary joined the police force because of the death of David Gundy and the unfairness of the justice system. Lisa associates the police work with health concerns indicating that indigenous people, for whom open space is a cultural imperative, are jailed in unhealthy conditions (*Scream Black Murder* 10-11). Lisa's observations highlight the social discrimination and cultural deprivation felt by non-whites (*Scream Black Murder* 122). The health issue is often raised by Lisa, whose mother-in-law died of cancer owing to a lack of medical care, and is also mentioned by Doctor Nick, a Greek-Australian who works in a rural aboriginal area, telling the story of a man who died of a diabetic coma in the waiting-room of a hospital because the medical staff assumed that he was drunk. Doctor Nick embodies the hyphenated Australian, his attitude and commitment to the indigenous, and destitute, population situates him on the margins of society and the mainstream. The exposure of various viewpoints and non-indigenous characters suggests that Australian society is dealing with the past either through innocence or guilt; the innocence of a people who did not participate in the crimes and dispossession of the indigenous population, and who is not involved in the colonizing process; the guilt of a people who feels responsible because of the exposure of the drama and trauma of indigenous people who were, and are still, denied the custodianship of their country.

Alan Jackson, the police Captain, feels compelled to tell Gary and Lisa that he is committed to the indigenous cause, endorsing the proposition that all Aboriginals should have the right to vote in the 1967 referendum. Jackson's statement exposes the guilt for past injustices and current attitudes towards indigenous Australians:

> "We are not all bigots and racists, you know," Jackson blurted out. "Some of us are thinking people with independent supportive views of Aborigines. You will recall the referendum giving Aboriginal people citizenship rights was won with an eighty percent majority. Well, I'm one of the eighty percent and so are most of my friends." (*Scream Black Murder* 78-79)

The plot focuses on positive figures to subvert racial tension and violence, showing that far from being unitary or monolithic, Australian culture is a cluster which can only be appreciated through an intercultural exchange. Such an exchange illustrates the development of the case when official investigative methods, computerised and profiling techniques, are associated to methods used by indigenous people. The investigation of the case demonstrates that both Koori detectives are also able to find and examine clues that the white police would never think significant and that will lead to the arrest of the evil character. Gary has the black tracker qualities in him, he is able to spot the killer by instinct (*Scream Black Murder* 64-66, 161) and is determined to catch him. He creates a "scanning wall" of the case (*Scream Black Murder* 141), pictures, locations, maps about the crime, in a chronological order. Such a technique is part of "the collective consciousness style of problem solving which Aboriginal society had successfully applied for thousand of years" (*Scream Black Murder* 142). The scanning wall, described by Lisa as "criminal dreaming" encourages collective effort:

> For hours people sat dreaming, looking at the wall. Without speaking they would walk to the white board, write notes, take a photocopy, leave the room. Later they would return to pin new material to the wall. Then they would sit, scan and dream, [. . .]. (*Scream Black Murder* 142)

Such a scene shows that what is foreign to white Australians becomes potentially familiar, that indigenous culture and practices can be disalienated through the acceptance of otherness. It also marks the breaking-down of boundaries, encouraging "a dialectical relationship between the "grafted" European cultural systems and an indigenous ontology" (Ashcroft et al. 195), the creation of an intercultural space, a space where cultural variables operate and where the figure of the people surfaces through the ambivalence of disjunctive times and meanings.

Scream Black Murder reflects moral, racial, social and ecological issues, suggesting that the postcolonial issue is no longer structural but discursive, giving voice to the voiceless and giving the colonial subject the capacity to transform imperial discourse. A police investigation becomes a voyage in the meanders of the past and the dominant white Australian discourse, a reality which is re-examined and appropriated to replace the marginalized, the forgotten others, the unhistoricized, at the centre of Australia's history.

Works Cited

Ashcroft, Bill, Gareth Griffiths, and Helen Tiffin. *The Empire Writes Back: Theory and Practice in Post-Colonial Literatures.* London: Routledge, 1989.

Ashcroft, Bill. *Postcolonial Transformations.* 2001. London: Routledge, 2002.

Bhabha, Homi K. *The Location of Culture.* 1994. London: Routledge, 1998.

——. "DissemiNation: Time, Narrative, and the Margins of the Modern Nation." *Nation and Narration.* Ed. Homi K. Bhabha. 1990. London: Routledge, 1997. 291-322.

Bennett, Bruce, Jennifer Strauss, and Chris Wallace-Crabbe, eds. *The Oxford Literary History of Australia.* Melbourne: Oxford UP, 1998.

Carter, Paul. *The Road to Botany Bay.* London: Faber, 1987.

Commonwealth of Australia. *Bringing Them Home: National Inquiry into the Separation of Aboriginal and Torres Strait Islander Children from Their Families.* Sydney: HREOC, 1997.

Fanon, Frantz. *Black Skin, White Masks.* New York: Grove, 1967.

Gelder, Ken, and Jane. M. Jacobs. *Uncanny Australia: Sacredness and Identity in a Postcolonial Nation.* Carlton, Victoria: Melbourne UP, 1998.

Glissant, Edouard. *Caribbean Discourse: Selected Essays.* Trans. J. Michael Dash. Charlottesville: UP of Virginia, 1989.

Kleinert, Sylvia, and Margo Neale, eds. The *Oxford Companion to Aboriginal Art and Culture.* Melbourne: Oxford UP, 2000.

Knight, Stephen. *Continent of Mystery: The Thematic History of Australian Crime Fiction.* Melbourne: Melbourne UP, 1997.

——. "Crime Writing Australia." *Australian Humanities Review* (August-October 1997). 24 February 2007 <http://www.lib.latrobe.edu.au/AHR/archive/Issue-August-1997/knight.html>.

Loomba, Ania. *Colonialism/Postcolonialism.* London: Routledge, 1998.

McLaren, Philip. Personal interview. 6 September 2004.

——. *Scream Black Murder.* 1996. Broome, WA: Magabala, 2001.

——. *Sweet Water–Stolen Land.* 1992. St. Lucia: U of Queensland P, 1993.

Muecke, Stephen. *Textual Spaces, Aboriginality and Cultural Studies.* Kensington, NSW: New South Wales UP, 1992.

Shoemaker, Adam. "Tracking Black Australian Stories: Contemporary Indigenous Literature." *The Oxford Literary History of Australia.* Ed. Bruce Bennett, Jennifer Strauss, and Chris Wallace-Crabbe. Melbourne: Oxford UP, 1998. 332-347.

Linguistic Damage
Fear of Other Languages in David Malouf's Works

Beverley Curran

Introduction

"Some translators are more visible than others," says Michael Cronin (2005), but "the visible translators are almost invariably those from developed Western countries" (254). Arguably, though, some of the least visible translators operating in the West are in Australia, a site rarely visited in translation studies research. The translation traditions noted in the *Routledge Encyclopedia of Translation Studies* (1998) include the African, American, Arabic, Canadian, Brazilian, Japanese, Romanian, Latin, Latin American, along with more than twenty others. No Australian tradition is included; Australian-born translation theorist and practitioner Anthony Pym (2004) writes the entry on the history of translation in Spain. However, translation activity in Australia is far from negligible if translation is seen to include interpreting, which it should:

> In a disci pline like translation studies that is dominated by the typographic cultures of highly-literate Western elites who speak majority languages, whole areas of translation practice, informed by residual orality in many different parts of the world, may be either misunderstood or sim ply ignored. (Cronin, 2002: 48)

In fact, the use of the term "community interpreter" began in the 1970s in Australia, when the country adopted a "non-discriminatory" immigration policy,[1] meaning anyone could *apply* to migrate to Australia. It is now widely used[2] to designate a linguistic mediator who works in varying contexts in social services related to legal matters, health, education, and environmental health (Corsellis 153). Australia started developing its community interpreting programs in the 1960s and 1970s in response to increasing levels of immigration, and it has become an integral part of its "border management" policy with regard to refugees and asylum seekers, in which the role of the linguistic mediator is that of a gatekeeper. Inside the gate, the paperwork is in English. However, as Edwin Gentzler (2002) has observed, much translation activity takes place off the record in officially multicultural but monolingual nations, between family and community members, who attempt to negotiate, remember, and linguistically survive by talking to each other.

The visibility of the translator in Australia can now be increasingly glimpsed in Australian writing. The fictional turn taken by translation in Australian writing in English is critically previewed in *Dark Side of the Dream: Australian literature and the postcolonial mind* (1990), when Bob Hodge and Vijay Mishra look at the linguistic damage that takes place when tongues are silenced by assimilationist policies or managed ethnicities. Hodge and Mishra trace "a difficulty in language" (187) in migrant writing in Australia that indicates the extent of "hidden countries" and linguistic diversity marginalized by institutional monoglossia. The "difficulty" reveals itself in the challenge of experimental writing; in gaps or thick lexical density; or in deliberate grammatical lapses. Among others, Hodge and Mishra mention the work of David Malouf (b. 1934), noticing a particular sensitivity concerned with the relation of tongue and skin under conditions where racism and assimilative pressure co-exist.

In this paper, I will look at Malouf's 1993 novel *Remembering Babylon*, which confronts Anglophone Australia's fear of other languages, provoking questions about language and place, assimilation and monolingualism. The metaphor of Babel is most often seen as an equation of multilingualism with punishment, confusion, or a fall from grace, dooming the process of translation to loss and failure. Reworking the notion of "a single monolithic rhetorical and grammatical 'system' underlying all theories of translation" (Robinson 21) and the comfort myth of a universal language, Malouf "remembers" a pre-Babel linguistic connection with the earth, in which language is embedded within the natural environment as an integrated rather than separate sign system.

Lost in Translation

In Australia, interpreting was present, of course, in the first colonial contact with Aboriginal people, with a view to gaining greater access and control of the land. "Whites made little effort to learn aboriginal languages" (Carter 327), and interpreters were usually found by capturing indigenous people so that they could "command the rudiments and rhetorical occasions of English speech" (Carter 327; for description of the (largely unsuccessful) case of Arabanoo, see Tench 1793). Speaking English, as Paul Carter observes, consigned the Aboriginal people to "historical silence" (Carter 327); there was no "shared intentional space in which translation could occur" (Carter 329). From another perspective, the superficial engagement in English meant that Aboriginal people could conceal, and protect, their collective and personal identity, and "[s]patially, if not linguisticially, the Aborigines informed the Whites at every turn" (Carter 337). Despite the suggestion of an upside, speakers of the more than two hundred distinct Aboriginal languages have dwindled to such an extent that, in Queensland, for example, there are now only four of the traditional languages have more than two hundred fluent speakers.

In the Northern Territory, Aboriginal people make up 27.5% of the population, over 70% of the prison population and more than half of all patients in the public health system hospital admissions (Spring 2001). Since almost 75% speak Aboriginal languages as their first or only language, this frequent contact with government health and social services, and legal, policing, and penal systems means that community interpreters are necessary for mediating between the English administration of these services and systems and the speakers of indigenous languages who use them. Such linguistic mediation, however, is often lacking, suggesting that the government-controlled language services more readily accommodate "new Australians" than Aboriginal people:

> Large numbers of Indigenous Australians are unable to access services or have any real participation in the legal and medical processes to which they are subject due to a lack of an appropriate interpreter service. The Commonwealth Government currently funds and operates the Telephone Interpreter Service (TIS) that provides interpreters in almost every world language 24 hours a day, 7 days a week. TIS does not cover even one indigenous language.
>
> The Australian Taxation Office provides tax information sheets in 18 languages. [. . .] the Centrelink Multilingual Service allows people to speak with staff in 20 languages other than English. Centrelink claim forms also have information in 20 languages. The Administrative Appeals Tribunal's website lists information pamphlets in 34 languages. Not one of the languages listed for any of these bodies includes an indigenous language. (Spring 2001)

Even when a community interpreter is available, the "neutral" position of government-approved translators may better serve official policy than those that need linguistic mediation to make their case. Here again, the issue of the direction of translation is im portant; although performed as a dialogue, the purpose of the mediation is to allow the English-administered service to run smoothly and thus "domesticate otherness" (Longley 30), which is, ironically, that of indigenous tongues.

Given the nature of the linguistic contact zones described above, and the circumstances of people who find themselves redefined as offenders, inmates, asylum seekers, or refugees, the interpreter often mediates between officialdom and those who are "emotionally scarred, extremely distressed, and have com pletely lost their bearings" (Roy & Kapoor-Kohli 2001), and may be engaged in a "social, joint narrative activity which is the remembering or retelling of a traumatic experience" (Wadensjö 1998). Significantly, in the fictional turn that is taking place in Australian writing—in addition to Malouf's *Remembering Babylon*, translation takes a fictional turn Yasmine Gooneratne's novel, *The Pleasures of Conquest* (1996), Noelle Janaczewska's bilingual play, *The History of Water/Huyên Thoai Môt Goòng nu'òc* (1995), and Annamarie Jagose's novel, *In Translation* (1994). The visibility of the language professional in Australia is also obliquely raised by the performance of high-profile Australian Nicole Kidman's performance in Sydney Pollacks's film, *The Interpreter* (2005)—and elsewhere, it is often the translator who is damaged and attem pting a reconstruction of his or her own self and story.

Fear of the "Other" in Australia

"Australian" seems to be a term difficult to access without a qualifier. According to a recent article (Guilliatt 2005) concerning incidents of violence on Sydney's beaches, "proud Aussies" described as "sunbleached locals" battled Lebanese Australians, seen as "swarthy [. . .] new immigrants" (15). Though, immigration from the Middle East to Australia has a relatively long history. Before 1926, Lebanese migrants to Australia were grouped as "undesirable Asians," along with Chinese, Japanese, and Indians. There was an increase in immigration during the Lebanese civil war in the 1970s, and since then, wars in Afghanistan, Iraq, and elsewhere have sustained migrant trajectories from the Middle East to Australia. Muslims of "Middle Eastern appearance," the report continues, "have supplanted [East] Asians as the new aliens to be feared" in Australia:

> In the 5,000-strong throng chanting 'Aussie, Aussie, Aussie,' were two Lebanese-Australian teenagers who had travelled [. . .] to partici pate, possibly out of an unwise spirit of irony. People demanded to know why they were there. As a crowd surrounded them, one white youth waved an Australian flag, proclaiming that his father and grandfather had fought for it.
>
> One of the besieged pair [. . .] smiled and explained that he was born in Australia, so it was his flag, too. When he reached out to touch the flag, however, the crowd punched and kicked him until he was rescued by two locals and police.
>
> The [. . .] mob, waving flags and singing "Waltzing Matilda" while beating up "Lebs" represented a darker side of patriotism, but Mr Howard remained insistent that it did not demonstrate any underlying racism in Australia. (Guilliatt 15)

The official and fictional record of overt racism (for a discussion of Australia's unofficial anthem, with "its strongly gendered national stereotypes embedded," see Hodge and Mishra 212; Dixson 1976) in Australia reveals an "im peccable genealogy stretching back to the initial confrontation with Aboriginal people" (Hodge and Mishra 180). Exclusionary policies against Asians have existed in Australia since the gold rush in the 1850s, when restrictions were placed on Chinese miners (Khoo 14), and later, in the 1900s, when language tests were designed with an intentional bias in favour of English-speaking and Anglo-European-educated immigrants (Khoo 16). These exclusionary language tests can be contrasted with one of the "privileges" accorded convicted felons in New South Wales during its colonization, when all criminal charges were required to be heard before a magistrate. As Malouf describes it in *A Spirit of Play: The Making of Australian Consciousness* (1998), linguistic leeway was possible at these hearings because the felons had the right "to use their own slang, their thieves cant, 'flash' or 'kiddy' language, which the Court, if necessary, translated" (121). This apparent "benevolence," however, hints at "something approaching panic, the chaos of unintelligibility" (Carter 318). Malouf also traces a trajectory of translation from an early convict performance of Shakespeare's *Henry IV* (1597) in Sydney on 8 April 1800 through to the contem porary annual manifestations of cultural code-switching in the huge spectacle of gay Mardi Gras, which "offers the crowd a reflected image of its own multi plicity, and all with in a spirit of carnival, a form of play" (Malouf, 1998: 114). It must be said, though, that *Remembering Babylon* represents Australia at neither its most playful nor its most "tolerant."

Somatic and Linguistic Tensions in *Remembering Babylon*

It has been argued that discriminatory practices against Asians in Australia have not been paid sufficient and sustained attention because the bulk of research on racialization in Australia continues to focus on the "tensions between black and white Australia, specifically addressing Aboriginal/settler-invader issues" (Khoo 16). In *Remembering Babylon*, Malouf does not shift that focus, but "undoes the polarizing of colonizing and colonized space" (Spivak 76) and com plicates the division between intrusion and dispossession. Malouf explains in an interview (1994),

> I wanted to tell the story of an in-between character who would have been in contact with [aboriginal] culture and would be able to stand for that but wouldn't be speaking directly for it. (Papastergiadis 92)

Gemmy Fairley, *Remembering Babylon*'s fictional translator, is thus a liminal figure, but the land and languages that he has been translated into truly ground him. This em phasis on the "local" is a move to imagine a mystical language, which Malouf locates in the hum of the beehive and its honeyed hexagonal perfection of communal geometry. It is what comes closest to Umberto Eco's (1995) descri ption of the pre-Babel tongue as an "effective language" (Berger 355), which not only says but *does*, by activating natural and supernatural forces.

Remembering Babylon is set in northern Queensland in the mid-nineteenth century. In the opening pages, Gemmy interrupts child's play by literally falling into Comet River, a small enclave of white settlers whose tight community bonds hold back fears stemming from being unwelcome intruders themselves. The unsettling ramifications of migrancy can be particularly marked when they involve changes in the stars and seasons, and in the local plants and animals, and Gemmy's sudden appearance in the midst of the community places "in question nearly everything that seems to be unquestionable to the members of the [. . .] group (Cronin, 2000: 45), including the certainties of their tongue and skin.

Malouf's fictional translator is initially unidentifiable. To the settlers, Gemmy first appears to be "a black," and then a thing "not even, maybe, human" (*Remembering Babylon* 2), a bird or a bewitched being whose transformance into a bird has been interrupted and is now "neither one thing nor the other" (*Remembering Babylon* 2). Gender, too, is unclear, although when "it" speaks a stuttering English—"'Do not shoot," it shout[s]. 'I am a B-b-british object!'" (*Remembering Babylon* 3)—identity hardens into that of a white man.

When, however, the community hears English followed by an utterance in "some whining blackfeller's lingo" (*Remembering Babylon* 4), their fear of the Other is replaced by fear of another language: if they "allowed the man to go on using it, he would see how weak they were and get the advantage of them" (*Remembering Babylon* 5). When the settlers have a better look at the intruder, they find "a man who had suffered a great deal of damage" (*Remembering Babylon* 7), with singed and smudged features, blackened teeth and a short twisted leg. One metaphoric message this body suggests is that colonization damages the people living in the invaded land, those who arrive, and the land itself. Poet John Daniels says in an interview (2004), "Damaged nature is very valuable because it shows us ourselves" (Satterlee 170), and Malouf's damaged fictional translator seems to have the similar function of revealing linguistic distress at the heart of multicultural Australia.

Like most of the Comet River settlers, who left behind hard lives in Scottish mining towns, Gemmy has escaped subsistence as a "maggot" on the factory floors of an industrialized London and then rat-catcher's gofer by climbing on a ship, but without knowing where he is bound. Falling sick aboard the ship, Gemmy is thrown overboard, and washes up on an unknown shore. He is found by a group of Aboriginal people and although he is not welcomed, he joins them and survives by letting go of English and then finding a new sense of belonging through the acquisition of several Aboriginal languages. The translator can be construed as a potential cause of cultural crisis (Gentzler, 1996: 117), and this seems precisely the role that Malouf intends for his fictional auto-translator in *Remembering Babylon*; that is, to cause trouble and initiate change. "I wanted to introduce [. . .] a kind of catalyst" (Papastergiades 88) that might accelerate the realization among anglophone Australians that migrancy entails a shift in consciousness and language.

The fear evoked by the translator's other tongue is not confined to the fledgling community in *Remembering Babylon*, of course. It is recognizable in societies suspicious of those whose languages are not understood. This fear can escalate to the extent that an "other" language can become "a national security concern [and] its speakers [. . .] defined as enemies" (Pratt, 2004: 422). Malouf's fictional translator confronts anglophone Australia's fear of other languages, provoking questions about language and place, assimilation, and monolingualism.

Linguistic Ecology

The tension between land and language needs to be resolved, and in *Remembering Babylon*, Malouf offers a prototype of how that link might be made through language learning. Language has also been linked to the land in the call for the preservation of languages. V. V. Ivanov asserts, "We should be concerned about preserving languages just as we are about ecology" (qtd. in Eco 338), and since the 1980s, linguistic human rights has largely been an issue of protecting the planetary loss of languages, particularly those of indigenous peoples, as part of efforts to protect the environment.

Many endangered languages have been neglected or abandoned because of their grounding in orality. *Remembering Babylon* offers a translator who cannot read or write; for whom English has been exclusively a language of oral expression. Gemmy then acquires several Aboriginal languages and a cultural context where the dynamics of orality are fully operative. Not only does his fictional presence suggest the value of indigenous languages as means to sustain and learn knowledge that may be crucial to survival, but also figures the oral community tongues hidden away in multicultural societies, covert or absent in school and workplace.

Tove Skutnabb-Kangas, a leading linguistic rights activist, has rather alarmingly described monolingualism as "a dangerous illness" (qtd. in Castles 1995) that needs to be eradicated. The focus of her efforts has been to obtain the European community's recognition of the rights of minority languages to survive. The im pact of Western European languages on indigenous ones in the Americas and Australia, however, has been much greater, and the rate of language loss much higher (Mufwene 2003). More widespread concerns about monolingualism have come to the fore since the destruction of the twin towers on 11 September 2001. For exam ple, in the area of language learning in the United States,

> the public education system [. . .] actually discourages the use of any language other than English. Education consists, then, of unlearning languages, not learning them. Before becoming an elite capable of mastering several languages, children must first pass into an elite of people who speak only English. (Johnson 32)

Or, as Mary Louise Pratt (2004) has flatly asserted, "The United Sates is a language cemetery" (422) in spite of being a multilingual and multicultural nation. "The English-only idea, for some an expression of patriotism and belonging, now appears as a prime cause of insecurity, error and ineptitude" (422). John Kinsella (2003) makes a similar observation about Australia when he says, "The myths of nation are firmly lashed to monolingualism":

> We hear the multi-ethnic nature of Australian society touted on a regular basis. However, in its national manifestation, in terms of projections of power, society is monocultural, as it's monolingual The fact of communities retaining their own birth-languages—spoken and written—does not signify diversity within the idea of the nation. Nation allows this in order to contain it: permission being "granted" in exchange for a loyalty to the language of power. [. . .]. The real constitution of Australia is written into immigration laws, into Customs regulations, into all those legalities that govern our movement. (Kinsella 2003)

In *Remembering Babylon*, Malouf suggests that insecurity, at least, precedes exclusive language policies in a place where "landscape reflected nothing back of their own humanity" (Papastergiadis 85). Com pare this with the closing lines of Margaret Atwood's poem from *The Journals of Susanna Moodie* (1970):

> *The moving water will not show me*
>
> *my reflection.*
>
> *The rocks ignore.*
>
> *I am a word*
>
> *in a foreign language.* ("Disembarking at Quebec" 11)

Remembering Babylon is a novel of gaps and silences, some due to grief or fear. It also locates speech in the body, specifically an alternative body. But crucially it reaches out, in a tactile move, to situate language as a relationship with others, all beings and with the land:

> There was no way of existing in this land, or making your way through it, unless you took it into yourself, discovered on your breath, the sounds that linked up all the various parts of it and made them one. (*Remembering Babylon* 65)

Malouf describes this relationship in *An Imaginary Life* (1978) as one

> that need[s] no tongue, a perfect interchange [. . .] as thoughts melt out of one mind into the other [. . .] with none of the structures of formal speech. (145)

Secret words are shared to imagine, and thus create, community. This sense of linguistic conspiracy identifies "those who breathe together" (Lubin xiii; he defines "conspire": "The word conspire comes from the Latin prefix com- (together) and verb spirare (to breathe). Hence conspirators are those who breathe together").

For Malouf, what is not put into words is crucial to meaning. Regarding *Remembering Babylon*, the author remarks,

> One of the things I am interested in is the different forms of language. It's not just the forms of actual speech: dialect language, the five or six Aboriginal languages that Gemmy speaks, which we never hear. But there is another kind of language which is the one I'm more interested in, and that is the language of gesture or the language of silence that doesn't require words. (Papastergiadis 90-91)

Viewing language from a number of possible positions, Malouf performs a task of translation attempted by disability studies: to "unsettle the hegemony of the normal and to institute alternative ways of thinking about the abnormal" (Davis 49). In imagining other linguistic options, Malouf reaches beyond the human to consider the beehive and its buzzing tongue.

Language Disabilities

Further, the colonizers, like the settlers in *Remembering Babylon*, do not see that "the continent had already been completely humanized by the people who lived there" (85), because they do not recognize the Aboriginal inhabitants as human:

> Even before the racial designation began to be scientifically assigned in the 1850s, natural science placed the natives of Tierra del Fuego and Aboriginal Australians together at the "zero order of civilization." The more "advanced" the primitive culture, [. . .] the closer it was to being classified as fully human and, more importantly, the more entitled it was to claim ownership to the land. (Schaffer 96)

In their inability to understand the land or its people, the settlers can be seen as second language immigrants who arrive in their new country unable to read and write and find themselves linguistically "disadvantaged."

Disability theorist Lennard Davis (1995) argues that the body with disabilities is a counter image not only to the domesticating ideal of a unified nation or cultural homogeneity, but also to the idea of "the body [. . .] as a site of *jouissance*, a native ground of pleasure, [. . .] that takes dominant culture and its rigid power-laden vision of the body to task" (5). Further, the body with disabilities is "not" seen:

> Rather than face this ragged image, the critic turns to the fluids of sexuality, the gloss of lubrication, the glossing of the body as text, the heteroglossia of the intertext, the glossalia of the schizophrenic. But almost never the body of the differently abled. (Davis 5)

A "language disability" is not distinguishable until a person "begins to engage in communication" (Davis 14), but Malouf renders it seen and heard in the case of his stuttering, limping fictional translator. What is most significant about this representation is the location of linguistic damage in the English speaker; it is only in English that Gemmy stutters, and the site of his trauma and abuse is England. That is, the damage arrives with him. Gemmy lets his English go and links himself to the land through the acquisition of indigenous languages. Thus his disability is in the eye and ear of the English-speaking Comet River community who construct him as such. From their perspective, Gemmy is somatically and linguistically damaged, while they assume themselves to be intact. "But the notion of an undamaged observer who is part of an undamaged society is certainly one to be questioned" (Davis 14), particularly in a colonial society.

In the specific terms of British colonies, and the multiple versions of England and English that have been constructed, Jamaica Kincaid (1988) puts it this way:

> [E]verywhere [the English] went they turned it into England; and everybody they met they turned English. But no place could ever really be England, and nobody who did not look exactly like them would ever be English, so

> you can imagine the destruction of people and land that came from that. (24)

Malouf uses his fictional translator to defamiliarize this scenario. The London-born Gemmy turns away from his origins to become a part of his new world. His contact with the Comet River settlement and the fear of his linguistic and somatic otherness, of his change and resemblance, triggers a communal identity crisis and the colonizers join the walking and talking wounded. Malouf's project in *Remembering Babylon* is how to make the connection between place and tongue—in the specific case of Australia, how does one acquire the language of the land? The objects of translation are "texts and utterances, rather than languages" (Zabalbeascoa 329), which means that variation, body language, and relationship are part of the event. Silence, the stutter, or, for that matter, excessive attention to speaking correctly, all demonstrate how social conditions affect the capacity to speak, be listened to, or be recognized or understood.

Malouf carefully traces the circulation and shifting capital of English words in different mouths and in different accents and makes explicit the connection between somatic and linguistic "impediment." For example, when Lachlan Beattie arrives in the Comet River community from Scotland, Hector Gosper, an older boy with a harelip, takes the ten-year-old under his wing:

> Lachlan, who was unhappy in the new place was grateful for it, but wary too, at first. His accent was the point on which he was tormented and he was concerned that what Hector might have in mind was a shared impediment. (*Remembering Babylon* 157)

Pierre Bourdieu (1991) locates a linguistic community not only in a shared language, but more crucially, where values and meaning *go without saying.* In *Remembering Babylon*, the tiny white settler community of Comet River tacitly pulls together as neighbours. The cultural capital of Jock McIvor, "one of the little inner band" (72), drops drastically when he offers Gemmy Fairley a place to stay. McIvor admits Gemmy into the community because the latter is essentially "white;" his decision to do so raises suspicions about McIvor because there is unspoken resistance to granting Gemmy that status, given his powerful cultural affiliations with Aboriginal people and tenuous linguistic links to the settlers. After aligning himself with Gemmy, the community looks at McIvor as if "a mark of difference or some deformity has emerged in him that they had failed till now to observe" (*Remembering Babylon* 73). Just as the others look for "signs of trespass" across invisible property lines, now they too scrutinize Jock McIvor and what he says. Gemmy's presence has the settlers asking each other, "Who (and what) is he?" but what Gemmy really calls into question is "Who are 'we'?" Who exactly is "Australian"?

An Ordinary Life: Language Beyond Tongues

In his discussion of deafness, Davis observes eighteenth century philosophers' interest in "how language began, how reason and thought intertwined into human essence," and the question, "Can a being be human without language?" (55). Research focused on " 'savages,' orangutans, wild children, and the deaf" (Davis 55). Malouf has also shown an interest in the beginnings of language and also in its endings. In his short story "The Only Speaker of His Tongue" (1985), a visiting lexicographer attem pts to speak to a man who is the last speaker of his tongue:

> Half a century back, when he was a boy, the last of this people were massacred. The language, one of hundreds (why make a fuss?) died with them. Only not quite. For all his lifetime this man has spoken it, if only to himself. The words, the great system of sound and silence [. . .] are locked up now in his heavy skull, behind the folds of the black brow (hence my scholarly interest), in the mouth with its stained teeth and fat rather pink tongue. (68-69)

In the figure of the "only speaker," language is embodied and made mortal; monolingualism is taken to its extreme, words found on but a single tongue. The lexicographer is curious about this man, whose linguistic isolation also makes the lexicographer aware of his own singularity as "a scholarly freak from another country" ("The Only Speaker of His Tongue" 70). He, too, is a linguistic oddity in this country. Suddenly frightened at being "cut off [. . .] from the use of [his] own tongue" ("The Only Speaker of His Tongue" 71), he whispers (Norwegian) words to himself to bring forth that northern world in his little rented room somewhere in the Anti podes.

Malouf's use of the term "freak" subtly connects the linguistic oddity with the "obviously disabled" (Davis 90). Davies reviews the assortment of specimens that the freak show offered:

> [N]ot only were the obviously disabled—the mentally delayed, the physically different—exhibited in freak shows, but also physically normal native peoples of colonized countries [. . .]. The notion of racial difference put them in the same category as the disabled. (90)

The incomprehensible tongue can also render the speaker a social aberration. Among the exhibits at the freak shows of the nineteenth century were wild children, usually hoaxes, presented as examples of extreme exotic. For the eighteenth-century researcher, "the wild child and the deaf provided living examples of the mind untouched by civilization" (Davis 55), and thus a way to understand the origins of humanity. Malouf joins cognitive scientists and other researchers, including literary scholars, who now see the body as a "crucial and contested boundary marker for the limits of language" (Berger 345), and are interested in what lies outside language in the fissure constantly covered. Controlled, and denied by its symbolic order.

In *An Imaginary Life*, Malouf shows his particular fascination with questions of language and being by imagining an encounter with a poet and a wild child. Ovid, with his wit, literary skill, and cosmopolitan tongue, finds himself silenced in his banishment to the margins of the Roman Empire:

> [N]o one speaks my tongue, and for nearly a year I have heard no word of my own language; I am rendered dumb. (17)

Here Latin, as a cosmopolitan, vehicular language of emprie, has run out of gas. In his writing, the historical Ovid maintains, "*Omine solum forti patria est*" (*Fasti* l.493-494) i.e. for the strong, all soil is home, but in Malouf's novel, his fictional counterpart finds himself "the least person here—a crazy, comic old man, grotesque, tearful, who understands nothing, can say nothing" (*An Imaginary Life* 17). The use of the word "grotesque" is interesting here, making a link between deviant tongue and body. Bakhtin famously associates the term with misrule, the unsettling of established order. Davis, however, sees "a thin line between grotesque and the disabled" (151). The former is aesthetic, the latter is somatic, but they both objectify.

A deaf person who learns sign language becomes a member of a linguistic minority and enters a community. In *An Imaginary Life*, the silenced poet becomes a reluctant language learner. The sounds of the language spoken around him are "barbarous, and [his] soul aches for the refinements of [the] Latin tongue, that perfect tongue in which all can be spoken, even pronouncements of exile" (*An Imaginary Life* 21). But Latin has its limits, for the land where his now lives "is a vast page whose tongue I am unable to decipher, whose message to me I am unable to interpret" (*An Imaginary Life* 17). Ovid prefers the prospect of learning the language of spiders than the "barbarous gutteral tongue" that he hears, but gradually does learn the "crude" tongue and starts to "see" the world through it. Instead of constantly comparing the vernacular with Latin, and in its difference, finding it inferior, Ovid now finds the language he is acquiring to be "oddly moving":

> It isn't at all like our Roman tongue, whose endings are designed to express difference, the smallest nuances of thought and feeling. This language is equally expressive, but what it presents is the raw life and unity of things. [. . .]. Seeing the world through the other tongue I see it differently. It is a different world. [. . .] I feel the ice of myself cracking. I feel myself loosen and flow again, reflecting the world. That is what spring means. (*An Imaginary Life* 69)

Translation merges with language learning, dwelling on the first steps into another world taken through language, rather than on mastery or manipulation.

We might compare this starting point with that of Gemmy, who also enters into a new language and through it, a new world. While Ovid is in command of Latin and recognized as a literary master, Gemmy has never really had anything but a "buttery" grip of English, the language of empire in *Remembering Babylon.* "He had never [. . .] possessed more than a few hundred words that were immediately needful to him, to fill his belly or save his skin" (26). That language "was not enough to hold him" (26) and Gemmy quickly learns that in this new place, thing and name and breath are inseparable.

Gemmy is comparable not only to the poet but to the Child in Malouf's earlier novel. *An Imaginary Life*'s Child lives in the forest and been raised by wolves; in other words, he is the wild child of the Enlightenment, who was such an object of curiosity to those interested in origins. Gemmy points towards an afterlife, repaired in the wake of damage. His linguistic impairment rather than innocence renders him a figure and site "both of social-linguistic trauma and of some kind of redemption of that reaches beyond language" (Berger 347). His auto-translation brings him *in touch* with the world, and makes him at home in his body.

Malouf is not just appraising the value of the acquisition of a new vernacular. Through the Child in *An Imaginary Life* and in his later novel, through Gemmy, Malouf suggests that language is not exclusively human, and moreover, that the languages of other beings can be learned if the body allows. In the Child's bird sounds, for example, Ovid sees a bird's life. "If he were to speak always as a frog or hawk or wolf, the muscles of his throat and jaw might grow to fit the sound, so intimately are the creatures and sounds they make connected, so deeply are they one" (*An Imaginary Life* 91). This is not mimicry. "In imitating the birds, he is not [. . .] copying something that is outside him and revealing the accuracy or virtuosity of his speech organs. He is being the bird" (*An Imaginary Life* 92). Language then is not to divide but to connect through a kinesthetic sense of being. A cosmopolitan tongue ostensibly promotes connection through common understanding, but its very structure can make it divisive and discriminatory. Ovid teaches the Child to speak by touch, by revealing the organs of speech in the body:

> [A]s I make the sounds I want him to imitate, and which he found such difficulty in drawing up to his lips, I place his fingers on my throat so that he can hear the buzzing of my voice there, I lay his fingertips to my lips so that he can feel the shape of them, the flow of breath. (*An Imaginary Life* 92)

At the same time that the Child locates communication in his own body, the poet sees the world as part of the Child's own being:

> It is his consciousness that he leads me through on our walks. It flickers all around us: it is water swamps, grass clumps, logs, branches; it is crowded with a thousand changing forms that shrill and sing and rattle and buzz. (*An Imaginary Life* 93)

The Child is in the hive, is part of the buzz.

While Malouf sets *An Imaginary Life* in a remote past and place, contemporary references implicit in the comparison of Latin and the local vernacular:

> When I think of the tongue that was taken from me, it is some earlier and more universal language than our Latin, subtle as it undoubtedly is. Latin is a language for distinctions, every ending defines and divides. The language that I am speaking of now, that I am almost speaking, is a language whose every syllable is a gesture of reconciliation. We knew that language once, I spoke it in my childhood. We must discover it again. (98)

The term "reconciliation" calls up the deeply troubled relationship between Aboriginal and invader in Australia, but Malouf thickens it with ecological implications. He sees the urgency of learning a language as a way to redress "our misuse of nature" and "put ourselves back in there—

inside nature and the rest of the creatures" (McDonald 54; see also "Three Talks 1984"), suggesting a process of translation that incorporates language into an ecological rather than an economic world system—twenty-five years later, at the 2003 MLA Convention, Masao Miyoshi proposes "to subsume knowledge production under an umbrella of ecology" (Pratt, 2003: 424). Malouf locates "reconciliation" in the syllables of a tongue that calls the Australian anglophone to learn a different language to relate to the land and Aboriginal peoples as part of the same eco-system; to learn a language that might link them to the land. This is a significant departure from the pervasive ideas of "possession" of a language and ownershi p of land, where the "master" pretends historically, through the rape of a cultural usurpation, which is always essentially colonial, to appropriate language in order to im pose it as "his own" (Derrida 23). What Malouf is proposing is not just learning a different language but a different way of being in the world.

This figure of a language learner/auto-translator, then, does more than straddle linguistic and cultural borders. Certainly, the border itself has been reconfigured in the past few decades.

> Our frontiers are now in the interfaces of cities and com puter networks; our border workers are mobile multilingual professionals, in virtual and yet doggedly urbanized societies. (Pym 2004)

Although Malouf positions Ovid on the margins of the em pire, and, in *Remembering Babylon*, balances Gemmy Fairley uneasily between two worlds, he is not as interested in border crossing *per se* as he is in understanding the nature of the connection between place and language and how that connection can be made through a willingness to admit change.

Imagining a "bilingual" self into existence through the presence of a damaged translator in the text, and creating a linguistic double that may or may not actually exist, involves the body in a kinetic performance of identity, where the performance is "about presence, not representation; [. . .] not [. . .] a mirror, but the actual moment in which the mirror is shattered" (Gómez-Peña 9). This version of auto-translation is distinct from the autonomy asserted by creative writers with "command" of more than one language, and acknowledges its dependencies rather than asserting its authority. Works by Vladimir Nabokov, who freely translated Lewis Carroll in Russian (1923) and faithfully rendered Alexander Pushkin in English (1964), as well as his own fiction in both languages, and those by Samuel Beckett, who wrote and re-wrote them in French and English, are examples of auto-translation "in all its infinite diversity" (Casanova 200), by authors who at least in part, maintain control of the transformation of their texts and, in the process, reassert their "absolute autonomy" (Casanova 200). The emphasis rests on creative licence and linguistic mastery. The fictional translator in *Remembering Babylon* reveals a writer exploring the constraint at the heart of more tenuous relationships with language and place.

Land Rights and Language Rites

In *Room for Maneuver: Reading Oppositional Narrative* (1991), Ross Chambers locates the issue of land rights—"the historical dispossession by the European invasion of land that had been occupied for 40,000 years by Aboriginal people and in relation to which their cultural identity was defined" (246)—at the heart of Australian history since colonial invasion. *Remembering Babylon* was published in 1993, the year after the *Mabo vs. Queensland* trial ended in a decision that refuted "the legal fiction on which the whole edifice of real property law came to be based in Australia" (Goodall 106). As Alice Brittan (2002) puts it:

> Mabo established, for the first time in Australian history, that the continent was not *terra nullius* (land belonging to no one) when the First Fleet arrived at Botany Bay in 1788 and that native land title was not automatically extinguished when James Cook took possession of the continent on behalf of the British Empire in 1770. (1159)

Just as the Mabo ruling was a retroactive challenge (Brittan 1159) to colonial claims of possession, so Malouf looks back to consider how one might enter a world without asserting and enforcing ownership. This involves discovering how to speak as well as how one might act.

It has been suggested that the fear that Gemmy instills in the Comet River residents stems from his racial ambiguity "but also, and crucially from the threat posed by his pidgin stuttering speech" (Brittan 1160). Certainly, racial ambiguity is a source of fear in the community:

> "He had started out white. No question. When he fell in with the blacks—at thirteen, was it?—he had been like any other child, one of their own for instance. (That was hard to swallow.) But had he remained white? [. . .] Could you lose it? Not just language, but *it. It.*" (*Remembering Babylon* 40)

Gemmy's struggle with English—his first language—is indicative of the extent of transformation possible in a man—in a white man, translated away from whiteness—and thus is very disturbing to the settlers:

> They looked at their own children, even the smallest of them chattering away, entirely at home in their tongue, then heard the mere half-dozen words of English this fellow could cough up, and even those so mismanaged and distorted you could barely guess what he was on about. (*Remembering Babylon* 40)

He does not sound white, which means he does not really speak English, and he does not look "right," that is, white, either. "The whole cast of his face gave him the look of one of Them. How was that then?" (*Remembering Babylon* 40). It is a face, it is suggested, shaped by other languages he has learned to speak.

However, what Gemmy speaks is not pidgin. Pidgin (thus named after the Chinese (mis)pronunciation of the English word "business") are contact languages that developed out of commercial activities between traders whose languages were mutually unintelligible. They were "improvised along cultural borderlines" (Pratt, 1992: 6) to facilitate communication, particularly for the purposes of commerce. As such they need to be recognizable and understandable. Gemmy's English, however, is not border talk:

> If you gave him a word for a thing, he could, after a good deal of huffing and blowing, repeat it, but the next time round you had to teach it to him all over again. He was imitation gone wrong, and the mere sight of it put you wrong too, made the whole business somehow foolish and open to doubt. (*Remembering Babylon* 39).

Yet he had been "living off the land, learning their lingo and all their secrets, all their *abominations* they went in for" to the extent that he now spoke five languages, his commitment obvious in the cast of his jaw which "had adapted itself to the new sounds it had to make" (*Remembering Babylon* 40). In other words, it is not his stammering English that poses a threat, but his other languages.

The question of Gemmy's loyalty is an important one for the white community of Comet River, and Gemmy recognizes that he must be selective about the information he shares. He is aware that this group sees him as a possible informant and when they attempt to pick his brains about the whereabouts of Aboriginal people in the vicinity, he deliberately skews the information he gives. At other times, though, he is simply incapable of furnishing the information desired because his listeners lack the necessary language:

> In fact, a good deal of what they were after he could not have told, even if he had wanted to, for the simplest reason that there were no words for it in their tongue; yet when as sometimes happened he fell back on a native word, the only one that could express it, their eyes went hard, as if the mere existence of a language they did not know was a provocation, a way of making them helpless. He did not intend it that way, but he too saw that it might be true. There was no way of existing in this land, or of making your way through it, unless you took it into yourself, discovered on your breath, the sounds that linked up all the various parts of it and made them one. (*Remembering Babylon* 65)

The limits of translation can be offset by a willingness to engage in language learning. Fear of languages, on the other hand, and suspicion of the translator leads to linguistic damage, physical violence, and ecological degradation and estrangement. The fictional translator in *Remembering Babylon* embodies a recuperative praxis that involves slow learning, attentive listening and contact.

Language Classes

In multicultural countries such as Australia, English promoted as powerful,

> the elite language that other language speakers aspire to master, as an indispensable means of access to cultural and other forms of capital. (Stanton 1268)

In the universities, animated discussion of difference with regard to sex, gender, race and ethnicity take place primarily in a single tongue, namely English. And yet, for a growing number of students, in particular, and citizens, more generally,

> English is a foreign, a second, an international, or a global language, not the language of a unitary mother tongue and culture. (Kramsch 1245)

In *Remembering Babylon*, Malouf implicitly juxtaposes Gemmy's profound acquisition of Aboriginal languages with the resistance to land and language shown by the settlement's schoolteacher, George Abbot.

When Jacques Derrida recalls his childhood in Algeria learning French in school, he says, "the master took the form, primarily and particularly, of the schoolteacher" (42). In colonial Australia, the "language of the master" is English, but it is a foreign language as taught by the British schoolteacher, with no relevance or resonance in the students' rough real lives in Queensland. Abbott is contemptuous and despairing of his charges' cultural illiteracy and dull refusal to learn, but continues to insist on their memorization of Shelley's poetry and the spelling of words like "mettlesome, benign, decorum, prudence" (*Remembering Babylon* 45). In his own free time, Abbot reads his foreign book, "usually a French one" (*Remembering Babylon* 81), in order to transport himself from a place which he detests for its lack of refinement.

Gemmy sees Abbot as a "sorcerer" (*Remembering Babylon* 177), at least when he is sitting at a desk with his pile of papers and "the bottle with the spirit that smelled like earth" (*Remembering Babylon* 177) and looked like black blood, and exerted too much power over his life and his death. The schoolteacher stands in striking contrast to Mr. Frazer, the settlement's minister, who is deeply interested in the natural world and the chances of revelations found within it. As a street child, Gemmy's survival skills included a gift for mimicry and he puts it to use when he finds himself in a new world:

> Relying on a wit that was instinctive to him and had been sharpened under harder circumstances than these, he let himself be gathered into a world which, though he was alarmed at first by its wildness, proved no different in essence from his previous one. (*Remembering Babylon* 26)

Mr. Frazer, Gemmy's own ad hoc intralingual community interpreter, has no such linguistic knack for learning Aboriginal languages:

> He did not open his mouth wide enough, or his tongue was in the wrong place or lolled about like a parrot's, or he put too much spit into the thing or too little. Gemmy was glad that none of the clan were there to hear it. (*Remembering Babylon* 67)

Further, the minister's interests in the world he asks Gemmy to show him are embarrassing, for Frazer is concerned with "women's business" and oblivious to the taboos attached to uttering words never "heard on a *man's* lips" (*Remembering Babylon* 67). However, seeing this "queer whitefella" painstakingly draw exquisite pictures of local flora, Gemmy finds

> satisfaction [in] the cooperation between them that made him the hands and eyes of the enterprise, the breath too when it came to giving things a name, as Mr Frazer was the agency for translating it out of that dimension, which was all effort, sweat and dirt [. . .] into these outlines on the page that were all pure spirit. (*Remembering Babylon* 66)

In his only deliberate performances as a translator, Gemmy teaches the minister the names of plants, but with several different Aboriginal languages in his head, he "has to ask himself which of those worlds he's going to let Mr. Frazer glimpse by giving him the name of the plant" (Papastergiadis 92). He also has to conceal things from the minister, too, out of reverence and caution, and does not point out things

> it was forbidden them to touch, since they were in the care of men whose land they were crossing; other that only women could approach; others again that were a source of more power then he could control. (*Remembering Babylon* 69)

This collaboration of translation and language learning is a profound shift in relating to the world from another direction, and with different intent. Less important than learning to speak is learning to listen carefully to voices and silences. This fictional translator is one with ecological interdependencies.

The Hum of the Hive: Under Linguistic Reconstruction

In *An Imaginary Life*, Ovid initially prefers the option of learning spider language to the prospect of acquiring a barbaric tongue. In *Remembering Babylon*, Janet McIvor tries to learn the language of bees. As a young girl, Janet is drawn to the hives, and experiences a moment of revelation when she is consumed in their hum. Covered in the bees, she is unafraid and understands through her body what the bees are doing and why. Janet continues her language studies, and years later, as a nun, she corresponds with a German priest doing similar research. However, it is wartime, and when her letters are confiscated and made public in the papers, the intricate unknowable language inscribed in the hum and motions of the bees turns "all explicable [. . .] as the language of an international conspiracy" (*Remembering Babylon* 189). In the face of fear, meaning is assumed. In the "cold print" (189) of the newspaper, Janet can see how her language learning efforts may appear odd. Fear of another language prompts a hostile response:

> [P]arents cancelling music lessons, anonymous voices shouting loyal obscenities. A youth on a bicycle rode up the drive [. . .] and put a stone through one of their windows wrapped in a Union Jack. (*Remembering Babylon* 189)

Janet is not the only one who appears threatening. A naturalized German pastry cook has his windows broken, as well, by a "gang of patriotic football fans. When he complained he was himself arrested, charged with disturbing the peace, and found guilty" (*Remembering Babylon* 189); to follow was deportation and confiscation of assets. The sadly predictable response in both cases shows a deep aversion to the "foreign" as a "local" danger.

The world of the bees suggests the architecture of a unifying language, a sonic structure that changes the way a human "sees" things. Or rather, as Janet understands it, the hum of the hive is "another life. She loved the way, while you were dealing with them, you had to submit yourself to *their* side of things" (*Remembering Babylon* 140):

> If she could escape, she thought, just for a moment out of her personal mind into their communally single one, she would know what it was like to be an angel. (*Remembering Babylon* 140)

Her understanding comes not from within herself. It can be read as a revelation similar to Antoine Berman's "experience of the foreign" which "signals neither exoticism nor colonialism but an opening of the self toward its own alterity" (Rajan 427), an erotic, ecological surrender; a most willing assimilation. However, Malouf goes further than the foreignizing translation *pulsion* espoused by Berman as he moves beyond border, nation, and the human to find a way back into the world. As a young girl, Janet, in her "moment of illumination" (*Remembering Babylon* 199), understands who she is in the hum of the bees, and fleetingly shares the secret of the single mind of the hive where home and being close in on each other. The world, she later thinks, has been separated into nations and languages, and yet we *all* hug this earth "on this night, now, in this corner of the world or any other" (*Remembering Babylon* 200). Acknowledging a mystery that can be called divine, Malouf locates the notion of "pure" language, the *pulsion* to translate, in the unifying spirit of the universe, which pulls the ocean towards the shore to touch its other life.

Malouf's longing for a planetary tongue does not allow him to deny the harsh conditions that reduce so many to damaged silence. The scabbed freckled skin of Janet, born in Australia, or her father or Laughlin, arrived from Scotland, is "the wrong skin" (*Remembering Babylon* 186) for a country of bright sun and heat; and somatic adaptation is a slow process. Gemmy enters the land through language, and sheds his skin to survive as a "ragged fragment" of the landscape "or its history or their own, some part of it that was still to come" (*Remembering Babylon* 194), finally at home. That landscape, in its turn is not an untouched wilderness, but rather a healthy renewal one, long under the stewardshi p of the Aboriginal people. The fictional translator as a steward suggests that language is something that also requires care to survive.

Gemmy's linguistic assimilation into an indigenous community may or may not have been enough to save his skin. Lachlan wonder if Gemmy might have been a victim of a "dispersal" by a group of cattlemen, though the story he uncovers is an uncertain one:

> The blacks had been ridden down and brought to earth by blows from a stirrup iron at the end of a stirrup leather—an effective weapon, when used at a gallop, for smashing skulls. (*Remembering Babylon* 196)

It is difficult for Lachlan to get any specific information from the Aboriginal people themselves. "He had only a few words of their language, picked up from Gemmy and poorly learned" (*Remembering Babylon* 196). There is no English newspaper report to verify or identify, a "dispersal" being "too slight an affair to be called a massacre" (*Remembering Babylon* 196), in the manner of an "evacuation" or "occupation" in another time and place. Lachlan hears the story told in another language barely understood, and located in a different consciousness. It is neither distinct with details nor written down, but "gathered [. . .] into the dreamtime of the land itself, a shadowy realm where the bones of facts had already drawn around them the skin of rock, of beasts, of air" (*Remembering Babylon* 196). But surely the violence disfigures that skin just as its telling might cause the tongue of a witness to falter. Gemmy's own stuttering English stems from other material conditions. In an urban industrialized London where he was both casually cared for and deeply abused, he sets fire to the room of his sleeping drunken keeper. His linguistic damage is neither unusual nor *unheimlich*; it speaks of damaged times.

Conclusion

Remembering Babylon was published in 1993, the year of the first World Trade Center bombing. The novel begins with Gemmy's unexpected arrival in Comet River, an event that changes everything in that community. Through the fictional translator, the novel imagines, rather than remembers, a way of communicating that links word and land, in a pre-Babel unity. The event of 11 September 2001 relocates the mythic destruction of the Tower of Babel in its "traumatic televised images of the fall of the World Trade Center towers burned into our minds" (Berger 354). Writer Don DeLillo (2003) has declared 9/11 the actual beginning of the 21st century:

> Because while the zeitgeist before the events was shaped by a belief in the omni present power of money and in America's invulnerability, [. . .] that belief has now been replaced by fear. (Henning 2005)

Fear of other languages is refined to fear of other languages spoken by "terrorists"—Arabic, Pashto, Dari, Farsi, Hazargi or Uzbek. Post-9/11, fear spreads quickly, and three days later, the Australian government invokes the ANZUS Treaty for the first time, and starts to look askance at "inaccessible" dialects spoken in neighbouring Indonesia and suspicious immigrant enclaves within Australia. In the wake of Babel there was confusion at the multi plicity of languages; in the wake of the destruction of the two 110-storey towers was a certain sense of vulnerability and helplessness. Further, the event brought home the inadequacy of monolingual education policies, demonstrated by a lack of translators in a multicultural country; in September 2001, there were only 614 students of these "other" languages in American universities.

In Australia, as in the States, the current scramble to find linguists and translators is motivated by fear of unknown languages, not an im pulse for dialogue. Those who speak these languages are suspected of having more than just "linguistic" links. The translator again is not to be trusted. There is a line drawn, too, between the community translator and the officially recognized linguist; that is between the "native speaker" and the "heritage speaker." Members of the intelligence communities reject the latter for their lack of expertise. At a meeting on "Translation and Terrorism" held in Atlanta during the American Translators Association meeting in November 2002, and attended by members of the FBI, CIA, and the Pentagon, Ronald Wolfe, a former US Air Force linguist, who translated the first round of al-Qaeda tapes made a scoffing distinction:

> [A] "heritage speaker" (or "kitchen table speaker"—presumably someone who learned a language other than English as a child of immigrant parents) is not a translator. Saying that "if you can speak a language, you can translate it" is like saying "if you can breathe, you can be a pulmonary specialist." (qtd. in Russell-Bitting 2002)

Dismissing the amateur, Wolfe advocates language services provided by the government, "just as in Australia."

Australian government language services are available to refugees and asylum seekers, but are em ployed in support of "border management." The exclusionary language tests administered to Asians in the 1900s find their contem porary counterpart in tests of linguistic identification that thousands of refugees undergo as part of the processing of their claims. According to linguist Tim McNamara (2004), the movement involved in human trafficking and dispersed communities can com plicate attem pts at national identification, but on the test, "the pronunciation of a small handful of words [is] sufficient to reject the asylum application" (1). *Remembering Babylon* finds a small, damaged boy washed up on a northern Queensland shore, who translates himself into the land, and the novel closes with a look out on the "ever moving, ever approaching, ever receding shore" (199) where the sea and land meet and touch each other's life. In the early twenty-first century, a nation of immigrants anxiously awaits the incoming "waves" of those from elsewhere, and refugee and terrorist blur in a unified language of fear. Talk about confusion.

Endnotes

[1] The "White Australia" immigration policy, which excluded Asians, was established during the ministries of the first two Prime Ministers, Edmund Barton (1901-1903) and Alfred Deakin (1902-1904). Until its revision in 1956, there was "a deliberate policy to discourage the immigration of people from countries seen as having a culture very different from Australia's" (Spring 2001).

[2] Although used widely, in the UK, the term has "attracted connotations of a lower standard or of a different and partial role" (Corsellis 153) and professionals there prefer the title "public service interpreter."

Works Cited

Atwood, Margaret. "Disembarking at Quebec." *The Journals of Susanna Moodie.* Toronto: Oxford UP, 1970. 11.

Baker, Mona, ed. *Routledge Encyclopedia of Translation Studies.* London: Routledge, 1998.

Berger, James. "Falling Towers and Postmodern Wild Children: Oliver Sacks, Don DeLillo, and Turns Against Language." *PMLA* 120.2 (2005): 341-61.

Berman, Antoine. *L'Épreuve de l'étranger: Culture et Traduction dans l'Allemagne Romantique.* Paris: Gallimard, 1984. *The Experience of the Foreign: Culture and Translation in Romantic Germany.* Trans. S. Heyvaert. Albany: State U of New York P, 1992.

Bourdieu, Pierre. *Language and Symbolic Power.* Trans. Gino Raymond and Matthew Adamson. Ed. John B Thompson. Cambridge. MA: Harvard UP, 1991.

Brittan, Alice. "B-b-british Objects: Possession, Naming, and Translation in David Malouf's *Remembering Babylon.*" *PMLA* 117.2 (October 2002): 1158-1171.

Carter, Paul. *The Road to Botany Bay: An Essay in Spatial History.* London: Faber & Faber, 1987.

Castles, Stephen. Introduction. Global Cultural Diversity Conference Proceedings. 1995. 25 July 2004 <http://www.immi.gov.au/ multicultural/_inc/ publications/confer/speech1a.htm>.

Chambers, Iain. "Citizenship, Language, and Modernity." *PMLA* 117.1 (January 2002): 24-31.

Chambers, Ross. *Room for Maneuver: Reading Oppositional Narrative.* Chicago, London: U of Chicago P, 1991.

Corsellis, Ann. "Training Interpreters to Work in the Public Services." *Training for the New Millennium: Pedagogies for Translation and Interpreting.* Ed. Martha Tennent. Amsterdam: John Benjamins, 2005. 153-173.

Cronin, Michael. "Deschooling Translation: Beginning of Century Reflections on Teaching Translation and Interpreting." *Training for the New Millennium: Pedagogies for Translation and Interpreting.* Ed. Martha Tennent. Amsterdam: John Benjamins, 2005. 249-265.

——. "The Empire Talks Back: Orality, Heteronomy, and the Cultural Turn in Interpretation Studies." *Translation and Power.* Eds. Maria Tymoczko and Edwin Gentzler. Amherst: U of Massachusetts P, 2002. 45-62.

——. *Across the Lines: Travel, Language, Translation.* Cork: Cork UP, 2000.

Davis, Lennard J. *Enforcing Normalcy: Disability, Deafness and Body.* London: Verso, 1995.

Derrida, Jacques. *Monolingualism of the Other; or, The Prosthesis of Origin.* Trans. Patrick Mensah. Stanford, CA: Stanford UP, 1998.

Eco, Umberto. *The Search for the Perfect Language.* Trans. James Fentress. London: Fontana, 1995.

Gentzler, Edwin. "What's Different about Translation in the Americas?" *CTIS Occasional Papers* 2 (2002): 7-17.

——. "Translation, Counter-Culture, and the Fifties in the USA." *Translation, Power, Subversion.* Eds. Román Álvarez and M. Carmen-África Vidal. Adelaide: Multilingual Matters, 1996. 116-137.

Gómez-Peña, Guillermo. *Dangerous Border Crossings: The Artist Talks Back.* London: Routledge, 2000.

Goodall, Heather. *Invasion to Embassy: Land in Aboriginal Politics in New South Wales, 1770-1972.* St. Leonards, NSW: Allen & Unwin, 1996 .

Gooneratne, Yasmine. *The Pleasures of Conquest.* Milsons Point, NSW: Vintage, 1996.

Guilliatt, Richard. "Battles on the Beach Unmask the Ugly Face of Australia." (*The Times*–Supplement) *The Daily Yomiuri* 25 December 2005: 15.

Henning, Peter. " 'Vielleicht Sehe ich Einiges Klarer und Früher als Andere.' Der Amerikanische Schriftsteller Don DeLillo über die Prophetische Kraft Seiner Bücher, den 11. September, Freundschaft unter Autorenkollegen und Seinen Neuen Roman 'Cosmopolis.' " *Frankfurter Rundschau* 20 November 2003: 28-29. Interview with Don DeLillo. Trans. Julia Apitsch. 12 December 2005 <http: perival.com/delillo/ddinterview_henning.htm>.

Hodge, Bob, and Vijay Mishra. *Dark Side of the Dream: Australian Literature and the Postcolonial Mind.* North Sydney: Allen & Unwin, 1990.

Jagose, Annamarie. *In Translation.* 1994. St. Leonards, NSW: Allen & Unwin, 1995.

Janaczewska, Noelle. *The History of Water/Huyên Thoai Môt Goòng nu'ò'c.* Sydney: Currency, 1995.

Johnson, Barbara. *Mother Tongues: Sexuality, Trials, Motherhood, Translation.* London: Harvard UP, 2003.

Khoo, Tseen-Ling. *Banana Bending: Asian-Australian and Asian-Canadian Literatures.* Hong Kong: Hong Kong UP, 2003.

Kincaid, Jamaica. *A Small Place.* New York: Plume, 1988.

Kinsella, John. "Refugees and Australia." Lecture. A Just Australia Campaign. June 2003. 12 December 2005 <http://www.johnkinsella.org/essays/refugees.html>.

Kramsch, Claire. "Alien Wisdoms in English and Foreign Language Programs." *PMLA* 117.5 (2002): 1245-1247.

Longley, Kateryna Olijnyk. "Fabricating Otherness: Demidenko and Exoticism." *"New Exoticisms": Changing Patterns in the Construction of Otherness.* Ed. Isabel Santaolalla. Amsterdam: Rodopi, 2000. 21-40.

Lubin, David M. Preface. *Shooting Kennedy: JFK and the Culture of Images.* Berkeley: U of California P, 2003. ix-xiv.

Malouf, David. *A Spirit of Play: The Making of Australian Consciousness.* Sydney: ABC, 1998.

——. *Remembering Babylon.* 1993. New York: Vintage, 1994.

——. "The Only Speaker of His Tongue." 1985. Ringwood, Victoria: Penguin, 1986. 68-72.

——, et al. "Three Talks: David Malouf, Les Murray and David Rowbotham." *Australian Literary Studies* 11.3 (1984): 316-325.

——. *Child's Play.* London: Chatto & Windus, 1982.

——. *An Imaginary Life.* 1978. Sydney: Pan Picador, 1980.

McDonald, Avis G. "Beyond Language: David Malouf's *An Imaginary Life.*" *Ariel* 19.1 (1988): 45-54.

McNamara, Tim. *UniNews* 13.1 (9-23 February 2004). 12 December 2005 <http://uninews.unimelb.edu. au/articleid'1204.html>.

Mufwene, Salikoko S. "Globalization and the Myth of Killer Languages: What's Really Going On?" 2nd Annual International Conference of the Graduiertenkolleg Postcolonial Studies. Evangelische Akademie Tutzing. 4-6 November 2003. 20 December 2005 <humanities.uchicago.edu/faculty/mufwene/publications/globalization-killer Languages.pdf>.

Nabokov, Vladimir, trans. *Anya v Stranye Chudes.* 1923. Trans. of *Alice Adventure's in Wonderland* (1865) by Lewis Carroll. New York: Dover, 1976.

——, trans. *Eugene Onegin*. Trans. of *Eugene Onegin* (1833) by Alexander Pushkin. Princeton, New Jersey: Princeton UP, 1964.

Ondaatje, Michael. "A Conversation with David Malouf." *Brick* 47 (1993): 50-58.

Papastergiadis, Nikos. "David Malouf and Languages for Landscape: An Interview." *Ariel: A Review of International English Literature* 25.3 (July 1994): 83-94.

Pratt, Mary-Louise. "Presidential Address 2003: Language, Liberties, Waves, and Webs: Engaging the Present." *PMLA* 119.1 (2004): 417–28.

——. *Imperial Eyes: Travel Writing and Transculturation*. New York: Routledge, 1992.

Pym, Anthony. "On the Social and the Cultural in Translation Studies." 10 January 2004. 1 July 2004 <http://www.tinet.org/~apym/on-line/translation.html>.

Rajan, Tilottama. Introduction. *Imagining History*. Ed. Tilottama Rajan and Linda Woodbridge. Spec. issue of *PMLA* 118.3 (2003): 427-435.

Robinson, Douglas. "Babel, Tower of." *Routledge Encyclopedia of Translation Studies*. Ed. Mona Baker. London: Routledge, 1998. 21-22.

Russell-Bitting, Alexandra. "Translation and Terrorism." *ITI Bulletin* January-February 2003: 20-23. 12 December 2005 <www.iti.org.uk/uploaded Files/events/terrorism.pdf>.

Roy, Ghislaine, and Angali Kapoor-Kohli. "Beyond Words: Bridging the Gap." *Critical Link 3 Papers* (2001). 12 December 2005 <http://wwww.criticallink.org/ English/cl3papers.htm>.

Satterlee, Michelle. "Seeing Local Nature: Interview with John Daniel." *Interdisciplinary Studies in Literature and the Environment* 11.2 (Summer 2004): 167-179.

Schaffer, Kay. *In the Wake of First Contact: The Eliza Fraser Stories*. Cambridge: Cambridge UP, 1995.

Shakespeare, William. *Henry IV, Part 2*. 1599. New York: Signet, 1987.

——. *Henry IV, Part 1*. 1597. New York: Barron's, 1985.

Spivak, Gayatri Chakravorty. *Death of a Discipline*. New York: Columbia UP, 2003.

Spring, Merie. "Evolution of Language Services: From Infant to Teenager." Paper presentation. "Interpreting in the Community: The Complexity of the Profession." International Conference, Montreal, Quebec, Canada, 22-26 May 2001. 12 Jan 2006 <http://www.criticallink.org/English/criticalLink3_papers. htm>.

Stanton, Domna C. "From Imperialism to Collaboration: How Do We Get There?" *PMLA* 117.5 (2002): 1266-1271.

Tench, Watkin. *Complete Account of the Settlement at Port Jackson.* 1793. 12 December 2005 <http://www.gutenberg.org/etext/3534>.

The Interpreter. Dir. Sydney Pollack. Perf. Nicole Kidman and Sean Penn. Prod. Sydney Pollack, G. Mac Brown, and Anthony Minghella. Universal Pictures, 2005.

Translation and Terrorism: A Town Hall Meeting. American Translators Association. Atlanta, Georgia. 25 November 2002. 12 December 2005 <http://www.atanet.org/chronicle/index2002.htm>.

Wadensjö, Cecilia. "The Social Organization of Remembering in Interpreter-Mediated Encounters." Paper presentation. *The Critical Link 2: Interpreters in the Community–Selected Papers from the Second International Conference on Interpreting in Legal, Health and Social Service Settings* (Vancouver, BC, Canada, 19-23 May 1998). Ed. Roda P. Roberts, Silvana E. Carr, Diana Abraham, and Aideen Dufour. Amsterdam: John Benjamins, 2000.12 Jan 2006 <http://www.criticallink.org/journalscl2/12.pdf>.

Zabalbeascoa, Patrick. "Dubbing and the Nonverbal Dimension of Translation." *Nonverbal Communication and Translation.* Ed. Fernando Poyatos. Amsterdam: John Benjamins, 1997. 327-342.

"A Breath Out of the Heart of the Country" The Landscapes of David Malouf

Jonathan Highfield

A sense of a national culture is an organic idea which grows as the nation develops. From the racist rhetoric of One Nation's Pauline Hanson to the lighting of the Olympic flame in Sydney in 2000 by Kathy Freeman, the sense of national character in Australia is still in flux. That the question of what kind of nation Australia will become is still subject to impassioned debate is unsurprising, given that the nation is only a century old and still grapples with the idea of breaking entirely from its former colonial master. The question of what sort of nation Australia will become, what its people will be like, has been debated since 1788. At the heart of this debate have been issues surrounding the original inhabitants of Australia.

Two novels by David Malouf (b. 1934), *Remembering Babylon* (1993) and *The Conversations at Curlow Creek* (1996), examine the resonances of Aboriginal thought in contemporary Australian culture. The novels can be read as interesting companion pieces: *The Conversations at Curlow Creek* is set at the height of the transportation era, when the majority of Australians were on the continent against their will, while *Remembering Babylon* is set in a farming community twenty years later. In both novels, Aboriginal culture is important, but in neither book does an Aboriginal character speak. This is, I would argue, intentional. One of the most important themes in the two novels is how genocide effectively destroyed an Australian landscape, since a way of seeing the land vanished with the destroyed Aboriginal peoples. If language and culture are the way humans organize the world, then the loss of over a hundred Aboriginal cultures and languages meant that the world will never be seen in the way it was by the Iora, Walumeda, Gwiyagil, and Dharuk. Those landscapes can never be seen again for they can never be spoken into existence.

At the same time, Malouf suggests that immigrants attuned to the rhythms of the land can over time see new landscapes and create the kind of native culture which Seamus Deane indicates is a necessary part of a national project (Deane 3).The landscapes they will bring into existence with their words and actions reveal their own heritage planted upon the Australian topography. What Malouf's novels, particularly *Remembering Babylon*, seem to argue for is a recognition of the continuing importance of the Aboriginal vision for the future of Australia. In both novels, the idea of *terra nullius* is explicitly voiced by certain characters only to be refuted dramatically by others.

In *The Conversations at Curlow Creek* Malouf is exploring the roots of Australia's founding through the observations of Michael Adair, a British officer sent to oversee a hanging in the Australian bush in 1827. The conversations of the title refer to the talk the night before the hanging between Adair and the condemned prisoner, as well as the conversations between the three soldiers guarding the prisoner. Beyond that, however, there is an ongoing dialogue throughout the novel between Ireland and Australia, and an ominous silence, broken once most dramatically, where the voice of the Aboriginal people should be heard.

When a group of bushrangers led by a charismatic Irishman named Dolan are finally killed, Adair, an Irishman himself, is sent to interview the gang's only survivor, Daniel Carney. Because of the attempted revolution in Ireland of 1798 and the transported Irish rebellion at Parmatta in 1804, the authorities want Adair to ascertain whether Dolan was a revolutionary or merely a criminal. Adair has a secret agenda in questioning Carney: he wants to discover whether the slain Dolan is his adopted brother Fergus.

There are resonances of Joseph Conrad's *Heart of Darkness* (1902) in *The Conversations at Curlow Creek.* Like Marlowe, Adair travels into the backcountry of a colony to discover the whereabouts of a promising man gone bad. There is also a "beloved" hovering over the two men—Virgilia Fitzgibbon, a childhood playmate—though in the case of Malouf's novel, there is the additional entanglement that while Virgilia is infatuated with the wild Fergus, Adair is in love with her. Though Adair and, through flashbacks, Fergus and Virgilia occupy the central place in the novel, there are several other important characters which Malouf uses to sketch out a sense of Ireland and the colony of Australia. In Ireland, Adair grows up around the revolutionary aristocrat,

Eamon Fitzgibbon, the butler, coachman, and gardener Paddy Magnan, and the peasant family of the O'Riordans whom Fergus adopts after the husband is transported. As a boy, Fergus declared, "I'd have made the world very different, if I'd had the making of it" (*The Conversations at Curlow Creek* 103), and it is the injustice of transportation, and his own wild nature, that drives him to try to remake the world in New South Wales.

New South Wales, Australia, however, is not an easy place to remake the world. The colony there is founded on class injustice, and, through the stories of the soldiers and the surviving gang member, it is evident that death and violence in New South Wales are always imminent. Significantly, two of the more important characters in the Australia segments of the book have already died before Adair arrives: Dolan, and Jed Snelling, the fourth soldier in the company.

Transportation to Australia was harsh sentence, and one usually reserved for the poor and political prisoners (Hughes 163). The cruelty of the penal system only perpetuates violence, transforming decent men like Mr. O'Riordan, transported for simple theft, into killers. The guards and soldiers are not spared either. Jed Snelling's death haunts the three surviving soldiers, though they cannot speak the horror they feel:

> The blacks' camp when they came upon it filthy enough but in no way remarkable, the argument, when it started, like a dozen others they had had along the way, with the same lot of difficult old men or surly young ones. But suddenly the shouting had got serious, things were out of hand, and Jed Snelling had with no warning become something unimaginable, a man with a spear in his neck who was on the rough ground, gurgling—praying maybe, or shouting for his wife or his mother, only you couldn't tell because the words were indistinguishable from the blood that was gushing out of him in an arc like a fountain, all sparkling in the sunlight but turning dark where it was sucked into the droughty earth.
>
> That is what he wanted to talk about. (*The Conversations at Curlow Creek* 15)

But to talk about the violence perpetuated by the Aboriginals on Snelling, the violence of Dolan's gang, and the brutal killing of the Aboriginals and bushrangers by the soldiers is to ask questions that challenge not only transportation and the penal system but class injustice and racism. As Carney awaits death, he wrestles with these very questions, not knowing exactly how to phrase them, but hoping Adair, as an educated man, can help him figure out the answers. In fact, Adair seems so sym pathetic to the plight of Carney, and after all both are Irish, that the other soldiers begin to worry that he is going to set him free, leaving them to chase and capture him again. Adair cannot forsake his duty and free Carney—despite his feelings that is left to his fictional counterpart O'Dare—but he is particularly drawn to Carney's discussion of the relationshi p between Ireland and Australia:

> "Ireland's a green place," he said, as if Adair might never had known it. "I think sometimes that this place—you know, is a punishment on a man just in itself. Like as if they'd taken Ireland and turned it into a place that made things as they could ever be in this world. I feel sometimes, as if maybe I've never really left it. Just got meself into a part of it, you know, that's meant for those that've gone wrong in life, taken a wrong turning. Could that be it, sir, do you think? When I first come here and see these natives, these black fellers, I thought they was just like us—you know, on'y starved and burned black as a punishment. (*The Conversations at Curlow Creek* 57)

For Carney, New South Wales is a mythical land, a magic place where the landscape is the opposite of Ireland. If were one to find the right passage, one could travel back to Ireland, back to a time free of the cat-o'nine-tails and the chains.

For Adair, Australia is unfinished, caught in the transformation from wilderness to civilization, a process which he thinks "might fail, all this, But then again, it might not" (*The Conversations at Curlow Creek* 61). Like Carney, however, his thoughts about the landscape stretching out before him are tied to the land of his birth. When he first arrives at the hut where Carney is being held, he contrasts the landscape and its memories with that of his home in Ireland:

> He had never in all his life felt so far from the things that were closest to him, from any object that gave him back the comfortable assurance of being in a world of his own kind, a habitable place crowded with other lives—even the lives of ghosts. (*The Conversations at Curlow Creek* 8)

What Adair cannot and will never see is that the stream he drinks from, the birds calling, and even the hills he rides over are part of an "old enduring faith," one that stretches back 30,000 years. The history Adair is concerned with is his personal history, the intertwining of his life with that of Fergus, and the possibility that Fergus has met his death calling for a revolution in the middle of this land em pty of stories.

But the land named Australia by the Europeans is anything but em pty of stories. In some ways this is the central idea in the novel. Some of those stories cannot be fully explained, like the death of Jed Snelling, some are cut short, like the ribald ballads of corrupted yet virginal Luke Cassidy, and some belong to the Aboriginals and will never belong to the white man. The ghost story Garrety tells belongs to this last category:

> I was crossin' this big paddock out Camden way. It was a place I knew well enough, I'd been there often enough. I was just walkin' across it. 'Bout four in the afternoon. I wasn't in a hurry. But somethin'—I don't know what—must of stopped me. I just stood there, I don't know how long, but it seemed long. I felt something strange was happening. Not to me but all round me. Like a wind had come up. Only it wasn't that. The air was still, stiller than it had been, in fact—no birds, no crickets. That's odd, I thought. I could hear grass-blades rubbing one against the other, a weird sound, that once you noticed it got louder and louder, like someone was going at a knife-blade with a stone—you know what that sounds like. Only loud. As if it was hundreds of 'em. Something made me look down then. I was standin' in blood. It was all around me, filling the whole paddock like a lake, I was up to me ankles in it! I smelt it then, and felt its wetness, the air was so thick I could hardly breathe. An' all of a sudden there were these voices, cryin' out something terrible, I never heard nothin' to touch it, all that cryin' and wailing.
>
> I knew what it was then. I'd stepped into a place where something terrible had happened, or was goin' t' happen, either one, I don't know which, I couldn' tell which. An' it didn't matter. I was there, that's all. (*The Conversations at Curlow Creek* 125)

But it is more than just being there. Garrety has seen into an Aboriginal tribe's fate, even if he does not understand what he has seen. His ability to see a landscape hidden to most white men has already unnerved Jonas, the Aboriginal tracker, and this time, in telling the story, Garrety unleashes a visceral reaction in Jonas:

> Away to their left, outside the circle, a high pitched wailing began, a weird sound, scarcely human.
>
> Clearly it was the black, Jonas, who was making it; the top part of his body, where he sat crosslegged in the dust, was swaying. But the sound itself was coming from a point several feet beyond him, out of the earth, and as his voice shifted pitch, the sound too shifted, came from another place altogether. (*The Conversations at Curlow Creek* 125)

The three soldiers and Adair sit stupefied by this event, until Langhurst goes to console Jonas. Even after the trooper sits with Jonas, the Aboriginal man "continued to sit, staring trancelike ahead" (*The Conversations at Curlow Creek* 126).

While this scene could be read in a way that would echo Chinua Achebe's criticism (1988) of Conrad's portrayal of Africans in *Heart of Darkness*, I would suggest that Malouf is doing something quite different. The fact that the crying seems to emanate from the land itself, along with the indication that Jonas is in a trance suggests not superstitious hysteria, as the soldiers seem to think, but a religious ceremony, performed by one who has seen a vision of the future. While Jonas has no dialogue, this "wailing," as Adair terms it, is both lamentation, a protest against the horrors perpetuated by the English on the Aboriginal cultures that began fifty years previously and still continue to this day, as well as affirmation, a prayer to the Dreamtime Spirits that despite this history of horror, Aboriginal cultures will survive. Jonas' invocation of his people, therefore, becomes one of the most im portant and poignant utterances in the novel, a response to the colonizers' conversation. Even though Adair is the primary character in the novel, he acknowledges that his transient nature limits the power of his own observations:

> What a place this is, Adair thought, his eye on Jonas. God knows what things have happened here and gone unrecorded by men, or on the way towards us. Will we ever know the true history of it? The secret history, stored away in the dark folds of the landscape, in its scattered bones, of a paradise found or lost. It struck him now that the real difference between himself and these others was that he could leave the place, and would leave it, but that they belonged and would stick. What he could afford to raise as an interesting question was the ground of their lives. (*The Conversations at Curlow Creek* 127)

This phrase, "ground of their lives" resonates with the current Aboriginal demands for land rights, as well as prefiguring the transformation of the continent which will be wrought by the settlers in the century after Adair's departure. As the ground of their lives, ultimately the new settlers, convicts, and soldiers must come to terms with the land, must make their eyes see the landscape, must form their mouths around new vocalizations, must tell new stories built out of the land. It is one such story that grows up to surround the execution of Carney:

> At the last moment Daniel Carney was saved—that was the nub of it. The Irish officer who had been sent out to oversee the hanging had all along been in on the thing, but had played so skillfully his part of lawman and public official that even the prisoner had been deceived [. . .]. Anyway, the officer, whose name was O'Dare, had become the hero of the hour, a true embodiment of the spirit of Irish resourcefulness and derring-do, and Daniel Carney was a martyr miraculously resurrected; or O'Dare was a hateful renegade and confounder of the rule of law and Carney a dangerous rebel, once more on the loose. (*The Conversations at Curlow Creek* 226)

The fictional counterpart to Adair has himself become part of the story that will create Australia, the story of defiant Irish building a city of freedom, exactly the opposite of Sydney, a English city built on bondage. The fantasies of Carney come to fruition in this story, for this "shadow Sydney" is a "green place," and even if the only way of getting there is through death or imagination, it provides a hope of another landscape, a landscape built not by law and chain, but by subterfuge and song. The legend will ultimately prove a more powerful story than the disci plining tale of the prison colony, and Australia will grow to be a country which celebrates the individual rather than the ordered mass of humanity.

The story of O'Dare also shows that even in the early years of the colony, a new culture is developing, for storytelling is the foundation of culture. Despite the attem pt by the authorities to execute Carney deep in the silence of the outback, his story, like that of the massacred Aboriginals, cannot be silenced, and the story that resonates out of the rocks and barbershops will accentuate the beauty and freedom in his last baptismal wash, not the horror of the hanging which follows and is absent from the narrative. Despite the best efforts, governmental authorities cannot control how a story is told and what kind of culture will grow out of the seeds it plants.

The last scene in the novel reaffirms that vision of culture. Adair's first thoughts about New South Wales focused on what was missing on this new continent and ended with the image of the lack of "warm, newly risen bread, on a plate with a blue Greek-key design on it like their everyday ware at Ellersey" (*The Conversations at Curlow Creek* 9). At the novel's close, the day before sailing back to Ireland and to Virgilia, with both the story of Fergus's death and a proposal of marriage, Adair wanders through the darkened streets of Sydney, pondering both the story of O'Dare and his own new desire "To be done at last with these years of moving from one place to another. To settle. To be at home" (*The Conversations at Curlow Creek* 229). His wanderings lead him to a bakery where the morning bread is being baked. After receiving a loaf of bread, Adair tastes it, and perhaps for the first time truly enters the new land:

> He pauses a moment and pinches off a corner of the loaf, the salty sweetness of the crust in his mouth a kind of blessing. He chews as he walks on, his saliva mixing with its sugars and driving new light into his heart, refreshing his mouth like common speech. (*The Conversations at Curlow Creek* 232)

The bread is not served on a China plate, but given from hand to hand. It still satisfies, however. Like the food shared with Adair by the O'Riordans, the bread offers a hope of charity beyond the misery of the imprisonment of class. It is common speech, this mixture of saliva and bread, and represents the new culture that is being formed in Australia. The things Adair noticed the absence of on his arrival, he now sees are coming, that the Australian landscape is being transfigured into those farms that grow grain, those bakeries that bake bread from the meal. English, Irish, and Scots farmers—to be joined by Germans, Chinese, Indians, Lebanese, and Eastern Europeans as the decades pass—are putting their roots down in this Australian soil and building a new landscape, a new culture. The question that rises up, like the howl of Jonas and the land, is what kind of culture will this mixture produce? Will it be a culture which embraces Fergus's ideal of justice, or one constrained by classism and racism?

It is this very question with which Malouf's novel, *Remembering Babylon* , wrestles. *Remembering Babylon* is set "in the middle of the nineteenth century, when settlement in Queensland had advanced little more than halfway up the coast" (*Remembering Babylon* 1). It is the story of Gemmy Fairley, an abandoned English sailor, who is adopted by an Aboriginal tribe. Gemmy is first discovered by the children Janet and Meg McIvor and their cousin Lachlan Beattie. When he emerges from the "Absolute Dark" of the bush, the children think he is an Aboriginal about to attack the settlement (*Remembering Babylon* 2). Gemmy is an interstitial being, hanging between the Britain of his childhood and the Aboriginal existence of his young adulthood. His first words inadvertently speak to his place in British society and ultimately his place in the community of settlers: "Do not shoot," it shouted. "I am a B-b-british object!" (*Remembering Babylon* 3). His life in England was lived not as a subject, but an object, a nameless orphan existing in the underbelly of the industrial imperial machine: "one of an army of little shitty creatures, mere bundles of rag and breath" (*Remembering Babylon* 146). For a homeless child in the early nineteenth century in urban Europe, there is not much of a chance of a different life. It is only after he accidentally "set himself loose in the world," that he becomes a boy on a series of ships, ending up cast off onto the Australian coast (*Remembering Babylon* 153).

Gemmy has always lived a life of adaptation, so his transition into the Aboriginal community does not strike him as unusual. After he is discovered by "a mob of naked women and gleaming big eyed children" (*Remembering Babylon* 22) washed up on the strand, Gemmy gradually insinuates himself into their society. For him, it is not much different than making a place for himself among sailors, being the ratcatcher's boy, or scrabbling for oil-coated sawdust in the bowels of a factory. For sixteen years he lives among the Aboriginals and gradually absorbs their philosophy and way of seeing:

> [H]e got into his mouth as much of its fat and flesh as he could manage, its names too, its breath. What kept you alive here was the one and the other, and they were inseparable: the creature with its pale ears raised and stiffened, sitting up alert in its life as you were in yours, and its name on your tongue. When it kicked its feet and gushed blood it did not go out of the world but had its life now in you, and could go in and out of your mouth forever, breath on breath, and was not lost, any more than the water you stooped to drink would cease to run because you gulped it down in greedy mouthfuls, then pissed it out. (*Remembering Babylon* 26)

To be able to name something is to control it, which allows you to survive. Gemmy learns his lessons well, and when he returns, again almost by accident, to the company of English people, he has to struggle to make his mouth form the unfamiliar patterns of English speech.

In white Australian society, Gemmy finds it equally difficult to force his life to fit into the structured existence of the close-knit society of farmers. Some view him as a spy for the Aboriginals, others are disgusted to see a white man behave like a "savage." Gradually, however, the community splits into two parts concerning him: "One lot wanted to make an ally of him in what they hoped would be an easy war" against the Aboriginals while the other group entertains

> a vision of plantations with black figures moving in rows down a field, a compound with neat whitewashed huts, a hallway, all polished wood, with an old grey-haired black saying "Yessir," and preparing to pull off their boots. (*Remembering Babylon* 62)

These are the alternatives—genocide or enslavement. Gemmy spends most of his time being shuttled back and forth between the two groups. He fears that anything he might say will prompt the farming community to unleash a pogrom against his adopted people.

The white settlers, many of them Scots, have come from a country where they were landless peasants. Australia represents their first opportunity to have land of their own, to choose which crops to raise and not be forced to give most of the harvest away. Even if most would probably agree with Ellen McIvor that "the conditions of her life here were harder than any she could have imagined at home because they were so different" (*Remembering Babylon* 110), few would abandon the freedom they had in this harsh landscape to return to the servitude of Britain. Gemmy represents the danger that the land and the freedom it represents could be stripped from them in a raid of "tribes of wandering myalls who, in their traipsing this way and that all over the map, were forever encroaching on boundaries that could be insisted upon in the daylight" (*Remembering Babylon* 9). The dream landscape the settlers imagine is that of fenced paddocks and neat garden plots, of rows of neat houses and fields of ripening grain. The farmers' paranoia and desire to build a small bit of Britain in Queensland leads them to both despise all things native and to plot for the complete extermination of the Aboriginal societies with which they share the land. To try to see the landscape Gemmy shares with the Aboriginal people is completely beyond the conception of most of the settlers, who are more horrified by him when they discover he is white than when they thought he was an ill-educated native. Gemmy is, the settlers think,

> a parody of a white man [. . .] imitation gone wrong, and the mere sight of it put you wrong, made the whole business somehow foolish and open to doubt. (*Remembering Babylon* 39)

There are two exceptions to this, two persons who begin to see the potentials of land not through European eyes, but through eyes that adapt to the environment. The first, Charlie Frazer, the minister, comes to this through the scientific method and his appreciation of Gemmy's abilities. The second, Janet McIvor, has her vision transformed through a mystical experience which leaves her forever changed.

For Mr. Frazer, who is an amateur botanist, Gemmy provides an entrance into the mysteries of the native flora and the native tongue. Gemmy takes Mr. Frazer out into the bush, showing him plants, teaching him their names and properties, and waiting patiently as he sketches them into a notebook. Gemmy is careful, however, not to allow Mr. Frazer to transgress the rules of the guardians of the land, taking great care to teach Mr. Frazer to articulate names properly:

> To get a name wrong was comic but it could also be blasphemous. In one case what emerged from Mr. Frazer's mouth was an old man's testicle, in another, the tuber came out as a turd. Of course he understood immediately that he had botched the thing and after a good deal of trying amended it, but so scandalously on one occasion that Gemmy was shocked, and looked about fearfully, since the word Mr. Frazer had hit upon was one the surrounding spirits should never have heard on a *man's* li ps, and he worried a little that some of these things might get into the book. (*Remembering Babylon* 67)

In aboriginal belief every feature in the landscape were created by the ancestors, and many were the ancestors themselves. To tram ple upon them unaware, without showing proper respect, was sacrilege. As with the rest of the settlers, Gemmy feels a heavy responsibility regarding Mr. Frazer. He must protect him in a landscape he does not understand.

At the same time, Gemmy enjoys his time with Mr. Frazer, feels satisfaction "at the co-operation between them that made him the hands and eyes of the enterprise, the breath too when it came to giving things a name" (*Remembering Babylon* 66). Mr. Frazer has a vision of an Australia not remade in the form of England. He writes in his journal of the necessity of learning from the Aboriginal culture:

> We have been wrong to see this continent as hostile and infelicitous, so that only by the fiercest stoicism, a supreme resolution and force of will, and by felling, clearing, sowing with the seeds we have brought with us, and by im porting sheep, cattle, rabbits, even the very birds of the air, can it be shaped and made habitable. It is habitable already. I think of our early settlers, starving on these shores in the midst of plenty they did not recognise, in a blessed nature of flesh, fowl, fruit that was all around them and which they could not with their English eyes, perceive, since the very habit and faculty that makes apprehensible to us what is known and expected dulls our sensitivity to other forms, even the most obvious. We must rub our eyes and look again, clear our minds of what we are looking for to see what is there. (*Remembering Babylon* 130)

Mr. Frazer dreams of orchards of native fruit, "to make this place too part of the world's garden, but by changing ourselves rather than it and adding thus to the richness and variety of things" (*Remembering Babylon* 132). He stands apart from most of the settlers in seeing an abundant landscape, not an empty land waiting to be refigured.

Despite Mr. Frazer's good intentions, he cannot see beyond the scientific. He cannot enter the Dreaming, and the stories which allow entrance into that landscape are disappearing into the land with the bones of the slaughtered native people:

> [The missionary L.E.] Threlkeld referred to one of the leading graziers in the colony who had openly told a public meeting in Bathurst that the best way to deal with the Aborigines would be to shoot them all and manure the ground with their carcasses. Women and children, he contended, should especially be killed so as to exterminate the race. (Willey 214)

The idealism of Mr. Frazer cannot contend with this. In fact when Gemmy is attacked in an attempted lynching, he can only ineffectually send his report to the Governor of Queensland, hoping to convince the authorities in his twinned vision of native knowledge and new varieties of cultivatable fruit. It is his wife who efficiently shifts Gemmy out of danger, into the care of the formidable Mrs. Hutchence.

It is also at Mrs. Hutchence's where Janet McIvor has the experience which will change her life, and open her eyes to the natural world. Janet, like Gemmy, represents what Mr. Frazer calls "*a true child of the place as it will one day be*"; in fact, Mr. Frazer's comment applies much more accurately to Janet, for as the novel closes in the early years of independence, the Aboriginal worldview has nearly vanished from Australia. Under the tutelage of Mrs. Hutchence, an independent lesbian living a life very separate from the settlers, Janet learns apiary, the art of beekeeping. The first moment the adolescent Janet sees the bees, she is drawn to them, sees in them creatures, like her, suspended between a British heritage and an Australian upbringing.

The honey those bees produce will be local, will emerge out of the combination of an English insect and Australian flowers, producing something new, a flavor which never existed before. The bees also produce a transformation in Janet:

> Suddenly there was a sound of a wind getting up in the grove, though she did not feel the touch of it, and before she could complete the breath she had taken, or expel it in a cry, the swarm was on her, thickening so fast about her that it was as if night had fallen, just like that, in a single cloud. She just had time to see her hands covered with plushy, alive fur gloves before her whole body crusted over and she was blazingly gathered into the single sound they made, the single mind.
>
> Her own mind closed in her. She lost all sense of where her feet might be, or her dreamy wrists, or whether she was still standing, as she had been a moment before, in the shadowy grove, or had been lifted from the face of the earth.
>
> The bees have their stomachs full, her mind told her, they will not sting. Stand still, stand still. It was her old mind that told her this.
>
> She stood still and did not breathe. She surrendered herself.
>
> You are our bride, her new and separate mind told her as it drummed and swayed above the earth. Ah, so that is it! They have smelled the sticky blood-flow. They think it is honey. It is.
>
> Mrs. Hutchence was only feet away. So was Gemmy. She could hear their voices calling to her through the din her body was making. But it made no difference, now, the distance, three feet or a thousand years, no difference at all; or whether she was a girl (a woman), or a tree. She stood sleeping. Upright. A bride. Then the bitterness of smoke came to her throat, and the cloud began to lift; and there, through the gaps in herself, was Mrs. Hutchence with coils of smoke pouring out of her sleeves, and Gemmy, open-mouthed with a frame in his arms, and the bees, one by one, then in fistfuls, rolling off her, peeling away like a crust, till she stood in her own skin again, which was fresh where the air touched it, and only a few dozen foolish creatures were left that had got themselves caught and were butting with their furry heads and kicking, in a panic at being alone.
>
> She felt Mrs. Hutchence's hands on her skin now, which was quite clear and unharmed but seemed new to her, and all through Mrs. Hutchence's fearful ministrations and Gemmy's whimpering cries, she remained a little out of herself—half-sleeping, regretful, her two feet planted square on the earth. (*Remembering Babylon* 142-143)

That last phrase "her two feet planted square on the earth" indicates that this moment has fully placed Janet on Australian soil, unlike her parents, or even her cousin Lachlan, whose hearts still remained tied to the Scotland they left behind. Janet's transformation remains uncomprehended by everyone but Gemmy, who like her sees how the moment has changed her.

The transformation of Janet also makes Gemmy take account of his life in the white settlement. Clearly, like the land itself, something new is growing out of the bee-fire which has consumed Janet McIvor, and Gemmy recognizes that this new life can bridge the vision of the white settlers and the demands of the land. He can never be a part of that new world, however, so he decides to return to the tribe that took him in when he foundered on the continent's shore. As he has learned from his time as a member of the Aboriginal culture, word and land are inseparable. If he has lost the proper words he will not be able to rejoin his adopted people because he will not see the landscape as it is; he will exist instead in the shadow world the whites move through, for:

> There was no way of existing in this land, or of making your way through it, unless you took into yourself, discovered on your breath, the sounds that linked up all the various parts of it and made them one. Without that you were blind, you were deaf, as he had been, at first, in their world. You blundered about seeing holes where in fact strong spirits were at work that had to be placated, and if you knew how to call them up, could be helpful. Half of what ought to have been bright and full of life to you was shrouded in mist. (*Remembering Babylon* 65)

When he was accepted into the Aboriginal clan, Gemmy's way of seeing gradually expanded. With each word he learned his sight expanded and a landscape of bounty and possibility opened before him. Now, after living with the whites, those possibilities have diminished. His life is as constrained as it was in the class-conscious England of his childhood. The words of power which allowed him to be more than just "Someone's Boy" have dried up on his tongue and without them he will never be able to return to the clan he left behind.

At the end of the novel Gemmy finds the words again and strides back into a living landscape and a culture which accepts him:

> A drop of moisture sizzled on his tongue: the word—he had found it. *Water.* Slow dribbles of rain began to fall. He was entering rain country. Soon the sky let down tangled streamers, and he was walking now in a known landscape: all the names of things, as he met them, even in their ashen form, shone on his breath, sprang up in their real lives about him, succulent green, soft paw and eyeball, muscle tense under fur. (*Remembering Babylon* 181)

The fate of Gemmy, like that of most Australian Aboriginals, is grim. A victim of a massacre, in death, as in life, Gemmy Fairley is cared for by the surviving members of his clan which bind up his bones in bark and give him a burial which ties him forever to the land. It is those ties to the land which continue to drive Aboriginal demands for justice today, for land rights on a continent shaped by the ancestors and containing the bones of their people. Like the Australian plants whose shoots reemerge from what seems to be a devastating fire, Aboriginal voices are reemerging as a "breath out of the heart of the country," demanding justice and a home in a land that belongs to them.

Works Cited

Achebe, Chinua. "An Image of Africa: Racism in Conrad's *Heart of Darkness*." *Heart of Darkness: A Norton Critical Edition*. Ed. Robert Kimbrough. New York: Norton, 1988. 251-262.

Conrad, Joseph. *Heart of Darkness*. 1902. Harmondsworth: Penguin, 1973.

Deane, Seamus, ed. Introduction. *Nationalism, Colonialism, and Literature*. Minneapolis: U of Minnesota P, 1990. 3-19.

Hughes, Robert. *The Fatal Shore*. New York: Knopf, 1987.

Malouf, David. *Conversations at Curlow Creek*. New York: Vintage, 1996.

——. *Remembering Babylon*. New York: Vintage. 1993.

Toynbee, Arnold. *A Study of History*. 10 vols. New York: Oxford UP, 1947.

Willey, Keith. *When the Sky Fell Down*. Sydney: William Collins, 1979.

Chandani Lokugé

"We Must Laugh at One Another, or Die" Yasmine Gooneratne's *A Change of Skies* and South Asian Migrant Identities[1]

This Essay examines identities of a category of Sri Lankan migrants to Australia through a reading of the novel *A Change of Skies* (1991) by a Sri Lankan immigrant writer in Australia, Yasmine Gooneratne (b. 1935). The protagonists of the novel make up a small but significant number of South Asian migrants to Australia: the westernized and Western- educated, upper-crust Sri Lankans. My concern here is with their self-identity, including the crises and transformations undergone in the course of their migrant encounter with Australia. I define "self-identity" in this essay not only as one's sense of self but as constituted, in the Lacanian sense, within the gaze of the other. When stylistically more appropriate, I will refer to self-identity as self-consciousness, which has been defined by Hegel as existing "*in itself and for itself,* in that and by the fact that it exists for another self-consciousness; that is to say, it *is* only by being acknowledged" (Hegel qtd. in Fanon 216).

Gooneratne's protagonists begin their journeys from the homeland as expatriates. Adopting a eurocentric perspective, and restricting the term to the affluent First World, Martin Stoddard (1992) defines expatriates as "voluntary exiles," romantics who, attempting to free themselves from such "smothering domesticity" as familial discontent or narrow nationalism, or "for the sake of individual expression," see fit to live away from their homeland (Stoddard 1).

Although from the Third World, the protagonists of *A Change of Skies*, like the confident "mimic men" (see Naipaul 1967) of the First World, comfortably fit the expatriate category that Stoddard addresses. Some background information in necessary here. Sri Lanka was under British rule from 1802 to 1947. The protagonists of *A Change of Skies* are descendants of the tiny minority of the indigenous upper-class cultivated by the British for the purpose of being "interpreters between [them] and the millions whom [they] govern[ed]; a class of persons, [Sri Lankan] in blood and colour, but English in taste, in opinions, in morals, and in intellect" (Macaulay 601; Macaulay's notorious "Minute on Indian Education" (1835) was aimed at India but can be applied equally to the Sri Lankan situation). The British carried out this enterprise with such characteristic competence and thoroughness that, when they left Sri Lanka in 1948, they left behind a class of Sri Lankan-British mimics who were more British than the British themselves. Here is Gooneratne herself, describing from first-hand experience the conditioning by the Raj of her own family, which belonged to this particular category:

> Cultivating English modes of living and thinking, the members of my father's clan had imbibed a very proper English prejudice against Jews, "frogs," "chinks," "niggers," "japs," "huns," "fuzzy-wuzzies," "wops" and "wogs" of every description. English upper-class scorn of the lower orders in British society was easily translated, in the context of Ceylon, into a wholehearted contempt for [. . .] members of "inferior" castes and even of [. . .] Sinhalese families such as their own who were not, unlike their own, "out of the top drawer." (*Relative Merits* 84)

The descendants of these people maintained allegiance to Britain even in independent Sri Lanka. One of them, Bharat, a protagonist in *A Change of Skies*, is not exaggerating when he says:

> Long before I saw Britain for the second time (as a postgraduate student), I knew London [. . .] I knew, long before I ever ate one, what muffins tasted like. Where Wordsworth's inward eye had been polished by memory, imagination had burnished mine: it flashed like images in a video on fast-forward, not just the skittish daffodils of his description but all the meadow flowers of Chaucer, Spenser, Shakespeare and Keats. For generations my relatives had been either going to, or returning from England. And so firmly had their gaze been focused on the metropolitan centre of a pale pink imperium that they had never so much as glanced in any other direction. To do so would have seemed the grossest laps of taste. (12)

Meanwhile, surveying his hill-country tea estates in the mid-twentieth century, and arrogantly cloaked in his British inheritance, Bharat's brother, Asoka, makes the remark to a reporter: "Raj? What Raj? Up here, [. . .] *I* am the Raj" (*A Change of Skies* 302). He gets away with such arrogance even in Independent Sri Lanka because the hierarchical Sri Lankan social system recognizes and venerates both his superior ancestral heritage and his acquired one: in his own eyes as well as in the gaze of the nation, to live and behave like a *suddha* (white man) brings ultimate prestige. In Ernest Macintyre's play *Let's Give Them Curry* (1985), the upper-middle-class Sinhalese immigrant to Melbourne says:

> we westernized Asians left over from the Empire [. . .] float very easily on the top, within Colombo. Like a slightly separate layer of cream on the top, different in texture though same in colour as the native brew underneath that supports us. But all part of the same brew, we have an identity. (96)

A Change of Skies deals with four main characters: Edward, who migrates to Australia in 1882 to return to Sri Lanka in 1887; his grandson Bharat and Bharat's wife Navaranjini, who come to Australia in 1964 as expatriates and take up permanent residence in the country eight years later, and Bharat and Navaranjini's daughter Edwina, born and brought up in Australia. This essay will focus on Edward, Bharat and Navaranjini.

Lifeline

Edward temporarily renounces his motherland as a young man to liberate himself from stifling domestic expectations. With his ex-servant Davith he boards the SS *Devonshire* in 1882 (the heyday of British rule in Sri Lanka) as a labourer contracted to a sugar plantation in Queensland. On board the *Devonshire,* he develops a friendship with Davith which displays all the markings of the stereotypical colonizer-colonized relationship. Edward is benevolent towards Davith but self-conscious in his superiority, while Davith calls him "*hamu*" (lord) more naturally than he calls him "*aiya*" (brother). If there is a crossing of class lines, it is mainly for the benefit of the authorities, from whose attention Edward, travelling in labourer's guise needs protective camouflage.

Edward's self-identity is damaged early in his contact with Australians. Australia seems to have "no means of distinguishing between two such different civilizations as Sinhalese *and* Chinese" (*A Change of Skies* 75). He is categorized by the white majority as a "coolie" along with poor Far East Asian labourers. His only difference from them in the eyes of the white majority is that he is more "dangerous" because of his knowledge of English, much more so than "the illiterate pig-tailed yellow skins," the growing number of whom was becoming a threat to the local people (*A Change of Skies* 75).

Disillusioned with this first experience of being forced to see himself as a generic subject in the gaze of the "Other," Edward roams without anchor "through the landscape of a still largely untamed Australia" (*A Change of Skies* 280). He is himself guilty of stereotyping Australia and Australians from the standpoint of British cultural superiority. Australians are seen by him as Brobdingnagians indulging in the crudest possible eating habits and the most peculiar of customs. Australia itself is a "cultural desert," "an alien and hostile land." He feels himself to be Ovid among the Goths (*A Change of Skies* 163).

But suddenly, as for Peter Porter's wandering Jew, the alien ceases to matter for Edward, because "truth and love, like miracles, need nowhere at all to happen in" (Porter qtd. in Bennett 25). Edward's identity crisis begins in Badagini, in Western Australia, where he re-lives the tragic death experience of some pioneer Sri Lankan immigrants who, unable to adapt to the climate of Western Australia, had died there of hunger and thirst.[2] Edward's epiphany, central to his identity transformation, takes place when his anglocentric complacency gives way to a non-anglocentric empathy for his own community. Stirred in spite of himself by their plight, he recognizes his compatriots as human beings of equal status and, in a moment of utopian self-transcendence, he "blesse[s] them unaware" (Coleridge, "The Rime of the Ancient Mariner": line 285). With this gesture, the imperial mimic identity that had distanced him from the majority of his own people falls from him; he finds himself "gloriously free." Now he is able to mourn Davith's death with the sorrow of a friend, and interact without class consciousness or intellectual superiority with Joe, a simple-hearted, illiterate Western Australian stockman, who seems to personify for Gooneratne an incorruptible Australia. The egalitarian ethos espoused by Joe persuades Edward to cast aside his fantasy of imperialism, a fantasy in which his family and friends were still trapped.

Liberated both in his own eyes and in the gaze of the "Other" from the foreign identity of his colonial inheritance, Edward can now seek the truth about himself and his homeland. As a Christian and a Western-educated colonial subject, he had been indoctrinated to regard the religion of his country, Buddhism, as heathenism and his language, Sinhalese, as primitive and crude. Now he begins to recognize the intrinsic value of his national culture and of Buddhism, and to be aware of that stunted part of his identity which might have been nourished by his mother tongue and culture. With the help of a Buddhist monk in the small Sri Lankan community on Thursday Island, he penetrates to the essence of his civilization, developing new ways of viewing it—and, in consequence, being viewed differently by that civilization.

Ultimately, demonstrating the truth of Sir James Emerson Tennent's words the "people cut off from the main stream of national life stagnate like the waters of a lagoon separated from the sea" (*A Change of Skies* 279), Edward returns to Sri Lanka in 1887. For all his transcendental self-realization, he is still "skewered, upon the duties of class and the responsibilities of inheritance" (*A Change of Skies* 292). But he returns as an Orientalist[3] committed to retrieving and reconstructing his submerged pre-colonial civilization. Thus his expatriate experience, although filled with disillusion and disharmony, is finally a lifeline.

Intersections

Edward's grandson, Bharat, accompanied by his wife Navaranjini, migrate to Australia in 1964 when the White Australian Policy is in force and where Australia is just beginning to be "Asia-literate." For the Sri Lankan elite and middle classes, the 1960s boded ill. In the resurgence of nationalism after independence, with Sinhalese being made the official language in 1956, they began to lose their high professional, if not social, status. The ethnic riots of 1958 only added to the general insecurity. And so began the first wave of migration by Sri Lankan professionals, their favoured destinations being Canada, USA and England (migration to Australia was something of a bad joke). In *A Change of Skies*, when Bharat's sister hears of decision to take up a five-year position as professor of linguistics at the mythical Southern Cross University in Sydney, she writes from New York:

> My dear child, it's a provincial version of the American Midwest. Maybe you can't imagine what that must be like. You'll be miserable. There's nothing there but koalas and kangaroos, sheep and (I think

> they call them) wombats [. . .]. And what about White Australia Policy? (*A Change of Skies* 33)

Vera concludes ironically: "Will you be regarded as honorary whites?" (*A Change of Skies* 33). For Bharat himself, Australia is the "dark side of the moon" from which, "after a few years of exile," he will "return to civilization" in Sri Lanka.

Bharat's sense of self when he leaves Sri Lanka is indeed that of an "honorary white" and can best be explained through "a doggy devotion to Britain" and the "accumulated experience of a profoundly Anglicized family" (*A Change of Skies* 12). And he bears with him his prestigious ancestral heritage, as symbolized by his name, Bharat Mangala Davasinghe.[4] His problems of self-awareness begin when he realizes that his identity is not recognized by white Australia. " 'Look,' " he snaps at his wife, " '*We're* Asians. *They're* Australians. When Australians meet us, that's what they notice first. Difference' " (*A Change of Skies* 118). Then he hears Ronald Blackstone,[5] a sociology professor from the University of Woop-Woop who "nicknamed a Sydney suburb 'Vietnamatta' because it was full [. . .] of Asians," lash out on the radio that

> Asians [. . .] pollute the air with the fumes of roasting meat. And we Australians must be alert to the dangers involved for our society if we allow Asians in who cannot assimilate and accept our customs. (*A Change of Skies* 120)

Bharat's identity crises and identity transformations in the mid-twentieth Century are more complex than Edward's (this is probably due to Gooneratne's first-hand experience of immigration during the 1970s and of the anti-Asian resurgence in 1988). From the moment that he hears of Professor Blackstone's anti-Asian policy, Bharat begins to realize that he has no substantial identity, that he is being pushed into a faceless Asian community. He sees himself in the gaze of the white majority as a subject of derision, as cannibalistic, if not Calibanistic. Whereas in his homeland he had held a position of authority, he is now relegated to a position as subject. His desperate flight from this truth is to resign himself to the order of things as preached by Blackstone, in order to assimilate to Australia and accept its customs. He seeks to identify as closely as possible with an acceptable Australian stereotype. Interestingly, Bharat's desire to assume white Australia's identity is in line with Fanon's exploration of Hegel's theory of self-consciousness, an analysis of which Yasmine Gooneratne, as a specialist in postcoloniality, is no doubt aware. Here is Fanon:

> As long as [man] has not been effectively recognized by the other, that other will remain the theme of his actions. It is on that other being, on recognition by that other being, that his own human worth and reality depend. It is that other being in whom the meaning of his life is condensed. (216-217)

Bharat's response to Australia's stereotyping of Asians resembles Fanon's to colonial stereotyping of the African. When, in *Black Skin, White Masks* (1952), a little white girl stereotypes Fanon as a terror-inspiring Negro, and cries to her mother: " 'Look, a Negro! [. . .] Mama, see the Negro! I'm frightened!,' " Fanon's response is "What else could it be for me but an amputation, an: excision, a hemorrhage that spattered my whole body with black blood?" (112). Entrapped in a similar hopeless mood at the shock of being seen as inferior in the gaze of the Other, Bharat withdraws "from his identity and his race in his total identification with the positivity of whiteness (see Bhabha's analysis of Fanon's heart-rending account of black-white collisions in "The Other Question" 1994).

In an effort to erase the foreignness figured in him, Bharat anglicizes his name (to Barry Mundy), falling back on the Australian custom of name swapping—explained by the author as "dating back to 1939 when after war was declared hundreds of German migrants anglicized their names practically overnight" (*A Change of Skies* 122). This is a statement laced with irony and resonating with the terrible underlying truth of what might have happened to the German migrants had they not changed their names and assimilated to the majority identity. It is worth noting that Bharat's new surname, Mundy, carries complex linguistic implications. It makes him a citizen of "the world," in Latin, a dead language in terms of friendly verbal interaction. However, in the more vibrant indigenous language, Sinhala, Barry Mundy turns derogatory: *barri* means "impotent," *mundi* "dregs" or "residue." Barry might change his name but, in the Sri Lankan estimation, he is reduced to the dregs: a dramatic let-down for someone whose class had been recognized as cream on the coffee. For his wife, who understood his name for its cultural associations and personal history, the name-change is something to regret. She realizes that, for both of them, the new "respectably Aussie" name is just a user-friendly means of getting by in day-to-day transactions, not a signifier of self-worth or true identity. Paul Carter's (1992) analysis of migrant names and their significance for identity might be applied to Bharat: the surname of R. A. Baggio, born in Victoria, Australia and the son of an Italian migrant, is subjected by white Australians to so many mispronunciations that it, and consequently his identity, becomes "unstable [like] one's sense of place"; "his name was a swag he shouldered, a means of travelling from one human situation to another, but it no longer provided him with a house of his own, a place from which he could speak" (Carter 12-13).

In an even greater effort to merge with white Australia, Bharat, as Barry Mundy, begins to imitate the stereotypical ego projection of the americanized Australian. Contact lenses (enhancing his beautiful long eyelashes) pave his way to TV fame as an Asia Expert. While he is recognized by academia for his serious research, his appeal for the average Australian viewer lies less in his intellectual prowess than in his exotic sexuality. He receives bags of mail from female fans. Intoxicated by his sexy public image, he begins to neglect his commitment to his academic career and his students at the university. He seems well on the way to developing into a popular stereotype: a "marketable product" (*A Change of Skies* 146). But his wife realizes the danger and sees his personality degenerating almost past repair, his "very substance being thrown into confusion."[6]

Sensing something of his own inner vulnerability, and seeking to "reorient" himself, Bharat returns to Sri Lanka eight years after first leaving it. He realizes that he has changed and that he cannot fit into the familial or social life there any more. Colombo is not what he remembers; it seems to have become promiscuous and addicted to TV, with everyone's favourite programme being the soap "Dynasty." There are also darker realities: ethnic crises, and insurgents disrupting the system and killing innocent people. Like Rushdie (1991), Bharat finds that "the past is [the] country from which [he has] emigrated." His Sri Lanka is now an imaginary homeland; he can. reclaim it only in his memory. He has the sense that his "present being [is] in a different place from his past, of his being "elsewhere" (Rushdie 12). Bharat decides to return to Australia.

However, back in Australia, he continues to be haunted by his imaginary homeland. Paul Carter (1992) endorses the truism that a sense of place is a highly significant factor in one's sense of self. In his exile, homeland had been for Bharat a past that he could reclaim and, in Carter's words, "a mothering space that both nurture[d] him and help[ed] define his own difference" (12-13).

Here is Bharat reminiscing about his home in Matara, Sri Lanka; note the exile's yearning for what Carter calls the remembered "haptic experience":

> Generations living and dying in the same ancient house, whose windows look out on an unchanging landscape, on one side green fields—our fields—stretching further than the eye can see, on the other the breakers pounding on a vide beach fringed with palms. Our duty to them and to those who worked on them gave a design to the seasons as they passed, while the echoing waves carried messages from the outside world that we could heed or not as we pleased. [. . .] We turned our backs upon the past, and yearned only to move away. The changes that occur within the self are things we cannot know beforehand. (*A Change of Skies* 152)

The migrant ceases to be an exile when the homeland loses its haptic meaning. Bharat's most significant metamorphosis of identity takes place where Gooneratne frees him from the constraints of the home space, "place ceases to matter," Bharat thinks,

> And that in itself is an incredible grace conferred by exile on the immigrant, because for a person like myself, I realize, place is—or used to be—everything. (*A Change of Skies* 152)

Only when the migrant is able to recede from the spaces of the past and can make a haptic experience of the new environment can he or she can be completely at home in it. In *A Change of Skies*, it is only when the Chinese immigrant poet from Malaysia began writing again, poems that "drew at last on his Australian experience," that "his life gain[ed] equilibrium" (*A Change of Skies* 284; the reference here is to Ee Tiang Hong). It is only when Bharat is able to respond meaningfully to the Australian space that he can think of Australia as home.

> I can only say that, gradually, I began, without quite understanding how or why, to see the world about me as whole and not fragmented, to see myself and Jean as part of that world and not aliens in it, and to perceive that in the enormous cracks, fissures, and towering mountains which sometimes ennoble and sometimes disfigure the landscape that surrounds, there are encoded images of human relationshi ps.

> [. . .] Gradually and with increasing contentment I [. . .] learned to feel in the unexpected lash of climatic change, to hear in the overwhelming crash of waves and the silence of the wilderness alike, expressions of power, of discipline and of tranquility that I had been hitherto unable to recognize as such anywhere but in my native land.
>
> [. . .] this land is calling soundlessly, through the gaps in its cultural life, through the echoing silences of ignorance and misunderstanding which beset fractured communities, for something that only persons like myself may be equipped to give. (*A Change of Skies* 286)

Those migrants who cannot escape their homelands, whose pasts or imaginary homelands continue to haunt them, are "mutated," as Rushdie would say, "into pillars of salt" (10). Both the Scots and Welsh immigrant poets in Gooneratne's novel, J. M. Couper and Hari Jones, "sink into the impenetrable silence" of their imaginary spaces, never to emerge from them (*A Change of Skies* 284).

Now Bharat is free to decide on his future, his earlier confusion about his identity, about seeing and being, seen, has vanished, Bharat's final liberation comes when, despite the pleasant pattern of academic life and warm personal relationships in the English Department, he decides to resign from Southern Cross University. Freed of his entire past–his name, his homeland, his identity, his job–Bharat moves out of the protecting whale and into a whaleless world (see Rushdie, "Outside the Whale" in *Imaginary Homeland* 87-101). He commits himself to teaching English as a second language to Vietnamese migrants to Australia whose illiteracy in English makes them more marginalized than he is:

> Even I have discovered that the hazards and difficulties of exile have compensating rewards [. . .]. One such reward, undoubtedly, comes directly from the abruptness with which exile brings immigrants face to face, ready or not, willingly or not, with worlds beyond those in which they have been brought up. Subjected to this experience, unwillingly I admit, I found myself gradually regarding with new eyes the vista that was opening before me. (*A Change of Skies* 284)

The fact that Bharat's self-realization takes place not through his interaction with mainstream Australian professional life but through his rejection of it, and through his professional interaction with other immigrant minorities, is a telling comment on migrant interaction with the white Australian majority. While Bharat seems blind to this issue, it is certainly one of the losses of his migrant experience. A Sri Lankan reading would show that the loss is just that much deeper for a Sri Lankan: Gooneratne herself would be fully aware, as a Sri Lankan, that Bharat's shift from the status of professor at a university to that of a freelance ESL teacher of Vietnamese migrants would be considered, by the more conservative of her compatriots at least, as a severe career demotion. However, my more serious concern is with Gooneratne's awareness that Bharat has no option but to join forces with other migrant communities before he can fully realize his new identity. And it is in these areas of the novel that she capitalizes most on her wide knowledge *of* migrant problems. She is possibly using a fictional strategy here, to illustrate a theory in relation to migrants described by researchers like Abdul JanMohamed and David Lloyd (1987). Here is what they say:

> minority individuals are always treated and forced to experience themselves generically. Coerced into a negative, generic subject position, the oppressed individual responds by transforming that position into a positive, collective one. And therein, precisely, lies the basis of a broad minority coalition; in spite of enormous differences between various minority cultures. (10)

"We must Laugh at one another, or Die"

If Gooneratne voices her irritation about migrants and migrant issues through Bharat, she prescribes her remedy for them through her female protagonist, Bharat's wife, Navaranjini. After a range of expatriate responses to racial/sexist stereotyping, from the emotional backlash of the Chinese-American Maxine Hong Kingston to the biting satire of the London-based Indian Salman Rushdie, the detached irony of Gooneratne is refreshing. As the Aboriginal writer Gill Rosser commented to Gooneratne after one of her readings of *A Change of Skies*. "What I think [the audience] responded to was that there was laughter directed at racism" (qtd. in Giese 17-18). Gooneratne's laughter is the irony of Jane Austen, with whose work she is intimately acquainted. Where Hong Kingston reacts violently to the stereotyping of the Chinese as "inscrutable, mysterious and oriental" with the cutting line "How dare they call their ignorance our inscrutability!," Gooneratne's heroine takes "oriental" in her stride (Kingston, "A Review of the Inscrutable Reviews of *The Woman Warrior*": privately circulated). Full of naivety, self-confidence, or her own racist prejudices (which seem as strong as white Australia's own), Navaranjini even occasionally exploits the white's sensual image of the East to her advantage, as when she slides a fully illustrated copy of the *Kama Sutra* into a showcase of academia, as a consequence of which what was predicted to be a very "boring" exhibition attracts a serpentine queue of fascinated white spectators. In another memorable "exotic" moment, she douses the developing passion for Bharat of one of his female colleagues with a show of oriental witchcraft.

Navaranjini's identity crises and transformations during migration signify, like Bharat's, loss and gain. She arrives in Australia as the indulged wife of an absent-minded intellectual. In her own eyes, as in the gaze of her husband's, she manifests a role, not personal identity. A Hindu and Tamil, originally from Jaffna, she is as deeply rooted in her Hindu *pativrata* (husband worshi pper) identity as in the anglocentric. As a wife, she considers herself to be of lower status than Bharat, and her way of seeing is com prehensively reflected in Bharat's behaviour. He calls her "*baba*" (baby), a pet name that relegates her to an inferior position. Since they "recognize themselves as mutually recognizing each other," there is no conflict in the marital relationshi p; but that is another story. What is relevant here is the fact that, in the role of wife, Navaranjini is self-confident and, within the limitations of their marriage, even enjoys certain liberties. Her approach to migration is equally coloured by self-confidence. Having taken a few swimming lessons and obtained her driving licence, she feels well-equi pped to carve out another little niche for herself in the foreign land. Like that leit-motivic presence in Gooneratne's novel, the South Asian "immigrant" mynah bird, which confidently makes its home in the lillypilly tree, sometimes resented by the owner of the tree but never aware of that resentment, Navaranjini determinedly goes about settling down in Australia. One of the first things she dose as a migrant in Australia is to familiarize herself with the Australian vocabulary by listening to Talk Back Radio.

In reality, she is doubly marginalized in Australia. She is the object of anglocentric racist *and* sexist stereotyping. Here is Maxine Hong Kingston's response to racist stereotyping:

> To call people exotic freezes us into the position of being always alien [. . .] by giving the "oriental" inhuman, unexplainable qualities, the racist abrogates human qualities, and, carrying all this to extremes, finds it easier

> to lynch the Chinaman, bomb Japan [. . .]. ("A Review of the Inscrutable Reviews of *The Woman Warrior*": privately circulated)

However, in Gooneratne's book, white stereotyping of the Eastern woman as exotic works differently. Navaranjini has no problems with being considered alien. She deals ironically with the stereotyping of her as woman and/or oriental Other, and, by ridiculing it, nullifies it. This is not too difficult for her, because she does not move in mainstream life and does not fully realize the extent of the majority's racist and sexist stereotyping of her as "a luscious little bit of foreign exotica" (*A Change of Skies* 131) on the arm of a white male, or of her bare midriff as "God's Gift to a deserving male" (*A Change of Skies* 101). She confronts racism at second-hand, on radio. Even then she is not particularly affected by it, because, for her, steeped in eurocentric cultural identity, only the Far Easterners, the "ching chongs" with "their slit eyes and sloping heads," could be Asians. Navaranjini is still conscious only of a oneness with white Australia. Thus, when she attacks the anti-Asian activist Professor Blackstone for his statement about Asians polluting Australia, she does so not because *she* is affected, but in defence of her husband, who is shattered by it.

The dialogue is exaggerated social comedy. If what is explicitly said is hilarious, what can be implicitly read in the dialogue is layered with ironical implications. By lending her naive heroine eloquence in Australian slang, Gooneratne gives herself the opportunity to use the interpretative process of irony that "bridges the two poles of saying one thing and receiving another—a process in which the reader sifts for a centred sign (for a brilliant introduction to the interpretative process of irony, see Mishra 36). The centred sign here is that racism hurts. And language is one of the most important factors in cross-racial relationships and integration into a culture, a theme reiterated in the novel. Not being at home in language can lead to irreparable communication breakdowns. The linguistic miscommunication in *A Change of Skies*, though comic, is black comedy exposing a fracture in interracial relationships. And not only that: Navaranjini has learnt "Australian" only to curse in it, like Caliban. While there is no Caliban complex in Navaranjini, she is perhaps projecting Gooneratne's warning to Australia to take heed of the catastrophe of migrant difficulties with the English language, without which language they are isolated, and with which, inadequately employed, they can be humiliated and harmed. The lack of proper knowledge of language can cause insurmountable cross-racial problems.

Somewhere along the way of her migrant experience, Navaranjini develops a voice of her own and sheds, as her creator says, her Sita and Savitri skins for the more spunky Draupadi of the Mahabharata (Gooneratne, 1992: 13). She develops into a celebrated culinary expert. Why does Navaranjini, a qualified librarian and potential artist, end up as a chef? In a Sri Lankan reading of *A Change of Skies*, Neloufer de Mel (1994) expresses the view that

> in cocking a snook at a brand of militant feminism through her heroine Jean who becomes a successful business woman in Australia by making a profession out of oriental cookery—that drudgery of most housewifes—Gooneratne asserts a woman's right to choice that jabs at "politically correct" stances which downplay and deny a vision and capability such as Navaranjini's. (251)

I would contest this view. I believe that the "development" of Navaranjini suggests Gooneratne's com plex strategies of dealing with her personal wish to transform Navaranjini from the "Western stereotype of Asian woman-hood as one-dimensional, sim ple-minded, sexy and servile: what Alison Broinowski in her *The Yellow Lady* has justly termed "the Butterfly Phenomenon" (Gooneratne, 1992: 14) into an individual, without stepping out of the "exotic" role—the title of Navaranjini's cookery book, *Something Rich and Strange*, tells its own story—and without countering white Australian expectations of migrants. I believe that, by making her heroine a culinary expert in Sydney, Gooneratne is also conforming to, and perhaps even ironically celebrating, Australia's notion of food, which, as Gunew (1993) notes, "has long been the acceptable face of multiculturalism" (16). Gooneratne thus skirts "one of the most, deadly weapons" stereotyping the immigrant writer: "the double bind, damned-if-you-do and damned-if-you-don't" (Kingston, "A Review of the Inscrutable Reviews of *The Woman Warrior*": privately circulated). Gunew writes that

> In Australia, one of the few unthreatening ways to speak of multiculturalism is in relation to food, in other words to say that all migrants have im proved the diversity of national cuisine. The usual way in which this diversity is celebrated is through a multicultural food festival. (16)

Replacing the festival in *A Change of Skies* is the launching of Navaranjini and Bharat's new restaurant and a lively article advertising Navaranjini's culinary expertise, which artfully mixed Eastern and Western ingredients. Thus Navaranjini's triumph finally signifies only that she moved into the immigrant mainstream. As Valli Rao (1992) says rather wryly, "it *had* to be a restaurant or a spice shop" for Navaranjini (39). Australia might not, at the time, have received Jean's more ambitious projects with the same enthusiasm and pride; because, as woman, Asian and immigrant, she could be thrice marginalized. As an Australian feminist academic in the novel observes:

> Women, abos, gays, kids, koalas, druggies, whales, and now the Asians. Endangered species, every one of them. The list of those marginalized by this rotten society gets longer every day. And does anyone give a damn? That's Australia for you! (*A Change of Skies* 131)

At the more personal level of the marital relationship, too, there is subtle avoidance of a head-on collision. Typically male chauvinist, Bharat might not have welcomed or tolerated anything more from his wife than a celebration of the domestic. As Navaranjini herself says rather wistfully to her daughter, "She was an artist," but "she was a also a woman" (*A Change of Skies* 324). And she chooses to submerge artist in woman. I would close Navaranjini's case with a modification of Spivak's assertion, "There is no space from where the subaltern [sexed] can speak," by saying that there is space where the [sexed] subaltern can speak—and that is only domestic space.

Epilogue

Gooneratne claims that she was inspired to write *A Change of Skies* by the "Asian immigration debate and a rash of anti-Asian graffiti on [her] university walls" in the 1980s. She remembers identifying with the feelings of Macquarie's Asian students at the time, many of them "Malaysian Chinese, very young and far from home." She also remembers how, as a post- graduate student at Cambridge, she suffered from a similar experience when Enoch Powell began speaking out about keeping immigrants out. "Until that time I had felt at home in England" (Giese 4).

A Change of Skies contains significant issues related to migrant identity in Australia. The epigraph to one of the novel's chapters is from

Wilson Harris: "We must laugh at one another, or die" (Harris is parodying Auden's famous line, "We must love one another, or die"). The epigraph, with all its ironic implications, contains Gooneratne's message to her readers: that, if we do *not* laugh at one another, we die. Her own words on the subject of humour and irony clinch this message:

> For me, irony isn't just a literary device, it's a form of defence, a means of keeping sane, of protecting the self against what is too obscene or horrible to contemplate squarely. Irony opens a door from horror into laughter, which helps you keep your emotional balance when passions pull you in different directions. (Giese 4)

Regretfully, the focus of this essay is not on the humour but on the serious issues connected with migrant identities that lie behind it.

ENDNOTES

[1] This paper was first published in *Shifting Continents/Colliding Cultures: Diaspora Writing of the Indian Subcontinent*, ed., Ralph J. Crane and Radhika Mohanram (Amsterdam: Rodopi, 2000) 17-34. The quote is taken from Wilson Harris by Gooneratne in *A Change of Skies* (Sydney: Pan/Picador, 1991) 115.

[2] There is a very fine line between history and fiction. While Edward himself is a fictional character, the adventures and misadventures of the earliest Sri Lankan migrants to Australia depicted in *A Change of Skies* are rooted in reality. For research on the subject, see Stanley J. Sparkes, *Sri Lankan Migrants in Queensland in the Nineteenth Century* (n.p.: The Author, 1988).

[3] As an Orientalist, Edward resembles James Alwis, a famous westernized Sinhalese who, having through an identity crisis in Sri Lanka, became an Orientalist.

[4] Navaranjini: "My husband's name, Bharat, means 'India' in just about every Indian language there is. But it means something more to us, for my husband had been named Bharat to commemorate his grandfather's scholarship in Indian languages [. . .]. Giving up Bharat seemed to us to be a betrayal of everything he had stood for" (*A Change of Skies* 119).

[5] Ronald Blackstone is a fictional synthesis of a number of activists during the revival of anti-Asian feeling in Australia in 1988: RSL leaders, conservative politicians, European migrants, and slogan writers who reflected the majority opinion. See Alison Broinowski, *The Yellow Lady: Australian Impressions of Asia* (Melbourne: Oxford UP, 1992) 204. This fact was confirmed by Yasmine Gooneratne in a private interview.

[6] Naim Kattan: "No one can change the language he speaks, the bread he eats, the colour of his sky, without his very substance being thrown into confusion" (qtd. in Gooneratne, 1992: 14).

Works Cited

Bennett, Bruce. "The Expatriate Vision of Peter Porter." *Poetry of the Pacific Region.* Ed. Paul Sharrad. CRNLE Essays and Monograph Series 2. Adelaide: CRNLE, 1984. 103-108.

Bhabha, Homi K. *The Location of Culture.* London: Routledge, 1994.

Broinowski, Alison. *The Yellow Lady: Australian Impressions of Asia.* Melbourne: Oxford UP, 1992.

Carter, Paul. "Lines of Communication: Meaning in the Migrant Environment." *Striking Chords: Multicultural Literary Interpretations.* Ed Sneja Gunew and Kateryna Olijnyk Longley. Sydney: Allen & Unwin, 1992. 9-18.

Coleridge, Samuel Taylor. "The Rime of the Ancient Mariner." 1798. 7 March 2007 <http://etext.virginia.edu/stc/Coleridge/poems/Rime_Ancient_Mariner.html>.

de Mel, Neloufer. "Women as a Gendered Subject and Other Discourses in Contemporary Sri Lankan Fiction in English." *Post-Colonial Women's Writing.* Ed. Anna Rutherford. Spec. issue of *Kunapipi* 16.1 (1994): 242-255.

Fanon, Frantz. *Black Skin, White, Masks.* Trans. Charles Lam Markmann. 1952. London: Pluto, 1986.

Giese, Diana. "Finding, One's Voice in a New Land." *The Weekend Australian* 17-18 August 1991: 4.

Gooneratne, Yasmine. "Constructing the Characters of Women in *A Change of Skies.*" *Australian Women's Book Review* 4.3 (September 1992): 13-15.

——. *A Change of Skies.* Sydney: Pan/Picador, 1991.

——. *Relative Merits: A Personal Memoir of the Bandaranaike Family of Sri Lanka.* London: C. Hurst, 1986.

Gunew, Sneja. "Feminism and the Politics of Irreducible Differences: Multiculturalism/Ethnicity/Race." *Feminism and the Politics of Differences.* Sneja Gunew and Anna Yeatman. St. Leonards, NSW: Allen & Unwin, 1993. 1-19.

JanMohamed, Abdul R., and David Lloyd. "Minority Discourse – What is to be Done?" Introduction. *Cultural Critique* 7 (Spring 1987): 5-17.

Kingston, Maxine Hong. "A Review of the Inscrutable Reviews of *The Woman Warrior.*" Privately circulated.

Macaulay, T. B. "Minute on Indian Education." 1935. *Sources of Indian Tradition.* Ed. William Theodore de Bary. New York: Columbia UP, 1958. 601.

Macintyre, Ernest. *Let's Give Them Curry: An Austral-Asian Comedy in Three Acts.* Melbourne: Heinemann Educational, 1985.

Mishra, Sudesh. "Riding in the Mahatma's Ox-ford: Irony and Post-Colonial Epistemologies." *SPAN* 44 (1997): 36-49.

Naipaul, V. S. *The Mimic Men.* London: Andre Dutsch, 1967.

Rao, Valli. "Change Within Changelessness: The Pattern of Interweaving in *A Change of Skies. The CRNLE Reviews Journal* 1 (1992): 37-44.

Rushdie, Salman. *Imaginary Homelands: Essays and Criticism 1981-1991.* 1991. London: Granta, 1992.

Sparkes, Stanley J. *Sri Lankan Migrants in Queensland in the Nineteenth Century.* n.p.: The Author, 1988.

Stoddard, Martin. *The Great Expatriate Writers.* London: Macmillan, 1992.

Displacement and Trans-placement
Jo e ohar's *Obiranje Limon*

Igor Maver

If home(land) is also and especially one's mother tongue, then this is certainly true of Jo e ohar (b. 1945), the Slovene migrant poet who has been living in Australia since 1968. His verse, however, proves that the limitations of his language are not also the borders of his world. Bert Pribac (b. 1933) and Pavla Gruden (b. 1921) are the other two best known migrant poets from Australia who have published both in Australia and especially in Slovenia (Maver 2002). As a contem porary Slovene migrant poet, ohar experiments with and researches the Slovene language potentials and thus constantly tries to expand the borders of his world and language by transcending traditional poetic aesthetics and by original linguistic self-awareness. Characteristic for ohar's poems written in Slovene is linguistic experimentation: palindromes, alliterations, vocal colouring, puns, homonyms and ornamental adjectives, as well as lexical and syntactic play. Experimentation is central to contem porary Slovene "poetology" and to ohar it in a way signifies even more: his personal freedom.

He could also be described as a migrant poet from the Prekmurje region, for *genius loci* is of great im portance in his verse: on the one hand of the Prekmurje region (the plain and the hills of the Gorièko region in Slovenia bordering with Hungary and Austria) and of Australia (the arid bush) on the other. ohar constantly moves between the two locales and identifies with each of them increasingly in his poems. The fact that the poet writes about his Prekmurje experience is significant, because this experience is like the region itself, close to the archetypal, elementary folk tradition, and the typical melancholy, mostly flat Prekmurje landscape as the landscape of the mind. In all three collections of his poetry, an element present strongly is the specific geographical environment, which appears in a dual relation: on the one side the poet's native Prekmurje and Gorièko, and on the other the Australian desert landscape, which he co-positions throughout. He wishes to be at the same time "one in two, be there and be here" simultaneously, something he considers a special yet agitating privilege.

In his very first collection of poems, *Aurora Australis* (1990), Jo e ohar states that he does not acknowledge the division between a "physical" and "spiritual" migration, since the two appear to him complementary, never appearing separately. In his almost erotic link with not only his native Prekmurje, but with all of Slovenia, which is to remain in him as "the eternal serpentine," he feels that the key question is how to reconcile within himself two countries. He became dis-placed and never finally trans-placed, remaining a cultural "hybrid," half Slovene and half Australian, which in his case represents a sort of homelessness (see Maver 1992; Jurak 1983 and 1997). It should be stressed that in the different thematic clusters of this first collection he already reveals a gift for linguistic experimentation, which suggests an allied formal significance, reflecting his dividedness between the "old" and the "new" homeland (Suša 1999). The initial homely sentimentality is replaced by the existential anguish of a migrant and a person *per se*.

ohar's second collection, *Veku Bukev* (1995; To the Crying of Beeches), which can mean a chronological definition of his youth spent among the beeches but also crying after it, i.e., an ode to a Proustian "time lost," time spent among the reeds, poplars and beeches (see Maver 1995 and 2003). Geographical locale is again of prime importance in the book and it appears in the typical dichotomic relationship: the Prekmurje and the Australian bush country are constantly being contrasted and juxtaposed. This second collection of the poet's verse represents his attempt to identify Australia as his new home; yet ohar remains caught "in between" and sings to the Australian "harem of camels in the desert, tombstones under the eucalypt trees, the waves broken on the shore, kangaroos, run away from bush fires" (*Veku Bukev*; my translation). ohar revives alliterative verse, amply uses paronyms (words that are identical but have a different meaning in a changed context) and palindromes (that can be read fowards and backwards and may have the same or a different meaning), amasses numerous homonyms, synonyms and uses onomatopoeia.

ohar's new verse collection *Obiranje Limon* (2004; Lemon-picking) shows that he has remained true to his bold linguistic experimentation. As a migrant he constantly tests the borders of the Slovene poetic expression, and in this book for the first time he uses rhythmical prose, representing the dark inventory of the poet's life via the metaphorics of lemon-picking in Australia. This rhythmical prose or poems in prose also represent some sort of reconciliation with the anguish of a migrant abroad and the significance of "homeland" for an emigrant as "one of us, displaced,with home away from home. Jernej. Domen. The tenth child. And much more" ("Wanderings" 49; my translation). ohar intimately yet only partly accepts Australia as his new homeland, because as a migrant he remains constantly displaced and not fully transplaced (Maver 2004). His sees his life as an endless process of saying good-bye here and there and writes that he is diminished each time he goes away, in Slovenia as well as in Australia, where as the prodigal son he tries to find his peace but where he also finds poetic inspiration:

> *Where you are now, there is June, when lemons and oranges become ri pe, time when you leave all behind and everybody leaves you behind, because you want it like this for a change. For you know full well that among lemon-trees sensually rich poems happen too. Find yourself shelter among them.*
> ("Com plaints, Conciliations" 29; my translation)

The poet's new collection of poems *Obiranje Limon* contains seven cycles or thematic clusters: "At Home! At Home! At Home! (The Two of Us)," "Sym posion," "From Apple-tree Orchards," "Indian Fragments," "Lemon-picking," "Nameless," and "Word Anguishes." The first cycle represents the poet's most explicit wording of his migrant experience and the overpowering sense of homelessness.

"Lemon-picking" consists of lengthy poems in prose, and the cycle "Nameless" features puns and linguistic experimentation. ohar's poems in rhythmical prose are a new form for him (and most other migrant poets from Down Under), where he shows his essential dividedness between the two "Homes":

> *You feel: there is less of you with each new coming back. Anywhere you go, you are merely saying good-bye. From everything and everybody. From bays and beaches.*
>
> *From the Blue Mountains, when they dwell cold in silence or when they speak out in fire.*
>
> *From the house which is the home of Home. From eucalypts,*

magnolia. From fences and walls between wordless neighbours.

From new roots. Yes: from new roots. You feel: there is no more of you with each new coming back. You bite into a ripe lemon,

Suck out its juice. The tongue pricks you. The tongue that is called [. . .]

You feel like crying. ("Lemon-picking" 35; my translation)

In "Word Anguishes" there are poems consistently written in rhymed stanzas, which once again, as in his earlier work, establishes an erotic relationship with his homeland personified as a woman:

Who is this coming back

down the muddy road? An old man

to see his bride. (65; my translation)

The cycle "Symposion," for example, reestablishes the image of a dark "aurora australis" (Australian dawn), the themes and the used allusions and elements taken from Greek mythology are, however, quite new for ohar. The third cycle "From Apple-Tree Orchards" inspires the poet with melancholy nostalgia, and not only one for home left behind (characterized by apple-trees) but also one for one's own lost youth at the realization of Man's fragility and transience, which drives him to an Australian pub where he does not find solace nor does he feel at home.

The cycle titled "Indian Fragments" represents an important novelty in ohar's poetic opus, although certain references to Buddhism (or Hinduism in his most recent collection) can already be found in the collection *Veku Bukev.* Man's anguish at the realization of his own transience suddenly strikes the poet, a Man, a migrant, as Everyman and as a pilgrim through life during his visits to India as less dense and pressing, for he seems to be able to find a way out of it in an after-life voyage and search for a new life after death.

Scented flames,

O, bright flames of cremation,

Anoint the body that through you

> *Offers itself to the gods.*
>
> *There is the time of search and migration.*
>
> *All the destinations and terminals are also the returns.*
> ("Pilgrimages" 18; my translation)

It is interesting that the speaker's experience and thinking about life (abroad) ends with a certain projection into the future, into what is for him a more "neutral" locale and culture, India—not Slovenia and not Australia. India represents for him, physically and symbolically, "something in-between," the phrase he uses to describe himself in a previous collection, a Slovene migrant to Australia ("Pilgrimages," "For Indira," and "Vishnu"). Jo e ohar's *Obiranje Limon* connects descri ptions of Man's existential anguish with questions of migration.

In the current processes of globalization and trans-nationalization, migrant literature appears particularly im portant, and this is of course true also of Slovene migrant literature in Australia (where the term migrant has been fittingly used for some time, unlike in some other traditional receptive countries, in oder to efface the emitive/receptive country and to stress the inclusive value of migrant transcultural/transnational contribution). Despite the "tyranny of distance" between the two countries, migrant literature should not be ghettoized, in either Australia or in Slovenia, and is, in fact, increasingly represented in the main-stream anthologies, published by major publishers, and receives major literary prizes, etc. Slovene migrant writers translate reality and their personal experience in two different systems, which is why their work can be regarded as an enrichment of both cultures, the source and the target one. Increasingly they are seen as "transcultural" authors in the best sense of the word, figuring both in the unified Slovene cross-border cultural space worldwide and the Australian multicultural society. These two, as ohar's most recent collection of verse *Obiranje Limon* am ply proves, are more and more becoming interchangeable.

Does the future culture/literature of the newly settled migrant countries such as the United States of America, Canada, and Australia belong to the melting pot, ethnic mosaic, some transnational hybrid or a new fusion of various ethnic identities? Recently introduced new concepts, in addition to the already well established multiculturalism, are polyvocality and hybridity. Homi Bhabha argues that the concept of hybridity as a form of cultural difference, while sometimes regarded as mani pulative, allows the voices of the Other/migrant, the marginalised and the dominated to exist within the language of the dominant group whose voice is never fully in control (Bhabha 1994). In recent theoretical debates diaspora and its writing have been frequently connected with the constructed and transnational nature of identity formation, since the concept refers to both voluntary and involuntary migrations and movements. In the future, migrant/diasporic writing should be examined for how it represents "otherness" in a text and how it brings this otherness to bear on the actual experience of reading. Contem porary theory of diasporic literature perceives Home as several locales, liberated of the spatial concept of location, which is at the same time deeply embedded in the cultural memory of a migrant and her/his own personal biography.

In Jo e ohar's poetry dis-placement and trans-placement and the fluid diasporic identity, as well as the changing position of the subject in the globalized world, show his contem porary "dynamic" global view. The sense of movement in his verse underscores his themes. The two remain in his poetic opus the source of an original and assured artistic inspiration.

Works Cited

Bhabha, Homi. *The Location of Culture.* London: Routledge, 1994.

Jurak, Mirko. "Slovene Poetry in Australia: From Terra Incognita to Terra Felix." *Acta Neophilologica* 19.1-2 (1997): 59-67.

——. "Poetry Written by the Slovene Immigrants in Australia: Types of Imagery from the Old and the New Country." *Australian Papers.* Ed. Mirko Jurak. Ljubljana: Filozofska Fakulteta, 1983. 55-61.

Maver, Igor. "Jo e ohar, Slovenski Izseljenski Pesnik med Prekmurjem in Avstralijo." *Obiranje Limon.* Jo e ohar. Ljubljana: Cankarjeva Zalo ba, 2004. 71-75.

——. "Jo e ohar, Izseljenski Pesnik med Prekmurjem in Avstralijo." *Sezonstvo in Izseljenstvo v Panonskem Prostoru/Seasonal Work and Emigration in the Panonian Space.* Ed. Marina Lukšiè-Hacin. Migracije 4. Ljubljana: ZRC SAZU, 2003. 423-428.

——. "Slovene Migrant Literature in Australia." *Acta Neophilologica* 35.1-2 (2002): 5-11.

——. "Zbirka *Veku Bukev* ali oda Izgubljenemu èasu, èasu med Bukvami, Topoli in Obmurskim Trstièjem." *Veku Bukev*. Jo e ohar. Murska Sobota: Pomurska Zalo ba, 1995. 52-57.

——. "Slovene Immigrant Literature in Australia: Jo e ohar's Aurora Australis." *The Making of a Pluralist Australia 1950-1990*. Ed. Werner Senn and Giovanna Capone. Bern: Lang, 1992. 161-168.

Suša, Barbara. "Literarno Ustvarjanje Slovencev v Avstraliji v Slovenskem Jeziku (Jo e ohar)." *Slovenska Izseljenska Knji evnost*. Ljubljana: ZRC SAZU; Rokus, 1999. 267-303.

ohar, Jo e. *Obiranje Limon*. Ljubljana: Cankarjeva Zalo ba, 2004.

——. *Veku Bukev*. Murska Sobota: Pomurska Zalo ba, 1995.

——. *Aurora Australis*. Ljubljana: Mladinska Knjiga, 1990.

Appropriating National Myths
Brian Castro's *Birds of Passage*

Marilyne Brun

Major changes in Australian immigration policy in the twentieth century greatly influenced Australia's national identity. Racial discrimination in immigration was decreased in 1947 and finally discarded in the 1970s. The end of Asians' physical exclusion from immigration to Australia has implied the need for Asian migrants, old and new, to find a place in a society that excluded them until very recently. Brian Castro (b. 1950), an Australian writer born in Hong Kong, addresses the question of Chinese presence in Australia in his first novel, *Birds of Passage* (1983). *Birds of Passage* presents the parallel narrations of Seamus O'Young, a part-Chinese Australian in search of his identity in the 1980s, and of Lo Yun Shan, a Chinese man who went to Australia during the 1850s gold rush. O'Young is an orphan whose identity seems to be forever escaping, and he develops a growing sense of alienation from the world and from his alcoholic adoptive parents. When O'Young discovers Shan's diary, the Chinese-language manuscript provides him with a parallel narrative that takes over his life. Shan's diary retraces his work in the goldfields, experience of racism and relationship with Mary Young. O'Young, alienated from the rest of society and ageing prematurely, finally experiences Shan's last moments in Australia. As O'Young and Shan's narratives intertwine, "impossible coincidences" enhance readers' understanding of both experiences (Pons 1990).

An interesting feature of the novel is that it deals both directly and indirectly with the national imaginary: O'Young's quest to understand his identity, placing his potential ancestor, Shan, at the centre, involves specific references to Australian national myths. The word "myth" has a variety of meanings. While many people use it today as a synonym for "illusion" and "fiction," "myth" also encompasses various primitive rites and allegorical understandings of historically-derived events. Anderson (1983) defined nations as "imagined communities" that are distinguished "not by their falsity/genuineness, but by the style in which they are imagined" (6). The imaginary nature of nations makes the narration of a national identity and of its legitimacy important stakes (Anderson 205). Nations, as "imagined communities," are therefore centred on unifying narrations of identity, which are often accompanied by political reinforcement of nationalist ideology through the media and education, among others (Anderson 113-114). In *Images et Symboles: Essais sur le Symbolisme Magico-Religieux* (1952), Mircea Eliade, who has worked on underlying primordial myths in various religious traditions, remarked that:

> La désacralisation ininterrompue de l'homme moderne a altéré le contenu de sa vie spirituelle, elle n'a pas brisé les matrices de son imagination: tout un déchet mythologique survit dans des zones mal contrôlées. (20)

i.e. "The uninterrupted desecration of modern man has altered the contents of his spiritual life, it has not broken the matrices of his imagination: a whole mythological waste persists in ill-controlled zones" (my translation). Such "mythological waste" can be found in religious behaviour, but also in adherence to national myths and to national imaginings. National myths present models of achievement, success and good behaviour for the community, thus codifying religious, social and moral concepts. They contribute in associating landscapes with national significance (Uluru in Australia, the Grand Canyon in the United States), and they ensure continuity between past and present and between different levels of reality, thus establishing unifying narratives. As Castoriadis (1975) remarked, national images and imaginaries are neither a double nor the reflection of reality, although they have a relation of representation to it (474).

National *discourse*, thus, targets a specific audience: minorities have often been excluded from identification with dominant national myths because of issues related to ethnicity, history, economy, and cultural difference. While Asians were long refused physical entry to Australia, another form of exclusion that affected (and still affects) them was (is) narrative exclusion. Indeed, Australian "textbook" history has eluded, and often still eludes, the question of Asian immigration:

public anxiety at the presence of Asians is rarely discussed, physical violence against Asians is hardly evoked, racist imagery and stereotyping is seldom acknowledged, and the legalised rejection of Asians is almost taboo. Asians are also generally excluded from the "official" history of Australia. A striking paucity in narrations of the nation is the tension between the constructive role of Asian immigrants in building and developing Australia and their complete absence from national myths. Finding it difficult to identify with white mythic figures, Asians have often felt rejected from mythic imaginings of their nation. Asian Australians were, and still are, despite growing activist movements, largely excluded from historical narrations of the nation. Given this absence of Asians in Australian national myths, how are references to national myths approached in Castro's *Birds of Passage*?

Birds of Passage contains many references to the Australian national imaginary. While some of these references are indirect, others are more explicit. First, the setting and the context of the novel refer to mythic times in Australian history: one of the two narratives of *Birds of Passage* takes place in the 1850s gold rush, thus referring to a mythic, egalitarian time; the second narrative is set in present-day Australia, and refers to flattering Australian self-projections through multiculturalism. National myths are also alluded to through the presence of certain themes. The theme of exile, an omnipresent concern in Australian national myths and in Australian history, is much developed in *Birds of Passage*. Exile pervades the text through Shan and O'Young's experiences of Australia. Shan's optimistic desire to gain experience in Australia is shattered upon his arrival as he is rejected and harassed by Europeans. O'Young, on the other hand, was born in Australia, but feels in exile:

> I am a refugee, an exile. My heart and my head are in the wrong places. There was no country from which I came, and there is none to which I can return [. . .] I am a truly stateless person. (*Birds of Passage* 8)

The motif of exile in the Australian imaginary is linked to convicts and early settlers who often found it difficult to be exiled from Europe. Convicts in particular could be qualified as "stateless"—they could not return to Europe, and were often rejected from Australian society. While O'Young's status does not work as a comparison of such cases, it inscribes the narration in national thematic traditions. O'Young's anxiety towards others can also be seen to reflect recurrent motifs in the Australian national imaginary: he believes that proximity destroys love, and that love can only exist in distance (Australia's geographical position to England); he lives through others, such as Shan and even the television (Australia's "cultural cringe" complex and reverence to England); he perceives himself as two different persons (Australia's double deference to England, the mother country, and to its own national development); and he undertakes a quest for an identity (Australia's obsession with defining a national identity).

Birds of Passage also addresses national myths in an explicit way. It refers to historical episodes that have come to be perceived as mythic: the gold rush (1851), Eureka Stockade (1854), Lambing Flat riots or massacre (1860-1861), and today's multiculturalism. Given the narrative structure of the novel—a present narration combined with a past narration that is accessed for clues about identity—mythic references deal with both myths about the past (the nation's origins) and myths about the present (the nations' distorted self-projections). Mythic references in *Birds of Passage* therefore deal with mythic past events, with the contrasting Asian reality behind these events, and with contemporary myths.

All mythic references in *Birds of Passage* contest the optimism of the myths. The novel presents decaying myths: egalitarianism, thought to be at its highest during the gold rush and largely glorified in Australian national perceptions, is confronted with the characters' greed and racism. Clancy's idealistic dream of a brotherhood in Australia is shattered by his own behaviour when he tries to murder Shan. While Shan is working in the goldfields, Clancy approaches him:

> [. . .] if only this idea of brotherhood could be enlarged [. . .]. Yes, that's my ideal. It's waiting to be created. A pastoral paradise without greed or fear. (*Birds of Passage* 116-117)

Later on, Clancy attacks Shan for being with Mary Young:

> They held him under the water for a long time, the bearded Clancy with a gap between his two front teeth and Carlos, a Spaniard who looked like a bull. (*Birds of Passage* 142)

Mateship, then, is limited to greed and xenophobia. In fact, the Chinese are more bound by the ideals of mateship than any other group in the novel: they work together, support each other and develop common rules to avoid interfering with European gold-diggers. The lack of equality is all the more acute in descriptions of the gold fields, where the Chinese were harassed by other groups. Eureka, which was regarded as, according to Bernard (1995), "the symbol of the victory of the oppressed against tyranny, and [. . .] the first step towards democracy," is imagined by cowards (Clancy) and realised by greedy gold-diggers (56). *Birds of Passage* confronts such fictional narrative with the mythic, thus questioning the validity of such myths. The novel seems to emphasise the irony contained in Australia's self-perception as a tolerant, egalitarian country. Myths of Australia as a place where everyone can have a "fair go" are disrupted by narrations of violence, inequality, greed and racism.

Thus, the general optimism of national myths sharply contrasts with the fictional reality presented in *Birds of Passage.* Asian figures are rarely present in evocations of Australian national myths, and the presence of Asian characters amid allusions to national myths in *Birds of Passage* disrupts usual imaginings of the nation. The juxtaposition of the narration of Asians and of national myths contests the established authority of myths and allows for a confrontation of myths and of their historical inspiration, for an evaluation of the relevance of national myths to Asian communities, and for a possible appropriation by these groups. The novel's use of precise historical references—Castro refers to the second opium war (7-8), the Phaeton ship and its captain Morrison (30), Eureka (122-123) and Lambing Flat (133)—inscribes it in national history. Descriptions of working and living conditions show the reality of early Australia with particular emphasis on the Chinese perspective. The novel mentions several issues: the disembarking of the Chinese just outside of Victoria to avoid paying tax and the difficult working and living conditions of the Chinese in Australia—they had to pay for a licence and for protection and there was little if no social order (101, 103). Such descriptions form parallel narrations to the national imaginings that are related to that time in history: Castro restores displaced narratives by giving a voice to the experiences of the Chinese. In fact, the novel not only gives a voice to the marginal and the excluded, but it allows the voice of the main Chinese character, Shan, to surpass that of any Australian character. *Birds of Passage* restores the "forgotten" narrations of the marginal and the excluded. "Forgotten/forgetting" is far from straightforward. As Anderson too reminds us that many events in national genealogies and myths are regarded as forgotten. However, the very fact of mentioning such events shows that they *are* remembered:

> A vast pedagogical industry works ceaselessly to oblige young Americans to remember/forget the hostilities of 1861-65 as a great "civil" war between "brothers" rather than between—as they briefly were—two sovereign nation-states. (Anderson 201).

Many such events and myths are evoked "to remind one of something which it is immediately obligatory to forget" (Anderson 201). Angel Island and other elements of Asian American history were largely forgotten, but have risen towards remember/forget episodes with the development of multicultural curricula.

Finally, *Birds of Passage* contests the optimism of contemporary myths. O'Young's confusion and alienation imply misconceptions about the efficiency of multiculturalism as well as the inadequacy of national myths to provide minorities with a stable identity. O'Young is rejected as alien and foreign in Australia: he has to insist on being Australian to his employer, while he is mistaken for "a Chinaman" and asked to do a reading test to be admitted at University (*Birds of Passage* 24, 61). The novel seems to denounce Australia's multiculturalist optimism. Myths of unity and balance in Australia do not reflect O'Young's everyday life and seem to bypass his need to be inscribed in the country's history and myths. While O'Young develops a neurosis, most (white) Australian characters are degenerate. In Shan's narrative, white Australians are idlers; while they work less hard than the Chinese, they are constantly resentful of the minority and indulge in provocation, violence and depravement:

> Next to the graves a party of drunken men is holding a competition. One of them has a watch in his hand. At his command, the men begin to urinate. They are trying to see who can urinate the longest without a break. (*Birds of Passage* 89)

O'Young's narrative also contains degenerate Australians: O'Young's adoptive parents, the Groves, are alcoholics and do not fulfil their parental role. The death of Jack Grove, on the other hand, is the result of stupidity and underlines the degenerate quality of the family. Jack dies because he drinks out of a brake fluid bottle that he mistook for alcohol (*Birds of Passage* 16). O'Young's neurosis and the degenerate nature of most Australian characters deconstruct the optimism of multiculturalist Australia.

Thus, O'Young's malaise implies a deceptive optimism in the "model minority" myth and in multicultural Australia. While Castro contests the optimism of myths, he takes his criticism of mythic structures much further. What is really at work in the novel is not just the presentation of a narration contrasting with national myths, but a deconstruction and an appropriation of national myths. Castro has qualified his writing, in an interview (2002), as "anti-myth":

> I try to reduce myth, particularly national ones, to rubble. And I do this by allowing what Deleuze and Guattari called a "minor" literature to operate, that is, a *literature in the minor key* written in a kind of deterritorialised yet appropriated language by characters who are outsiders within a minority and who are also excluded from that minority. (Barker 243)

Castro (1999) is anxious to escape categorisation and works in his novels to "write [him]self out of crippling essentialist categorisations" (*Looking for Estrellita* 115). He is interested in transgressive figures, such as the hybrid and alienated characters:

> Alienation, anomie and spiritual homelessness are opportunities to escape normalisation in order to reformulate thinking about the myth of community. Without this questioning, there can be no art movements. Alienation, anomie and spiritual homelessness are transformative values with an individual, linguistic and artistic base. (*Looking for Estrellita* 220)

Castro's writing therefore tends to resist national myths and does so by operating a minor literature and by escaping categorisation and normalisation in order to re-evaluate "the myth of community."

In *Birds of Passage*, Castro's resistance to national myths largely relies on the ultimate impossibility to categorise his characters and to fit them in defined groups. O'Young and Shan are indeed "outsiders within a minority." Being an orphan of part-Chinese ancestry with blue eyes, O'Young can hardly be categorised. When he is unemployed, he lives in a state of destitution and is offered some food by a homeless man; however, he is even rejected by the homeless when he fails to help the man and is distrusted for carrying books (*Birds of Passage* 34-36). Shan is also an outsider within his own community. Once he leaves for Australia, he progressively sets himself apart from the Chinese: "I begin to set myself apart [. . .]. My survival is with these, my people. Yet it pains me to speak to them, so apart am I from their beliefs"

(*Birds of Passage* 80). Shan and O'Young are hybrids and excluded from a minority. Then, O'Young resists nationalities: although an Australian citizen, he is "a refugee, an exile [. . .] a truly stateless person" (*Birds of Passage* 8). He escapes reality and cannot be categorised: as a child, he is believed to be mentally disabled because of his appearance; later, he hears voices and contracts diseases that are rare and unique—unknown to science (*Birds of Passage* 9). He ages prematurely and suffers from Hume's syndrome. As Michael Deves (1999) has argued,

> Hume's Syndrome' is another of Castro's jokes. There is no medical condition known as Hume's syndrome: he has invented a syndrome and named it for David Hume, "the eighteenth-century philosopher who bored me to death at university. He was an empiricist and a positivist and detested metaphysics [. . .]. So Hume's Syndrome was that perverse state of being utterly in touch with common sense and reality and [. . .] ultimately [. . .] extreme boredom and rapid ageing." (91)

To an extent, O'Young even escapes reality and categorising in the way he reads:

> I had always read [. . .] with three or four books open. I jump from one book to another, catching the mood from one and then linking up to another. After a while, passages from different books interconnect. I have then a good picture of several interlinked worlds as I read, the momentum generated by each carrying me through them. Different worlds open up. I inhabit all of them. (*Birds of Passage* 52)

Finally, he progressively loses his ability to perform all primary functions: he stops eating, becomes partly paralysed, is not sexually active and loses his voice. Such a condition seems to result from his genuine need to escape reality and categorisation: being impossible to categorise, O'Young resists national myths and the "myth of community."

Castro's resistance to national myths and their categorisation is not only visible in O'Young and Shan: Castro seems to refuse the imposition of authority and set structures. The revelation that Shan is O'Young's ancestor is questioned by the inclusion of puns: Edna thinks that O'Young's name is "sham," and it is most likely that O'Young's ancestor would be called Ouyang and not Shan (although O'Young could be a reference to Mary Young) (*Birds of Passage* 135). Castro also plays with historical and mythic references: in the boat to Australia, the

Chinese hold onto and drown in tea, a possible ironic reference to China's history; and O'Young has to read from a text called "The Yellow Race" for his university interview (*Birds of Passage* 40, 61). The novel's concluding chapter celebrates imagination:

> And I think now that I have found the significance for which I was searching: not in the audacity of mere words, not in the belief in existences that transcend the human, but in the celebration of not searching, in the wonder of the imagination. (*Birds of Passage* 157)

Castro thereby celebrates the importance of escaping categorisation, of using imagination to overcome imposed structures. His use of language to resist such structures draws from the margins and effectively enacts his conception of culture: "The whole notion of culture is that it only grows outwards, at the margins" (*Looking for Estrellita* 32).

Castro's resistance to national myths is extended by his deconstruction of the myth of an Australian brotherhood. Castro has remarked on Australia's lack of intellectualism, which, according to him, results in static myths:

> In most spheres of artistic endeavour there are usually three phases: the establishment of mythology, the debunking of this myth by oppositional subcultures and the eventual parody of and absorption of debunking. In Australia phase two is commonly avoided, perhaps out of concern for intellectualism's low status. Phase three is reached through an almost invisible compromise with apathy. (*Looking for Estrellita* 221-223)

The use of parody and debunking in *Birds of Passage* seems to challenge Australian myths. Castro is rather fond of parody, and has used it in several other novels. Indeed, *Pomeroy* (1990) was designed "to parody all the genres it could possibly accommodate" (*Looking for Estrellita* 105). Besides, Tseen-Ling Khoo (2003) has argued that Jaime Pomeroy, the main character in Castro's *Pomeroy*, is an interesting deconstruction of Australian myths. Pomeroy, a hesitant, hardly heroic journalist, represents Australia in Hong Kong, which upsets Australian national conceptions of masculinity as white and heroic (Khoo 130). Castro has also used parody in most of his other novels, including *Drift* (1994) and *The Garden Book* (2005). *Birds of Passage* parodies the figure of the bushman. An important figure in Australian national myths, the bushman is a generous, strong, honest worker. Castro presents two figures of the bushman, Clancy and Jack Grove. Clancy is an idealist and was on site when the Eureka stockade was erected in 1854 by gold-diggers as a reaction against the digging licence, work rules and repression. In reality, the stockade lasted some fifteen minutes when attacked by troops (Bernard 56). Although Eureka "[. . .] did not have the revolutionary impact that it was often conferred" (Le Cam 79), it was understood as "the symbol of the victory of the oppressed against tyranny, and [. . .] the first step towards democracy" (Bernard 56). It also enhanced the mythic side of the rebellious Australian hero and placed the concept of mateship as a key element in the national imaginary (Le Cam 79). However, Clancy is incapable of action at Eureka,

> A few idealistic men like himself cowered in their tents while their comrades screamed in their shepherd's holes, exposed to the fire and steel of Her Majesty's forces [. . .]. He knew he was totally incapable of action and this understanding of himself tortured him, the foundations of his idealism crumbling into a pit of depression. (*Birds of Passage* 82-83)

Incapable of enacting his idealistic principles, Clancy is a wanted man and is reduced to hiding and obsessing about the past. While Clancy is a pitiful Australian hero, he is related to another parodic character, Jack Grove: Jack's twin brother is called Clancy or Fitzpatrick, just like the character of Clancy (whose real name is also Fitzpatrick), and both Jack and Clancy have gapped front teeth. Jack Grove is also a parody of the Australian bushman: his hands are "the size of a shovel," and he is ridiculously strong:

> He hammered heels into shoes made for clubbed feet with his fists, fashioned and worked the leather with his fingers, pulled out nails with his teeth which had convenient gaps in the front. (*Birds of Passage* 13)

It is therefore through parody that Castro subverts the figure of the Australian bushman. Kam Louie (2005) similarly remarked that Castro's "apparently marginalized and vulnerable heroes in *Birds of Passage* betray a deliberate attempt by their creator to question accepted cultural norms and symbols of manhood" (186).

Finally, mythic perceptions of Australia are disrupted. Clancy dreams of a brotherhood. In a fling of universalism, he tells Shan about his ideal of "a brotherhood that made no distinction between race or religion" (*Birds of Passage* 115). Clancy presents his ideal Australia:

> "There's been a lot of talk about an Australia, a country, a united Australia Felix," Clancy went on, his voice rapturous, trembling. "Yes, that's my ideal. It's waiting to be created. A pastoral paradise without greed or fear." (*Birds of Passage* 117)

Such descri ption will not fail to evoke common images of Australia as a brotherhood and a pastoral paradise in the Australian imaginary: Clancy's ideal largely recalls Australian national myths. Clancy imagines the potential of collaboration:

> If only this idea of brotherhood could be enlarged; if only the white man could learn from your methods without feeling besieged, threatened by a close-knit group of com petitors, by the authorities, then something good could come out of this society. (*Birds of Passage* 116-117)

Clancy feels that the brotherhood could be achieved if everyone communicated (*Birds of Passage* 117). There is even a sense of communion between Clancy and Shan: "Yet in some strange way he felt he was understood" (*Birds of Passage* 117). However, the narrative of *Birds of Passage* disrupts any belief in the creation and even the possibility of such a brotherhood. Clancy ruins his ideal by attem pting to murder Shan at the end of the novel. All elements of Clancy's ideal Australia are shown to fail in the novel: no one tries to learn from the Chinese, Australia is far from being a pastoral paradise and communication is jeopardised by Clancy's very actions. In fact, communication is com promised right after Clancy's monologue:

> Centuries of human history had sparked one small covenant in the souls of two men for a brief moment. The wind prevented the spark from catching. (*Birds of Passage* 117).

Interestingly, wind is always present when major events take place in *Birds of Passage.* Wind is present when O'Young evokes his mythological mother (42), when Shan and Clancy meet and fail to communicate fully (117), when Edna tells O'Young the name of his ancestor (135), when O'Young is released from Shan's presence (144), when O'Young and Mrs. Bernhard achieve erotic fusion (154) and when Shan returns to his home village (157).

Though, enacting the "brotherhood" never takes place; the idea remains at an early imaginative stage. References to the brotherhood also represent a mockery of Australian idealism. Castro's deliberate presentation of degenerate Australian characters, his parody of the figure of the bushman, the impossible categorisation of his characters, and his criticism of Australian national myths through Clancy's idea of a brotherhood questions the validity of mythic structures and subverts national mythic narrations. Such deconstruction represents a playful manipulation of national myths, an effective appropriation of mythic references.

Castro's desire to avoid categorisation is interesting: his refusal to acknowledge a mainstream and to marginalise minorities by categorising them contrasts greatly with Asian American attempts at self-definition and with the process of fragmentation that is taking place in many multicultural states (Taylor 122-123). At the end of the novel, O'Young has finally found a place in society, but Castro does not present it as a possible alternative for reality. O'Young's model to overcome social alienation is limited to the novel. Castro does not, in any of his novels, suggest models for reality or cultivate a political outlook. As Eliade, *Aspects du Mythe* (1963), observes:

> On devine dans la littérature, d'une manière plus forte encore que dans les autres arts, une révolte contre le temps historique, le désir d'accéder à d'autres rythmes temporels que celui dans lequel on est obligé de vivre et de travailler. (234-235)

i.e. "In literature, much more powerfully than in any of the other arts, one can perceive a rebellion against historical time, the desire to access other temporal rhythms than the one in which we are forced to live and work" (my translation). It is this desire to transcend personal and historical time, to "writ[e] [one]self out of crippling essentialist categorisations" (*Looking for Estrellit* 115) that dominates *Birds of Passage.*

Works Cited

Anderson, Benedict. *Imagined Communities: Reflections on the Origin and Spread of Nationalism.* 1983. London: Verso, 1991.

Barker, Karen. "Theory as Fireworks: An Interview with Brian Castro." *Australian Literary Studies* 20.3 (May 2002): 241-248.

Bernard, Michel. *Histoire de l'Australie de 1770 à nos Jours: Naissance d'une Nation du Pacifique.* Paris: L'Harmattan, 1995.

Castoriadis, Cornelius. *L'Institution Imaginaire de la Société.* Paris: Editions du Seuil, 1975.

Castro, Brian. *The Garden Book.* Sydney: Giramondo, 2005.

——. *Looking for Estrellita.* St. Lucia: U of Queensland P, 1999.

——. *Drift.* Melbourne: Minerva, 1994.

——. *Pomeroy.* Sydney: Allen & Unwin, 1990.

——. *Birds of Passage.* 1983. London: Angus & Robertson, 1989.

Deves, Michael Ian. "'Apart from the Expected': The Novels of Brian Castro." PhD thesis. Flinders U, 1999.

Eliade, Mircea. *Aspects du Mythe.* Paris: Gallimard, 1963.

——. *Images et Symboles: Essais sur le Symbolisme Magico-Religieux.* 1952. Paris: Gallimard, 1980.

Khoo, Tseen-Ling. *Banana Bending: Asian-Australian and Asian-Canadian Literatures.* Hong Kong: Hong Kong UP, 2003.

Louie, Kam. "Decentring Orientalist and Ocker Masculinities in *Birds of Passage.*" *Culture, Identity, Commodity: Diasporic Chinese Literature in English.* Ed. Tseen-Ling Khoo and Kam Louie. Hong Kong: Hong Kong UP, 2005. 183-204.

Le Cam, Georges-Goulven. *L'Australie et la Nouvelle-Zélande.* Rennes: Presses Universitaires de Rennes, 1996.

Pons, Xavier. "Im possible Coincidences: Narrative Strategy in Brian Castro's *Birds of Passage.*" *Australian Literary Studies* 14.4 (October 1990): 464-475.

Taylor, Charles. *Le Malaise de la Modernité.* 1991. Trans. C. Melançon. Paris: Les Editions du Cerf, 1994.

Lost and (then) Found
The Quest for Home in *Benang*, *Tirra Lirra by the River* and *Requiem for a Rainbow*

Reema Sarwal

Multiculturalism as a State Policy in Australia is now more than three decades old. Though Australia has been home for numerous communities and diverse peoples in terms of race, ethnicity and religion since a long time; multiculturalism, is "still a contested idea,"

> a public policy which enables all [. . .] Australians, irrespective of their differences on the basis of culture, religion, history, and other variables, to have the opportunity to partici pate equally in the political, social and economic life of this society. (*WA Charter of Multiculturalism* 2)

It is essential to make this distinction between the mere co-habitation of different peoples, and co-habitation in an egalitarian society. The latter is signified by the term multiculturalism. But what do multicultural writing and studies mean? Multicultural studies often involve looking at migrants and aborigines—the so-called "ethnic" Australians. However, white settler or Anglo-Australian is as much an ethnic identity as aboriginal, Greek, Lebanese, Chinese, Indian, and so on. Merely the anthologies/collections of "black" writings, "migrant" writings, or the writings of "New Australians" (as the third generation and contem porary migrants are called), cannot be said to constitute the multicultural writings of Australia. Further, these ethnicities are not homogeneous categories and there are further distinctions within each. By definition, "multicultural" is inclusive of *all* groups/communities, including whites, and any kind of multicultural study must, therefore, include diverse Australian voices.

The three basic categories of multicultural writings can be identified as white settler, aboriginal and migrant. In a broader sense, white settlers have also been called migrants. However, this paper maintains a sharp distinction between the two on the grounds that unlike the settlers, migrants recognize the governing systems of the host country and accept the rules, regulations and the authority of the existing population. Settlers, on the other hand, defined Australia as uninhabited, *terra nullius* and claimed the continent as their own by right of being pioneers. They made their own laws and governing structures for themselves as well as for the pre-existing population. This distinction needs to be made because otherwise, the migrant argument can be stretched to include even the aborigines as they too came from outside, even though many centuries earlier.

At first glance, the writings emerging from, and about, these different ethnic groups of Australia seem so different from each other that it is difficult to believe, especially for an overseas reader, that they are descriptions of the same country. One is tempted to explain away the matter by concluding that there are indeed many Australias, though politically and geographically there may be one territory. However, a deeper consideration reveals certain predominant characteristics and pre-occupations, inseparable from the fact of being Australian. Without falling into the trap of universalizing on nationalistic grounds, one can discern shared concerns and anxieties. The writings show that Australia as home has not been a fixed, steady, unproblematic entity for any of her citizens, whether settler, aboriginal or migrant. Morag Fraser (2004) says,

> It is that lightness about being Australian [. . .] a condition of lightness that acknowledges the experiential rather than the essential nature of who we are [. . .]. (98)

And this lightness leads to a rather precarious conception of Australia as home. This paper looks at the quest for "home" in Australia and the instruments used for this quest such as exploring memory to rediscover the past, the act of writing and so on, in Jessica Anderson's (b. 1916) *Tirra Lirra by the River* (1978), Kim Scott's (b. 1957) *Benang* (1999) and Satendra Nandan's (b. 1939) *Requiem for a Rainbow* (2001). The first two are works of fiction written in the autobiographical mode while the last is an autobiography. Though the purpose of the quest is the same, its nature and result are rather different for different peoples as can be seen by looking at these three texts written by Australians of very different ethnic origins.

I

Nora, the white protagonist-narrator of Anderson's *Tirra Lirra by the River* comes back to her "home" in Brisbane, simply because

"Anything else is too much trouble." Thwarting reader expectations, it is not a homecoming for this old woman in her seventies to return to the house she grew up in. Even as a young girl she tolerated the place just because she was sure that she would leave it as soon as she grew up. It was this attitude that led her elder sister to call her "Lady Muck" who thinks herself "too good" for the place. The all pervasive question throughout the book is, "Who does she think *she* is?" Though the answer to this oft repeated question keeps changing, it is much more than an individualistic story. It tells much about the "un-settler colony" established by the settlers.

As the seventy-something woman is recovering from pneumonia in the house she grew up in, she decides that it is high time to spin the "globe of her memory" and explore the "nether side," to come to terms with all the things that she has refused to think about before she dies. In other words, she decides to revisit her memory to make sense of her life, to redefine who she is, and where she belongs.

Even as a child, she is not alone in feeling stifled by the suburb, a forced imitation of the English countryside, with the weakest kind of veneer of gentility. Dorothy Irey, her elder sister's friend whom everyone thinks to be a "gentle" and contented girl, confesses to Nora that as soon as she gets her inheritance, she'll be off. However, Dorothy gets married before that and is too busy looking after "the babies" to have a chance of moving out. If Harley takes respite in driving around the old routes with his uncles, Nora and Dorothy walk about the landscape to cope with their imprisoned situations. Nora persuades herself that she is in love with a suitor from Sydney and gets married to "escape." Her stingy, impotent husband accuses her of being "frigid" and therefore unable to have a baby, but when she begins to respond, she is told that a man doesn't like to be married to a "whore." Yet, she does feel at "home" in Potts Point in Sydney, with a house of her own and her frequent visits to the neighbouring dressmaker's house where she enjoys helping with the work and talking to the assortment of artists living there. Nora at this point is a proud housewife and amateur dressmaker. She does not work professionally because that would hurt the "self-respect" of her husband but does derive genuine satisfaction from the work itself. Later, the Depression makes them shift to the house her mother-in-law and she is reduced to a petty thief, stealing coins from her husband's trouser pockets and mother-in-law's purse to be able to visit her friends in the city. Again, she is not alone in this: a popular contemporary journal cracks regular jokes at wives stealing their husbands' hard earned money. Years of wasting begin till finally her husband announces that he wants a divorce to marry another woman. Nora feels freed but she is now homeless. In the first flush of freedom at the age of thirty-five, she decides to go to London, not because she particularly wants to, but because she feels that no one can stop her. She plans to come back after a year.

It is significant to note the way historical events affect the lives of different people. In 1936, the year the Spanish Civil War began, Nora finds herself in London, recovering from an abortion, while her childhood friend Olive discourses on communism and is shocked by Nora's frivolity in caring so much for her dressmaking in such times. 1936 is also the year an Aboriginal Act is passed in Australia to define the term "natives." It is this act according to which persons of less than "quadroon" (one-fourth aborigine) descent born before 31 January 1936 are declared exempt from the aborigine "protection" laws and Ern's ambition to have the first white man in the family line is thwarted as his son is born a few months *after* the deadline of 31 January. He must therefore wait for a grandson. For more than one reason, the year 1936 is etched in Australian history. If the aborigines were turned homeless in their own homes, the white settlers, who claimed the *terra nullis* as their own, too could not find a home to belong to. When Nora asks Olive why she does not return to Australia, the prompt reply she receives is that Olive wants to live in an "important" country. Olive is a writer of romantic novels dealing with "delicate nuances of feeling" but Nora points out tersely that those nuances of feeling would certainly be affected if the lovers had to stop to use contraceptives, of which Olive knows nothing. Nevertheless, Nora is proud that her best friend of childhood can write. Reading had always filled her imagination and later, narrating her past life to friends at "number six" in London helps her deal with her grief. Later, she writes letters to her friends from Brisbane. But finally, it is the narrating and putting into words her "forgotten" memories to herself that helps her find a home.

Nora's attempt to go back to Sydney after her training as a dressmaker is thwarted because of war, sickness and the depression in Sydney. Now robbed of her youthful looks, beginning work as an old woman in a depression hit Sydney seems hardly possible. She actually tries to commit suicide. Years later when she finally returns to Brisbane, she comes to know that around the same time she attempted suicide, Dorothy Irey murdered her husband and children with an axe before gassing herself in the oven. A "gentle" woman like Dorothy doing such a horrendous deed shocks the entire community, though later, it is identified as a case of "suburban neurosis." Such a term is an acknowledgement of the fact that there was something about living in suburban Australia at that point in Australian history that could lead to such a diseased state of mind.

Though Nora lives for more than three decades in London among a beloved group of friends, the desire to go back is never entirely lost. London has been a "home" and gives her an identity—"Nora Porteous-Dressmaker"—but it no longer wants her when she turns too old to work. Her old home at Potts Point in Sydney has changed beyond recognition with modern changes and all her old friends are dead. As she hopelessly returns to her suburb, all her worst expectations are met in the first glance. However, as she allows the "nether side" of her globe of memory to come to light and also discovers that she has been actually remembered in the suburb by the embroidered wall-hangings she had once gifted to some of the neighbours, she does develop a sense of belonging, and is able to make the old house her home.

Memories slowly flood her consciousness. She finally remembers her father and her father's funeral, which she had not been able to recall all these years. It is as if the journey within her memory allows her to find the way she lost long ago. The poem "Lady of Shallot" had evoked a landscape "in her mind" when she was a girl, though she never associated it with the real brown river along which she had walked. That landscape never left her mind and she still feels grief at the loss of it. For she never found either Camelot or Sir Lancelot, even if Sydney provided a substitute for Camelot for a few years. These lines have stuck in her mind:

> *"From underneath his helmet flowed*
>
> *His coal-black curls as on he rode,*
>
> *As he rode down to Camelot.*
>
> *From the bank and from the river*
>
> *He flashed into the crystal mirror,*
>
> *"Tirra lirra" by the river*
>
> *Sang Sir Lancelot."* (qtd. in Tirra Lirra by the River 9)

The step of the horse, the feathered plumes that have so often haunted her now merge with the memory of the feathered plumes of the horses on which rode the mourners at her father's funeral. She finds some solace for her grief in the memory of the ceremony. And the memory of her father somehow restores the home, something she had never thought possible.

II

The "first white man born," Harley the narrator-protagonist of *Benang: From the Heart* has a mixed heritage—Nyoongar and white—but has been raised to remember and carry on only one. He is the product of A. O. Neville's plan to "uplift a despised race" by careful breeding and segregation from aborigines. Ernest Solomon Scat, or Ern carries out this plan, records the following observation in his notes:

> Breeding Up. In the third or fourth generation no sign of native origin is apparent. The repetition of boarding school process and careful breeding [. . .] after two or three generations the advance should be so great that families should be living like the rest of the community. (*Benang* 28)

Ern assumes that the white genes are dominant and quickly do away with the inferiority of the "native" genes. With his "scientific method" and careful records of "genealogical diagrams," he judges that his grandson Harley is one-sixteenth aboriginal but has inherited only the "dominant" characteristics of the whites: characteristics including not only the colour of his skin, but the fondness for reading and drawing. Harley is the "successful end of a long line of failures" (*Benang* 13)—failures at being "white." When sixteen year old Harley accidentally discovers the truth about Ern, who insists on being called Dad, he is completely devastated. He finds records in his grandfather's study with statements like: "The need for both biological and social absorption. Dilute the strain" (*Benang* 29). Harley's first response is the wish to reverse this upbringing and to prove himself his "grandfather's failure." He finds himself floating in the air, with no history to hold on to, no home to belong to. His so-called "Dad" has fathered countless number of children with any number of aboriginal and white women, but has chosen him from among all of them, simply because he is the living proof of the success of his "experiment." The bed-and-breakfast place that Ern runs with the help of his various women "business" partners looses whatever little sense of home it had ever provided for Harley. At the same time, he does not know his other heritage. His father had left him in the care of Ern when he was seven under the condition that he would not be allowed to meet his father or any of his other relatives.

Scott displays a masterful use of language when he takes A. O. Neville's phrase "uplift and elevate these people to our own plane" (*Benang* 13) literally to mean that Harley is lifted off the ground and set afloat. Harley's first reaction is anger and anguish, so that he even hurts Ern physically and mentally. Ultimately, it is writing that comes to his rescue—writing his family history as narrated by his two Uncles, Will and Jack, supplemented with meticulous "facts" from Ern's records. He is conscious that he does not know the Nyoongar tongue and must write in the language that has been used so cruelly to misrepresent his ancestors:

> I have written this story wanting to embrace all of you, and it is the best I can do in this language we share. Of course, there is an older tongue which also tells it. (*Benang* 497)

It is through words that Ern trapped the destinies of Harley and so many others and hence, more words are needed to counter the earlier ones, like those proposed by Ern to advertise his new bed-and-breakfast place:

> "We have pristine beaches; turquoise waters and white sand. Granite outcrops. We can offer the history of the place's pioneers, explain

> how once there was an unofficial port where the enterprising Mr. Mustle welcomed the whalers, sealers and other adventurers in the very earliest days of settlement. They used rum for currency [. . .]."And so he went on. Adventure, enterprise, vision. (*Benang* 26)

It is the grand narrative created by these three evocative, powerful words—adventure, enterprise, and vision—that has been used to glorify the settlers and to obliterate the history and carnage of aborigines, and it is this grand narrative that the author's/Harley's words must counter. Although he says that he is writing "a simple family history, the most local of histories" (*Benang* 12), the narrative effectively reflects on not just his own personal history but on the histories of so many aborigines and ultimately, the history of the entire nation. It is a history of the violence, rape and atrocities perpetrated in the name of "assimilation" and "welfare" of the aborigines as well as of the attempt to rob them of their history. It is a recognition of the power of the written language in "the way words can blur, and shift, and welcome you among them" (*Benang* 18).

It is important to note that Harley himself has received the white man's education and also has the assurance of inheriting all of Ern's wealth, but material security alone can never be a substitute for a "home" and a sense of belonging. Especially when Harley now knows that he has been selected from among so many children that Ern has helped "create," simply by the virtue of his "whiteness." It is the same need that his great-great grandparents had felt when forced to move away from the land that was their home: "So much more here than at the goldfields or the drier land to the east. But not quite like home" (*Benang* 280). Harley's quest for home involves listening to the stories of his Uncles sitting around campfires as they drive along the old routes taken by their ancestors and the roads which they helped build, though their contribution remained unacknowledged. The same event is narrated differently by the two Uncles and sometimes, Harley himself remembers the event from his childhood. It is these various perspectives and stories that need to be then woven together and one of the strengths of the book is that this process of composition is made available to the reader. Further, an old and invalid Ern must listen to the stories of Will and Jack around the fires, powerless to interrupt, as well as to the written drafts which Harley reads out to him when they are alone.

The novel thus incorporates the activities of oral narration, listening, writing and finally even reading into its fabric so that Harley the writer has at least one reader/listener, however unwilling, within the narrative structure. It is quite plain that this whole writing-reading process is an essential part of the quest for home and it is the words themselves which are instrumental in Harley's finding his lost home and realizing that he can also be a part of a continuation, and not the "end" of a line. It is a process of "scratching and tapping from within the virtual prison of my grandfather's words" (*Benang* 497), which lets new words make him welcome among them.

III

Satendra Nandan is a Fiji Indian New Australian. It might be contested whether Nandan's *Requiem for a Rainbow: A Fiji Indian Story* can be considered Australian writing at all. It could be seen merely as the story of a Fiji Indian grieving the loss of his country from Australia, arguing that it could have been written from anywhere else as well. However, the fact remains that it was written from Australia because he was welcomed there. It is as much a story of having found a new home, as of losing the older one and perhaps feeling the more for it because of the loss. Besides, any writing by a migrant is inevitably permeated by the memories of the home and the dear ones left behind. So while Nandan's *Requiem for a Rainbow* can certainly be classified as Fijian Indian or as Expatriate Indian, it is also as much Australian. Nandan migrated to Australia in his late forties after the two coups in Fiji in 1987. Having been a minister in the government that was overthrown, he found it difficult to get a job in Fiji, though the decision to leave was made more because of the mental torture suffered by him and his family. To migrate, relatively speaking, at such a late stage of life itself makes it quite difficult to think of the new country as "home" and it is indeed to the credit of any nation that it made this possible. It is also, of course, yet another inspiring instance of human resilience and adaptability.

As in *Benang*, the author here to says that he is writing as much for himself as for his children. Further:

> I hope it inspires others to write their stories of the tragic events that have wrecked Fiji particularly the life of Fiji Indians—a people whose narratives are woven with sorrow and betrayal but also with hope and inspiration. (*Requiem for a Rainbow* 6)

Writing then is not only for the purpose of Art but for recording histories, to "Gather up the fragments that remain, that nothing be lost" (*Requiem for a Rainbow* 6) and to inspire others who have lived through the same national catastrophe of the coups of 1987 in Fiji. Kavita Ivy Nandan, in the introduction to the work says,

> They [migrants] remember in their life stories, knowing how unstable the reality of home is, that the only grounds they have to stand upon is language, remembrance, a haunted imagination [. . .]. [Satendra Nandan's] writing has certainly given me a sense of creative security, a belief that writing can change one's sense of reality [. . .] writing is a way in which diasporic writers and their children, who are even further removed from these receding realities, can revisit these spaces and places of the past [. . .]. (*Requiem for a Rainbow* 7-8)

It is the revisiting of the old home—not physically but through memory and writing, which can make possible the acceptance of the new home. Words become essential for finding home, for a "movement forward."

The narrative shifts between three countries: India, Fiji and Australia, along with a few incidents from London, where he went briefly for studies. It begins with the description of the coup which led to the loss of the home that till then had always been taken for granted. It is the loss that forces Nandan to rethink about Fiji and his connections with that country, about the girmits, the indentured labourers from India, among whom came his four grandparents, about the lives of his parents who managed to provide their children with an education without which this story could never have been written. Then begins the attempt to excavate the ancestors' story as well as his own:

> They had come from obscure villages: they had left no great manuscripts except their lives, if only one could decipher them. My own knowledge of Fiji history came very late: we were not taught Fiji history or geography. Literature, we were told, we had none. We'd only one culture: agriculture, so we were told [. . .]. (*Requiem for a Rainbow* 113)

It takes this homeless "*ghaasphoose ke daaktor*" (as a "well-wisher" calls this doctor of philosophy) to write about the Fijian landscape and history, however personal the account may be. His grandparents came from India to Fiji to work in farms owned by CSR, an Australian company and his father worked on a leased farm, again from the same company. So he grew up thinking none too well of Australia as CSR took away so much of the share of the farm produce from their Fijian farms. And though he now expresses warm gratitude to Canberra, the relationship with Australia has not been unproblematic. Yet, the coups in Fiji were meant to discriminate against Indians there and Nandan's belief that the best answer to give to racists "is to live well and ensure that your children get the best" made him move to Australia. And over a period of more than a decade, it became "a healing home for all of us" (*Requiem for a Rainbow* 226).

Requiem for a Rainbow uses three metaphors for migration: of "transplanted trees amidst the native bush," of arranged marriage, and of a migratory bird. It is significant how the metaphor of birds takes on different meanings in the three texts. In *Benang*, the bird is the curlew, whose cry denotes death so that Harley wonders initially if his singing is nothing but like that of the curlew since to "create" him, so many aborigines have been killed. He feels that he is just the "end" of the line. Later the song of the bird is identified as telling the tale of the dead aborigines which has been left unsung by others and so, it is Harley who can show the children "where and who we are." It is an embroidered magpie from her childhood that shows Nora that she did create something even from that house in suburbian Brisbane which made the people remember her. The image of a bird gives her the sense of roots, though she is terrified to "fly again." Another recurring image is that of water—Nora and Nandan grow up near rivers that often flood over but they also flood their imaginations and are inextricably linked to their memories of childhood. Harley grows up near the ocean—the ocean is from where the white man entered Australia. But it is not just that. It symbolizes the determination of the Nyungars to "return, return, and remain" no matter how hard anyone tries to exterminate them.

IV

The quest for home is not an easy one for any of the three narrators. Their "shifty" narratives keep moving between the past, present and future. It is the loss of the old home and the old identity which sparks the quest but that quest leads to hope and a re-assertion of their different identities. Words become essential not just to express, but also to discover, to find out and to create for themselves their home. A home that can be inherited, not just physically but psychologically by many more than their own children, and is, at the same time, a home for the dead ancestors who will now be remembered through their words. These words, indeed, are the markers of a dynamic multicultural Australia.

Works Cited

Anderson, Jessica. *Tirra Lirra by the River.* 1978. Ringwood, Victoria: Penguin, 1980.

Bird, Delys. Rev. of *Tirra Lirra by the River,* by Jessica Anderson. *Westerly* 25.4 (December 1980): 78-80.

Government of Western Australia. *WA Charter of Multiculturalism.* Perth: Office of Multicultural Interests, 2004. 7 March 2007 <http://www.equalopportunity.wa.gov.au/pdf/wa_charter_multiculturalism.pdf>.

Fraser, Morag. "Correspondence: 'Made in England.' " *Quarterly Essay* 13 (2004): 98.

Nandan, Satendra. *Requiem from a Rainbow: A Fijian Indian Story.* Canberra: Pacific Indian, 2001.

Scott, Kim. *Benang: From the Heart.* 1999. New Delhi: Penguin, 2003.

Messages from the Inside? Multiculturalism in Contemporary Children's Literature

Sharyn Pearce

The Beginnings

At the start of the 1950s, a massive intake of one and a half million European migrants was assimilated into the Australian community, effectively and permanently eroding Australia's Anglo-Saxon-Celtic composition. To gain some sense of the enormity of the changed demographics it is salutary to note that at the end of the World War II the population of Australia was only seven and a half millions, and over ninety-five percent of Australians came from British or Irish stock (McGregor 323). By the late 1980s, after further waves of immigration, only 47% was British and "Old Australian," 23% was composed of non-English-speaking migrants and children, while 30% was a mixture and "growing" (Hirst 228). In the 1950s many Australians were firmly convinced that their way of life was unique because it was based upon the mores of a homogenous community, and they were determined to prevent these norms from being broken down by the admission of large numbers of unassailable elements. And so these lucky immigrants were tolerated if they embraced the Australian way of life as enthusiastically as the author of *They're a Weird Mob* (1957), a book of such immense popularity that it was reprinted 13 times in its second year of publication, and was later made into a highly successful family film (the novel was originally written for adults, but many children and teenagers also read it, and it subsequently became a favorite text in the secondary school English curriculum). The fervently nationalistic bravado of these mid-century times is reflected in the words of the narrator Nino Culotta, one-time Italian journalist and now a successful "New Australian" (in reality an Anglo-Australian writer called John O'Grady):

> There are too many New Australians in this country who are still living in their homelands, who mix with people of their own nationality, and try to retain their own language and customs. Who even try to persuade Australians to adopt their customs and manners. Cut it out. There is no better way of life than that of the Australian. I firmly believe this. The grumbling, growling, cursing, profane, laughing, beer-drinking, abusive, loyal-to-his-mates Australian is one of the few free men left on this earth. He fears no one, crawls to no one, bludges to no one, and acknowledges no master. Learn his way. Learn his language. Get yourself accepted as one of him; and you will enter a world that you never dreamed existed. And once you have entered it, you will never leave it. (*They're a Weird Mob* 204)

The novel concludes with Nino's recognition that Australia is really God's Own Country, and that God himself is the biggest "Ocker" (that is, stereotyped beer-bellied Australian male, usually in blue singlet, shorts and rubber sandals) of them all:

> There are hundreds of ways we could spend this sunny Sunday afternoon. Or we could just stay at home and do nothing, and perhaps that would be best of all. To rest on the seventh day. To thank God for letting us be here. To thank Him for letting me be an Australian. Sometimes I think that if I am ever fortunate enough to reach Heaven, I will know I am there when I hear Him say "Howyergoin'mate, orright?" (*They're a Weird Mob* 204)

Now, at the beginning of the third millennium, this evangelising assimilationist (and masculinist!) zealotry would thankfully seem to be no more: relegated, together with the paternalistic and patronizing attitudes so popular half a century ago, to the realms of the quaint past. Australia is now one of the most cosmopolitan and ethnically diverse countries in the world, and for nearly three decades multiculturalism has been its officially dominant discourse. Multiculturalism is part of the everyday currency of Australian life, where tolerance of cultural differences and respect and understanding in cross-cultural contacts are promoted as ideal civic virtues, and migrants and their children are ideally integrated into an effectively harmonious society without alienating them by unreal assimilationist expectations. Because for the most part Old World disputes have not been seen to be transferred to the New Land, and a large number of differing cultures have been accommodated without overt conflict, and because, also, of the immense economic advantages which have ensued, immigration and the subsequent adoption of multiculturalism as public policy have been hailed by many commentators as Australia's greatest post-World War II policies and achievements (Patience 34).

Definitions of multiculturalism are slippery, and have in fact changed in recent years: while the term used to imply Non-Anglo-Celtic, representing people whose first language is not English, this is no longer necessarily the case, and, as Jon Stratton (2000) argues, many British migrants, eager to retain an entitlement that was once naturally theirs, now assert that as their society and culture is not the same as Australian society and culture, they should be treated like other migrant groups to the country;

> British self-ethnicization [. . .] is an attempt to gain a new status, this time one which places British-Australians on an equivalence with other ethnic groups in Australia, arguing for the same rights and treatment accorded non-English speaking migrants by asserting their own ethnic backgrounds. (23-24)

It is usually argued that multiculturalism was eventually welcomed and celebrated largely because it appealed to traditional Australian values such as easy-going tolerance, and egalitarian informality; in short, the tendency of the locals to defend everyone's right to have "a fair go" (Hirst 228). Recent developments have, however, tended to dim the picture of a people triumphing over their tribulations and prejudices to embrace diversity and tolerance with an egalitarian generosity, and to confirm instead the pessimistic view that the never entirely dormant nostalgic hankering for a pre-1950s monocultural, assimilationist lifestyle has of late been gaining crucial momentum. The view from what social commentator Hugh Mackay calls the "rose-colored rear-window" (qtd. in Dale 316) currently seems attractive to a significant number of Australians who apparently have reached saturation point with the narratives of difference, and yearn instead to return to Nino's Australia—to a world which reflects the cultural homogeneity of the past rather than the enriched cultural diversity and hybridity of the present. Yet the impatience with multiculturalism appears to have specific, highly visible and highly "different" targets within its sights: Central European migrants are accepted, mostly without question, but Asian and Middle Eastern ones often face a different reception, for reasons which are deeply embedded in the national psyche. Rich, empty Australia, tantalizingly close to some of the most populous nations in the world, has, over the last century or so, seen adroit political manipulation of the old anxieties and fears about being over-run by non-whites, but few have been more recent or more breathtakingly cynical than in the 2001 Federal Election, when the ruling Conservative Coalition parties, which had previously been languishing in the polls, retained power via a campaign which presented them as the stout defenders of Australia against a deluge of invading Asian hordes—in this case, desperate Afghan asylum-seekers, fleeing to Australia in scrappy, make-shift boats, who were successfully demonized as threats to the nation's well-being. Moreover, since the attacks upon the World Trade Centers in New York on September 11, 2001 and the repercussions which have reverberated about the globe, intakes of non-Europeans, non-whites and non-Christians have tested community tolerance, and multiculturalism is on uneasy ground, with a raft of right-wing commentators calling for an end to that bedrock achievement of the last forty years, the racially and religiously non-discriminatory immigration program (Sheridan 11). It could be argued, as the country bunkers down once more into Fortress Australia mode, that some migrants are now more equal than others. The movement to return to the core values of the formerly ascendant Anglo-Celtic cultural and political past gathered great momentum from the mid-1990s onwards. In her maiden speech in the Federal Parliament Pauline Hanson, leader of the ultra-conservative, anti-Asian immigration One Nation Party, declared:

> a truly multicultural [country] can never be strong or united [. . .]. We do not want little ethnic islands. We want migrants who can integrate, not congregate, or the country will start falling apart because of violence, gang warfare and ethnic separatism. (10 September 1996)

One in four Queenslanders voted for Hanson's party in the State elections in 1998, and it may be argued that the 2001 Federal election was won because the Conservative parties successfully hijacked One Nation's policies.

Nonetheless, despite the swirling tides of White Australia revisionism fuelled by vociferous media commentators and paranoid "shock jocks," multiculturalism still remains, for the moment at least, a desirable social value which should be inculcated in child readers. It is, in fact, a judicious exercise to examine the progress of multiculturalism in books for children and young adults, for while it may be seen that literature rarely initiates trends, it certainly responds to societal changes, and books can legitimately be viewed as crucial agents of socialization of the young into appropriate channels of behavior and deportment or as valuable conduits of altered or enlightened governmental policies. Over 10 years ago, in a germinal article entitled "Advocating Multiculturalism: Migrants in Australian Children's Literature after 1972," John Stephens (1990) demonstrated that as the complexion of Australian society was changing, the inclusion of themes of migration, identity and cultural differences into literature for children became more relevant and necessary. Just as Australia's political and educational institutions adopted multiculturalism, he argues, so did Australian children's literature. Yet Stephens also contends that while the texts of the 1970s and 1980s reveal an increasing acceptance of "difference" and heterogeneity, they were still, in the main, written by Anglo-Celtic authors, few of whom were actually of the classes, races or even demographic areas represented in their stories. Stephens also wryly observes that the focalisers in these "multicultural" narratives are overwhelmingly members of the majority culture, that "the privilege of narrative subjectivity is rarely bestowed upon minority groups" (181), and that the usual plotline is that of a person from mainstream society being influenced, in some positive way, by the exotic "Other." Moreover, he notes that novels tend "to rewrite social and cultural history for the purpose of shaping the present" (181):

> The books certainly recognize that racism has been deeply ingrained in Australian culture, but construct situations in which it is invariably physically or morally defeated. In addition, the books characteristically generate motifs or significant objects or incidents which function as symbols or metaphors for the ideology of multiculturalism, usually standing for some way in which the coexistence of cultural difference offers mutual enrichment. (181)

In summary, he concludes that despite the fact that there is a significant corollary between the development of a personal identity and that of a national (that is, multicultural) identity, multiculturalism in texts of the 1970s and 1980s is rarely treated in a radical way, but is invariably presented in a superficial or cosmetic fashion.

Warming to this topic for a second time some five years further on, Stephens once again notes a continuation of this tendency for more recent texts to disclose inherent multicultural tendencies in earlier Australian history, particularly in pre-mass migration eras. He also detects a significant shift in the treatment of positionality: now the experiences of members of minority communities are more frequently depicted from an insider perspective, with a significant number of texts being narrated, or focalised, by a member of a cultural minority (1996: 3-4). Yet, as Stephens is also aware, while first person narration by a member of a minority community is indeed a very powerful method of expressing subjectivity, this achievement is nonetheless a limited one when in many instances the representation of people from other cultures continues to be mediated by British-Australian authors. Benign or commendable though their intentions might be, mainstream dominant majority writers can still legitimately be accused of appropriating other cultures and silencing or erasing them by speaking in their place. By imposing their own interpretations, mainstream authors can have the effect of being oppressive, and of reinscribing the marginalization of minorities through overwriting according to their own forms and norms. Bearing this in mind, what I propose to do in this paper is firstly to examine two texts which illustrate that even today Stephens' findings remain apposite, and then, in the final part of this paper, I propose to add a third stage to Stephens' closely-argued multicultural progression. In particular I will disagree with another critic in this field who contends that:

> we are still a long way from a realistic portrayal in children's literature of Australian multicultural society [. . .]. Most writers are Anglo-Australian and their books make only small tokenistic gestures towards multiculturalism. You have to wait for the authentic voice to come from the cultures themselves. (Starke 24)

A Tale of Two Histories

Whether for children or adults, Australian writing has traditionally been predicated upon the perpetual themes of displacement and dislocation, the reconciliation of personal and national identity, and the establishment of a sense of belonging. It comes as no surprise, then, that the end of the second millennium (a thoughtful time, one could say) has witnessed, in Australia, the publication of a welter of historical texts for children and young people which focus particularly upon these themes. To celebrate the 2001 Centenary of Federation (amid much celebration, Australia relinquished its colonial status in 1901 in order to become a fully-fledged member of the British Commonwealth of

Nations), Scholastic Press produced a new series of historical fictions presumably designed primarily for school classrooms. This series explores seminal periods of history through the observant jottings of young female authors, and one of these texts, Nadia Wheatley's *A Banner Bold* (2000), is an exemplary instance of the anachronistic approach described by Stephens in his two analyses. Set in the turbulent and colorful times of mid-nineteenth-century Australia, this piece of engagingly blatant proselytising endeavours to demonstrate that Australia has always been a multicultural society. The novel is based upon actual historical events: during the days of the Gold Rushes in the colony of Victoria, miners had to pay a monthly license fee of thirty shillings for the right to dig for their fortunes. This fee was enormously resented, particularly because it was so rigorously enforced by the police and governmental authorities. In December 1854 men from a range of countries including Ireland, America, Canada, France, Italy, Germany and England refused to pay the miners' fees, and in an act of rebellion against the repressive colonial government flew their own flag, the Southern Cross (so-called after a constellation of stars seen only in the Southern hemisphere) above the Eureka gold diggings. Although this revolt was quickly suppressed, it has subsequently garnered hugely symbolic significance in Australian history, as an iconic moment linked in the minds of many with the beginnings of republicanism, with egalitarianism, and with the rejection of Empire.

The hero of Wheatley's tale is Rosa Aarons, a secular German Jew, who writes a journal for her friend Jenny Marx (daughter of the more famous Karl Marx, who had some connection with the events depicted in the novel in that in 1855 he actually wrote an account of this riot for a German newspaper called the *Neu Oder-Zeitung*). Freedom-loving Rosa is already multicultural—or at least a citizen of the world—as she is of German birth, yet she speaks English fluently, together with a number of other European languages, including Yiddish. Moreover Rosa is, like her father, a committed republican and a staunch anti-imperialist. When the new Governor of the colony of Victoria, Sir Charles Hotham, arrives from England, Rosa disapproves of the "Royalist circus" that accompanies him, echoing her father's question—"When will these people demand the right to elect their own rulers?" (*A Banner Bold* 22). Like her parents, she abstains from singing "God Save the Queen" and "Rule Brittannia," and while at school, much to her teacher's chagrin, she sews "All Power Proceeds from the People," rather than the usual Biblical or patriotic text, onto her needlework sampler. Rosa quickly makes friends with children from a range of nationalities, and together they form a theatrical group which originally intends to perform a play written by Rosa, about Judith, the Jewish heroine who rescues her people from tyranny. Following the incendiary political events, however, they perform the story of the valiant Eureka uprising instead. Moreover, the children are not merely witnesses to "History in the making" (*A Banner Bold* 122), and they do have a real part to play, because Rosa suggests the Southern Cross design for the rebels' flag, while she and her friends are also responsible for helping the leader of the uprising, Peter Lalor (later to become a respected member of the Victorian Parliament), to escape from the soldiers.

In some ways *A Banner Bold* is situated neatly within the social and cultural milieu of nineteenth-century Australia. Wheatley adroitly presents the radical-nationalist nineteenth-century longing for the country to be the earthly equivalent of the Promised Land, a utopian world freed from the deformation of class exploitation, a haven from the Old World hatreds, tensions and prejudices, a "working man's paradise" (this is the title of an enormously popular book published in 1892 by the utopian socialist and editor of the *Worker*, William Lane) where all men can prosper in egalitarian harmony. She harnesses the Legend of Eureka to the distinctively Australian ethos of mateship, born in that same century of the need for a cultural hero in a newly evolving society, and developed and extended by first-generation Australian authors and critics anxious to stress a new national identity. Yet in the Historical Note which appears at the end of the novel, Wheatley deliberately creates a multicultural Australian history, linking migration from its beginnings with the indigenous Kulin people settling in what was later to be called the Ballarat Goldfields, to the miners with their polyglot backgrounds. This "melting pot" version of the past, complete with its romanticized, eulogized and totally partisan account of Eureka's place in the national identity appears to be designed to prove attractive to a modern-day generation, particularly one currently weaned upon contemporary debates about Australia's future in terms of the hotly-argued republicanism versus monarchist debates of the 1990s. It should be noted that in the years preceding the Centenary of Federation in 2001, the Australian public was subjected to much (often acrimonious) debate concerning the nation's political future, particularly whether it should become a republic or remain a constitutional monarchy with the English Queen as its Head of State. Although republicans were in the slight majority, a referendum in 1998 voted to maintain the existing arrangement, largely because the pro-republican organizations squabbled over the methods of electing the nation's first President (who would, if their campaign proved successful, replace the English monarch as the leader of the people).

In some important respects, then, Wheatley's story amounts to a revisionist chronicling and whitewashing of the past. Against much evidence to the contrary, for example, she paints a picture of nineteenth-century Australian life where the much-vaunted egalitarianism and mateship includes all races, even Dr. Wong, whose Chinese medicine cures Rosa's critically ill baby brother. Wheatley ignores the over-riding concern for racial purity at this time, the prevalence of the notion of "race-suicide," (that is, that the Anglo-Saxon race was being outbred by Asian races), the fears of and the consequent paranoia about miscegenation, or, as one contemporary put it, the "unnatural mongrelizing" of races (Gilmore 9), which would inevitably lead to Australia's decay. There is no indication at all that this was a time in which the stereotyped apparition of the rapacious Asian (seen perhaps most clearly in the cartoon depiction of the coolie-hatted Mongolian Octopus, its tentacles reaching out to ensnare all that defenceless, innocent White Australia held dear), was regularly invoked in the magazines of the day. The goldfields witnessed ugly outbreaks of racial violence, notably the Buckland River and Lambing Flats riots in 1857 and 1861, where the Chinese, the largest non-European group in Australia, and distinctive in their appearance, language, religion and customs, encountered great hostility. They were condemned as a social and economic threat (as sweatworkers and debauchers of white women) and had to pay special entry taxes which applied solely to them. The recent Australian unease about non-white boat people has its historical roots, after all, but Wheatley chooses to erase this unpalatable fact in her desire to inculcate the "right" values in her young audience.

Gary Disher's *The Divine Wind* (1998) is another fascinating text, if for different reasons. Like *A Banner Bold*, this less polemical novel adheres to Stephens' schema by advocating an ideology which is pertinent to contemporary Australia but generally anachronistic for the earlier historical periods. Yet instead of glossing over Australia's awkward racist history, *The Divine Wind* confronts it more or less directly. Disher's novel is set in the pearling town of Broome, in the north-west of Western Australia, against the backdrop of the World War II, and, in keeping with another of Stephens' observations—namely that multiculturalism is often advocated through harnessing the forms of a popular genre (16)—it is primarily a love story about an inter-racial relationship between Hart Penrose, the white son of a pearling boat captain, and Mitsy Sennosuke, the daughter of a Japanese diver employed by Hart's father. In 1941, Broome was a unique and exotic racial mix, as a result of the generations of Japanese, Aboriginal, Malay, Chinese and Indonesian workers who flocked to the hot, balmy tropical town to work for the pearling masters (interestingly, it is now a major tourist destination, where foreigners and other Australians alike come to marvel at its robust fusion of races and ethnic identities, as well as its beautiful beaches and idyllic scenery).

Disher writes about a unique pre-1950s experience of different cultures, yet he does not offer an idealised picture of a community in harmony. He successfully recreates the character of Broome, with its steamy heat, long white beaches and swampy mudflats, and its bungalows on stilts, their broad verandahs choked by shady creepers. He shows that while the children have acclimatised and are "naturally" multicultural, the adults are hampered by outmoded and Old World notions of racial superiority (this generational device also appears in *A Banner Bold*, where Rosa adapts happily to her adventurous new life, never feeling displaced or dispossessed, while her mother is much more cautious and apprehensive). Hart's mother, with her English gentility and class-ridden pretensions, is particularly out of place— "unlike the rest of us she did not have red dirt, mangoes or pearls in her blood" (*The Divine Wind* 2) and "we were too careless, too casual, too democratic for her tastes" (*The Divine Wind* 3). Dabbing at the perspiration on her brow with a delicately-scented lace handkerchief, Mrs. Penrose walks the town, parasol in hand, covering miles in her attempt to escape (when she does manage to return to England midway through the novel, she is shortly afterwards killed in an air-raid, proving that you can never, *ever* go back home again). As part of his rites of passage, young Hart rejects not only those colonial snobberies and prejudices associated with an isolated colonial wife living in the tropics, but also the overtly racist attitudes endemic among the powerful men of the region, including their preoccupation with eugenics, with creating a "Little England," breeding a "superior Australian type" of "good English stock–

–not your continental rubbish" (*The Divine Wind* 27). Hart (surely the nomenclature is not accidental?) rebels against the men's prejudices and appalling treatment of non-white workers, yet his liberal attitudes are sorely tested after Japan becomes Australia's wartime enemy and his sister Alice, now a nurse, goes missing after Japanese planes bomb her hospital shi p. In the face of mounting war losses and enemy attacks upon undefended Broome Harbour, Japanese like Mitsy begin to assume a kind of "shape-shifting" (*The Divine Wind* 125), and even Hart starts to believe the propaganda about the Japanese, who are demonized every evening in Department of Information broadcasts which sound astonishing to a modern-day ear:

> The Japanese violate our deepest and most fundamental instincts. The princi ple of White Australia shall never be overturned by armed aggression. An enemy setting foot on Australian soil will find himself up against a manhood of unparalleled strength and determination. Australia shall remain forever the home of a people whose descendants came here, to southern waters, in peace and established an outpost of the British race [. . .].
>
> Japan is not interested in peaceful co-existence with Australia. We are too valuable to them for that. In fact they hate us, vilely and savagely. But we do not hate. We find the Japanese too loathsome for hatred, and shall not rest until they have been cleared from the earth. (*The Divine Wind* 123-124)

Seeing these kinds of racist attitudes, it is not surprising that when Arthur Caldwell, Australia's first Minister for Immigration, famously qui pped "Two Wongs don't make a White" (in defense of his decision to deport Chinese refugees in 1947), his remark was greeted with general good humor and approbation.

Given that most multicultural novels to date have dealt with far less controversial European-Australian tensions, *The Divine Wind* is unusual in focusing upon Australian and Asian relations, and it is actually rather brave. This novel seems to be mirroring mid-1990s Australia, before the current conservative backlash, when there was an increased political and economic recognition of Australia's place as part of Asia, and an increasing presence of immigrants and refugees from Asian countries. Yet there is also at times a discernible tentativeness about Disher's novel, and it is highly debatable whether Disher shows enough understanding of Asian cultural differences. Part of the problem is that the love affair is seen entirely from a white Australian male perspective, and because of this limited focalization strategy, readers never really get an understanding of Mitsy, or her dilemma of being caught between two worlds. Mitsy is the classic "narrative object" to whom Hart, as a representative of the dominant group, extends understanding and "the privilege of narrative subjectivity" (Stephens 181) never applies to her. It is significant too, that in keeping with the unfinished colonial moment, the novel does not end with a conventional closure. In postwar Australia Hart and Mitsy are about to meet again, after Mitsy has been released from internment as an "enemy alien," but future happiness is by no means certain. The last two sentences of the novel make for rather glum reading: "It won't be easy. We may not make it" (*The Divine Wind* 151).

Moving On

While both these previous texts disseminate multiculturalism by disclosing inherent multicultural tendencies in earlier Australian history, or by attempting to delineate personal histories via transformations from an intercultural subjectivity to a multicultural subjectivity, one final novel deserves attention because it, far more than the previous two, demonstrates that third stage of the multicultural progression that I indicated earlier. At this present moment, as well as Stephens' earlier stages (for I would argue very strongly that these progressions are more shard-like than seamless) some texts are being produced where "authentic" ethnic voices are created by authors who themselves come from minority ethnic backgrounds. Although in writing this I am also mindful of Wendy Morgan's (1995) warning that to authorize a story as authentic by pointing to the (ethnic) identity or knowledge of the author behind it is to forget that the meanings of a text are not so definitively determined, and that it is readers who realize a particular meaning (272). Most importantly, instead of offering generic models of newcomers adapting to a new society and culture or unique diasporic cultures surviving in an ersatz Australian culture, novels such as this one reveal that what is Australian is not the cultural purity, but the *mix*.

These new novels are not "ethnic" texts, but texts about a social world (school, homelife, friends and leisure pursuits) which would be recognized by many, if not most Australian readers. While they feature minority groups in subject positions, multiple focalizations, and are told from an insider perspective, above all else they are important because they actually take their multicultural social contexts for granted as they get on with their plots (they are, in this respect, similar to a number of Australian films of the 1990s, like *The Heartbreak Kid* (1993), where ethnic identity is implicit rather than explicit). The characters' cultural heritage is incidental rather than pivotal, one of a number of factors influencing their subjectivity. After all, as French-Australian writer Sophie Masson (1995) comments:

> People aren't only "nesbies" (Non English Speaking Backgrounds) or "ethnics" or whatever: they are themselves, with their own circumstances. My non-English speaking background and experience has been an important catalyst in my life: but so has my interest in religion and mythology, my love of music, my dislike of smugness and complacency. (14-15)

Matt Zurbo's *Idiot Pride* (1997) is representative of this trend. It never refers in any explicit or jarring way to the cultural backgrounds of the characters, and it is devoid of cultural clichés or emphases upon its characters' exotic or alien lifestyles and behaviours. Instead it incorporates ethnicity in a low-key manner, as a "normal" part of social life, and presents none of that hackneyed and hoarily problematic interface between ethnic identity and mainstream Australian life. There is a total absence of those often tokenistic cultural stereotypes where multiculturalism is largely presented as a spectacular form of ethnicization involving costumes, customs and cooking—the so-called "pasta and polka" approach to migrant culture (Jupp 330). Zurbo's characters are not alien to Australian society but feel very much a part of it. *Idiot Pride* (shortlisted for the Children's Book of the Year for Older Readers in 1997) deals with the lives of second-generation migrant families of Hungarian, Italian, Greek and Russian extraction, and in particular a group of seventeen-year-old boys (Gianpi, Johnny, Carlo, Serge and Matt) living in grimy inner-city Melbourne. With its tales of "grubby little working-class kids" (*Idiot Pride* 14), "scruffy mongrels in the inner-city Commission flats" (*Idiot Pride* 70), "depressing, rundown, four-smelly-old shops shopping centres" (*Idiot Pride* 57), broken homes, little money, and mothers on welfare, this novel foregrounds issues of class (and hegemonic masculinity) rather than ethnicity. Very much a text of its time, *Idiot Pride* speaks on behalf of disillusioned and disempowered youth and emphasizes life dominated by boredom and aimlessness, reflecting the "grunge" fad of the mid-to-late 1990s: "we're doing nothing, going nowhere" (*Idiot Pride* 64) and "the day's going nowhere" (*Idiot Pride* 111) as well.

Idiot Pride is a novel about streetwise young men searching for their identity, about how they hate school and are bored by its sheer irrelevance to their lives:

> "We sit around each lesson, scratching our balls and fannies, going insane, as a wog who has trouble with Aussie tries to read some dumb-arse language that died hundreds of years ago." (*Idiot Pride* 123)

The novel is primarily concerned with boys' relationships with their peers, their casual experimentation with sex and anxieties about sexual performance, especially for first-timers (it is especially good in indicating that the "I-fuck-therefore-I-am" mentality of many testosterone-fuelled teenage boys, of whatever ethnic background, is not all-inclusive). *Idiot Pride* is about camaraderie, dreams, and regrets, its rather retrospective air reminiscent of actor Carrie Fisher's remark that "the very best thing about going off the rails as an adolescent is that you get over it while you're young, then you talk about it for the rest of your life" (qtd. in Harlen 11).

In Zurbo's novel the characters are not contrived to serve ethnic stereotypes, and the lack of any patronizing generalizations leaves the characters free to use terms such as "wog" (Australian slang for a non-Anglo migrant) without offense or selfconsciousness. Instead of being there as devices to show foreignness or isolation, the characters reveal the multi-faceted reality, the multi-ethnic composition of contemporary Australian inner-city communities. In the words of one reader, this novel illustrates the point that:

> you cannot single out one group as other or outsider, our identity as Australians is defined by the fact that we are all other. We cannot all claim to be white AngloSaxons, with similar spiritual and social beliefs. It is our acceptance of the differences in our midst, our ability to maintain a separate cultural identity whilst still functioning in a diverse society that make us typically Australian. (Pase 9)

In recent novels like the one discussed above, I would argue very strongly that the intertextuality of gender, ethnic and familial themes resonates with readers even if they do not share those same gendered, ethnic or family experiences. This particular point is reinforced in Pieter Aquilia's (2000) analysis of *Head On* (1998), a recent Australian youth movie which deals with a gay Greek-Australian boy living in Melbourne

> in working across the usual line between an "ethnic" "minority" topic and the Anglo "mainstream" it begins to redefine what Australian national cinema and Australian national culture are, inscribing the Greek-Australian identity as equally central to any experience and not marginal or different. (108)

The crucial difference between these kinds of texts and those representing the earlier stages is that in texts like these *ethnicity is not a marker of cultural difference, but an accepted part of Australian life.* Instead of crossing the boundaries between "us" and "them," Hungarian-Australian or Italian-Australian experiences are fully commensurate with Anglo-Australian ones. In texts like this, where second and third-generation non-Anglo-Australian writers are finding their places in shaping a national identity, we seem to have reached a point where non-Anglo-Australians are no longer seen as in any way undesirable or suspect, marginalized or displaced, but reveal that creolization rather than ghettoization or assimilation is nowadays the norm. Ethnic otherness, once implicitly depicted as "deviating from a norm and therefore inevitably subordinate" (Stephens 4), has been domesticated at last. Given that these multicultural texts are sites where the meanings of a plurality of cultures are being contested, reworked and renegotiated, one would hope that a further progression would include Asian-Australian families in this same naturalistic, all-inclusive way.

Final Forebodings

It remains to be seen whether the events towards the end of the first decade of the New Millennium in Australia and elsewhere will produce a triumphant counter-discourse of assimilation and/or exclusion, and whether the tolerant pluralism of the multicultural society, so comparatively recently and arduously asserted, is exposed as fragile and illusory. In the future, Australians might continue to accept and embrace diversity, or we might harken back to the hegemony of the old Anglo-Celtic order, those old stereotypes of national identity, the insularity and xenophobia and close-mindedness of a bygone era, where migrants were tolerated as long as they merged into society as soon as was decently proper, and where appropriately grateful, well-educated English speakers were cordially received, but the attitudes towards immigrants not fitting these rigid criteria were grudging and uncharitable. A children's literature reflecting a society intent upon renovating the fading picture of a homogenous Australia, one peopled by junior Crocodile Dundees saying, like Nino's God, "Howyergoin'mate, orright?" (*They're a Weird Mob* 204) really would be a step backwards.

Works Cited

Aquilia, Peter. "Wog Drama and 'White Multiculturalists': The Role of Non Anglo-Australian Film and Television in Shaping a National Identity." *Journal of Australian Studies* 65 (2000): 104-108.

Culotta, Nino [John O'Grady]. *They're a Weird Mob.* Sydney: Ure Smith, 1957.

Dale, Leigh. "Mainstreaming Australia." *The Australian Legend and its Discontents.* Ed. Richard Nile. St. Lucia: U of Queensland P, 2000. 311-325.

Disher, Garry. *The Divine Wind.* Sydney: Hodder, 1998.

Gilmore, Mary. "The Race or the Mongrel?" *Worker* 24 December 1914: 9.

Harlen, Jonathon. "A Writer's Perspective." *Magpies* 12.2 (May 1997): 11.

Head On. Dir. Ana Kokkinos. Prod. Jane Scott. Palace, 1998.

Hirst, John. "Aborigines and Migrants: Diversity and Unity in Multicultural Australia?" *Australian Book Review* 36-37 (February/March 2001): 30-33.

Jupp, James. "Immigrant Society." *The Australian Legend and its Discontents.* Ed. Richard Nile. St. Lucia: U of Queensland P, 2000. 326-338.

Masson, Sophie. "Writing from Another Culture." *Viewpoint* 3.3 (Spring 1995): 12-15.

McGregor. *Profile of Australia.* Ringwood, Victoria: Penguin, 1966.

Morgan, Wendy. " 'You've Come a Long Way, Baby': Multicultural Literature for Children." *Australian Journal of Language and Literacy* 18.4 (November 1995): 270-280.

Pase, Cristiana. "Your Mother Must be a Good Cook." *Viewpoint* 7.1 (Autumn 1999): 8-9.

Patience, Alan. "Politics of Recognition." *Australian Book Review* 34-35 (December 2000/January 2001): 227.

Sheridan, Greg. "No Grounds for Racial Paranoia." *Australian* 20 December 2001: 11.

Stratton, Jon. "Not Just Another Multicultural Story." *Journal of Australian Studies* 66 (2000): 23-47.

Starke, Ruth. "What is a Multicultural Book?" *Viewpoint* 3.1 (Autumn 1995): 22-24.

Stephens, John. "Advocating Multiculturalism: Migrants in Australian Children's Literature after 1972." *Children's Literature Association Quarterly* 15.4 (1990): 180-185.

——. "Multiculturalism in Recent Australian Children's Fiction: (Re)connecting Selves Through Personal and National Histories." *Other Worlds, Other Lives: Children's Literature Experiences.* Ed. Myrna Machet, Sandra Olen, and Thomas van der Walt. Pretoria: Unisa, 1996. 1-19.

The Heartbreak Kid. Dir. Michael Jenkins. Prod. Ben Gannon. Roadshow Entertainment, 1993.

Wheatley, Nadia. *A Banner Bold.* Sydney: Scholastic, 2000.

Zurbo, Matt. *Idiot Pride.* Ringwood, Victoria: Penguin, 1997.

Reading Kerry Greenwood
The Fisher Queen of Australian Crime Writing

Toni Johnson-Woods

Australia has a particularly long association with crime fiction; especially crime fiction written by women (see Sussex 1989). And since the 1980s, female writers of crime fiction have continued to garner attention and critical praise. In *Killing Women* (1993) Delys Bird considered the influence and output of prominent female crime writers: Marele Day (b. 1947), Claire McNab (b. 1940), Susan Geason (b. 1946), Kerry Greenwood (b. 1954), Finola Moorhead (b. 1947), and Jan McKemmish (b. 1950). Of all the successful Australian female crime writers, why focus on Kerry Greenwood? Because her interpretation of the crime genre warrants further investigation. For too long she has remained under the critical radar, perhaps ham pered by her accessible style. What Greenwood provides is a more domestic literary space in which to consider how women articulate their social, political and sexual agendas. Second, her high sales figures and continued popularity demonstrate that Greenwood's blend of crime, history and humour appeals to readers in both Australia and in the USA. As American reviewer David Pitt (2007) noted

> Australian crime fiction is becoming increasingly popular in North America, but Greenwood's series, thanks to its sparkling evocation of how the 1920s roared Down Under, manages to stand apart from the crowd. Anyone who hasn't discovered Phryne Fisher by now should start making up for lost time. (http://www.amazon.ca/Green-Mill-Murder-Phryne-Mystery/dp/1590582403)

Greenwood is praised for her stories' rollicking good fun, her feisty heroines and her ability to weave a deft crime story with a social consciousness. But despite popularity, sales and glowing reviews Greenwood has received little critical attention; this chapter seeks to redress this imbalance.

Australia's first international best-selling *Mystery of a Hansom Cab* (1886) by Fergus Hume (b. 1859 – d. 1932) was set in Melbourne and it is in Melbourne that Greenwood sets her novels. Kerry Greenwood is a lawyer-cum-writer who has published nearly forty novels, twenty of which are detective novels. Nearly twenty years ago, Greenwood started writing crime, by accident. After publisher Hilary McPhee read a manuscript Greenwood had submitted for the Vogel Literary Award (a yearly prize awarded for an unpublished manuscript), she contacted Greenwood. During their talk, McPhee told Greenwood she did not need historical novels but asked Greenwood if she could write mysteries. Greenwood "agreed so fast that the words echoed off the wall" ("On Phryne Fisher" 2004-2005).

Protagonists

On her way home from their meeting, Greenwood sat on a Melbourne tram and planned her character. She believed that once she had the character right, the rest would follow. Disgruntled with female roles in detective fiction, Greenwood decided to make her own detecting rules. Though a fan of Dorothy L. Sayers (b. 1893 – d. 1957), she disliked the fact that Lord Peter Wimsey had to rescue Sayers' damsels in distress. She wanted to create a female character who had all the advantages of the male adventurer and so she created a Simone Templar, a Jane Bond, a Phillipa Marlowe, Phryne (rhymes with briny) Fisher.

The Hon. Phryne Fisher is named after a famed courtesan in Ancient Greece. Her second name, Fisher is a multi-facted pun, as Greenwood explains

> Her second name is derived elaborately as a scholastic joke. She is a Fisher of Men, as all detectives are. Her name also reflects the Grail Cycle Roi Pêcheur, the Sinner or Fisher King. I have always liked that absurd pun on Sin (pécher) and Fish. And there was a street in Paris called la Rue de la Chat qui Pêche which was a good place to find a gigolo—all of the information had come to me piecemeal from various sources. ("On Phryne Fisher" 2004-2005)

Phryne is a wealthy socialite-turned-sleuth residing in Melbourne in the 1920s. She is beautiful, sophisticated, titled and versed in the arts of armed combat. Basically she is someone who has all the talents and capabilities of male adventurers, only female. She smokes gaspers, drinks cocktails, drives fast cars and flies faster aeroplanes. She is unafraid of heights, depths or any dangers that are presented to her. She might not leap tall buildings at a single bound but her super-hero qualities is a response to other contemporary female detectives whom Greenwood found too guilt-ridden

> The modern women detectives are afflicted with self-doubt, neglect their diet, worry about exercise, think they may be growing fat as if fat was a disfigurement, and are generally afflicted with low self-esteem and guilt. I wanted a character without guilt, with boundless self-esteem, as a role model, perhaps. ("On Phryne Fisher" 2004-2005)

Critics have noted that Phryne has become increasingly so perfect, so much a cipher, that she is almost a parody. Phryne's aristocratic heritage harkens back to the early days of crime fiction when only the privileged had the leisure and freedom to indulge their interest in crime solving.

Australian readers and writers show a marked preference for the amateur sleuth—that is to say, the person who solves crimes not for money or because it is their job. Stephen Knight (1997) posits that this stems from Australia's criminal beginnings, and that our literature mirrors Australia's distrust of the police figure, and he has traced the "vanishing policeman" in Australian literature; he contends that "suspicions of authority developed through the forms of the convict novel" (128). So it is not surprising, given our literary heritage, that Greenwood's stories minimize the role of the professional police force. Her books focus on the female protagonists and their flirtation with crime. In some ways, the stories might best be described as female adventure stories rather than crime detection, as there is little in the way of overt detecting. When Phryne is confronted with an enigma, she sets out to find who did what to whom and when and then settles it all with remarkable aplomb. Corinna Chapman, on the other hand, is a very reluctant sleuth and her first book ends with the words "I quit."

Phryne's historical adventures are in direct contrast to Greenwood's later invention, Corrina Chapman. Fifteen years after the glam Phryne first appeared, Greenwood started another mystery series starring accountant-turned-baker Corinna Chapman. Corinna is far removed from the glamorous Phryne. She is rotund, works for a living and lacks social standing, technological gadgetry and fast cars. She is not trained in armed combat but bakes a mean loaf of bread. Corinna is more irritable and less perfect. She is Phryne's contemporary equivalent—without the trappings of perfection. Corinna lacks Phyrne's physicality—she does not dash from place to place solving crimes, the most energetic thing she does is to rise at 4am to bake bread. Corinna's sleuthing is more of the cerebral kind—crimes come to her, she doesn't need to seek it out. What they both share is a penchant for the comforts of life.

In *Sleuths in Skirts* (2002), DellaCava and Engel noted that the female protagonists often reflect the writer's alter ego (xi). Greenwood freely admits that Phryne is a wish fulfilment (Schwartz 1992): she is slim, always impeccably dressed and socially adept. She is surrounded by doting relatives and supportive friends; she is generous and likeable but still wholly her own woman. She dispenses kindness and justice in equal measures. While Phryne is happy with her life, Corinna is content. Her bakery is a success, she has a constant and dashingly handsome lover and a loving cat. Her apartment is generally not beset by strangers and dangers; she lives a life of comparative ease. The two protagonists present idealised lives: they both have the money and emotional support to do exactly what they want to—and are a far cry from the female detectives of yesteryear. They are, to use Stephen Knight's phrase, "Utopian fantasies" for professional women.

Adding a piquant dash to the fantasy is the protagonist's sensuality. Greenwood rejects the virgin-whore binary assigned to women in the hard-boiled school of crime fiction, she finds it "exceptionally offensive" (Schwartz 11). She also scorns the sexual neutrality of the maiden-aunt school of sleuthing, for example Miss Marple created by Agatha Christie (b. 1890 - d. 1976). She therefore gave both of her protagonists healthy and fulfilling sexual relationships—though of a differing kind. Phryne takes partners as her desire takes her. In *Cocaine Blues* (1989) Phryne dallies with Sasha a deliciously beautiful Russian ballet dancer. In *Urn Burial* (1996), she sleeps with another young man, only to find him dallying with another man a few chapters later. In *Ruddy Gore* (1995), she saves a man who will become her regular lover, Lin Chung. Lin Chung marries—*Murder in Montparnasse* (2002), but the marriage does not disrupt their relationship. However, Phryne continues to warm her bed with a string of lovers, young and old, radical and conservative. She therefore has the best of both worlds, a constant and devoted lover and a string of exciting new partners to keep her amused during her various investigations. On the other hand, Corinna, is much less sexually adventurous. She has one steady lover, Soup Run guard Daniel. The two meet and fall in love in the first book and so far Daniel remains her faithful though sometimes absent lover. Sex Greenwood-style is satisfying, exciting and uncomplicated.

Aside from wonderful men, both women enjoy consoling baths, self-pampering and scrumptious food. Greenwood devotes considerable fictional space, often up to a page, describing food feasts:

> Laid out on the buffer was the Cold Collation of the Gods. Small cups of perfectly seasoned vichyssoise were gathered at one end of the white draped buffer. Pump pink prawns studded the seafood aspic as thickly as daisies in a springtime meadow. A whole baron of beef squatted glistening in a bed of dark green bitter lettuce, rare paper-thin slices rolling from its side. An entire salmon, sliced and decorated with radish flowers lay shining in a silver dish. A nearby salve held oysters, freshly opened, with lemon juice in a jug beside. Little squares of rye-bread toast, sliced onions and hard boiled eggs accompanied the black pearls of the Beluga caviar, a gift from the Russian ambassador, where piled with a lavish hand onto their silver dish bedded in crushed ice: the manner in which Phryne always served caviar. An aspic gallimaufry of poultry [. . .] reposed on a broad salver, a golden jelly which trembled slightly. (*The Castlemaine Murders* 61)

Phryne's table is littered with the trappings of wealth, from the expensive salmon and prawns to the silver salvers. The carefully arrange table highlights Phryne's sensibility, she "always" serves her caviar in crushed ice, the beef is "paper-thin." The banquet also reinforces her social position; the Russian ambassador has seen fit to gift to her a quantity of one of the world's most prized delicacies, Beluga caviar. In this story she has no dealings with the ambassador and thus his present underscores her social standing. Items such as the seafood aspic and gallimaufry of poultry reflect Greenwood's attention to historical detail. Food is equally important to Corinna, perhaps even more so because feeding people is germane to her business. While her tables are not as exotic as Phryne, her bread and muffin concoctions are described in mouth-watering detail.

Accompanying the many meals is a host of exotic and tasty sounding cocktails, usually Phryne's are whipped up by her eponymously-named manservant, Mr. Butler. His "Considering Cocktail" recipe is printed at the end of *The Castlemaine Murders* (2003). Likewise recipes for muffins and soup appear at the end of the Corinna Chapman stories. Food and drink are not obsessions, indeed the heroines consume modestly; they are markers of wealth and social standing and sources of comfort. They are dispensed in times of crises; food and drink are civilising.

Furthermore, a soak in a bath with appropriately scented products is central to soothing shattered nerves—*Death Before Wicket* (2005)—or to instigating sexual activity—*Heavenly Pleasures* (2004). Increasingly in the protagonist's hectic lives, they allow themselves restful naps, long baths, soothing cocktails, exquisite lovemaking—fictional pamperings that provide the reader a vicarious slice of their utopian ideals.

Secondary Characters

Clever and capable as Greenwood's heroines are, they need a posse of helpers to help them solve crimes. Phryne has Bert and Cec—two ex-wharfies (wharf labourers) who provide the muscle and underworld information that Phryne needs to solve crimes. Bert and Cec are honest, hardworking heroes the antithesis of the idle, indulgent and corrupt upper classes. When her family is placed in danger Phryne uses the service of Pi, Lin Chung's Shaolin monk. Corinna's companions are drawn from the helpers on the Soup Run, Daniel and the other heavies and nuns who nightly provided sustenance to Melbourne's indigent and Phryne is aided by Scotch female doctor, Dr. MacMillian who provides medical assistance and information; Corinna has a Wicca witch to give her alternative medical advice. And of course amateur sleuths cannot always work outside the law. Phryne meets Detective Inspector Jack Robinson during her first foray into crime; and though he's resentful of her intrusion into his cases, he comes to respect her abilities and in later books seeks her help. Indeed, she helps him solve a domestic crisis in *Queen of the Flowers* (2004). Similarly Corinna adopts Senior Constable Lepidoptera White as her aid-in-law; and as the series progresses so does Corinna's relationship with White. Her bakery assistants give her the street cred and the gossip she needs. Thus, Greenwood creates extended networks which become increasingly familial.

Phryne and Corinna's families are similarly unconventional. Phryne has two adopted daughters, a personal maid whom she treats more as a confidante but who likes to keep an appropriate distance. Phryne's cook and butler, sister and adopted daughters create a proto-family which surrounds and supports her. Corinna is estranged from her commune-dwelling hippy parents; instead, she finds companionship with the neighbours in her Romanesque apartment block. Both households have a menagerie of pets, dogs and cats some of which have contributed to solving crimes. These familial relationships are, as DellaCava and Engel noted, essential elements in the female-centred crime fiction (35).

Dotted throughout the stories are less conventional characters than those typically found in detective fiction. There is Phryne's gay sister and her philanthropic lover who worked with the poor in London, the ex-circus performer turned nun (see *The Castlemaine Murders*); Mable the kind prostitute who saves Dorothy and the female elephant trainer Dulcie

Fawnshawe (see *Queen of the Flowers*); Meroe, the Hungarian Wicca witch, Mistress Dread the gender ambiguous dominatrix; Monk the elderly and erudite classics professor who offers insightful Latin qui ps; the elegant Mrs. Sylvia Dawson who demonstrates the old age is not synonymous with senility or bad clothes. These com plementary characters invite readers to consider their own prejudices. Mr Burton a circus dwarf who is writing a PhD on disjunction between literary depictions of the poor and the "real social conditions," he explains his PhD topic

> most prostitutes stop being prostitutes when they have, for instance paid off their debts, saved enough to open a business, accepted a proposal of marriage [. . .] inherited money or decided to move to another city and get a straight job. Prostitutes do not kill themselves at a greater rate than the general population. But what is even more curious is, from Dickens onwards, the authors know that they are not depicting the truth, if they have done any research at all, they know that they are just people. (*The Castlemaine Murders* 58)

The sophisticated Mr. Burton therefore offers more to the reader than the label "dwarf" while discoursing about the stereotyping of prostitutes. Perhaps the most obvious feature of Greenwood's worlds is their abundance of female characters. Women populate her stories at all levels. In this way, Greenwood provides a myriad of female role models. In the *Queen of the Flowers,* there is the ex-circus performer turned nun, the kindhearted prostitute Mabel, Phryne's lesbian sister and her philanthropic friend. Phryne's house has one male, Mr. Butler, and five females (Phryne, her two adopted daughters, her maid Dorothy and Mrs. Butler). Corinna too lives in a female dominated world—there are eight females and three male households in her Insula apartment building. Only one apartment has a mixed couple, and that's a father and daughter. The men play a supporting role; they are intelligent, fun and sexy but not the focus of the novels.

Social, Moral and Political and Class Issues

DellaCava and Engel noted that one of the traits of contem porary female crime fiction is the propensity for the protagonists to become embroiled in crimes which highlight women's issues and concerns. With a female-centred cast, it was inevitable that the crimes in Greenwood's books most often im pact upon women. When readers are first introduced to Phryne in *Cocaine Blues*, she has carefully secreted one of Marie Stopes devices, a diaphragm so that the customs official will not confiscate it. The diaphragm becomes emblematic; Phryne prevents Dorothy from murdering her would-be seducer (and then hires her as a maid) and she brings to justice a backyard abortionist who has been butchering pregnant women. In a later story, *Queen of the Flowers*, an abandoned pregnant woman goes mad after giving birth. Spousal abuse also provides material for several stories. In *Death by Wicket* (2005), Dorothy's sister escapes the drudgery and abuse of married life and goes to work for the notorious Sydney prostitute Tilly Devine not as a sex-worker but as an instructor; her job is to teach Tillys' girls etiquette because their job demands a certain level of sophistication. Child abuse is central to the themes of *Murder on the Ballarat Train* (1991), *Away with the Fairies* (2001) and *Queen of the Flowers*. Corinna's brush with abandoned and abused children has been a feature in her crimes. Throughout the series, Greenwood's protagonists demonstrate an admirable social consciousness—Phryne and Corinna help people in distress, abandoned and abused children, single mothers, drug addicts and the homeless.

Crime is "conservative, moralists, simplistic and punitive in its values (Bird and Walker 9) but crime-solvers' morals are remarkably mutable. While their job is to find evil doers and see they get their just desserts, they have, like Superman an ethical code which is just shy of the legal system. Phryne and Corinna share a highly developed moral code. When they solve crimes, they ensure that justice prevails. When it seems that the law promises to be an ass, they step in. For example in *The Green Mill Murder* (1993), an evil-doer accidentally plunges to his death when he loses his footing in the dark; Phryne does not report his death because it means his hermit brother would inherit the family fortune and have to leave his idyllic bush existence. She often muses on the shortcomings of the legal system and has her protagonists solve crimes for the somewhat incapable Melbourne police force.

Greenwood's political agenda is usually viewed through asides and metaphors. Corinna's assistants are as "thin as a politician's promise" (*Heavenly Pleasures* 32); she ponders that "isn't a world with George Bush in it bad enough" (*Heavenly Pleasures* 53). Corinna's ex-husband is a money grasping banker and she delights when he almost bankrupts himself with his shady dealings. Phyrne's sympathy with strikes and workers' issues shows her political hand—*Death at Victoria Dock* (1992). Her heroines might have money but they also have generosity in abundance.

Though Phryne might enjoy wealth and Corinna financial independence, they have at heart working-class sensibilities; they are offended by the rich and the privileged. When Phyrne receives an invitation from a wealthy Melbourne couple, she notes its "tasteless and flamboyant" engraving and is even more appalled by the purple ink and ill-formed handwriting. After phoning her acceptance she is unimpressed by the "social pinnacle" of Melbourne which she decides is "grim" (*Cocaine Blues* 53). Her impression does not improve when she see their ostentatious house and the grasping hostess who has asked two of her guests, Russian ballet dancers, to perform for their supper. This breach of etiquette shocks the unflappable Phryne. In *Murder in the Dark* (2006) the eccentric and aristocratic Templar twins are post-decadent in their Beardsley-esque lifestyle—one cannot help but shudder at their constant striving to be "outrageous." Despite the tempting food, the expensive gadgetry and the fabulous clothes, Phryne finds the trappings of wealth vulgar and seems more at home in the circus or the theatre or the hospital than she does in the drawing room.

Place and Setting

As Stephen Knight has noted, place and setting are of primary importance to Australian crime fiction. The terror and beauty of the bush provides the ideal atmospheric play for the mystery needed for crime fiction (158). Traditionally, the Australian landscape has been fictionalised and realised as female (Schaffer 1988)—the virgin land offered opportunities for men to penetrate its mysterious interior and to plunder the land for its wealth. Increasingly, though, cities have replaced the bush as the loci of crime. Since the 1950s, the highly settled urban areas and their mean streets have come to be recognised as masculine. In the fiction of Greenwood, the increased anxiety about the city reflects the increased cultural awareness that the city streets are often mean—as Knight notes, the mean streets are replaced with a non-anxious urbanity (147). Greenwood, however, wrests the streets from male clutches. Phryne lives in the not-so-reputable suburb of St. Kilda and Corinna in her inner city bakery and residence. Phryne's house is close to the widest variety of "characters" and from her Calico Lane location Corinna she more closely interacts with the contemporary social problems of inner-city—drugs, nightclubs, and homelessness. The protagonists might venture into the Greenwood's streets are mean but not vicious; she prefers not to dwell on the grittier realism common in many contemporary novels. Greenwood's stories celebrate Marvellous Melbourne whether in 1928 or 2008.

Occasionally Phryne ventures outside Melbourne to solve crimes. She has weekended in a gothic mansion in the Victorian countryside (see *Urn Burial*), taken a train journey to Ballarat (see *Murder on the Ballarat Train*), travelled to the goldfields (see *The Castlemaine Murders*) and enjoyed a P & O cruise to New Zealand—*Death by Water* (2005). But perhaps her most confronting visit was her trip to Sydney in *Death Before Wicket*. Traditionally Sydney and Melbourne are rival cities and so it is no surprise that the thoroughly Melbournian Phryne finds Sydney brash. It is a crowded, humid and grimy place where the taxi drivers are over familiar and the students too bohemian; however, it is saved by the harbour which Dot extemporises as a "patchwork quilt. A huge, beautiful, complicated appliqué that changes every minute" (*Death Before Wicket* 5). Greenwood's cityscapes reflect that Australia is the one of most highly urbanised nation in the world, a fact ignored in the bush-literature of the nineteenth century—her stories reflect the reality of the twenty-first century and not the romanticised notions of yesteryear.

Style

Greenwood dislikes the stark reality of the hard-boiled school of crime fiction; she prefers happy endings, romantic subplots, and lush details—all of which serve to offset the suspense which is considered essential in crime fiction (Schwartz 11). Simon Caterson (2006) found her "chatty and relatively free of suspense" style "exasperating" though he admitted it "is all a matter of taste, of course, but I much prefer terse to twee" (24) and Stuart Coupe (1998) agreed that Greenwood was not his "cup of Hemlock." That two critics, both male, do not like her style is not surprising; her stories are guilty of being "chatty," domestic, and "superficial [. . .] but pleasing nonetheless" (Vernon 88). This style is part of the Greenwood charm—the sleuthing is done "between times" of orgies, dressing, eating and just being jolly (Vernon 88). Readers who have laboured through decades of gritty realism and bloody serial murder stories find Greenwood's mix a comforting antidote.

Greenwood also commits an almost unpardonable crime and mixes her genres. She laces her crime stories with generous helpings of romance. The blend doubles the potential readershi p—crime and romance readers can enjoy elements of what I term "crimance." Crimance was most notable in the successful Stephanie Plum series of USA author Janet Evanovich which debuted in 1994. One of the hallmarks of romance fiction is, of course, the happy ending and Greenwood's explanation of her endings reinforces the comfort and solace which her novels and style offer "What makes a happy ending for me is that sense of, yeah, of comfort and order. Someone's cooking something, the door is shut, the bad guys are gone and everything is back to where it ought to be" (qtd. in Cremen 17). And just in case the reader thinks Greenwood is unaware of the elements of crime fiction; she salts her tales with sly references. One character in *Urn Burial* is named Miss Mary Mead in reference to the fictional home of Agatha Christie's Miss Marple, and in *Ruddy Gore* one of the stage hands volunteers to be Phryne's "irregular," an homage to Baker Street irregulars who run errands for "the Great Detective" Sherlock Holmes.

Pace varies considerably in crime fiction. Plots can be high-octane stories which leap from action-packed event to event. This is not the case with Greenwood's plots. Her plots are as leisurely as a Phryne Fisher bath. The meandering pace is created by Greenwood's narrative diversions, the lush descri ptions which halt the text and defuse the suspense. Paragraphs are devoted to depictions of food (as above) and clothing

> It was a deep claret, edged with dark mink; evidently a design by Erte [. . .] the deep décolleté was artfully concealed with strings of jet beads [. . .] it had a train but not so long as to be inconvenient, and the huge sleeves, inspired by an Im perial Chinese robe, slid gracefully together at the front to make a muff for her hands. The deep colour contrasted effectively with Phryne's pale skin and black hair, and as she moved the liquefaction of the satin flowed over her limbs, moulding her as if in gelatine. It was a perfectly decent but utterly erotic dress [. . .]. (*Cocaine Blues* 57-58)

These narrative asides have become hallmarks of Greenwood's fiction and allow her to incorporate the extensive research which gives her stories an historical authenticity and which pleases so many readers and reviewers (Turnbull 2003; Barlow 2003). As DellaCava and Engel noted, mystery readers are generally affluent college graduates who try to learn something from whatever they read (viii). At the end of most books, Greenwood now includes bibliographies which demonstrates the breadth of her research; this is not grandstanding, she imagines the reader, like herself, has in interest in learning. Greenwood admits that she likes to writes stories that educate readers:

> My favourite detective writer, Dorothy Sayers, always included a slab of solid research in her books and I decided, in homage, to do that too. In each of my novels you will find out something different about Melbourne in 1928, as well as the detective story. It is not so much a mission as a gift to the readers. ("On Phryne Fisher" 2004-2005)

Capitalising on her research, Greenwood usually includes epigrams from appropriate sources to unify the novel's theme. Thus *Ruddy Gore*, a story tracing a death in the theatre during a performance of Gilbert and Sullivan's supernatural opera "Ruddigore, or The Witch's Curse" (1887), is studded with Gilbert and Sullivan quotes and *Urn Burial* has quotes from Sir Thomas Browne's *Hydriotaphia, Urn Burial or a Discourse of the Sepulchral Urns Lately found in Norfolk* (1658). Greenwood's close attention detail and historical research have earned her a loyal readershi p.

Publishing History

It is no wonder Hilary McPhee wanted Greenwood to write mysteries in 1989, the demand for female detective fiction had been increasing steadily. In their quantitative analysis, DellaCava and Engel calculated that between 1890 and 1979 there were 45 female sleuths; they added ten times that number (477) after 1980. In 1992, female crime stories were the "publishing rage" claimed *New York Times* critic Marilyn Stasio (1991). Though she only had a contract for two mysteries, Greenwood has written sixteen Phryne Fisher books.

At first, Greenwood's novels appeared without little fanfare; however, after six novels in as many years, critics were regularly reviewing her latest offering. Reviews listed at Factiva newspaper database demonstrate her increasing popularity: reviews jum ped from three for the first Phryne novel in 1989 to twenty-eight in 2002 (see *Away with the Fairies*) and her latest book *Murder in the Dark* has eighteen reviews. Allen and Unwin reckons Greenwood's Australian sales at around 200,000—a substantial number for an Australian author. However, she fares even better overseas where USA publisher Fawcett has print runs of 250,000 for each title. Reader reviews at the Amazon.com site demonstrate that Greenwood's formula works just as well in the USA as it does in Australia.

While many enjoy Greenwood's novels, the most common com plaint is the style over substance; Hanrahan found *Away with the Fairies* "clever" but "the writing is a bit pedestrian"; Cremen acknowledges that Greenwood's stories probably won't win awards (17) but still they are "definitely not fluff and nonsense" (Mulligan 2004). Greenwood devotees do not find her digressions about fashion, food and bathing annoying and forgive the breach of crime etiquette; they welcome the "fantasy" element and overlook the "slightness" of the plot (Rev. of *Earthly Delights* 2004).

The original McPhee Gribble covers of the Phryne Fisher books demonstrate the perverse nature of the publishing industry. Despite having a female heroine, males dominate the first releases—on *Urn Burial* a bearded miner holds a kerosene lamp and on *Ruddy Gore* a elegantly dressed male grasps a walking stick. All are "realistic" photographic covers; designed to convey to readers a masculinist and historical but unidentifiable period. They are unimaginative at the best and misleading in the extreme. Clearly, McPhree Gribble was hesitant about putting a female detective on the covers; in the twenty-first century, Allen and Unwin had no such qualms. Allen and Unwin revamped the covers for their reissues in 2003. Beth Norling perfectly captures the glamorous and winsome Phryne in her covers. The art-deco backgrounds, the detailed dresses and the languid poses capture the essential Phryne. She sits where she belongs on the covers of the books an appropriate visual rendition of her stories.

In keeping with contemporary marketing practices, Allen and Unwin have also given Phryne and Corinna online websites (see http://www.phrynefisher.com and http://www.earthlydelights.net.au). At the Fisher website one can browse Phryne's horoscope, a cast of characters and a glossary of Australian sayings. Recipes are available at both websites and Corinna reminds readers to "obey your hunger." The Earthly Delights website has the added advantage of downloadable chapters.

Conclusion

Greenwood has produced a different kind of detective fiction. In her two series, she presents her readers with different ways to read crime. In Phryne, the flapper with a pistol in her garter, Greenwood recreates an exciting past crammed with exotic food, designer clothes and jolly orgies. Just as nineteenth century writer Mary Fortune recreated the goldfields for readers; so too Greenwood recreates Melbourne in the Jazz Era. In Corinna, Greenwood offers her readers the comforting smells and tastes of inner-city Melbourne, sure it is a rough and sometimes cruel place but things are always set to rights by the reluctant but capable baker. In total Greenwood has written twenty detective novels—and in 2003 Greenwood was awarded the Ned Kelly Lifetime Contribution to Crime Writing.

Greenwood explores the "female" dimension of Australian crime writing. Her concerns are not those of the bush but of the city–it is not flooding plains that breathe danger but predatory males and abortionists. The bush is not melancholy but silent. It is part of Australia's criminal past. Instead, she invites readers to warm their toes at the hearthside of an innercity Melbourne, a pleasing city of historical significance, considerable charm and some naughty criminals. But never fear, there is always the diamond-sharp Phryne or the domestic-goddess Corinna to sort out the baddies. In her crime writing, Greenwood offers solace and shelter to the crime-weary. She has recovered the domesticity of the hearth and home and serves to her readers a considering cocktail with a hefty splash of redem ption.

Works Cited

"Ruddigore, or The Witch's Curse." Creators. William Schwenck Gilbert and Arthur Seymour Sullivan. Savoy Theatre, London. 21 January 1887.

Barlow, Genevieve. "Mining history for Intrigue." *Herald and Weekly Times* 25 June 2003: 67.

Bird, Delys. *Killing Women: Rewriting Detective Fiction.* Pymble, NSW: Angus & Robertson, 1993.

Bird, Delys, and Walker, Brenda. Introduction. *Killing Women: Rewriting Detective Fiction.* Pymble, NSW: Angus & Robertson, 1993.

Browne, Thomas. *Hydriotaphia, Urn Buriall or a Discourse of the Sepulchral Urns Lately found in Norfolk.* 1658. 12 May 2007 <http:/ /penelope.uchicago.edu/hydrionoframes/hydrion.html>.

Caterson, Simon. "Devilishly Short on Vice." *The Age* 21 January 2006: 24.

Coupe, Stuart. "Crime Gets a Payoff." *Sydney Morning Herald* 20 June 1998: 4.

Cremen, Christine. "A Sleuth on the Trail of Detail." *Sydney Morning Herald* 28 June 2003: 17.

DellaCava, Frances A, and Madeline H. Engel. *Sleuths in Skirts: Analysis and Bibliography of Serialized Female Sleuths.* London: Routledge, 2002.

Greenwood, Kerry. "On Phyrne Fisher." *Murder Down Under.* Spec. issue of *Mystery Readers Journal* 20.4 (Winter 2004-2005). 2 May 2007 <http://www.mysteryreaders.org/Issues/australia.html#greenwood>.

——. *Devil's Food.* Crows Nest, NSW: Allen & Unwin, 2006.

——. *Murder in the Dark:* A Phryne Fisher Mystery. Crows Nest, NSW: Allen & Unwin, 2006.

——. *Death by Water.* Crows Nest, NSW: Allen & Unwin, 2005.

——. *Queen of the Flowers:* A Phryne Fisher Mystery. Crows Nest, NSW: Allen & Unwin, 2004.

——. *The Castlemaine Muyrders:* A Phryne Fisher Mystery. Crows Nest, NSW: Allen & Unwin, 2003.

——. *Murder in Montparnasse: A Phryne Fisher Mystery.* Crows Nest, NSW: Allen & Unwin, 2002.

——. *Away with the Fairies: A Phryne Fisher Mystery.* Crows Nest, NSW: Allen & Unwin, 2001.

——. *Earthly Delights.* Crows Nest, NSW: Allen & Unwin, 2004.

——. *Heavenly Pleasures:* A Corinna Chapman Novel. Crows Nest, NSW: Allen & Unwin, 2004.

——. *Death Before Wicket.* St. Leonards, NSW: Allen & Unwin, 1999.

——. *Raisins and Almonds.* St. Leonards, NSW: Allen & Unwin, 1997.

——. *Urn Burial.* Ringwood, Victoria: Penguin, 1996.

——. *Ruddy Gore.* Ringwood, Victoria: McPhee Gribble, 1995.

——. *Blood and Circuses.* Melbourne: McPhee Gribble, 1994.

——. *The Green Mill Murder.* 1993. Scottsdale, AZ: Poisoned Pen, 2007.

——. *Death at Victoria Dock.* Ringwood, Victoria: McPhee Gribble, 1992.

——. *Murder on the Ballarat Train.* Ringwood, Victoria: McPhee Gribble, 1991.

——. *Flying Too High.* Ringwood, Victoria: McPhee Gribble, 1990.

——. *Cocaine Blues*: A Phryne Fisher Mystery. Melbourne: McPhee Gribble, 1989.

Hanrahan, John. "Darn Good." *The Age* 2 April 1994: 8.

Hume, Fergus. *Mystery of a Hansom Cab*. Melbourne: Kemp & Boyce, 1886.

Knight, Stephen. *Continent of Mystery: A Thematic History of Australian Crime Fiction*. Melbourne: Melbourne UP, 1997.

Mulligan, Eileen. "My Other Job as a Crime Writer." *Illawarra Mercury* 10 July 2004: 48.

Pitt, David. Rev. of *The Green Mill Murder*, by Kerry Greenwood. *Booklist* 103.13 (2007). 1 March 2007 <http://www.amazon.ca/Green-Mill-Murder-Phryne-Mystery/dp/1590582403>.

Rev. of *Earthly Delights*, by Kerry Greenwood. *Canberra Times* 18 January 2004: 19.

Schaffer, Kay. *Women and the Bush: Forces of Desire in the Australian Cultural Tradition*. Melbourne: Cambridge UP, 1988.

Schwartz, Larry "The Rise and Rise of the Female Sleuth." *Sunday Age* 14 June 1992: 11.

Stasio, Marilyn. "Murder Least Foul: The Cozy, Soft-Boiled Mystery." *New York Times Book Review* 18 October 1991: 42.

Sussex, Lucy. *The Fortunes of Mary Fortune*. Ringwood, Victoria: Penguin, 1989.

Turnbull, Sue. "Murder in Many Colours." *The Age* 21 June 2003: 5.

Vernon, Mary. "Murder in the Dark." *Townsville Bulletin* 21 October 2006: 88.

"In Their Different Ways, Classics" Arthur W. Upfield's Detective Fiction[1]

Carol Hetherington

Arthur W. Upfield (b. 1890 – d. 1964) is arguably the most successful, if not the most prolific, Australian writer of popular detective fiction in the twentieth century, whether the success be measured in financial terms, in terms of local, Australian readership, or in terms of international popularity and recognition.[2] By the time of his death in 1964, noted with sadness in obituaries in most major national and international newspapers, including the London *Times* and the *New York Times*, Upfield had published thirty-three novels, numerous articles for newspapers and magazines, and more than twenty short stories. Several novels serialised during his life-time were published after his death and his last unfinished novel, *The Lake Frome Monster* (1966), was completed using "the copious and detailed notes which Arthur Upfield left for this purpose" (verso of title page), and published posthumously. Translations of the novels have been published in more than a dozen countries and new editions continue to appear in French, Japanese, German and even Vietnamese. Upfield's novels were consistently nominated for crime writing awards—for example *Sands of Windee* (1931) was the June Book-of-the-Month choice for the Crime Book Society; *Winds of Evil* (1937) was the *Chicago Sun*'s critic's list of top ten whoduits for 1944 (qtd. in Lindsey 161). Upfield himself was admitted to the exclusive Mystery Writers of America Inc. and in 1962 his American publisher Doubleday Doran, presented him with a pair of gold cuff-links engraved with his initials and the logo of their Crime Club. Upfield's success derives from his series of twenty-nine novels featuring the fictional detective Inspector Napoleon Bonaparte who first appeared in Upfield's second novel, *The Barrakee Mystery*, in 1929. In these novels Upfield gives a uniquely Australian embodiment to several key elements of the classic detective story: the strongly-drawn, larger-than-life sleuth, the detailed and intrinsically interesting setting and atmosphere, and the carefully-plotted "clue-puzzle" (Knight, 1997: 13) mystery of the murder.

Bony, as he is known by his friends—"all my friends call me Bony" (*Death of a Swagman* 28)—is of mixed race: part-Aboriginal, part-European, with dark skin and piercing blue eyes. Bony was found as a baby in his dead mother's arms, under a sandalwood tree in the Queensland outback. Raised on a mission by a redoubtable matron—"the finest woman who ever lived" (*Winds of Evil* 78), Bony received a standard, English education and took a Master of Arts degree from the university in Brisbane. After coming to the attention of the police force for his skills as a tracker, Bony eventually becomes a Detective Inspector with the Queensland police and begins a career in which he is regularly dispatched to other parts of Australia to assist in solving the most puzzling and previously unsolvable crimes. This "man of two tribes" has inherited the best qualities of both—gentleness, keen powers of observation and an instinctive knowledge of "The Book of the Bush" from his Aboriginal mother; and the logic and a capacity for deductive reasoning from his white father. He is also cultured, though slightly pedantic, sympathetic, courteous, possessed of a sense of humour and fair play, and amazingly vain: "I never fail" (*Winds of Evil* 79) he boasts, "If everyone had heard of me there would be no murders" (*The Barrakee Mystery* 63). He admirably fulfills the requirements of American crime writer S. S. Van Dine that a fictional detective should be "a character of high and fascinating attainments—a man at once human and unusual, colourful and gifted" (qtd. in Symons 102).

Bony was an audacious creation in the context of 1920s and 1930s Australia. Upfield's high regard for the qualities of Aboriginal people was unusual and the social conditions of Aboriginal Australians meant that the existence of a character like Bony, an educated, half-caste, senior policeman, was highly improbable. This might well have been an obstacle to the novels' acceptance but it proved not to be the case.[3] Readers everywhere loved him. For Anthony Boucher, himself a noted crime writer and influential reviewer for the *New York Times*, he was "my favourite fictional detective of the past twenty years" (1957: 18) and "one of the rare detective figures with stature as a man" (1962: 16). Within the conventions of the genre a character needs to be possible, rather than probable, credible but not necessary realistic. Elements of flamboyance, eccentricity, even caricature, are there in all the best fictional sleuths—Agatha Christie's Hercule Poirot, Dorothy Sayers's Lord Peter Wimsey, Colin Dexter's Inspector Morse.

The character of Bonaparte also provides Upfield with another key ingredient for the detective fiction genre: the ambivalence and outsider status of the sleuth that allows him to insinuate himself into the crime situation, to draw out its mysteries and clues, and yet possess the authority to restore the disrupted social order, albeit through his own unorthodox brand of justice. Bony, neither white nor black, is not completely accepted by either society but able to move between both worlds in the course of an investigation. He is city-educated, but he has an instinctive affinity with the bush and has lived in the outback long enough to know its ways. He is comfortable in his dealings with urban police officials, but has the bushman's touch when dealing with the outback communities, both black and white, and their people. He has access to the forensic services of the metropolis, but he is an expert in reading the "Book of the Bush" and the clues provided by the land and the seasons. Perhaps more importantly in the Australian context, he has the power and resources of a police inspector, but is outside the ranks of the rule-bound, plodding bureaucrat. One of his favourite and often-repeated lines is: "I am not a real policeman" (*Winds of Evil* 158), and in the words of his long-suffering superior Colonel Spendor: "My worst policeman [. . .]. My best detective" (*Wings Above the Diamantina* 224). Even so, in the majority of the books, Bony arrives at the scene of the crime incognito—possibly an additional insurance against rejection by the traditionally anti-authoritarian Australian ever reluctant to deal with officialdom in any form. He can easily slip into whatever role or disguise is required: a pastoralist on a solitary holiday—*The New Shoe* (1952) and *The Mountains Have a Secret* (1948); a swagman looking for casual work— *Winds of Evil* (1937) and *Death of a Swagman* (1945); and an itinerant horse-breaker—*Death of a Lake* (1954) and *The Sands of Windee* (1931). While the country policemen with whom Boney works—Constable Lee in *Winds of Evil*, Sergeant Marshall in *Death of a Swagman*—are worthy and admirable, if limited, Watsons to this "Bush Sherlock," the "city detectives," wedded to regulations and red tape are totally at a loss out of their urban environment and worthy merely of contempt. Detective Sergeant Redman looks only for fingerprints—he does not see that on "the clean page of the Book of the Bush are printed the boot prints of a man" (*Death of a Swagman* 52); the bullying, bombastic Sergeant Simone is a "mountainous fool," a "gutter-bred Charlie Chaplin detective" (*Winds of Evil* 155).

City/country opposition pervades much of Upfield's fiction and the vividness and accuracy of his varied settings, the representation of rural communities, and the all-important role of landscape in his novels, the intense sense of place, are firmly rooted in his own experiences. Arthur Upfield arrived in Australia from England in November 1911. In the period until August 1914, when he enlisted in the AIF, Upfield lived and worked in outback and rural South Australia and New South Wales, employed as a labourer on a wheat farm, a rouse-about, a station cook, a fencer on the dingo fence and an itinerant swagman. This period laid the foundation for a relationship with the Australian bush that was to dominate his life. After his discharge from the army in October 1919 and a short time in England, Upfield returned to Australia at the beginning of 1921 with his Australian wife, an army nurse whom he had married in Egypt in 1915, and an infant son. He was briefly employed in a factory where "a bell issued orders four times a day" but walking though a park one evening he walked "through a wisp of smoke arising from a little heap of smouldering gum-tree leaves" ("Tale of a Pommy" 87). "After that," he says, "the damned bell could ring until it was cracked ("Tale of a Pommy" 87). Upfield left his job and, temporarily, his family and followed "the lure of the Bush"; he worked on the dingo fence, tried opal-mining, trapped foxes and rabbits, and worked as a drover and as a station cook in New South Wales. In 1927 he moved to Western Australia where, until 1931, he was employed patrolling the rabbit-proof fence (designed to prevent the incursion of rabbits into the state) in a camel-drawn dray. It was a solitary existence and it suited Upfield who had continued to write through all this post-war period. Although he left the bush in 1931, and in 1934 took up a short-lived position with the Melbourne *Herald*, Upfield never lived in a city. He lived on the outskirts of Melbourne, in the Dandenong Ranges, on the coast at Airey's Inlet in Victoria and Bermagui in New South Wales, and finally in the small community of Bowral where he died. He had two more expeditions to the outback: in 1947 he was part of an expedition to Birdsville and the Diamantina River and in 1948 he led an Australian Geographic Society party on a 5000 mile tour of the north-west of Western Australia.

Some critics have accused Upfield of perpetuating the myth of the noble bushman fostered by Henry Lawson and the *Bulletin* writers who glorified an era that had passed even as it was being recognised, but Upfield, unlike Lawson, was not a sentimental "City Bushman" (1900). He depicts a world he knew and lived in, small rural communities as well as lonely outposts and large stations. His rendering of their character and language is sure and accurate. The country doctor or priest, the motherly cook or the local policeman's wife are as much a part of the novels as the weather-beaten old loners, like Dogger Smith in *Winds of Evil*, one of the "immortals" "created in the 1860s, hardened by a diet of meat, damper and tea, and an annual "drunk" at a bush pub" (179). But as Upfield says himself, it was above all the country, the bush, which captured him. He refers to it, in his unpublished autobiography "The Tale of a Pommy," as "Australia Proper" for which he developed "a passionate love [. . .] which will burn until the end, a love stronger than love of family" and which had made him "its slave in the company of many white men as well as all the blacks and members of the mid-races" (88-89).

"Location," according to Stephen Knight (1997), "is one of the major dynamics in crime fiction" (143), and while Upfield's settings range from New South Wales coastal towns, to farms in the West Australian wheat belt, to the inland deserts, they all have a non-urban, specifically Australian quality. They are as memorable in his novels as the Oxford of Dorothy Sayers, the Paris of Georges Simenon or the Venice of Donna Leon. Place is crucial. Upfield is a fluent and vivid writer and his passion for the landscape and its many moods and variables always comes through powerfully and effectively—though Upfield himself made no claims to be a stylist and some reviewers, even those who praised his books, have noted stiltedness of style, but none have denied his descriptive power. The qualities of light and wind, sunsets and sunlight, sounds and silences are what create the strong presences in the novels and they require considerable descriptive powers. The classic Upfield scene might be the quiet noises of settling birds in the trees near a water-hole in the hour before darkness, or the silent activity of a colony of ants moving tiny, sun-heated stones down their holes for warmth, or the gentle hissing whisper of wind moving sand in the moonlight and the regular clanging of a windmill turning. Knight (1997) has dubbed Upfield the "classic tourist thriller writer," suggesting, whether deliberately or not, that Upfield exploits the sensational elements of his settings for a "foreign" audience (159). Dangers there are—floods, fires, heat—for these are ever-present realities of life in Australia, then as now, and "Australian" animals abound but there are no gratuitous snakes, spiders, or crocodiles: indeed the most common animal in the novels might well be the rabbit, an animal not native to Australia, but one which has become part of the Australian psyche since its introduction with British settlement. Place in Upfield's novels is deftly and convincingly evoked, both genuinely felt and explored and exploited in ways traditional to literature and while his settings are all recognizably and pervasively Australian, they are at the same time remarkably varied. Within the confines of the genre and its formulae, Upfield's novels are surprisingly individual. It is hard to generalise without distorting but two novels I shall discuss here *The Sands of Windee* and *The Death of a Lake*, illustrate in different ways some interesting and important features of Upfield's writing and career.

Within the confines of the genre and its formulae, Upfield's novels are surprisingly individual. In all novels the social background, the people of the bush and the small town, are of great importance but each of the other elements of plot, setting and atmosphere is more prominent in some novels than others. It is hard to generalise without distorting but three novels I shall discuss here—*The Sands of Windee*, *Winds of Evil* and *The Death of a Lake*—illustrate these different emphases and some interesting and important features of Upfield's writing and career.

The Sands of Windee, the second Bony novel, published in London in 1931, was the June Book-of-the-Month for the Crime Book Society, assuring it good sales in Britain. Despite its excellent reception in Britain, the book was dismissed in Australia in patronizing terms by one of the most influential of local reviewers, Nettie Palmer (1931: 179). The incident marked the beginning of a resentment on Upfield's part towards the literary establishment lasting his whole life.[4] *The Sands of Windee* is a novel in which intricacies of plot are paramount. The mystery, is complex and original. There is no body to be found, although it is known that a murder has been committed. In fact, the body has been disposed of by burning it together with animal bodies, any metal bits dissolved in nitric acid, the bones ground up in a gold-miners dolly pot and the dust scattered. The book became linked with a sensational murder case. During the writing of the novel, Upfield had discussed with a fellow worker on the rabbit-proof fence the need to find the perfect method of disposing of a body. Also present on this occasion was an individual who was later charged and convicted of a murder in which this means had been employed. Upfield was called to give evidence at his trial. Set on a sheep station in New South Wales, the novel involves Bony in a mystery where his knowledge of Aboriginal lore, and his ability to inter-act with local tribal Aboriginals, is crucial to a solving the murder—something that is often a factor in the books. As well, his acute powers of observation, his infinite patience and his willingness to make "Time" his ally, allow him to unravel the mystery. Typically, he operates "under cover." Posing as an itinerant and expert horse-breaker, Bony is able to step into the breach when the station cook goes off on a drinking spree (he makes a creditable pastry crust), and still finds time to strike up an intellectual relationship with the region's Catholic priest (with whom he discusses philosophy and the classics). There is a love interest in the novel and characteristically Upfield treats this in a rather stilted, romantic manner. Women, especially "good" women, are usually idealised in the novels. Despite his enormous vanity, Boney resists finalizing the case in an official sense, something that happens frequently with the unorthodox inspector. Of course he knows the answer but decides that justice, as he interprets it, has been served and that bringing things to a correct legal conclusion will only cause pain. The verdict from the London reviewer: "well-written, absorbingly interesting in a score of ways, and, above all else, intensely human" (Graeme 7).

If *The Sands of Windee* has the most famous Upfield plot, *Winds of Evil* has a greater focus on atmosphere and symbolism. In the far western New South Wales community of Carie, a killer, a strangler, is at large. He strikes at intervals, always when a fierce sandstorm envelops the town, reducing visibility to nil in a hissing, red-brown fog, unnerving the people of the town and surrounding country with its highly charged atmosphere, and ensuring that all trace of this unseen killer are obliterated by the winds. Itinerant swagman Joe Fisher arrives in the midst of such a storm. Despite the warnings from fellow travellers on the track, he makes camp at Catfish Hole, the scene of two previous murders. Beautiful in the calm windless daylight, and previously a traditional Aboriginal camping ground for generations, the billabong is now shunned by black and white alike. After the death of the first victim, Alice Tindall, a part-Aboriginal girl, her people leave, fearful of the monster, the legendary bunyip whom they blame for this inhuman crime. Confirming local fears, the killer strikes again, although it is not the swagman but a local girl who is the subject of the attack and who narrowly escapes becoming the third corpse.

Clear views of the crime are obscured in a variety of ways. The clouds of dust and sand dust hide the perpetrator and the winds sweep away traces of his movements. For the arrogant, oafish Sergeant Simone, facts and clues are obscured by clouds of stupidity and racial prejudice; he suspects Joe Fisher, because of his colour, and eventually arrests Elson, an innocent man. As another wind-storm approaches the town waits nervously, particularly the town matriarch, Mrs. Nelson, the local hotel proprietor and property owner. Alone on the hotel veranda, "the throne from which she ruled Carie" (*Winds of Evil* 21), she waits and watches, apprehensively it seems, for a drama to play out to its end.

Not very much is as it seems in Carie. Who is Joe Fisher? Joe Fisher is Bony and he spreads his net to ensnare the murderer, but other questions and puzzles abound. Who is Dennington, the Englishman with the unknown past who is employed as a fence-rider on Wirragatta station? Is the murderer an outsider, like him, or is he to be found within the community? The strangler appears to wait for his victims in trees near Catfish Hole, swinging from tree to tree like a gorilla and dropping on his unsuspecting victims. Is he the physically deformed, unnaturally strong Hang-Dog Jack, the Wirragatta cook, ugly, snarling, scowling, a "human travesty" (*Winds of Evil* 60)? Or is he the bush bunyip, as the Aboriginals believe, "that horrific thing, half-dog, half-human, which, during the daylight hours, lurks invisibly in the heart of the bush, behind a tree, at the foot of the mirage, and at night takes material form" (*Winds of Evil* 226), to stalk the venturesome lone wanderer? There is "something about this foul Strangler which was almost supernatural" (*Winds of Evil* 142) Bony reflects as he struggles to maintain the reasoned logic of the white man's world and fight against the ancient primeval superstition of the black: "Bony's aboriginal blood tingled and Bony's white man's mind fought to still the tingling" (*Winds of Evil* 139).

Bony is "Tortured by inherited superstition" about the "monstrous figure slinking through the shrouded world of wind and noise" (*Winds of Evil* 225). But just as the whirling sands hide the evil-doer and conceal his tracks, so other records have been concealed and destroyed by human agency. Traces of older crimes have been obliterated just like the tracks of the strangler. Pages that relate to the true identity of station owner Martin Borrodale have been torn from the medical record books; and evidence of the profound derangement of his real father, the disfiguring scars on Mrs Nelson's neck, have been kept hidden by the high buttoned necklines of her black silk dresses.

Disguise, concealment, deformity, disfigurement, disruption and distortion are at the heart of the mystery, integral to the crime. The search for the solution to the mystery is a parallel one—Bony seeks the strangler and Martin Borradale seeks the truth about himself. Finally they are one and the same, the monster at large in society is the monster lurking within the depths of Martin Borradale's misshapen psyche, a phenomenon no less mysterious and inexplicable than the existence of the Bunyip. *Winds of Evil* was selected by American crime writer Craig Rice as one of the top ten "whodunits" of 1944 (the year of its US release) because of its outstanding atmosphere and it is tempting to overplay the extent to which Upfield manages to fuse the realistic and symbolic elements in the novel. But although there are times when the work moves towards the allegorical, when the disturbances in the natural world suggest a mirroring of the social and psychological disruption, it never quite realises its potential in this respect. The imaginative synthesis that would have allowed this to become a very good literary novel is never quite achieved and *Winds of Evil* remains securely within its genre, but a powerful example of it.

In *The Death of a Lake* (1954) the focus is different again, the plot is slight and the psychological tension sustained but centre stage is the countryside that "dwarfs any human activity, superbly observed and described" (Offord 23). Here is place, location, becoming a key element in the work involving a perennial Australian pre-occupation—drought. The setting is an inland lake, one of several in central Australia that at times, for a year or so, are full of water after floods, attracting abundant and brilliant wild-life, oases of fertility and colour in a desert and then for years bare, stark, bleached salt pans. This novel describes the slow death by evaporation, of a lake and as the water level falls, tension mounts and the expected discovery of a body in the lake draws closer. Unusually for a Bony novel, there is a strong sexual element in the tension. Jealousy and greed are key factors in the crime and women are to blame. For the first time "bad" women make an appearance–two women who are "schemers," "Proper trollops" (*Death of a Lake* 44). Suspense is intensified by the reactions of the birds and animals to the atmosphere, the heat, the drought and the receding waters. Publisher Michael Duffy reprinted *The Death of a Lake* in 1988. He has called it "probably the best book I've ever read about drought in Australia."[5]

Death of a Lake was published first in America (in February 1954) and somewhat later (June) in Britain. It was the interest of American publishers, beginning with the publication of three novels in 1943–*Murder Down Under* (originally titled *Mr. Jelly's Business*), *Wings above the Claypan* (originally titled *Wings above the Diamantina*) and *The Mystery of Swordfish Reef*–that gave Upfield a secure financial basis for his writing. Locally, Upfield made money from the regular serialisations of his novels in newspapers and magazines and many Bony mysteries were read on local and national radio and adapted as radio serials. But despite accolades in Britain and a wide following for his work in Australia the economics of publishing, typically, made American sales a necessity for commercial success. Upfield was proud of his ability to sell his work and of his status as one of the very few Australian writers who could support themselves by their craft. However, all his life, he was conscious that his work was not regarded as "literary." Upfield has not received the prominence within Australian literary history that he deserves. Some of various reasons for this include ostracism by the "literati" in the 1920s and 1930s, a dismissal of popular fiction genres by critics as unworthy of study, and later a reluctance to engage in discussion of Upfield's treatment of Indigenous issues, even of the character of Bony himself. Some of Australia's most respected critics have made delivered favourable verdicts on Upfield's work. Geoffrey Dutton (1985) chose *Man of Two Tribes* (1956) as one of the hundred best Australian books and wrote: "Upfield's novels are frequently dismissed as mere thrillers. Such a book [. . .] is far more and has a secure place as a work of art" (226). While Morris Miller (1940) saw that even in his early works Upfield "shows a talent that may ultimately find the art of synthesis" (573). And Clem Christesen commented that while Upfield was "generally recognised as a competent writer on the 'popular' level. I personally consider him rather more than this" (qtd. in Lindsey 195). For Colin Roderick (1950), Upfield "raised the Australian standard" in crime fiction, and judged that "We have had no such promising work since Fergus Hume's celebrated *Mystery of a Hansom Cab*" (139). Despite this, very few critical articles on Upfield have appeared and the only full-length study has been published in America (see Browne 1988). This was certainly not a matter of indifference to Upfield. In a draft letter (18 June 1954), probably to Colin Roderick and referring to *Death of a Lake*, he asks a question which still needs to be answered:

> I would much appreciate your opinion on whether this particular type of mystery story [. . .] could take its place in National Literature. If, of course, it be possible for a crime story to be included in National Literature.[6]

ENDNOTES

[1] The quote has been taken from Geoffrey Dutton, *The Australian Collection: Australia's Greatest Books* (Sydney: Angus & Robertson, 1985) 8.

[2] The "pulp" fiction author Alan G. Yates, who wrote as "Peter Carter Brown," is Australia's best-selling author, writing approximately 300 novels and novelettes from the early 1950s to the early 1980s. For more details, see Toni Johnson-Woods, "The Mysterious Case of Carter Brown, or, Who Really Killed the Australian Author," *Australian Literary Studies* 21.4 (2004): 74-88.

[3] Indeed the acceptance of *The Barakee Mystery* (1929), in which a white woman has a relationship with an Aboriginal man, is itself surprising considering the outrage provoked by the depiction a mixed-race union between a white man and an Aboriginal woman in Katharine Susannah Prichard's *Coonardoo*, published in the same year, and the responses to Xavier Herbert's *Capricornia* some ten years later.

[4] *An Author Bites the Dust* (Sydney: Angus & Robertson, 1948) is a biting satire, in the guise of a murder mystery, on the literary establishment and literary pretensions.

[5] "The Arthur Upfield Mystery: Bony," *Books and Writing*, Narr. Ramona Koval, Australian Broadcasting Commission, 12 May 2002, 7 April 2007 <http://www.abc.net.au/rn/arts/bwriting/stories/s550978.htm>. Upfield

lived near one such lake, Meenamurtee Lake, in his first years in Australia, and witnessed the teeming wildlife; he had also seen water in Lake Eyre on his 1947 outback expedition. The early Australian explorers searched, with often fatal consequences, for a great inland sea. In May 1954 when its first serialised installment appeared in the major daily, the *Sydney Morning Herald* (22 May 1954), the facing page carried an interview with an old bushman recommending the flooding of Lake Eyre as a solution to problems of drought. As I write this, in March 2007, the morning newspaper has a feature on the movement of floodwaters into a drought-stricken Lake Eyre (see Sproull and Wahlquist 7).

[6] Draft letter to Roderick, probably Dr. Colin Roderick, later Professor Roderick, 18 June 1954. Archive of Don Uren, Mansfield, Victoria.

Works Cited

"The Arthur Upfield Mystery: Bony." *Books and Writing.* Narr. Ramona Koval. Australian Broadcasting Commission. 12 May 2002. 7 April 2007 <http://www.abc.net.au/rn/arts/bwriting/stories/s550978.htm>.

Boucher, Anthony. Rev. of *The Will of the Tribe*, by Arthur W. Upfield. *New York Times* 29 July 1962: (Section 7) 16.

——. Rev. of *The Bushman Who Came Back*, by Arthur W. Upfield. *New York Times* 23 June 1957: (Section 7) 18.

Browne, Ray B. *The Spirit of Australia: The Crime Fiction of Arthur W. Upfield.* Bowling Green, Ohio: Bowling Green State U Popular P, 1988.

De Hoog, Kees. "Arthur W. Upfield." 7 April 2007 <http://pandora.nla.gov.au/pan/48745/20050420/www.collectingbooksandmagazines.com/upfield.html>.

Dutton, Geoffrey. *The Australian Collection: Australia's Greatest Books.* Sydney: Angus & Robertson, 1985.

Graeme, Bruce. "The Crime Book Society's Selection for June is *The Sands of Windee* by Arthur W. Upfield." *Crime Book Society Magazine* June 1931: 3, 7.

Herbert, Xavier. Capricornia. 1937. Sydney: Pacific, 1969.

Hume, Fergus. *The Mystery of a Hansom Cab.* Melbourne: Kemp & Boyce, 1886.

Johnson-Woods, Toni. "The Mysterious Case of Carter Brown, or, Who Really Killed the Australian Author." *Australian Literary Studies* 21.4 (2004): 74-88.

Knight, Stephen. *Continent of Mystery: A Thematic History of Australian Crime Fiction.* Carlton South, Victoria: Melbourne UP, 1997.

——. "Upfield, Arthur William (1890-1964)." Australian Dictionary of Biography. Vol. 12. Carlton South, Victoria: Melbourne UP, 1990. 305-306.

Lawson, Henry. "The City Bushman." *In the Days When the World was Wide and Other Verses.* Sydney: Angus & Robertson with Australian Book Co., 1900. 147-157. 7 March 2007 <http://www.gutenberg.org/dirs/etext95/dwwww11.txt>.

Lindsey, Travis Barton. "Arthur William Upfield: A Biography." Diss. Murdoch U, Perth. 2005. 7 March 2007 <http://wwwlib.murdoch.edu.au/adt/browse/view/adt-MU20051003.113934>.

Miller, Morris E. *Australian Literature from Its Beginnings to 1935.* Melbourne: Melbourne UP, 1940.

Offord, L. G. Rev. of *Death of a Lake,* by Arthur W. Upfield. *San Francisco Chronicle* 21 March 1954: 23.

Palmer, Nettie. Rev. of *The Sands of Windee,* by Arthur W. Upfield. *All about Books* 3.9 (September 1931): 179.

Prichard, Katharine Susannah. Coonardoo. 1929. Sydney: Angus & Robertson, 1957.

Roderick, Colin. *An Introduction to Australian Fiction.* Sydney: Angus & Robertson, 1950.

Sproull, Richard, and Asa Wahlquist. "Wildlife Follows the Dark Tide towards Lake Eyre." *Australian* 9 March 2007: 7.

Symons, Julian. *Bloody Murder.* London: Faber, 1972.

Upfield, Arthur W. "Tale of a Pommy." Archive of William Upfield, Melbourne.

——. *The Lake Frome Monster.* London: Heinemann, 1966.

——. The Will of the Tribe. Melbourne: Heinemann, 1962.

——. *The Bushman Who Came Back.* 1957. New York: Berkley, 1963.

——. *Man of Two Tribes.* Melbourne: Heinemann, 1956.

——. Draft Letter to Colin Roderick. 18 June 1954. Archive of Don Uren, Mansfield, Victoria.

——. *Death of a Lake.* 1954. London: Pan, 1967.

——. *The New Shoe.* London: Heinemann, 1952.

——. *The Mountains Have a Secret.* New York: Doubleday, 1948.

——. *An Author Bites the Dust.* Sydney: Angus & Robertson, 1948.

——. *Death of a Swagman.* 1945. Sydney: Pacific Books, 1964.

——. *The Mystery of Swordfish Reef.* Sydney: Angus & Robertson, 1939.

——. *Winds of Evil.* 1937. Sydney: Pacific Books, 1968.

——. *Wings Above the Diamantina; Or, Wings above the Claypan.* 1936. London: Pan, 1972.

——. *Mr. Jelly's Business; Or, Murder Down Under.* 1932. New York: Doubleday, 1943.

——. *The Sands of Windee.* 1931. New York: Scribners, 1985.

——. *The Barrakee Mystery.* 1929. London: Pan, 1970.

Malathy Anandavalli

Writing the Land
Western Australia as Textual Space in Tim Winton's *Dirt Music*

> [. . .] his eye is drawn to the page between his hands. Australia. The continent is a craggy frown and half that frown is Western Australia. (Winton, *Dirt Music*: 160)

> This state, says Horrie, is like Texas. Only, its big! (Winton, *Dirt Music*: 246)

The land and the human relationship with it have always figured conspicuously in the Australian consciousness. A spiritual relationship with place and a holistic sense of interconnectedness of man with the land have been distinctive aspects of aboriginal culture throughout the long period of the continent's history that predated European colonization. Traditional and contemporary aboriginal narratives, song cycles and art reflect this view of human beings as totally identified with the land and the natural environment. However, Australia's history as a settler colony and a modern nation has been marked by a confrontation between man and the land, between human and non-human life, and writing this confrontation with the environment has been a major preoccupation of modern Australian literature. Myths of the frontier and the pioneering experience celebrated the triumph of the human spirit pitted against a relentlessly harsh environment. Literary texts that write the colonial and nationalist periods of Australian history are resonant with motifs and metaphors related to possessing and taming an essentially difficult and harsh landscape that resists human occupation. Aboriginal literary texts however avoid the vocabulary of confrontation, control and mastery in depicting the relationship with the land and the natural environment, but reflect the harmony and easy understanding of the land that has always typified aboriginal culture.

An engagement with place, no longer seen in terms of the bush or the city/bush dichotomy as in the nineteenth and early twentieth centuries, continues in later decades in writers like Eleanor Dark (b. 1901 - d. 1985), Xavier Herbert (b. 1901 - d. 1984), Randolph Stow (b. 1935), David Malouf (b. 1934), Elizabeth Jolley (b. 1923 - d. 2007), Kim Scott (b. 1957) and Tim Winton (b. 1960). Again, aboriginal life writing, and the work of poets like Judith Wright (b. 1915 - d. 2000), Les Murray (b. 1938) and the Jindyworobaks are marked by a strong sense of place. Twentieth century writing of place has tended to focus on specific regions of the country—Western Australia in particular, has witnessed a remarkable output of regional writing and a textual space that is distinctively Western Australian is easily recognizable within the Australian literary landscape. As in American and Canadian literature, the "West" has acquired a peculiar significance for Australian literature. Early settlers and colonists who recorded their perceptions of the land in letters and diaries, and an entire galaxy of writers among whom may be included Katharine Susannah Prichard (b. 1883 - d. 1969), D. H. Lawrence (b. 1885 - d. 1930), Randolph Stowe, Robert Drewe (b. 1943), Elizabeth Jolley, Dorothy Hewett (b. 1923 - d. 2002), Fay Zwicky (b. 1933) and Tim Winton—writers who have spent some time or lived their entire lives in Western Australia, have carved out a distinctive "Westralian" fictional space. Aboriginal writers of the region—who form an equally impressive group, and among whom some of the most conspicuous names are Kim Scott, Sally Morgan (b. 1951), Doris Pilkington (b. 1937), Rosemary van den Berg (b. 1939), Kay Walley and Ivy Dodd—have written the "other side" of the West Australian story, often seeking to explore issues of rootedness, community, belonging and identity through their place writing. Coming as they do, from a culture whose spirituality is primarily a spirituality of place and whose consciousness is intimately bound with the landscape, they write the region differently. Their mapping of place is marked by an easy and comfortable sense of identification with the land and natural forces. They are not as concerned with "Western Australia"—a product of the colonial project—as they are with the numerous aboriginal territories and identities of the region, its bioregional realities and its spiritual mapping. Their concern in fact is with—to borrow a phrase from John Jackson—"the vernacular landscape" of this part of Australia.

The Fremantle Arts Centre Press (1976-Present) and cultural journals like *Westerly*(1956-Present) which are committed to publishing the work of the region's writers and which have been instrumental in "discovering" talented young writers, have been to some extent at least, responsible for creating this vibrant body of Western Australian writing. Delys Bird and Dennis Haskell (2005) point out how the increasing sophistication of creative and critical work in Western Australia is partly due to the existence of *Westerly*: "[. . .] publication in a major magazine validates and encourages a writer's work and *Westerly* has been privileged to help the development of writers as diverse as Elizabeth Jolley, Edwin Thumboo, Alf Taylor, Shirley Geok-lin Lim and Phili p Salom" (10). Institutional support has therefore been crucial in creating a corpus of literature that is distinctly Western Australian.

Western Australia is for many of these writers, not merely the "setting" of their work, but the creative space out of which they write, which is why Veronica Brady (1982) sees the West not merely as a geographic entity, but an imaginative one as well (105). Beth Watzke (1992) also remarks how many of the region's writers "[. . .] share an awareness of the landscapes of Western Australia as unique and vital in the shaping of their awareness of themselves as writers. Out of this process and awareness have come their individual visionary literary worlds [. . .]" (28). While Watzke sees an awareness of space, of a unique landscape distinct from other areas of Australia as the shared expression of place in the works of Western Australian writes like Peter Cowan (b. 1914 - d. 2002), Elizabeth Jolley, Dorothy Hewett and Tim Winton (24), Delys Bird's (1998) assessment of the meanings Western Australia assumes in the work of some of its women's writers, reveals some of the significances of the region as a textual space.

> For them, the West generates meanings not only in its physical life, its political and geographic significance, but also in its symbolic life. It is an imaginative and creative space, a place of the writer's mind as well as of her body, so that the tension between the external and internal spaces of the West , palpable in a place where the natural world is very evident, the population very small, and the settlement history very short, gives their work particular qualities (3).

Tim Winton represents one of the strongest voices of contem porary Western Australian literature. He has also been actively involved in environmental activism for the protection of the land and the preservation of its pristine quality. Several times winner of the Miles Franklin award and twice short-listed for the Booker Prize, Winton writes out of the Western Australian land where he lives. Winton's writing of Western Australia has been deeply influenced by American regional writing of the South and the West. Western Australia is in his own words the creative space out of which he writes. In an interview given to Ron Hogan, Winton said: "I've always written out of the place. The characters come after the place for me. I am more interested in the landscape and the characters are sometimes just an excuse for me to indulge in bouts of landscape" (Winton, 2002: 2). Winton's fictional oeuvre includes such contemporary classics as *Shallows* (1984), *That Eye, the Sky* (1986), *Cloudstreet* (1991), *The Riders* (1994) and *Dirt Music* (2001), collections of short stories and children's books. Many of his books are counted among the most popular and outstanding fictional texts in recent Australian writing. At least part of his appeal as a writer lies in his creative engagement with the Western Australian land and its life and his sensitivity to the nuances of Western Australian vernacular. His non-fictional work—books like *Local Colour* (1994), *Land's Edge* (1998), and *Down to Earth* (1999) are also suggestive of his deep commitment to the land and its values.

A "regional" writer of national and international repute and recognition, Winton agrees that there is a stigma attached to regional writing everywhere, which holds good for West Australian writing as well, though, he adds, he has found the isolation from the metropolitan centres, very useful (see Winton, Interview: 2001). As Robert Dixon (2005) points out, Winton locates the national in the regional or elevates the regional to national significance (258) rather than seeing regionalism as an inhibiting factor. It gives his work a refreshingly earthy and folksy flavour and an autochthonous quality that is lacking in the more "intellectual" preoccupations in the writing of "metropolitan" authors. Family relationships, childhood, sexuality, community and isolation are typical concerns in his novels which have a lyrical and almost visionary quality, and occupy the luminous territory between fiction and poetry.

Winton's acclaimed novel, *Dirt Music,* is the story of modern Western Australia at the turn of the century, rooted in a capitalist ethic and the ethos of a late- industrial society. The novel explores sexual relationships and family bonds in a liberated and permissive modern West Australian fishing community. The relationship that develops between Georgie Jutland, a former nurse and partner of Jim Buckridge, chief fisherman in White Point, a town on the long West Australian coast north of Perth, and Luther Fox, a "shameteur" (the local word for a poacher) form the basic plot. Georgie realizes the precariousness of her position as Buckridge's partner when his son turns hostile to her and tries to ease her emotional trauma by drowning herself in drink and by endless surfing on the internet. Luther Fox has also been through a phase of life that has scarred his soul and the two come together instinctively for support and strength. Luther is almost caught for his poaching, and in a bid to be free from all the troubling ties to the community, he strikes out, somewhat in the manner of Heriot in Randolph Stow's novel *To the Islands* (1958), to the wilderness of the North West, to lose himself in a life close to nature and the land.

The scenic evocation of Western Australia is a crucial component of the text. The seascape, desert and wilderness of Western Australia are not just the "setting" but the soil from which the characters and the action spring up. *Dirt Music* bears witness to Winton's intimate awareness of the nature of the land, the seasons, the weather, the winds and the behaviour of the sea. The title refers to a kind of roots music that could be played on simple unsophisticated instruments, and itself carries a suggestion of the land. The overwhelming sense of natural life, the sheer beauty of the region, its vastness and the variety of physical landscapes are evoked in the description of Luther's flight to the north.

In his essay "The Beholding Eye: Ten Versions of the Same Scene" (1976), the cultural geographer D. W. Meinig suggested ten different ways in which people see landscapes—while acknowledging that more are possible—landscape as nature, as habitat, as artifact, as system, as problem, as wealth, as ideology, as history, as place and as aesthetic (47). These, says Meinig, are the cultural constructs through which people perceive places. It would be interesting to see whether all or some of the "ways of seeing" suggested by Meinig, are adopted in *Dirt Music* to build up the textual landscape of Western Australia.[1] Seeing landscape as place, according to Meinig, involves seeing its individuality and unique flavour (Meinig 53-54). This way of seeing is constantly built into the fictional discourse of *Dirt Music* to evoke various landscapes in the Western Australian region and subtly suggest their singular essence. Though Winton emphatically states that White Point is not a location on the map, the unique character of a small fishing town on the West coast is built up in several ways. The feel of the wind, the smells, the play of light and shade, the sounds, the activities performed, the spatial system, the location, the sense of connection to other places—all help to create the identity of the place. The character of White Point as a coastal fishing town is built up through several touches. For instance, Georgie steps out on to the terrace of the Buckridge home in the town

> [. . .] where the air was cool and thick with the smells of stewing seagrass, of brine and limey sand, of thawing bait and the savoury tang of saltbush [. . .].White Point sat in the teeth of the Roaring Forties. Here on the Midwest coast the wind might not be your friend but it was sure as hell your constant neighbour. (*Dirt Music* 5)

The overwhelming presence of the sea is crucial in creating the identity of White Point. The white sandy beaches which give the town its name are evocatively drawn. When Fox returns from one of his boating tri ps, he is described as pressing "[. . .] on along the soft, em pty beach with the roar of surf in his head. The sand is white, blinding, endless" (*Dirt Music* 151). The scorching heat of the Western Australian summer as it "shudders upon the land" (*Dirt Music* 152), adds to the sense of place. If White Point is the quintessential Western Australian fishing town, the identities of other landscapes of the region are constructed by the sensitive evocations of unique locations such as the wheatbelt, the Pilbara and the Kimberley, places traversed by Fox on his journey northwards. Having left the coast behind them, Fox and his com panion, "[. . .] drone through floodplain country and into the beginnings of rich soil where late crops stand brassy in the sun" (*Dirt Music* 217-218). Again, further north, "[. . .] without noticing the transition, Fox sees that the country has become vivid, dramatic. The Midwest is behind them. This is the Pilbara. Everything looks big and Technicolor. Ahead the stupendous iron ranges" *(Dirt Music* 227).

The changes in soil colour and types sometimes indicate transitions in landscapes. At Meekatharra, the earth is red, staining the tar streets, the vehicles and the buildings. Near Port Hedland, Fox comes upon the low flat flood plain "[. . .] bleached yellow, the color of a dried biscuit" (*Dirt Music* 238). Often, the change in place is suggested through changes in human activities and occupations. As Fox and his com panion enter the Western Australian wheat belt, the scene changes quite dramatically and "[. . .] harvesters raise clouds of chaff and dust across the rolling hills" (*Dirt Music* 218). Further on, in sheep farming country, it "[. . .] grows dry and low and wheat gives out to sheep paddocks which seem thinner and more marginal until only squat mulga scrub remains [. . .] "(*Dirt Music* 219). Still further up the road they come into mining towns where "[. . .] diggings and slagheaps become landscape" (*Dirt Music* 225). Very often the character of a new place is suggested through flashes of colour and visual effects. One of the most striking instances occurs in the passage where Fox enters the Opthalmia ranges "[. . .] whose bluffs and peaks and mesas rise crimson, black, burgundy, terracotta, against the cloudless sky. Gully shadows are purple up there and the rugged layers of iron lie dotted with a greenish furze of spinifex [. . .]. The colours burn in his head" (*Dirt Music* 228).

Bioacoustics are an integral aspect of the identity of a place and Winton often gets the reader to listen to the sounds of nature as experienced in various places in the Western Australian region. When Fox goes out on to the verandah of his home at White Point, the reader hears with him "[. . .] paddocks thrum with cicadas, crickets, birdwings. Up from the creek comes the chirr of frogs" (*Dirt Music* 86). If sounds are suggestive of place- identity, so is the stillness of a place at restful times of the day. When Fox approaches the town from the sea, "Nothing moves ashore at White Point. There's only this prevailing painterly stillness. Deserted beach. Norfolk pines immobile" (*Dirt Music* 130). Winton acknowledges community to be an excellent indicator of the identity of a place. The multicultural and multiethnic com position of modern Western Australian communities is subtly suggested. When Fox reaches Broome he notices that the "[. . .] the faces hereabouts are red, yellow, black [. . .]" (*Dirt Music* 294). The aboriginal presence in the region's communities is acknowledged only in very few instances, but there are very crucial suggestions of the aboriginal past, as in Fox's discovery of the dynamic cave paintings. It is through the aboriginal youth Axle, who prides himself on his ability to hunt goannas and birds, dig out sugarbag from the beehives, and instinctively knows the berries, and declares em phatically, "*Dis,* my country," that the relationshi p of aboriginal culture with the land shows through.

Western Australia is a region that encom passes a variety of landscapes, and by adopting the perspective of landscape as place, Winton recognises the unique essence and character of each of them.

Seeing landscape as process, or in Meinig's words, as "a complex, cumulative record of the work of nature and man," in a particular place and looking at the cumulative effects of processes working on the elements of a locality (Meinig 52-53) is a "way of seeing" adopted occasionally in *Dirt Music*. The transformation of White Point into a fancy lobster boom town is described from just such a point of view. The town is favoured by nature—it is the only safe anchorage on that part of the coast. Originally a shanty town, a bunch of tin sheds in the lee of the foredune, late twentieth century capitalist enterprise has created a "lobster boom" in White Point—every fisherman is rich now and lives in a "trophy house." White Point is now a town of "pink brick villas" of prosperous fishermen many of whom owned "[. . .] a million dollars' worth of boat and licence, a new Landcruiser and six weeks in Bali every season, families who owned city pubs and traded in gold, whose TVs were the size of pianos" (*Dirt Music* 18).

The way of seeing landscape as nature, says Meinig, considers nature as "primary, fundamental, dominant, enduring" and the viewer of a place tries to "imagine what the area *really* is like. It is an old view which separates man and nature. Ideologically it had its greatest vogue in eighteenth century Romanticism, in that longing for wilderness, in the view of nature as pure, fine, good, truly beautiful" (Meinig 47-48). Winton is deservedly acclaimed for his sensitive responsiveness to the natural life of Australia, especially of Western Australia. This sensitivity comes across in *Dirt Music* as well in some superb prose that is often lyrical. But Winton's reading of nature differs from the Romantic "way of seeing" landscape, which Meinig carefully qualifies as "separating" man and nature. Avoiding the Romantic position of man as passionate or worshipful observer of nature, Winton reveals a deeper empathy for nature and sees humans as one of several species whose habitat is nature. Winton's favoured perspective to read Western Australia, is in fact, to see landscape as nature and as habitat.

To ease his troubled mind and to get over his numbness Fox instinctively seeks out the wilderness, what Thoreau calls the "tonic of wildness," and he travels great distances to get to one of the most isolated areas in the region. "If you want to be left alone," he says to himself, "then clear out. Go somewhere clean. A place where you can stand alone, completely alone [. . .]. The idea of a place to be truly alone in—wilderness" (*Dirt Music* 294). Fox is, as Jules Smith (2003) rightly points out, yet another Winton character whose journey of self-discovery is connected to his relationship with the natural world (see "Tim Winton - Critical Perspective"). The wilderness, he seems to acknowledge, is his true habitat, the return to which is significant in his attempts to heal his troubled self. As Cheryl Glotfelty points out in *The Ecocriticism Reader* (1996), the modern discipline of eco-psychology sees the estrangement from nature as a major contributor to our psychological ills and advocates a re-integration with the world of nature as their remedy(xxi)

Fox is unusually alive to the rhythms of natural life. Even as a boy, he could sense "[. . .] the ooze of sap, the breathing leaves, the air displaced by birds" (*Dirt Music* 104). He remembers the times when, as a boy, he would stand "stump- still, mind clean as an animal's, and hear melons splitting in the heat" (*Dirt Music* 104). At his hideout in the far Northwest, Fox's life is lived according to the tide, and he surrenders himself to the physical environment. He learns to read the behaviour of animals and plants around him to foretell a coming storm or cyclone. Fox leads the life of a hunter- gatherer, eating nuts, berries and green ants which he gathers and fish that he catches. He is totally bereft of all trappings of culture—but he does not find it easy.[2] There are times when he curses himself for having brought no books with him and nearly drives himself crazy, craving for something to read. In the absence of any troubling ties to society and community, his instinctual biophilia develops further. He learns to savour the natural pleasures of the island and love its trees and creatures. The hot warm boles of the young boab trees, their shapes, the asymmetrical splendour of one particular old tree—all are sources of delight. There are other pleasures as well on Fox's island. He sports with a pack of sharks, recklessly enjoying the "carnal sociability of the buggers."

Maps and map-sense are a crucial part of the novel's textual space. Fox's journey northwards, the route he takes, the towns he passes—Mount Magnet, Wittenoom, Kunnunnara, Broome—are all precisely mapped. Each location is defined with reference to its distance from the ocean, from Perth or from Broome. Through this accurately mapped journey, the text conveys a sense of the immense stretch of the state, and we realize like the character Horrie, that the state is "big." At Broome, Fox loses his maps—they are destroyed by the aboriginal youth Axle. This is crucial—it signifies that Fox will now discard the cartographic sense which has brought him up to Broome, and surrender himself to an experiential place sense which is almost aboriginal, and which gives him a surer sense of the land, its contours and its creatures than any map would.[3]

Flashbacks, memories, stories of familial tensions, relationships between parents and children, of wounded sexuality—are all in Winton's fiction, firmly anchored to natural life. Winton, as Jules Smith rightly points out, "[. . .] places human stores within natural history [. . .] Tim Winton brings his human and environmental themes together in ways that are always intensely realized and touching" (Smith: 2). Winton situates what D. H. Lawrence (1914), in his study of Thomas Hardy terms the "little human morality plays" within the larger natural context, constantly reminding us that our lives are rooted in nature, from which we alienate ourselves at our own peril. Such an ecocentric position, seeing humans as integrated with nature, rather than controlling or mastering it, is in accordance with the ecological position and an implicit critique of the dualisms inherent in the anthropomorphic attitudes of Western thought of the past centuries. Winton thus supports the environmental cause both through activism and through his creative writing. Some of his novels, especially *Blueback* (1997) and *Shallows* are explicitly about environmental concerns, his stories in general are implicit, impassioned pleas for preserving the fragile ecosystems of the Western Australian region.

Winton, in *Dirt Music*, thus adopts several "ways of seeing" which are not mutually exclusive but together offer a multifocal perspective of the West Australian region and a deep awareness of its various realities—the novel is an example of "dialogic narratives involving multiple ways of seeing" (McGrath 163). What the text foregrounds however, is the bioregional sense of Western Australia, as a unique, strangely beautiful, fragile land which is the habitat of several species of life including humans. In this book as in most of his work, Winton's signature is his topophilia and the resonance of his being with the land where he lives and its life. The tone of confrontation with a "hostile" environment, so characteristic of much of Australian writing of the earlier centuries is nowhere seen in Winton. As Mark Tredinnick (2004) says:

> Australian geographies have their characteristic musics, and rarely, it seems to me, have our prose writer caught those musics—or their colours and forms [. . .].

> We haven't let the land take possessions of our imaginations so that when we speak of it in prose, what we express is the land itself, and our own reconciliation with it. As Indigenous Australians have done for millennia, of course. As our poets, especially Judith Wright and Robert Gray and many others now have done. ("Catching the Lyric of the Country")

Winton is a novelist who has caught the music of the Western Australian land; a writer, who, as Judith Wright (1965) says, is at peace with his landscape (11).

Endnotes

[1] In "Ten Ways of Seeing Landscapes in *Walden* and Beyond" (2000), James McGrath approaches Thoreau's Walden from a similar perspective based on Meinig's ten ways of seeing.

[2] In "The Edge of the World" (1997), a documentary film on Tim Winton and his work, Winton talks about an ongoing writing projects (which eventually develops into *Dirt Music*), and mentions that the novel would tell the story of a character who has to cope with a difficult and isolated environment with no human interaction: "What happens when all the other stuff's gone, when all the trimmings are left out, when the only conjunctions you have are your relationshi p to the landscape and the physical environment around your. Just the business of shelter, food? What happens to you then? I wonder, I really wonder" (*The Edge of the World* 1997).

[3] In his seminal ecocritical work, *The Environmental Imagination: Thoreau, Nature Writing and the Formation of American Culture* (1995), Lawrence Buell studies the significance of maps and map-sense in Barry Lopez's *Arctic Dreams*, a classic text in modern environmental writing. Lopez, says Buell, '[. . .] recognizes the superiority of aboriginal place-sense to western cartography in this respect: "the evidence of continued intimacy with a local landscape – a practical knowledge of it, a sensitivity toward it, a supplication of it"(271).

Works Cited

Bird, Delys. "The Spirit of the Place: Women Writers of the West." *Women's Writing* 5.2 (1998): 240-251.

Bird, Delys, and Dennis Haskell. "Fifty Years with a Blue Pencil." *Westerly* 50 (2005): 9-12.

Brady, Veronica. "Place, Taste and the Making of a Tradition: Western Australian Writing Today." *Westerly* 27.4 (1982): 105-110.

Buell, Lawrence. *The Environmental Imagination: Thoreau, Nature Writing and the Formation of American Culture.* Cambridge: Harvard UP, 1995.

Dixon, Robert. "Tim Winton, *Cloudstreet* and the Field of Australian Literature." *Westerly* 50 (2005): 245-260.

Glotfelty, Cheryll, and Harold Fromm, eds. *The Ecocriticism Reader: Landmarks in Literary Ecology.* Georgia: U of Georgia P, 1996.

Jackson, John. *Discovering the Vernacular Landscape.* New Haven: Yale UP, 1984.

Lawrence, D. H. *Study of Thomas Hardy and other Essays.* 1914. Ed. Bruce Steele. Cambridge: Cambridge UP, 1985

McGrath, James G. "Ten Ways of Seeing Landscapes in *Walden* and Beyond." *Thoreau's Sense of Place: Essays in American Environmental Writing.* Ed. Richard J. Schneider. Iowa City: U of Iowa P, 2000.

Meinig, D. W. "The Beholding Eye: Ten Versions of the Same Scene." *Landscape Architecture* 66 (January 1976): 47-54.

Quin, Rod, and Robyn Quin. "*The Edge of the World*: Viewing Notes." 17 August 2006 <http://www.filmaust.com.au/programs/teachers_notes/6058_edgeworldnotes.pdf>.

Smith, Jules. "Tim Winton - Critical Perspective." *Contemporary Writers.* British Council Arts. 2003. 23 March 2007 <http://www.contemporarywriters.com/authors/?p=auth03c7l3937126351 04>.

Stow, Randolph. *To the Islands.* London: MacDonald, 1958.

The Edge of the World. Dir. Geoffrey Bennett. Prod. Don Featherstone. Film Australia, 1997.

Tredinnick, Mark. "Catching the Lyric of the Country: A Natural History of Australian Nature Writing." ASLE-ANZ. 2004. 23 September 2006 <http://www.asle-anz.asn.au/resources/resources.htm>.

Watzke, Beth. "Writing the West: Regionalism and Western Australia." *Westerly* 1 (Autumn 1992): 21-29.

Winton, Tim. Interview. By Ron Hogan. *Beatrice Interview.* 2001. 17 August 2006 <http://www.beatrice.com/interviews/winton>.

——. *Dirt Music.* Sydney: Picador, 2001.

——. *Down to Earth: Australian Landscapes.* Fremantle, WA: Fremantle Arts Centre P, 1999.

——. *Land's Edge.* Sydney: Picador, 1998.

——. *Blueback.* Sydney: Pan, 1997.

——. Local Colour: Travels in the Other Australia. St Leonards, NSW: Allen & Unwin, 1994.

——. *The Riders.* Chi ppendale, NSW: Pan Macmillan, 1994.

——. *Cloudstreet.* Melbourne: McPhee Gribble, 1991.

——. *That Eye, the Sky.* Melbourne: McPhee Gribble, 1986.

——. *Shallows.* Sydney: George Allen & Unwin, 1984.

Wright, Judith. *Preoccupations in Australian Poetry.* Melbourne: Oxford UP, 1965.

The Poet as a Public Critic
A Study of Christopher Brennan

Phillip A. Ellis

In the conclusion to her review of *The Prose of Christopher Brennan*, the 1962 volume of Brennan's critical and other prose, Sybille Smith makes the following point: "[Christopher Brennan] stands, not only at the beginning of, but unrivalled in, Australian literary criticism" (70). She argues that Brennan eschewed the sort of im pressionistic criticism that had prevailed at that point, and that he followed a course of criticism that was characterised by a number of salient points; she is positive in this review, almost glowing, and, unlike Wallace Kirsop (1963) in his review, she avoids a steady look at Brennan's failings. Brennan should deserve no introduction, given his im portance to Australian literature, yet it may help to know something of him.

Brennan was born in 1870, the eldest son of a brewer. A Catholic, Brennan was educated first at parish schools, thence Riverview College; he entered Sydney University, where he achieved honours in classics. After a brief period as a teacher in Goulbourn, he returned to university study, achieving both his Masters of Arts degree, and a travelling scholarshi p. He then went to Berlin, to study, having taken up poetry by this time. While in Berlin, he met his wife-to-be, and encountered the poetry of Mallarmé, which was to have a decided effect upon his vocation as a poet.

Returning to Sydney, without a degree, and awaiting his fiancée, Brennan eventually joined the staff of the Public Library as a cataloguer. During this time he worked for the university, despite failing to achieve a position there, and he also took up a number of public lectures. In 1908, he finally achieved a position as lecturer in French and German. By 1914, when his major volume of poetry, *Poems*, was published, he was taking on more students, and concentrating upon his teaching work. Around this time, Brennan's marriage began to disintegrate; he had married in 1897, but the combination of his wife's neglect, and the pressures of living with an ill-disposed mother-in-law, helped push Brennan towards drink.

By 1920, Brennan achieved a position as an Associate Professor of German and Comparative Literature. Both the pressures of Brennan's drunkenness, and the after effects of a tragic affair with Violet Singer, led to Brennan's divorce, and his dismissal from his post, in 1925. For a period, Brennan lived in poverty, but the combination of some teaching work at schools and a series of public collections, as well as a small literary pension, afforded to make his final years ones of some small comfort. He died, in 1932, of stomach cancer, a neglected, but revered poet.

Now, the average undergraduate may not be familiar with Brennan the poet, let alone Brennan the critic. Such critical works on Brennan as Randolph Hughes' *C. J. Brennan: An Essay in Values* (1934), and A. R. Chisholm's *Christopher Brennan: The Man and His Poetry*(1946) are long out of print, and rarely accessible to the average undergraduate. Yet, for the Brennan scholar, the importance of such poets as Baudelaire, Mallarmé and the German Romantics on both Brennan's poetic and critical thought, has become somewhat of a commonplace, so much a commonplace that it is little discussed now. Few critics have come close to Katherine Barnes examination of these sources, in her study *The Higher Self in Christopher Brennan's Poems* (2006). Brennan is, of course, more familiar as a poet, rather than a critic, if he is familiar at all. Hence, then, the importance of the companion volume to the *The Verse of Christopher Brennan* of 1960, both as a corrective to the view that Brennan is solely a poet, or, rather, a widening of that same view into more critical territories. For, as Smith (1963) highlights for us, "we receive a powerful complementary image to that of Brennan the poet; the image of Brennan the critic and interpreter" (65). And Kirsop agrees in principle: "The Brennan that emerges from [*Prose*]" he writes, "is essentially the critic" (209-210).

We see this importance as a critic partially from the work that Brennan produced. There is the critical material that he contributed to *From Blake to Arnold*(1900), an anthology of poetry that he edited with his friends J. le Gay Brereton and J. P. Pickburn. There are, also, his public lectures; of this, only the 1904 series on "Symbolism in Nineteenth Century Literature" has been published, in the 1962 *Prose* volume. Then there are his articles. Brennan produced a number of these, around a hundred, roughly, and they vary in importance. Some, like his "Newer French Poetry" series of 1899, covered late Nineteenth Centurc poetics, others covered contemporary Australian literature, or looked at Classical work, like his important "On the Manuscript of Aeschylus" of 1894. Part of Brennan's importance lay in the fact that he was a university critic. A good portion of his critical work was produced in, and for, the university, and this work and emphasis helps in the creation of the Brennan legend. He was, in one way, a university critic, and a university scholar.

Brennan certainly was important as a university critic, as a critic's critic, so to speak, but he also played the role of a public critic. He did so in two main ways: by supplying critical articles for publication, and by public lectures on critical topics. It is possible, as a result, to partially reconstruct a sense of that role through *The Prose of Christopher Brennan*. For, with it, we can make some conclusions about his criticism apparent. Such include recognising the importance of the public lectures for his critical legacy, even if we judge solely from the 1904 lectures on Symbolism. There is also an emphasis upon English, French and German poets in such public venues as the *Bulletin*, and other periodicals. There is also a sense of a basic division of his criticism into two main periods punctuated by the World War I: there is material, such as the extant lectures, that pre-date it, and point towards the development of Brennan's critical interests, and there is material that follows thereafter, pointing towards a cementing (or ossification) of these same interests. Brennan was in his forties when that war occurred, so it is no real surprise to consider his abandonment of new critical interests in favour of the consolidation and reinterpretation of his existing ones. Finally, there is a sense of the importance of Brennan's criticism for the exegesis of his own poetry. Brennan's critical thought illuminates his poetry, and it helps us understand what may seem difficult or obscure.

Of course, there are limitations: the prose volume is hardly complete. There have been, as Kirsop argues, a number of items left out. And imbalances of analysis occur, naturally, when we look at the respective bulk of topics in *The Prose of Christopher Brennan* and consider that same material that is lacking: some topics are ill-represented, such as German literature, and others, such as Classical literature, fail to reflect the nature of Brennan's involvement with the material. Yet, overall we can gain a fair measure of Brennan not only as a critic, but as a public critic, and we can see his importance as a man of letters. Brennan found himself fulfilling a role as a public critic, and, in doing so, he illuminates one role that the public intellectual can still take in contemporary society.

Brennan demonstrates a clear ability as a critic, and as a public critic. Aside from the work produced in association with the University of Sydney, and with his early philological studies, in many ways much of his critical work was produced with a public arena in mind. There are his public lectures, for one; there is *From Blake to Arnold* (1900), produced in association with J. le Gay Brereton and J. P. Pickburn; and there are his articles in the more popular venues, such as the *Bulletin*.

Brennan demonstrates a number of characteristics that typify his criticism at its best. Smith highlights the "combination of powers" that he was to demonstrate: the

> range and depth of scholarship together with sensitivity of response; a sense for patterns of development and relationship together with the ability for close textual commentary [. . .]; a basic good-will; and finally, scrupulous honesty and commitment. (65)

He was, as Kirsop states, "Beyond mere impressionism" (203). Smith goes on to note that "His criticism is both interpretive and evaluative, and he has also a craftsman's approach, a professional interest which gives added solidity to his judgements" (65). In addition, where he is not being vindictive, as in his attacks on both Heine and the *Nibelungenlied* (*The Song of the Nibelungs*), Brennan in attack is "pungent, agile and witty, but also fair," and, in praise, "generous but discriminating" (Smith 66). But Kirsop differs, stating that Brennan

> was comparatively rarely induced to state his position in some detail. When he did, as in his 1904 lectures or in the definition of German Romanticism, he hardly ever failed to be illuminating. (204)

The rest of the time, Kirsop notes, we get "intermittent flashes of insight" in his "numerous rapid and not infrequently sketchy applications of general principles" to his various subjects. (204)

Yet Kirsop is not all negative: he notes specifically how:

> Beyond his superficial pronouncements, his prejudices and sheer bad temper [. . .], his virtual silence on post-Symbolist literature, there is a faculty of analysis and of sympathy rare amongst men of letters, rare still amongst scholars. (204)

Looking at the divergences between Smith and Kirsop, it is possible to gain a clearer insight into where and how Brennan succeeds and fails as a public critic. Brennan had a range of abilities that mark him as an important critic, and as an important public critic. Where he could, he demonstrated a range of faculties, such as that "faculty of analysis and sympathy" in his work that Kirsop praises, and these help distinguish the best of Brennan. Yet Brennan's impact was limited in turn by his choice of venues. He shone, in a sense, but ephemerally: his work graced the public lecture hall, and the fleeting journal, but it lacked, until thirty years after his death, a more permanent venue, the volume of his prose.

It can be seen through a study of that volume that Brennan's public criticism falls into two main phases—pre-World War I, and the decade following, the 1920s. Closer inspection reveals that over half of this material was published in the 1920s. With *The Prose of Christopher Brennan*, the division of the material by subject area partially obscures this chronological division, despite Kirsop noting that "it is possible to follow the progressive definition and elaboration of Brennan's critical position without difficulty" (203). That such is true in the areas of division should be apparent, but a wider, more chronological view of Brennan patterns of activity is, nonetheless, ham pered.

Com pared to the poetry, where there are large periods of silence, this pattern of activity demonstrates that Brennan was productive throughout his life. Where he was active in both areas, prior to the World War I, he wrote less critical material; he concentrated more upon public criticism later on, as a means to an end—to help, at first, codify his thought, then, later, more for monetary motives—rather than as an end in itself. Indeed, in his review of *The Prose of Christopher Brennan*, Kirsop makes the point that "there is am ple evidence that Brennan was, at different moments of his career, far from unproductive" (203). And this is supported by a superficial analysis of Brennan's bibliography.

The first period saw, in 1898, five items later reprinted in *The Prose of Christopher Brennan*. The following year, twelve items are published, that later appear in *The Prose of Christopher Brennan*. 1900 sees the publication of *From Blake to Arnold*, from which the introduction is sam pled, and the other critical material neglected (a number of the critical essays and notes appear later in Sturm, 1984: 227-255). Five items are reprinted from 1902-1903, and only one, "A Regular Hash!" from 1914. There are a number of other items during this period by Brennan, but these remain neglected by *The Prose of Christopher Brennan*, for whatever reason (some appear, or are excerpted in, Sturm 1984). Speaking of the 1899 criticism, Clark notes that Brennan was "in most cases developing ideas and executing plans he had formulated in previous years" (144). Though why Clark should necessarily see this as a drawback is beyond me: there is no reason why there should be a continuity, or a development of earlier interests.

During this period, too, there were a number of public lectures. There are some indications of these beyond the survival of the 1904 lectures on Symbolism. There are, for example, syllabuses for two series of lectures: there is the *Sydney University Extension Lectures: Syllabus of a Course of Six Lectures on Symbolism in Nineteenth Century Literature* of 1904, and there is the 1906 *Sydney University Extension Lectures: Syllabus of a Course of Six Lectures on the Homeric Question.* However, for the most part, the evidence for the lectures has not survived, with the exception, perhaps, of scattered notes in the manuscript collections.

This period also saw an emphasis upon French poets, particularly through the brief series, "Newer French Poetry" of 1899. Clark sees this first major sequence as arising out of the latter half of Brennan's stay in Berlin (144), but this is a development, rather, of the interests of that period, rather than a form of critical atavism. Overall, the articles have a tendency to exhibit the same basic faults as later articles. "Rolling the Stone from the Sepulchre" is, for example, in Kirsop's view, "almost ludicrously cavalier and inexact in its characterisation of classical French literature" (204). And the treatment of some poets, such as Verlaine "remains slight and, finally, unsatisfying" (Kirsop 204).

There is also an emphasis upon Anglophone literature in this period. For instance, the critical anthology *From Blake to Arnold* was intended as a textbook for the New South Wales Junior Examination, but was never set (Clark 154). It contains a good deal of critical material by Brennan about the English poets, both in the introduction and the critical essays and the notes to the individual poems. It also includes a succinct statement about what poetry is, given in the process of defining it: it is Brennan's "central theory" about poetry (Smith 67); he writes that "poetry is the expression of imagination in language, acknowledging that this is not a definition, but a text for explanation" (Brennan, 1962: 14), and in the process of doing so he attempts a definition of Symbolism as he perceived it (Clark 154). According to Clark, Brennan

> considered poetry as the way to a true understanding of the universe, a means to that monistic metaphysic which he had not been able to find in Catholicism or in philosophy. (154)

Whilst Brennan was not to produce the same quantity of critical material, that is preserved in *The Prose of Christopher Brennan* as he was to do later on during this period he was to develop some major pieces central to an understanding of his thought and poetry. What matters now is an understanding of that later period, the 1920s. Again, a superficial examination of Brennan's bibliography can be helpful.

1920 saw ten items published, that are later collected in *The Prose of Christopher Brennan.* Although only three items were published the following year, they are all collected, and 1922 saw only one item that was not likewise collected (it is reprinted in Sturm, however). 1923 saw two items (that appear in *The Prose of Christopher Brennan*) as well as an uncollected third item, and 1924 sees another ten items that are collected. 1925 sees nine items collected, with only three more items, though there are a number of uncollected pieces, for the rest of the decade.

Of these items, the bulk of the surviving critical material was written for payment. They were, in Brennan's piquant phrase, "pot-boilers that boiled a merry pot" (qtd. by Chisholm 31). Again, there is a definite lack of extant transcripts and notes of public lectures; there are no syllabuses either, and this lack of transcripts, notes and syllabuses leads to an over-emphasis on the critical articles. This emphasis, however, the articles fail to support: they are, in Kirsop's words, "journalistic, superficial" (204). During this period, too, there is the second major sequence on French poets, "Studies in French Poetry, 1860-1900," which covers similar ground to the earlier sequence. They can be read as elaborations, renewed and further reflections upon a topic important to Brennan. There is, too, an emphasis upon German and Italian literature, arising out of Brennan's position as a lecturer in comparative literature, which he was to lose in this period. And, unlike the earlier material, there is less importance in his critical material of this period for his poetry.

With the publication of *The Prose of Christopher Brennan*, it became easy to see the importance of Brennan's criticism for the exegesis of his own poetry. This is recognised by Smith, as early as 1963:

> One's first tendency, now that Brennan's prose is available, is perhaps to focus it back onto his poetry, to look for revelations of his thought which will throw light on the more problematical aspects of his work. (65)

Yet, at same time as illuminating his own work, the criticism's primary importance is the illumination of the work so addressed (Smith 65). Kirsop also reflects upon this in his review; he states that the items in *The Prose of Christopher Brennan*

> allow us to grasp clearly the philosophical and aesthetic principles that guide the poet's enthusiasms and dislikes, his literary affinities and ultimately his practice. (203)

Thus the introduction to *From Blake to Arnold* contained Brennan's "general sketch of the symbolist doctrine" as he understood it (Brennan in a letter to F. S. Delmer, 14 December 1900; qtd. in Clark 154): "the image should be directly expressed, without introduction of unnecessary matter" (Brennan, 1962: 315). Further, although German Romanticism is important for our understanding of Brennan's *The Verse of Christopher Brennan*, the late appearance of articles about it does not diminish this importance. Unlike the other early material, which has a direct bearing on the circumstances of the writing of *The Verse of Christopher Brennan*, the collected work on German Romanticism is revelatory in hindsight. Although Brennan intimately understood German Romanticism, and (as Robin Marsden pointed out in a critique of a draft of this essay) though it informs *The Verse of Christopher Brennan*, and his lectures on it reveal a "reliable historical account and analysis" of the essential concepts contributing towards it, we see this only after the immediate circumstances of the poems' composition, after the fact, as it were. The section of *The Prose of Christopher Brennan* dedicated to German Romanticism is seen by Smith as one of the two "most sustained and interesting sections of the book" (66; the other is the section on French Symbolism), and Smith further notes how Brennan "is speaking to a remarkable degree from within Romanticism, from a basically Romantic temperament" (69). Brennan's wider criticism helps us understand his poetry, and the importance of some movements, both of German Romanticism and of French Symbolism, to its exegesis. This, perhaps, is the major reason why we still read it, although it is not the only reason, and it serves to highlight Brennan's achievements as a critic, not only in understanding others' work, but his own as well.

Brennan, in essence, created his own audience. In the same critique, Marsden noted that Brennan was a reader, thence collector, thence contributor to a number of periodicals of his time, in doing so creating his own audience, his own public for his public criticism. He did scorn the "general" public, the "unwashed crowds," largely, as a result of the silence of his fellow critics about him. But such silence was of the lion cubs in the presence of the lion, of inferiors in the presence of their better, and their attitude was tinged with an element of envy. Although there were some open disagreements—A. G. Stephens considered that Brennan did not know his Mallarmé—there was at the same time some respect: Stephens accepted most of Brennan's contributions, and published them in the *Bulletin*.

Of course, Brennan has many achievements as a critic. And it is easy enough, following Smith's example, to list them, and to say, as she does, that

> The ability to show the unity of a work in all its aspects, even the most technical, to reveal "the totality which is nothing else than the poem," is one of Brennan's major achievements. (68)

Yet it is harder to assess Brennan's importance as a public critic only from the selection gathered together into his *The Prose of Christopher Brennan* volume. It does not serve us well in addressing the importance of Brennan's public lectures, for example. We have to look elsewhere, in addition, to gain an understanding of this. There is the emphasis upon the English, French and German poets in his public criticism, criticism which, in the later period at least, has a tendency towards superficiality. This point about the later period reminds us of that division into two periods, each with their own emphases and importance, the former especially for the elucidation of Brennan's own poetry, a major aspect of his critical function. Yet Brennan stands at the beginning of the development of public criticism in Australia. Although there were some, like John le Gay Brereton, and Stephens, who also fulfilled the role of public critic in the Australia of Brennan's time, they seem pallid in comparison to him. In comparison, A. G. Stephen's criticism seems, for example, mere boosterism,and Brereton that of a lesser light. There were others, but they remain in Brennan's shadows, lessers rather than equals, with more faults and failings, and less virtues than Brennan Yet, although Brennan may have had his faults and failings, as Smith reminds us, "Brennan's opinions command respect and attention" (70).

Works Cited

Barnes, Katherine. *The Higher Self in Christopher Brennan's Poems: Esotericism, Romanticism, Symbolism.* Boston: Brill, 2006.

Brennan, Christopher. *The Prose of Christopher Brennan.* Ed. A. R. Chisholm and J. J. Quinn. Sydney: Angus & Robertson, 1962.

——. "[What is Poetry?]." *The Prose of Christopher Brennan.* Ed. A. R. Chisholm and J. J. Quinn. Sydney: Angus & Robertson, 1962. 12-19.

——. "Newer French Poetry: VII: Henri de Régnier (b. 1864)." *The Bulletin* (21 October 1899). *The Prose of Christopher Brennan.* Ed. A. R. Chisholm and J. J. Quinn. Sydney: Angus & Robertson, 1962. 318-322.

——. "Newer French Poetry: VI: Stéphane Mallarmé (1842-98)." *The Bulletin* (9 September 1899). *The Prose of Christopher Brennan.* Ed. A. R. Chisholm and J. J. Quinn. Sydney: Angus & Robertson, 1962. 312-317.

——. "Newer French Poetry: V: Arthur Rimbaud." *The Bulletin* (12 August 1899). *The Prose of Christopher Brennan.* Ed. A. R. Chisholm and J. J. Quinn. Sydney: Angus & Robertson, 1962. 306-312.

——. "Newer French Poetry: IV: Paul Verlaine." *The Bulletin* (1 July 1899). *The Prose of Christopher Brennan.* Ed. A. R. Chisholm and J. J. Quinn. Sydney: Angus & Robertson, 1962. 301-306.

——. "Newer French Poetry: III: Cold Parnassus." *Bookfellow* (31 May 1899): 33-38, 40-44. *The Prose of Christopher Brennan.* Ed. A. R. Chisholm and J. J. Quinn. Sydney: Angus & Robertson, 1962. 296-300.

——. "Newer French Poetry: II: The Lazaretto of Romanticism." *Bookfellow* (29 April 1899): 31. *The Prose of Christopher Brennan.* Ed. A. R. Chisholm and J. J. Quinn. Sydney: Angus & Robertson, 1962. 290-295.

——. "Newer French Poetry: I: Rolling the Stone from the Sepulchre." *Bookfellow* (25 March 1899): 27. *The Prose of Christopher Brennan.* Ed. A. R. Chisholm and J. J. Quinn. Sydney: Angus & Robertson, 1962. 286-290.

——. "Symbolism in Nineteenth Century Literature." *The Prose of Christopher Brennan.* Ed. A. R. Chisholm and J. J. Quinn. Sydney: Angus & Robertson, 1962. 48-173.

——. *Sydney University Extension Lectures: Syllabus of a Course of Six Lectures on the Homeric Question.* Sydney: n. p., 1907.

——. "The Homeric Question." *Sydney University Extension Lectures.* University of Sydney, 1906.

——. *Sydney University Extension Lectures: Syllabus of a Course of Six Lectures on Symbolism in Nineteenth Century Literature.* Sydney: n. p., 1904.

——. "On the Manuscri pt of Aeschylus." *Journal of Philology* 43 (1894): n.pag.

Brennan, Christopher, J. le Gay Brereton, and J. P. Pickburn. *From Blake to Arnold: Selections from English Poetry (1783-1853).* London: Macmillan, 1900.

Chisholm, A. R. "Biographical Introduction." *The Verse of Christopher Brennan.* Ed. A. R. Chisholm and J. J. Quinn. Sydney: Angus & Robertson, 1960: 1-38.

——. *Christopher Brennan: The Man and His Poetry.* Sydney: Angus and Robertson, 1946.

Clark, Axel. *Christopher Brennan: A Critical Biography.* Carlton, Victoria: Melbourne UP, 1980.

Hughes, Randolph. *C. J. Brennan: An Essay in Values.* Sydney: P. R. Stephenson, 1934.

Kirsop, Wallace. "Brennan, Critic and Scholar." *Southerly* 23 (1963): 203-210.

Marsden, Robin. Personal communication. 5 March 2007.

Needler, George Henry, trans. *Nibelungenlied.* 1904. 22 February 2007 <http://www.authorama.com/nibelungenlied-1.html>.

Smith, Sybille. "Brennan's Stature as Critic." *Quadrant* 7.1 (Summer 1963): 65-70.

Sturm, Terry, ed. *Christopher Brennan.* St. Lucia: U of Queensland P, 1984.

Once More with Feeling
The Strange History of Manning Clark[1]

Mark McKenna

We give what we have. The rest is the madness of art. (Clark 1967)[2]

Among the portraits and photographs that hang in the living room of Manning Clark's former home in Tasmania Circle, Canberra, there is a pencil sketch by Charles Blackman, "Drifting." Out on the water, two men sit in a boat; no land is in sight. Another figure, completely white, stands just behind the bow: an apparition defying the current. Manning Clark saw himself as much like the ghostly figure in Blackman's sketch, as the artist-historian seeking a solitary understanding of the human condition. Clark's was a singular vision—emotive and mischievous, tortured and divine—like that of no other historian or writer of his generation.

Manning Clark relished cultivating an image of himself as the lone outsider. When he sought to place his work in the context of Australian historiography—even on the first occasion, at a Melbourne University seminar in 1954—he dismissed nearly all the writing of Australian history that had gone before him as the product of the dead hand of British imperialism and Protestantism. He could see little cause for optimism in his own generation: the radical historians were wedded to a rigid creed that denied the mystery in human experience and lacked a great theme (Clark, 1980: 3-19). Three years later, in the introduction to *Sources of Australian History* (1971), he wrote that Australian history after 1919 was "like an uncharted sea" (ix). Clark was adept at leaving himself as the last man standing, the only historian with sufficient insight and breadth of interest to rewrite Australian history. This task was made all the more noble—in his eyes, at least—by virtue of the fact that its execution was entirely cut off from conversation with his contemporaries. In private, Clark heeded the advice of his colleagues, but he chose not to acknowledge other historians in his work, continuing with the pretence that he was writing history from a tabula rasa.

Clark warned historians not to read what others had to say until they'd completed their early drafts, "and maybe not then." The duty of the historian was to create history anew from primary sources; he insisted that historians should never "start arguing with what others have to say." But Clark went much further than merely shying away from argument. In his histories, he could not even bring himself to discuss the research and work of others. To do so would only obscure the individuality of the historian's voice, one cast in the mould of nineteenth-century European romanticism—Beethoven, Goethe and Caspar David Friedrich–that of the artist-hero who stands alone on the cliff and gazes out to sea, seeking sublime inspiration (Clark, 1992: 60).

In his Boyer Lectures, delivered in 1976, Clark listed the writers that had sparked his interest in writing a multi-volume history of Australia: Chekhov, Hardy, Dickens, Dostoevsky, Tolstoy, James. Not one historian of Australia—not one scholar—is mentioned, though Henry Lawson, Patrick White, Henry Handel Richardson and Martin Boyd are credited with providing inspiration. Although Clark spent 30 years within the academy (in 1949 he was appointed professor of history at Canberra University College, now the Australian National University, and remained there for the rest of his career), he preferred to place his work in the company of artists. And most historians who have written about Clark's place in Australian historiography seem happy to leave him there, hovering in a no-man's land, somewhere between nineteenth-century literature and an antiquated form of epic history. There is a broad consensus that Clark simply does not fit into the schema of Australian historiography in any significant way.

Stuart Macintyre and Alan Atkinson have both drawn attention to the fact that few historians have sought to engage with Clark's work, save for one or two embarrassing attempts to imitate him (see Macintyre 1987 and 994). Historians have ignored Clark in much the same way that Clark ignored the work of others. In the multi-volume Bicentennial history *Australians: A Historical Library* (1987), Clark's six-volume *History of Australia* (1962-1987), by then complete, received little attention. Reviewing the posthumously published *A Historian's Apprenticeship* in 1992, Geoffrey Blainey described Clark as ploughing a "lonely furrow" and being "deliberately deaf to many of the questions that excited social scientists."

True to form, Clark was out of step with the intellectual fashions and preoccupations of his colleagues. He was the great generalist in a time of increasing specialisation. The revisionist history of the 1960s and 70s had little impact on his work, while his dogged pursuit of a prose style recalling Macaulay or Carlyle was already passé by 1962, when volume I of *A History of Australia* was published. Richard Waterhouse has neatly characterised Clark's work as "a belated attempt at an Australian national history" (see "Controversies in Australian History") in the mode of George Bancroft, replacing Bancroft's emphasis on progress with an unfolding tale of "the collapse of social purpose." As Stuart Macintyre wrote in 1994, "in bypassing the work of others, [Clark] created a gulf that few specialists sought to cross" (26).

Manning Clark's audience was not the academy. Like the village parson and the local MP, he spoke often of his connection with ordinary people. Today, publishers would bid furiously for the work of a historian who saw himself as akin to "an actor on a revolving stage" (see Crawford et al., 1988: 66). Historians, said Clark (1984), "should be judged by their success in increasing wisdom and understanding and their capacity to entertain" (133). Clark wrote for the public gallery, and his prose is ever conscious of its presence, even to the point of inserting the applause, guffaws and shouts of abuse from an imagined public chorus into his narrative. And to keep his audience entertained, it was sometimes necessary to be flexible with the facts. Clark's eye was first and foremost on the dramatic impact of the narrative. Humphrey McQueen once told me, "I would never go to Manning to look up dates" (Personal interview 2006).

My own experience with Clark has been similar. When I first read him, in my early twenties, I did not rush off to read the work of other Australian historians. Instead, I went to listen to Bach's *Well-Tempered Clavier*, and to the final movement of Sibelius's Fifth Symphony. If I went to Clark to look anything up, it was to find the pieces of music that he found inspiring. Years later, working on my doctoral thesis, I discovered that chasing the trail of Clark's footnotes was a fruitless task. Like many before me, I could not crack Clark's code. Quotes frequently appeared in his work that seemed to bear no relation to the sources in the notes—or, as was more often the case, they blended so seamlessly with his own prose that it was impossible to tell who was speaking. It seemed that he saw primary sources as something akin to a musical score, a mere form of notation upon which he would improvise, providing a magnificent libretto for another Clark oratorio. All of this raises important questions: If Manning Clark's work is not seen as a reliable historical account, and is rarely used in schools and universities in the teaching of Australian history, what might we go to it *for*? What is it that makes Clark's work memorable? And how are we to understand the value of his work?

Finding Inspiration

> I would like to be a writer—But how! My style is poor, my vocabulary lamentably small, and my ideas indistinct. Yet I do receive inspiration, by which I mean my mind becomes filled with an idea, and I want to develop it—then I am excited [. . .] to achieve my goal I must (i) discipline myself—no excesses—an artist should observe, (ii) Note down my ideas and impressions, (iii) Not be dependent on people. (Clark 1942)

After all that has been written on Manning Clark, it seems trite to claim that his work needs to be critically understood as literature rather than history. As Peter Munz perceptively wrote in 1979, Clark's work demonstrated that Australian history was "but a variation on the universal themes of life and death, greed and hope, curse and vengeance"—he had effectively created Australia's past as "a series of myths" (13). Despite the brutalising history of convictism, frontier violence and a harsh environment, Clark showed, as Humphrey McQueen claimed in 1987, that Australia could still be "a mythopoeic site" (3). Certainly, Clark's work is literary in its imaginative scope, its field of reference and its depth of feeling. In positive reviews, *A History of Australia* is described as a literary masterpiece. In critical reviews, it is condemned for being clichéd, derivative and repetitive. Still, as Michael Cathcart noted in 1995, for all the references to Clark's literary imagination, "no one has really managed to articulate the translucent quality in [his] work [. . .] or quite identified how his literary imagination works, or why it gives the history a value which is not undermined by its idiosyncrasies and inaccuracies" (Cathcart to Carl Bridge, 1995; see also Cathcart, "Big Ideas": 2003).

One way of appreciating how Manning Clark's literary imagination functions is to examine his personal voice. It is a feature of his work that was frequently commented upon by critics, especially in the context of his literary skill. On the publication of volume I of *A History of Australia*, Max Crawford (1962) noted "the very distinctive personal vision" (7) that Clark brought to his subject. As each subsequent volume appeared, Crawford's remarks were replayed. Reviewers described volume

II as "personal and burning, and fascinatingly readable," "highly personal," "idiosyncratic" and "highly original world view" (see also reviews in *News Weekly* 1968; *Sydney Morning Herald* 1968; Serle 1974). Exactly how Clark's personal voice functioned, few sort to tease out. In what sense then was Clark's work personal?

The first-person pronoun never appears in the six volumes. Yet Clark's work was deeply personal long before historians such as Greg Dening, Miriam Dixson, Peter Read, Inga Clendinnen or Tom Griffiths, among others, began to bring personal experience and reflections into their prose. Nor was Clark's voice in any way transparent or self-reflective. Indeed, he warned budding historians not to discuss the problems of writing with the reader: "the narrator must learn to shut up" (1992: 40), he proclaimed, and this from an author whose volumes were steeped in personal comment. But if Clark's work was *political*, it was so in a unique way. Consider, for example, the bold statements of position by some of Clark's contemporaries. History is "the struggle between the organised rich and the organised poor" (Fitzpatrick 1940); "I am for the weak not the strong, the poor not the rich, the exploited many not the select few" (Ward, 1987: Preface); "This book is deliberately biased" (McQueen 1974); "This history is critical not celebratory. It rejects myths of national progress and unity. It starts from a recognition that Australian settler society was built on invasion and dispossession" (Burgmann and Lee, 1988: Introduction). Nowhere in Clark's histories did he seek to reveal his political sympathies so openly, yet it is he who is remembered by some as the most politically prejudiced historian of the post-war period——a memory preserved by John Howard, who has attacked Clark's alleged communist sympathies and his bleak view of "the Australian achievement."[3] To a large extent, Clark earned the ire of conservatives not only because his history cast the Labor Party as the engine of Australia's national progress, but because his public statements characterised the non-Labor parties as little more than moneychangers and philistines. In its intent, however, Clark's *History of Australia* was less overtly political than the work of many left-leaning historians who were writing at the same time.

If Manning Clark's voice is personal, this quality emerges in his telling of history, in his selection of primary sources, in his presentation of conflict, and in his endless search to understand the inner life of his protagonists, a search that led him to employ emotional language which lacked the one quality that historians of his generation tended to admire: "sober restraint" (the words "sober restraint" belong to Macintyre, see 1987: 21). Clark's personal voice was not grounded in political statements or in any prefiguring of post-modern scholarship, but rather in a profound religiosity, and it is this highly individual understanding of the religious—ecumenical and spiritual, in the broadest sense–that gives Clark's work its depth of feeling and its distinctive, redeeming personal quality. It is also a feature of his oeuvre that takes shape very early. Clark opened *Puzzles of Childhood* (1989), the first volume of his autobiography, with a story he told many times. He remembered his mother telling him as he sat on the lawn in the backyard of his parents' house at Burwood in Sydney's inner-west (he was no more than four-and-a-half years old), "Mann, dear, you are a very special boy. There's nothing you can't do if you want to do it" (*Puzzles of Childhood* 1). Of course, like all his autobiographical writings, the truth of this recollection is uncertain. But it still captures an essential truth about Clark—his belief in his unique powers of perception and insight, something that was evident from the moment he began to write, in his early twenties:

> [I am thinking of writing a] short article on Australian culture [. . .] but it is an artistic experience, not a conclusion from evidence [. . .]. My idea is: in Australia we are uncertain of everything, we feel insecure. What is the cause of this? [. . .]. First [. . .] geography, the hostile environment, the fear experienced when alone [. . .] second, the doubt, do we belong here, perhaps this is geography, perhaps history [. . .] third, Australia as the harlot, raped by the Europeans, coarse, vulgar, meretricious [. . .] I should write this when in an inspired mood. (Clark, Diaries: 15-22 February 1943).

In his early diaries—from the time of his arrival in Oxford, in 1938, until he began teaching the first full course in Australian history at the University of Melbourne, in 1946—Manning Clark wrote frequently of the fits of inspiration that would descend upon him, the words racing through his mind "like water with the light shining on it" (Clark, Diaries: October 1942). It was something that he described frequently as being received, "images rising before [his] mind" (Clark, Diaries: October 1942; see also Clark's diaries throughout September and October 1942 for similar comments), in the manner of a painter facing a blank canvas. From the beginning, Clark found writing a struggle. Inspiration came, but he often railed against his inability to express on the page the thoughts that possessed him. This sense of failure and dissatisfaction with his work remained with him until the end of his life. But he had no choice other than to follow the flashes of inspiration that he received.

Gazing at paintings or photographs, standing before monuments or historical sites, conversing with friends and colleagues, Clark was fired by inspiration that came from an unknown but implicitly divine source. He claimed that he wanted to understand what had moved men, had inspired and defeated them, believing that "what happens and has happened in life mocks the fitness of things" (*Speaking Out of Turn* 65). These words, echoing Ecclesiastes—"All is vanity"—not only articulated his motivation as a historian. They also expressed the drama and conflict of his personal life.

From Clark's six volumes, and particularly his writings on history (he wrote more on the writing of history than most historians), there is the familiar refrain of Manning Clark, Historian: the seeker of the heart and soul of human beings (usually men), the worrier over the question of faith and what it meant to live in a Godless world, the tragedian, the writer who drew inspiration from art, literature and music and who, following Carlyle, saw history as the "true epic poem of mankind" and himself as "one of the muses" that could "communicate a vision of the world" (*Speaking Out of Turn* 58, 66). What remains uncertain, however, is the extent to which Clark's highly personal historical voice was shaped by his personal life.

Several historians have hinted at the autobiographical dimension of Clark's work. Reviewing volume II, Geoffrey Serle (1974) referred to the "depth of personal experience" that informed Clark's work. In *Suspect History* (1997), Humphrey McQueen gives the well-known example from volume IV, where Clark has Robert Burke suffering from a "fit of the sillies," before claiming that "Clark carried concerns from his life and memoirs into his history" (129). More recently, on Radio National, Michael Cathcart (2003) insisted that the great theme of Clark's history—"the struggle between Catholicism, Protestantism and the Enlightenment"—was really Clark's "lifelong struggle." Manning Clark admitted this much to be true. In 1976, he acknowledged that the central conflicts in his history—especially that of the English inheritance versus the native born—were, as he put it, "in my veins" (*Occasional Writings and Speeches* 36). Beyond the obvious tension between the different family backgrounds of his parents, the personal quality of Clark's historical voice was connected intimately with his personal life.

The polyvocal element of Clark's history—or, as Peter Craven (1999) once called it, his "point-of-view writing"—is one example. Clark's later volumes teem with voices simultaneously playing variations on a theme. Like a Handel Oratorio, they rise up to take their designated role in the score, given an added touch of Clarkian drama here, an extra bit of Clarkian pathos there.[4] The voices within his text mirror those within his mind: Clark often referred to himself as a "polyphon," a man of many voices. He claimed to hear the future-of-humanity voice, the sceptical voice, the eye of pity, the voice of doubt about everything, the voice of "Mr. Passion" and countless other nondescript voices within "Mr. Passion." In Clark's mind, the music of these voices played constantly, usually in unresolved tension, conveying "an eternal restlessness and discontent." Just as he could never discipline the voices in his text, he had little control over the voices within his head (for Clark's many voices, see Clark, 1980: 60-61).

Clark presented many of his lead characters (Wentworth, Lawson, Curtin) as divided personalities brought down by the predictable "fatal flaw," and his private correspondence reveals that he thought of himself in much the same way. In letters to his friends and to his wife, Dymphna (24 December 1972), he refers to "the Double" (a description taken from the title of an early short story by Dostoevsky), the other Manning Clark who is usually saddled with responsibility for the drinking and sinful behaviour that brings the more virtuous Clark down (this correspondence is held by the family). As the voices arose in his text, slowly taking shape and life as different characters, so the voices within his mind fought for dominance, embodying the potential persons that he might become. They also serve to displace responsibility for his behaviour.

Many of the leading characters in Clark's histories are animated by the same inner conflicts and dramas that racked Clark. They personify his inner struggles. Driven from elsewhere, by some unknown force, they struggle to attain a moral sensibility and control over their own destiny. They fight to assert their own conscience, naively cling to the dream of human perfectibility, doubt the existence of God, and strain to find purpose and meaning in life. They suffer because of their knowledge of human beings' capacity for evil (a capacity which they know is also inside of *them*), and they are confronted with the conflict between the desires of the flesh and the needs of the spirit. And, now and then, they are brought down by a fit of the sillies.

Clark, prompted by Kathleen Fitzpatrick (20 November 1962), a great fan of Henry James, Clark became fond of borrowing James's phrase, the "felt life." He believed that he could not write history as art until he had accumulated a sufficient quantity of felt life. He needed a bank of his own excitements and disappointments, his successes and heartbreaks, before he could write about the inner life of others, before he could inform their world with the shared experience of his own life. In this sense, Clark's historical voice is personal like few other historians. The past becomes the site for expressing and working through his deepest feelings. His lifelong fear of the wolves—the critics whom, he imagined, would tear his work to pieces—points to the deeply personal nature of his history. Having invested so much feeling, so much of his inner self in his work, he felt that he had laid himself open, and he trembled like a child in search of approval at the thought of his creation being subjected to censure or derision.

Epiphany and Revelation: The Story of Kristallnacht

> I think that's what you've got to get over in a history—those moments, those epiphanies in human experience. (Clark 1987)

In the last 20 years of his life, after his retirement, Manning Clark began to construct his own mythology—as historian, writer and public figure. When he tried to tell the story of why he became a historian, and explain the personal vision that drove him to write *A History of Australia*, he often recited a series of personal epiphanies. In Clark's telling, these are moments of profound intellectual and spiritual revelation. They arrive like the words of an angel, shrouded in mystery, in a process that remains partially hidden—even from Clark himself. Through their telling, and in the contemplation of the morals they contain, Clark navigates his way through life. The epiphanies provide inspiration and ultimately, they serve as the *raison d'etre* of Manning Clark: historian, both informing and guiding his personal voice need to find circumflex.

There are many Clarkian epiphanies. First, there are the epiphanies of place: visiting Cologne Cathedral for the first time, awestruck at the beauty created by man to praise God; standing on the South Head of Sydney Harbour, the sight of the turbulent sea making him want to write about what was inside the hearts and minds of the convicts; gazing at the ruins of Yorkshire's Whitby Abbey and dreaming of telling the story of how the Europeans had brought those two Great Expectations—Catholic Christendom and the Enlightenment—to the ancient continent of Australia. There were the library epiphanies: discovering the Hindu fables about the world to the south of Java in a museum library in Jakarta; crying after reading that Magellan's "black eyes wept" when he realised he had found a way through to the Pacific; seeing John Henry Newman's pencilled notes on truth in an 1864 article by Charles Kingsley in *MacMillan's Magazine*, the genesis of Newman's *Apologia Pro Vita Sua* (1866). There were also the epiphanies that came through the meeting of fellow artists—James McAuley (b. 1917 - d. 1976), Patrick White (b. 1912 - d. 1990), David Campbell (b. 1915 - d. 1979) and many others, bonds and friendships created by a spark of unspoken recognition and understanding rather than being earned slowly over time. Finally, there are the numerous epiphanies which relate to Clark's encounters with art, music and literature–listening to Bach's B Minor Mass or the slow movement of Beethoven's Sonata Opus 111; hearing Henry Handel Richardson read from *The Fortunes of Richard Mahony* (1930); viewing Sidney Nolan's *Riverbend* (1964-65) or standing before Rembrandt's *Return of the Prodigal Son* (1662) in the Hermitage Museum in St. Petersburg; reading White, Hope, Chekhov, James or the usual suspect, Dostoevsky—all of these encounters made Clark realise that history must always run second to art as a form of human expression. Yet of all Clark's epiphanies, there is one that stands out for its allegorical power. It is the one that he tells most often, the one he invests with the most significance, especially because it explains the genesis of his life's work as a historian (for Clark's various epiphanies, see *A Historian's Apprenticeship*, especially chapter 1, although the first three chapters contain a succession of them; his list of musical works, for example, appears on 50).

Of all Clark's epiphanies, though, there is one that stands out for its allegorical power. It is the one that he told most often, the one he invested with the most significance, especially because it explains the genesis of his life as a historian. So far as I can tell, Clark first told the story publicly in 1978, in an unpublished background piece he prepared for Rob Pascoe, who was then writing a profile of Clark for the *National Times*. Pascoe's article, "The History of Manning Clark," led with the story, describing the 23-year-old Clark arriving at Bonn on the morning after Kristallnacht, on 10 November 1938: "Clark made his way amid the debris throughout Bonn in a state of disbelief." Two years later, in 1980, the background article Clark had prepared for Pascoe was published under the title "Themes in A History of Australia" in Clark's *Occasional Writings and Speeches* (1980). Throughout the 80s, Clark was invited to reminisce about his life and career in the national media, and he told the Kristallnacht story many times. In 1987, interviewed by John Tranter on Radio National, he offered a typically powerful telling:

> What really got me going was that when I was about 22 or 23 I went to Germany to meet the woman I was going to marry, and I happened to arrive at the railway station at Bonn am Rhein on the morning of Kristallnacht. That was the morning after the storm-troopers had destroyed Jewish shops, Jewish businesses and the synagogues. Burned them and so on. And I came up out of the Bonn railway station, my head stuffed with these myths about progress and so on. And there I was confronted with these storm-troopers. Of course they didn't menace me, or threaten me. But I saw the fruits of evil, of human evil, before me there on the streets of Bonn.
>
> Over the next three or four years, I gradually had to abandon all the myths I'd grown up with. That my world, my intellectual equi pment, my spiritual equi pment, couldn't cope with what I'd seen in Germany. And all the things that had meant a great deal to me and probably still do mean a great deal to me, like *Hymns Ancient and Modern*, the Old Testament, the King James Bible, the Dry Souls of the Enlightenment, as Carlyle called them, the hopes about things better, the belief in the British——all this had to go and I had to start on a new pilgrimage to see, was there anything which could replace these myths which I think I found then didn't correspond with the world as I'd come to know it.

This telling of the Kristallnacht epi phany is similar to the version in *Occasional Writings and Speeches*, as are the lessons Clark draws from the encounter, except that in the published article, Clark wrote about himself in the third person ("the author"), more consciously creating a figure of myth. One year after the Tranter interview, the story appeared again in R. M. Crawford and Stuart Macintyre's *Making History* (1985), in Clark's brief paper explaining his approach to the writing of history:

> When I came up out of the Bonn railway station on the morning of 11 November I was confronted by men in military uniforms who had machine guns in their hands. They were wearing huge breeches. They would have made marvellous shepherd rucks for Carlton in the old

> days. That morning in the *Volkischer Beobachter* Dr. Goebbels explained that the German people had taken their revenge on the Jews for the attem pt by a Jew named Grunspan to assassinate a member of the German Embassy in Paris. Once again [. . .] I found myself chewing over the question of human evil. There were at least two people inside me—the optimist and meliorist, and, dare one say it, the part-time messianic; and the other pessimistic, gloomy, the person who saw no answers to the problem of evil, or, as I liked to put it in those five volumes, "the madness in men's hearts." (1980: 57-58)

After telling the Kristallnacht story on ABC TV and radio on several more occasions in the 80s, it appeared for the final time in the second volume of Clark's autobiography, *Quest for Grace*, published in 1990. At the last moment, in his ink scrawl, Clark had added the following words in the margins of the volume's final typescri pt draft:

> Dym phna was there on the platform at the Bonn railway station when I stepped off the train early in the morning of 8 November 1938 [. . .] we were in for a rude shock, it was the morning after "Kristallnacht" [. . .] glass was everywhere on the footpath [. . .] there were trucks with men in uniform standing in the tray. (68-69)

If there is one personal experience that explains Clark's life and work, it is his experience of Kristallnacht, the point when the Nazi persecution of Jews turned towards the Holocaust. In a small village outside of Dresden, the diarist and literary scholar Victor Klem perer described his fear and sense of im pending horror after the events of the night. Many of his friends "had been arrested and taken away." Klem perer himself was arrested but later released. He was "free," he wrote, "but for how long"? Like many Jews, he was "tormented by the question [. . .] to go where we have nothing [or] to remain in this corruption?" As the persecution of Jews spread, Klem perer, under curfew from noon till 8 pm, felt that he "could not bear it any more—I really felt as if I could not breathe" (263-266). For Manning Clark, the encounter in Bonn sends him on a journey to seek an understanding of the human condition. It is his Creation story, taking him back to the ancient classics, the Old Testament and Shakespeare. Witnessing the aftermath of Kristallnacht, the shards of glass still on the street, Clark confronts Conrad's heart of darkness, and he doubts the capacity of the Enlightenment to deliver human beings peace and happiness. It is the "beginning of an awakening [. . .] the moment when the author realised that he would have to start to think again about the whole human situation. He would have to base his beliefs on something more solid than those superficial, shallow ideas picked up in Melbourne" (*Occasional Writings and Speeches* 84). For Clark, history needed to be much more than an empirical or scientific endeavour: it also needed to be spiritual, a work of individual artistic expression that remained true to the personal voice and feelings of the man within. This was his credo.

In early 2006, I was reading correspondence from the 30s between Clark and his wife-to-be, Dymphna Lodewyckx. In late 1938, Clark was at Oxford's Balliol College, reading history, while Dympna was in Bonn, studying German literature in preparation for her doctorate. The two scholarship winners, deeply in love, had sailed together from Australia in August 1938. It was late and I was tired, struggling as usual with Clark's handwriting. Reading one letter from Dymphna to Clark, dated 12 November 1938, I suddenly realised that Clark had not been in Bonn on the morning after Kristallnacht. At first, I thought I'd made a mistake. Like many others, I had taken Clark at his word. I had even quoted the Kristallnacht story in my published work. I re-read Dymphna's letter carefully, checked Clark's diary entries, and saw that it was impossible for Clark to have been in Bonn on the morning of 10 November. As his own diary confirms, he did not arrive in Bonn until 26 November, more than two weeks after Kristallnacht (which, as we know, was the night of 9 November). It was Dymphna Lodewyckx, not Manning Clark, who witnessed the immediate aftermath of Kristallnacht. She wrote to Clark on 12 November 1938, when he was still in Oxford, and she wrote again on 24 November, two days before Clark arrived in Bonn. In the letter of 12 November, she described the scene:

> The violence was over when I came—but the crowds were everywhere—following the smiling SS men, children shouting in excitement, grown-ups silent, except for children. We went along lots of streets, & saw about 15 smashed shops—mercers, frock shops, & laundry, a silk shop etc. Then we went down to the Rhein and saw the smoking ruins of the synagogue. Behind it the rabbi's house was burning [. . .] Weitergehen! Weitergehen! [Keep moving!] from the police was the only sound to be heard except the shuffling feet of hundreds of curious sightseers, so we left the Rhein where the grey evening mist was just rising over the poplars & factory chimneys and the western sky was all rosy [. . .] I went home but couldn't work [. . .] on the way to the forest, I passed a second, smaller synagogue, gutted like the first [. . .]. (this correspondence is held by the family)

Later, in the company of a friend, the Swiss student Hans Ehrenzeller, Dymphna walked the streets of Bonn to "see the sights." She enclosed the article by Josef Goebbels that Clark referred to in one of his tellings of the Kristallnacht aftermath, describing it as "a gem" before remarking that "gentlemen in uniform were not very conspicuous during the actual venting of righteous wrath." Although she did write that she had heard one girl say that "gentlemen in black poured the oil on the synagogue here, & others set it on fire" (12 November 1938).

I felt a sense of disbelief and disappointment at having been misled, but this did not last long. When I told two of my friends, both historians, about my discovery, the response was the same: "Oh, no!" they said, sighing. Like me, they wished that Clark had been there; they wished that the historian, of all people, would not play with the truth in such a way. When I told two other friends, both novelists who had known Clark, the response was different: "Isn't that fantastic?" they said. "Typical Manning—theatrical, playful, pulling your leg. What a great subject for a biography!" It was as if they could imagine Clark laughing from beyond the grave. The novelists made me stop my rush to judgement. I began to see Clark's untruth as the most revealing parable of all.

Manning Clark not only placed himself in Bonn on the morning after Kristallnacht; he also appears to have used some of the material in Dymphna's letter, mixed it with his own recollections, and made it his own. In *Quest for Grace*, for example, he describes walking the streets of Bonn with Dymphna and Hans Ehrenzeller after Kristallnacht, as well as a later meal with two Irish students in a university *mensa*. These events seem to be taken directly from Dymphna's account (*Quest for Grace* 69). More importantly, Clark, by claiming the story as his own, denied Dymphna the voice of the narrator. Three years after Clark died, she wrote to Carl Bridge (the head of the Menzies Centre for Australian Studies at King's College, London), trying to dispel what she called "the myth of Manning's rejection of Oxford." But her letter revealed much more. She wrote to Bridge,

> In December-January 1938-39 [Manning] certainly took an extended Christmas vacation to come to Bonn, but he returned willingly to Balliol and left only when the outbreak of war made it necessary for him to find a job. (14 November 1993)[5]

"December-January," not November. This letter demonstrates that Dymphna's memory was quite different from Manning Clark's. Dymphna Clark was not one to play with the facts. And, reading her blunt and occasionally caustic editorial comments on his manuscripts, it is difficult to imagine that, sometime between 1978 and his death, in 1991, she did not question Clark's recollection (See Dymphna Clark's comments on the *Quest For Grace* manuscripts). Given her nature, it is possible that one morning at Tasmania Circle, Dymphna climbed the ladder to Clark's study, confronted him and said, "Manning, you weren't there, you know you weren't there. What do you think you're doing?" Exactly why she chose to remain publicly silent is an intriguing question. The most obvious answer is probably the right one: she was so loyal to him that she could never betray him. There is another, related question. When Clark told the Kristallnacht tale, he did so in the context of telling his life story. He had retired and was already a significant national figure. Why could he not have told the story of Kristallnacht through Dymphna? Why did he need to reduce her to a woman who was simply waiting on the steps of the railway station to marry him? Why did he need so desperately to be the one who was there? Most likely, Clark, the great historian, needed to be there to make the parable of Kristallnacht more powerful, to draw from the events the great lessons he had undoubtedly drawn. In this sense, there is no fabrication. The impact of Kristallnacht on Clark was genuine and profound, somehow pushing aside the mere fact that he was not physically present. In the same way that Clark felt he could not write about events in the past without visiting the places where those events had occurred, he felt he could not speak of the significance of Kristallnacht for his intellectual and spiritual development without having been present. Clark needed to be *the* witness—the only way he could make meaning of the past was to inhabit it—and he willed himself to be there. Here, another question arises: How conscious was Clark's invention?

Traces of Truth: Understanding the Kristallnacht Epiphany

> [The historian] cannot invent facts, or put into the mouths of characters words which they never used. If he does, he slides into fiction or imaginative biography. (Clark, *Boyer Lectures*: 1976)[6]

In a life-long partnership, a couple's memories can sometimes become one, and through Dymphna, Manning Clark no doubt felt he *was* there in Bonn on the morning after Kristallnacht. He had, after all, arrived in

Bonn only two weeks later, on Saturday, 26 November 1938. His diary entry for that day reveals a young man shocked by what he saw:

> I walked round the town, struggling against the oppressiveness, the sea of hostile, hard faces, and the strangeness of my surroundings [. . .] uniforms, pictures of Hitler, notices in form of command, not of request. And yet life went on here very much the same as in England. It was very bewildering, almost frightening. (Clark, Diary: 25-26 November 1938)

Months later, he was certainly dwelling on the question of evil. He wrote in his diary on 15 February 1939, "I have been worried lately by the problem of evil, the existence of which we are apt to ignore in our frantic search for the ideal." When Clark arrived in Bonn, he saw the Nazi storm-troopers and was frightened by them; he also saw and heard evidence from several people of the Nazis' persecution of the Jews; and he was torn over the best means of resolving the political crisis between Germany and England—to appease or not to appease. His experience in Nazi Germany is the beginning of the polyphon. As he told an audience at Melbourne University in 1980, "after the experience in Bonn in November 1938, followed by quite an epiphany in Cologne Cathedral in the same year, my mind was rather like a fugue in four voices" (Clark, 1980: 60). For Clark, it is the beginning of his confrontation with the "age of unbelief." Kristallnacht, the portent of the Holocaust, is mankind's fall from grace. In this sense, there is considerable truth in Clark's account of it. The truth lies in the felt part—the emotional and moral truth—and the conclusions drawn. He did not see the glass on the street or the smoke rising from the burning synagogues on the morning of 10 November, but he certainly experienced its aftermath and the increasing terror of the Nazi dictatorship.

At the same time, there is also something typically, comically Clarkian about the whole affair. Each time Clark tells the story, he has himself arriving in Bonn on a different day. In *Quest for Grace*, he arrives in Bonn on 8 November; in *Making History*, he arrives on 11 November. On other occasions, he arrives in "early November" or on "one of the mornings after Kristallnacht" (*Quest for Grace* 68). Many years later, after reading *Quest for Grace*, a friend of Hans Ehrenzeller wrote to Dymphna, noting that Hans had lived for another four years after the date Clark had given as his death.[7] It is also highly unlikely that Dymphna met Clark at the *Hauptbahnhof* in Bonn, as he claimed. Clark's journey from London would have taken him through Belgium and across the border to Cologne. Here, Clark would have needed to change trains in order to get to Bonn, a journey of a little over half an hour on a regional train. Dymphna had written to him shortly before he left Oxford for Bonn, on 18 November, telling him that she would meet him in Cologne (18 November 1938; this correspondence is held by the family). Clark's details and dates, as usual, are unreliable. But as always with Manning Clark, the dates are not the issue. He seems to have streamlined these minor details in his telling of the story, in order to dramatise his arrival. Typically, he describes it in theatrical terms—coming up out of the darkness of the underground onto the streets of Bonn, meeting his waiting lover, confronting the portent of the twentieth century's greatest horror. The scene is operatic—both romantic and tragic—like Verdi doing Shakespeare. But it is also deeply existential. In late 1938, Clark was afraid of the onset of war. He feared for Dymphna's safety, and for his own. On a much larger scale, he feared for Europe and the future of civilisation. His Anglican upbringing and Enlightenment beliefs were no match for the Nazi terror. In this sense, the desolation Clark feels as he tells the Kristallnacht story half a century later is for the sake of the future and not for the sake of understanding the past. The question he asks—Where to now?—he asks of himself and of human society. And even as he tells the story, he does not believe he has found the answer.

In the late 80s, Clark began to consult his diaries and letters as he worked on his autobiography. In the preface to *Quest for Grace*, he explains that in writing the volume he had "made use of diaries begun in April 1941" (Preface). This date suggests that in writing *Quest for Grace*, Clark did not have access to the first volume of his diary, begun in Bonn in late November 1938 and proving that he arrived there two weeks after Kristallnacht. But the date he gives is also odd, given that the second volume of his diary begins in May 1940, not in April 1941. Clark appears to be plucking the date out of thin air. There is no volume of his diary that begins in April 1941. It is possible, but unlikely, that he managed to find all of his diaries from the late 30s and 40s, bar one. Yet, even if it were true that Clark did not have access to his first diary while writing his autobiography, there is no doubt that he drew on Dymphna's correspondence from the same period. In *Quest for Grace*, Clark's memory of Dymphna's visit to the home of the art historian Dr. Busslei draws from a letter she wrote to him in October 1938.[8] "I had heard about him in letters from Dymphna," Clark writes. At one point, recalling a belligerent outburst by Busslei, he quotes almost verbatim from her letter. That letter was kept together with others from Dymphna written in October and November 1938, including the one she wrote to him on 12 November 1938 that describes her experience of Kristallnacht. Given that Clark's account of Kristallnacht closely resembles that of Dymphna's, and that in writing *Quest for Grace*, he drew on her correspondence from the same period, it seems unlikely that he did not sight the letters she wrote to him in November 1938.

If Manning Clark chose to place himself on the streets of Bonn, knowing that he was not there, this was his inner lie. He had told the story in public and traded on his audience's trust in him as a historian. In 1997, Carl Bridge, another scholar who took Manning Clark at his word on Kristallnacht, presciently summed up Clark as "part mystic, part fraud. He had to be. This was how he made us aware of his and our versions of the truth." Referring to Clark's intellectual larrikinism and his penchant for preaching on the meaning of life, Bridge argued that this was part of his greatness. Clark revelled in the power of myth (Bridge 1997).

I believe that the older Manning Clark did possess some awareness of the fact that he was not present on the morning after Kristallnacht. But to claim to know the *extent* to which he was conscious of it is to claim to know the inner depths of his mind. At times, I can see his memory slipping, shifting and struggling to recall; at others, his recollections are clear. I know I can never recover what he truly remembered, the memory of his inner voice, the voice that only he heard. But it is precisely this tension and uncertainty—fed by the shadowed, fallible nature of memory—which makes the story so fascinating.

One of the most interesting aspects of the Kristallnacht story is that Clark first alluded to it in fiction. In the 60s, Clark began to write short stories "for relaxation," as he told Beatrice Davis, his editor at Angus & Robertson. In 1966, he published "Two Visits," a thinly veiled autobiographical story of the exploits of Charles Hogan in Bonn in 1938.[9] The story's tone is oddly aggressive, occasionally misogynist and at times consumed by self-loathing. Like Clark in his twenties, Hogan is "tormented by his own impotence" and frustrated by his time-wasting in Bonn. He seems incapable of producing the great work he believes himself destined to write. Hogan wanders Dostoevsky-like through the streets of

Bonn. He is "never quiet": "Some demon inside him drove him on the whole time he was there." While he does not mention Kristallnacht, Clark drew similar conclusions from Hogan's experience in Germany to those he drew for himself when he first began to tell the Kristallnacht parable in the late 70s. Of Hogan, he writes:

> I think it likely that Hogan did discover things about himself in Germany; that first visit did confront him with the question: what is the source of human evil? Is the imagination of man's heart evil from the start, so that questions of social organisation, political systems, moral codes are but the scum on the pond of human life—not the wellspring? (Clark, "Two Visits": 102)

Hogan struggles to come to terms with the brutality of Nazi Germany. He is a man without faith, an "unbeliever" in "Protestant Christianity" deeply sceptical of any utopian vision "for the future of humanity." Clark seemed to know himself better in fiction. He writes of Hogan in Bonn that his "flair for dramatising his life" was really "one sustained effort to draw attention to himself." And then this: "His flair for the dramatic often caused his memory to play him tricks" (Clark, "Two Visits": 105-106). Indeed. Clark's experience in Germany, recounted first as fiction, is fleshed out and becomes autobiography a decade later. Finally, like much autobiography, it reveals itself as ultimately a strange and unavoidable amalgamation of both fact and fiction. In Clark's case, however, this trajectory seems entirely appropriate. Whatever Clark wrote—fiction, history, autobiography, criticism, newspaper opinion or political oratory—he blended fiction and fact in his attempt to communicate feeling, insight and historical understanding. Nevertheless, it is significant that Clark's memory of Kristallnacht is told in the context of autobiography, a notoriously imperfect and fraught enterprise at the best of times.

Setting out to write her three-volume autobiography, Doris Lessing (1994) was decidedly uncomfortable with the genre. Among novelists, she is not alone. J. M. Coetzee (2001), for example, preferred to fictionalise his autobiographical writings, believing that "fiction has better resources for dealing with unconscious forces than discursive self-analysis" (295). In the process of writing her autobiography, Lessing found that it exposed "the worst deceiver of all—we make up our pasts" (12-13). Well aware of the black holes and "shifting perspectives" of memory, she remained adamant, like Coetzee, that "fiction makes a better job of the truth" (12-13). But unlike Coetzee, she persisted with autobiography, largely out of her instinct for "self-defence," given that at least four writers were then working on biographies of her. The unreliability of memory is the unreliability of autobiography, a necessarily apocryphal genre. Distanced by time, the self who is created by the narrator becomes a character, even a complete stranger to the person who writes. Details, dates and places are lost in the fog; the felt life is often a more abiding memory than the minutiae of the lived life. Jerome Bruner's (1990) work on "autobiography and the self" best expresses the fundamental strangeness of the genre. "There is something curious about autobiography," writes Bruner,

> It is an account given by a narrator in the here and now about a protagonist bearing his name who existed in the there and then, the story terminating in the present when the protagonist fuses with the narrator [. . .]. The self as narrator not only recounts but justifies. And the self as protagonist is always, as it were, pointing to the future. (121)

The "self" created by Clark was certainly busy justifying and pointing to the future, but even more importantly, he was busy *revealing* profound truths. Clark was not so much concerned with reliability as he was with insight.

As a historian who saw himself more as an artist than a fact-grubber, Clark showed no signs of discomfort with the genre of autobiography. Its potential for truthfulness seemed to him just as great, largely because, unlike Lessing, he rendered his life as narrative not out of necessity but willingly. As he told John Tranter in 1987, "the only gift I had was to tell a story" (Clark 1987). In the late 80s, with his six-volume history complete, he turned to write autobiography at a time when the genre was experiencing extraordinary popularity. Writers such as Clive James (b. 1939), Barry Humphries (b. 1934), Geoffrey Dutton (b. 1922 - d. 1998), Donald Horne (b. 1921 - d. 2005), Jill Ker Conway (b. 1934), and Bernard Smith (b. 1916) had all turned their hand to memoir, often, as Bruce Bennett (1998) has pointed out, tracing their life "as part of a national allegory" (255). In the lead-up to the bicentenary, Clark became a celebrity and Australia's most public intellectual. Having told the nation's story, the nation now demanded Clark's story, and he relished the opportunity to tell it.

Writing autobiography allowed him to do with his own life what he had already done with his historical actors: create himself as a character, and employ the same literary devices—particularly the epiphany as a moment of "new consciousness"—to reshape his life through literary reminiscence (the words "new consciousness" belong to Bruner, 1990: 121). In the process of recollection, and in the creation of his life as story, he was able to invest new meaning in past events. Many of the events from his past that the septuagenarian Clark saw as significant in the late 80s were not invested with the same significance at the time they occurred. Clark's diary entry after his visit to Cologne Cathedral on 9 December 1938 makes no mention of the painting of the Madonna or of the Heinrich Heine poem that allegedly moved him to tears:

> We saw the cathedral, beyond description [. . .] we walked round the town and saw the notices [. . .] "Juden werden nicht bedient" [Jews will not be served] on shop windows. Everything looked very prosperous and very lovely in the soft glow of twilight, with the darkness of the buildings against the blue of the sky and the pink clouds. The dome of the cathedral seemed to cast a spell on the whole town, and the darkness came down quietly, and one felt safe.

This is a far cry from the memory of Cologne Cathedral recited by Manning Clark in 1987. In other diary entries from the late 30s, he is moved by a triptych of Rubens' paintings depicting the Immaculate Conception, the birth of Christ and his crucifixion ("Mary, in horror—that it should [come] to this"), and by Chartres Cathedral, "which inspires that sense of awe and wonder" (21 July 1939). "I thought of the powers of inspiration of the Catholic Church," wrote Clark, "of the issues between Catholicism and Protestantism—authority & beauty against liberty of thought & dullness" (1 August 1939). These entries reveal the traces of truth in his later recollections, and perhaps this is the best that the author and reader can hope for in autobiography: traces of truth.

For Clark, and for every writer of autobiography, there are two competing truths: one's past life as it was perceived and lived (mostly lost from view), and one's past life as seen from the time of writing, a truth that leans on the paper-thin house of memory. Despite the fact that Clark had access to his diaries as he composed his autobiography, he was more concerned with the latter truth: making his life behave as literature. The older Clark shifts the time and place of many his early encounters in Europe, then condenses and embellishes his visions into one or two Earth-moving epiphanies as he reinvents his life before a public audience.

On every occasion in the last years of his life that he tells the Kristallnacht story, he tells it together with the Cologne Cathedral epiphany. In 1987, two months before his interview with John Tranter, he appeared on ABC TV, interviewed by the arts presenter Peter Ross. Telling the story of the two epiphanies, Clark wept:

> Clark: I went to Germany to see the girl, or the woman, I was going to marry—Dymphna—at the University of Bonn, and I happened to get there on the morning of the ninth or tenth of November [. . .] I got there and came out of the Bonn Railway Station onto the footpath, the road, and it was one of the mornings after Kristallnacht, when the SS in Germany had conducted this savage vendetta against the Jews for the murder, or the attempted murder, of a member of the German Embassy in Paris.
>
> Ross: You saw the broken glass?
>
> Clark: I saw the broken glass and I saw those troops with their revolvers and their sub-machine guns and so on, on the back of trucks [. . .] I was absolutely overwhelmed by it. I could scarcely speak, and in the long run—it's difficult to work it out, Peter, isn't it, when you're really [. . .]. But it was some time then, within the next few days or certainly within the next few weeks, that I realised that all the things I'd been brought up with [. . .] *The Book of Common Prayer*, *Hymns Ancient and Modern*, and all the hopes and aspirations of those dry souls of the enlightenment [. . .] all this was just pitiful equipment with which to face up to the phenomenon of human evil.
>
> Ross: So the scales came from your eyes?
>
> Clark: Yes the blinkers, the blinkers of being a member of British civilisation overseas, of being a simple boy from the Australian bush—all this had to go [. . .]. A few days after that, I went with Dymphna to Cologne, and remember I was a Church of England clergyman's son and a State school boy and a Melbourne Grammar boy, as it were, I walked up those steps of Cologne Cathedral [. . .] I went into the Cathedral [. . .] and I [. . .] yes [. . .] I was overwhelmed.
>
> Ross: You're overwhelmed now, as you recall it.
>
> Clark: Yes, I am.
>
> Ross: It must have been an extraordinary occurrence.
>
> Clark: Yes, it was. I'd find it difficult to put into words.
>
> [It was at this point that Professor Clark wept.]
>
> [Clark then tells the story of seeing, behind the high altar in the cathedral, Stefan Lochner's painting of the *Madonna and Child* (1450),

which inspired the famous lines Heinrich Heine's poem "Ziemlich langsam" ("Quite Slow"). He translates the one line that had always remained with him: "Inside the cathedral there stands a picture / painted in golden leather / and in the great wildness of my life / it's always shone brightly."]

Clark: That episode in the cathedral in Cologne which had moved me so deeply—in fact, so deeply that I have never been able to speak about it since—it, I think, was germinal in writing the History, because then and subsequently I realised that I had to dispense with what had carried me through life so far, what I call my "great expectations," either of Christian belief or the Enlightenment, and that I had to [. . .] find another way. And that, really, in a sense the History became an account of how all we in Australia became citizens of the Kingdom of Nothingness—believing in nothing—but that doesn't mean nothing in one sense [. . .]. It's the opposite of nil. It's really giving up the great expectations and asking yourself, what then?

Clark seems to admit at one point that he is uncertain as to exactly when the encounter in Bonn revealed its mysteries to him ("It's difficult to work it out, Peter"). We see him in the act of fashioning memory anew, bringing himself to tears in the telling. He wrote to Kathleen Fitzpatrick shortly after, "I made an attempt to talk about what I had never talked about to anyone before [. . .] [I] am still shaken by what happened during the interview" (Davies, 1996: 107-108). Clark had never spoken before about the experience in Cologne. To some extent, he was discovering its significance as he told the story to Peter Ross. In 1978, he wrote of his visit to Cologne Cathedral, but made no mention of the mystical experience he described in 1987. He seemed to create the emotionally shattering vision at Cologne in the act of performance (see Clark, *Occasional Writings and Speeches*: 79-88).

When Peter Ross questioned him directly, he insisted that he *was* there in Bonn on the morning of 10 November ("I saw the broken glass"); then, at another point in the interview, he claimed that two days later, he was out cycling with Dymphna. "It was Armistice Day," he told Ross. In freezing cold weather, he and Dymphna came across a memorial to German soldiers. Clark claimed that this introduced him "to the whole idea of *mittel-Europa* and German civilisation and what it had been like to be a German" (1987). But Clark was no more in Germany on Armistice Day than he was in Bonn on the morning after Kristallnacht. Once again, he places himself in a key historical moment in order to dramatise his moment of revelation. When he tells the story of Cologne Cathedral in *Quest for Grace*, it also follows closely behind the Bonn epiphany—"From the day I saw evil in Bonn am Rhein there would be no putting back to harbour: I launched further into the deep when I stood in front of the painting of the Madonna and Child behind the high altar in Cologne Cathedral" (*Quest for Grace* 75). Dymphna, aware of the "tempests" raging within her lover, retires to the back of the building, apparently unable to partake in such a shattering moment: "inside the cathedral I was strangely moved. Dymphna, noticing what was going on inside me, left me alone to feast on it all in my heart" (*Quest for Grace* 75). This epiphany in Cologne is, in fact, almost a reincarnation of Dostoevsky's experience in Basel in the late 1860s, a fact of which Clark must have been aware.

In 1867, while travelling from Baden-Baden to Geneva, Dostoevsky visited Basel and there saw Hans Holbein's *The Body of the Dead Christ in the Tomb*, painted in the early 1520s. The painting depicted Christ's emaciated body in the tomb, the holes still visible on his blackened hands and feet, his gaunt and bearded face looking upwards in doubtful hope. Dostoevsky remained haunted by the image for the rest of his life, just as he was by his memory of Raphael's Madonna in Dresden, a painting which he described in *Crime and Punishment* (1866) as bearing a kind of "mournful religious ecstasy." Dostoevsky was moved and overwhelmed, unable to articulate the mystery he sensed within Holbein's work. Yet he is also plagued by the doubt that arises within him: What if Christ did not rise from the dead? Then man is truly alone. In the back pages of his copies of *Crime and Punishment*, *The Idiot* (1869) and *The Possessed* (1866)—still on the shelves of his study in Canberra—Manning Clark noted the page numbers of Dostoevsky's writings about Holbein's and Raphael's paintings. Clark is drawn to Dostoevsky's mysticism and to his doubt; like him, he is eternally divided over the question of faith and belief. But even more importantly, he emulates his search for truth, cultivating (sometimes consciously) an artistic sensibility in which art, literature and metaphorical language are the one true source of spiritual revelation. Like Dostoevsky, Clark is moved but does not fully understand the experience: it is mystical, forever hinting at profound truths destined never to be resolved. Manning Clark visited Basel in 1956 and viewed the Holbein. In 1961, during a lecture on Dostoevsky, he told ANU students how Dostoevsky's wife, Anna, had been present with the writer in Basel on the day he first encountered Holbein's work. As Clark told the story, Anna "withdrew" from Dostoevsky: "she knew who he was, what came up from inside the man." Thirty years later, when Clark told the story of his own epi phany before the painting of the Madonna in Cologne, he has Dym phna withdraw in the same manner as Anna, creating the memory of his own life in the image of Dostoevsky's (on Dostoevsky, see Rowlands, 1985: 52-53; see also Dostoevsky, *Crime and Punishment*: 492; Clark, "Fyodor Dostoevsky": 158-159; Clark, "Melbourne: An Intellectual Tradition": 17-21, in this article (on page 19) Clark mistakenly places Holbein's painting in Baden instead of Basel).

The two epi phanies, Kristallnacht and Cologne Cathedral, are spliced by Clark into an almost filmic scene of self-discovery, one representing the inadequacy of Protestant teachings and the Enlightenment to solve the problem of human evil, the other holding out the potential spiritual solace and com passion of the Catholic faith, a faith Clark would continue to dance with (but never embrace) for the remainder of his life. Like the Spanish poet Federico García Lorca (1955), with his notion of *duende*–which Lorca described in 1930 as "a momentary burst of inspiration, the blush of all that is truly alive [. . .] what Goethe called the 'demoniacal' [the 'dark force' that rises from within the poet] [. . .] needing the trembling of the moment and then a long silence" (vii)—Clark is rendered speechless by the visions and inspirations that rise before his eyes. "I could not speak of the experience then to anyone" (*Quest for Grace* 75), he writes of the epi phany in Cologne Cathedral. "Was there anyone who could understand? Many years later when I risked talking about the experience my whole body shook" (*Quest for Grace* 75). Clark sought and depended on *duende*, flashes of inspiration that brought the pain and suffering of a deeper awareness of the human situation but at the same time served as his intellectual and spiritual guiding lights. Writing and the act of creation was not only intellectual but emotional and physical, a whole-body experience. He had no alternative but to write from the gut, to feel the physical sensation of trembling and shaking, because his was a poetic imagination. The historian's inspiration is the artist's sensibility, made real and truthful through the repetition necessary in public performance. The details of Clark's life, like Australia's past, are adapted to suit his dreams and mystical visions. Manning Clark, Australia's greatest self-mythologiser, was a daddy-long-legs spinning his thread.

Far from being out of place or shocking, Clark's misrepresentation of his presence in Bonn on 10 November 1938 is entirely in keeping with the spirit and intent of his life and work. Rather than diminishing Clark, it reveals him. He fictionalised his life, just as he played with primary sources in writing his histories. He lived out the life of his greatest character, himself, the historian whose potential greatness was constantly undermined by his fatal flaws. Both his *History of Australia* and his autobiographical writings are unreliable as historical sources. But this should come as no surprise: where Manning Clark's life is concerned, the last person we should trust is Clark himself. He created himself as myth, cultivating a theatrical persona of the people's priest and sage, telling history as parable. And as the Kristallnacht epiphany reveals, the moral of the parable always mattered more than the facts.

The true story of Kristallnacht reveals the true nature of Manning Clark's voice: the voice of the heart and mind, the inner man seeking "higher truths." Voices spoke to Clark—from within him, from the past, from the present—and he struggled to play them back to us, mediated through his unique emotional intelligence and sensibility, so that we might hear them, too, as if for the first time. Clark's *History of Australia* is a flawed attempt to write history as a revelation of the human condition. It is a search for the time when the veil, for a brief moment, is pulled back, and life is seen for what it is. This is the translucent quality of Manning Clark's work.

Endnotes

[1] I would like to thank the following friends and colleagues for their assistance in writing this essay. Bain Attwood, John Blay, Sebastian Clark, Ann Curthoys, Humphrey McQueen, Ockert Meyer, Stuart Macintyre, Jan Nicholas and Penny Ramsay.

[2] Clark paraphrasing Henry James, see *Speaking Out of Turn: Lectures and Speeches 1940-1991* (Melbourne: Melbourne UP, 1997) 85.

[3] See, for example, John Howard's Australia Day Speech 2006, or his *Quadrant* 50th anniversary speech, 3 October 2006, both speeches are available on Howard's website at http://www.pm.gov.au.

[4] Edmund Campion was probably the first to compare Clark's work to an Oratorio, see "Manning Clark," *Scripsi* 5.2 (1989): 183-187.

[5] With kind permission of Carl Bridge. Dymphna's friend, who informed me of Dymphna's comments on Clark and Kristallnacht, prefers to remain anonymous.

[6] See also, Clark, "The Discovery of Australia," *Occasional Writings and Speeches* (Melbourne: Fontana Collins, 1980) 71.

[7] Letter undated and the correspondent's name difficult to decipher, but it was certainly mailed from Basel to Dymphna Clark sometime in 1991, most probably January; NLA MS 7550, Series 18, Box 176, Correspondence relating to *Quest For Grace*

[8] Dymphna Lodewyckx to Manning Clark, undated letter but certainly some time in October 1938 (Clark is still in Oxford, she in Bonn)

[9] Note from Beatrice Davis, 18 October 1967, regarding a phone conversation with Clark on 12 October 1967; Angus & Robertson Papers, Second series, Mitchell Library, MSS 3265, Vol. 186, "Charles Manning Hope Clark 1946-1969." See also Manning Clark, "Two Visits," *Summer's Tales 3*, ed. John Iggulden (New York: Macmillan St Martin's P, 1966) 90-113.

Works Cited

"Charles Manning Hope Clark 1946-1969." Angus & Robertson Papers. Second series, Mitchell Library, MSS 3265, Vol. 186.

Anonymous. Correspondence with Dymphna Clark. January 1991. NLA MS 7550, Series 18, Box 176.

Atkinson, Alan. "A Great Historian?" *Manning Clark: Essays on His Place in History*. Ed. Carl Bridge. Melbourne: Melbourne UP, 1994. 122-135.

Bennett, Bruce. "Literary Culture Since Vietnam." *Oxford Literary History of Australia*. Ed. Bruce Bennett and Jennifers Strauss. Melbourne: Oxford UP, 1998. 239-264.

Blainey, Geoffrey. Rev. of *A Historian's Apprenticeship*, by Manning Clark. *Weekend Australian* 17-18 October 1992: n. pag.

Bridge, Carl. "Manning Clark and the Ratbag Tradition." 1997. 24 April 2007 <http://www.api-network.com/cgi-bin/page?archives/jas55_bridge>.

Bruner, Jerome. *Acts of Meaning.* Cambridge, Mass.: Harvard UP, 1990.

Campion, Edmund. "Manning Clark." *Scripsi* 5.2 (1989): 183-187.

Cathcart, Michael. *Big Ideas* (forum on Manning Clark). ABC Radio National. 16 February 2003. 25 April 2007 <http://www.abc.net.au/rn/bigidea/stories/s781897.htm>.

——. Personal communication with Carl Bridge. 30 March 1995.

Clark, Dymphna. Comments on the *Quest for Grace* manuscripts, by Manning Clark. n.d. NLA MS 7550, Series 25.

——. Correspondence with Carl Bridge. 14 November 1993.

Clark, Manning. *Speaking Out of Turn: Lectures and Speeches 1940-1991.* Melbourne: Melbourne UP, 1997.

——. *A Historian's Apprenticeship.* Melbourne: Melbourne UP, 1992.

——. *The Puzzles of Childhood.* 1989. Ringwood, Victoria: Penguin, 1990.

——. A History of Australia. 6 vols. Carlton, Victoria: Melbourne UP, 1962-1987.

——. Interview. By John Tranter. ABC Radio National. 17 June 1987.

——. Interview. By Peter Ross. *The Arts on Sunday.* ABC TV. 12 April 1987.

——. *Occasional Writings and Speeches.* Melbourne: Fontana Collins, 1980.

——. *Making History.* R.M. Crawford et al. Melbourne: McPhee Gribble, 1980.

——. Correspondence with Dymphna Clark. 24 December 1972.

——. Telephone conversation with Beatrice Davis. 12 October 1967.

——. "Two Visits." *Summer's Tales 3.* Ed. John Iggulden. New York: Macmillan St Martin's P, 1966. 90-113.

——. "Melbourne: An Intellectual Tradition." *Melbourne Historical Journal* 2 (1962): 17-21.

——. *Sources of Australian History.* 1957. Melbourne: Oxford UP, 1971.

——. Diaries. Clark papers. 1942-1943. NLA MS 7550, Series 2, Box 28.

Coetzee, J. M. *Youth: Scenes From Provincial Life II.* 2002. London: Penguin, 2003.

——. "Doris Lessing." *Stranger Shores: Essays 1986-1999.* London: Secker & Warburg, 2001. 295. 284-303.

——. *Boyhood: Scenes From Provincial Life.* 1997. London: Penguin, 1998.

Craven, Peter. "A Man of Contradictions." *Australian Book Review* August 1999. 25 April 2007 <htpp://home.vicnet.au/-abr>.

Crawford, Max. Rev. of *History of Australia* Vol. I, by Manning Clark. *Australian Book Review* November 1962: 7.

Davies, Susan, ed. *Dear Kathleen, Dear Manning: The Correspondence of Manning Clark and Kathleen Fitzpatrick 1949-1990.* Melbourne: Melbourne UP, 1996.

Davis, Beatrice. Note. 18 October 1967.

Dostoevsky, Fyodor. *Crime and Punishment.* 1866. Trans. David Magarshack. London: Penguin Classics, 1972.

Fitzpatrick, Kathleen. Correspondence with Manning Clark. 20 November 1962. MS 7550, Series 18, Box 156, Folder 4.

Howard, John. Australia Day Speech. 26 January 2006. 26 April 2007 <http://www.pm.gov.au/>.

Howard, John. *Quadrant* 50th Anniversary Speech. October 3 2006. 26 April 2007 <http://www.pm.gov.au/>.

Lessing, Doris. *Under My Skin.* 1994. London: Flamingo, 1995.

Lodewyckx, Dymphna. Correspondence with Manning Clark. 12 November 1938.

Lodewyckx, Dymphna. Correspondence with Manning Clark. 18 November 1938.

Lodewyckx, Dymphna. Correspondence with Manning Clark. n.d.

Lorca, Frederico Garcia. *In Search of Duende.* 1955. New York: New Directions, 1998.

Macintyre, Stuart. "Always a Pace or Two Apart." *Manning Clark: Essays on His Place in History.* Ed. Carl Bridge. Melbourne: Melbourne UP, 1994. 17-29.

Macintyre, Stuart. "The Writing of Australian History." *Australians: A Guide to Sources.* Ed. D. H. Borchardt. Sydney: Fairfax Syme & Weldon, 1987. 1-29.

McQueen, Humphrey. *Suspect History: Manning Clark and the Future of Australia's Past.* Kent Town, SA: Wakefield, 1997.

——. "The Old Dead Tree and the Young Tree Green." Rev. of *History of Australia*, Vol. VI, by Manning Clark. *Continuum: The Australian Journal of Media and Culture* 1.2 (1987). 22 April 2007 <http://wwwmcc.murdoch.edu.au/ReadingRoom/1.2/McQueen.html>.

——. Personal communication. September 2006.

Munz, Peter. "Gesta Dei Per Australianos." *Australia 1888 Bulletin* 3 (December 1979): 13. 5-27.

Pascoe, Rob. "A History of Manning Clark." *The National Times* 2 June 1978: n. pag.

Rev. of *History of Australia* Vol. I, by Manning Clark. *News Weekly*, 12 June 1968: n. pag.

Rev. of *History of Australia* Vol. I, by Manning Clark. *Sydney Morning Herald*, 15 May 1968: n. pag.

Rowlands, John. *Holbein: The paintings of Hans Holbein the Younger.* New York: Phaidon, 1985.

Serle, Geoffrey. "One Man's Window on our Past: Manning Clark's Third Volume." *Meanjin Quarterly* 38.1 (Autumn 1974): 86-88.

Waterhouse, Richard. "Controversies in Australian History." Unpublished public lecture. <http://www.sl.nsw.gov.au/publications/pdf/waterhouse.pdf>.

Becoming Postcolonial
Getting Lost for a While with Stephen Muecke's *No Road* and Remaking Australia

Lisa Slater

Stephen Muecke's *No Road* (1997) is a travel book that generates profoundly new ways of thinking about Australia. Muecke proposes that if Australia is to become postcolonial than we must change the stories we tell and the way that we tell them. To take up the challenge he transforms the archetypal journey into a road that leads nowhere and explores instead an Australia overflowing with stories and potentiality. *No Road* is a hybrid text that weaves together Muecke's real and imagined travels throughout Australia, travels in which he pursues a dialogue between Indigenous and non-Indigenous histories. It is an experimental text, which juxtaposes memoir, theory, poetic reverie, letters, anecdotes, historical enquiry, personal speculation and Aboriginal oral narrative, positioning itself between fact and fiction. Muecke generates a critical practice that does not survey and classify Australia, but rather partici pates in and produces new cultural practices. He suggests:

> Something new begins when the answer the local gives is not forced into a universal language of rationality in order to have an understanding determined by this interrogator from a more powerful place.
>
> Something new begins if such interrogators have to invest something of their subjectivity, if they have to negotiate, change, and learn to belong. (*No Road* 184)

In this paper I pose the questions: *what* begins when one attem pts to learn to belong through negotiation and investing one's subjectivity in the local and Indigenous world? In assembling such disparate texts, voices and stories, what is Muecke *making* of Australia and subjectivity? How does changing the stories we tell transfigure inhabitation?

Storytelling is a way of attempting to transform space into place. Generating knowledge of a country is a way of belonging and inhabiting the country. Thereby, for all fictocriticism's interrogation and unsettling of Western knowledge, the writing subjects are participating in inscribing their presence in the country. As Muecke travels the country he encounters other subjects and other knowledge and self-reflexively records the effects of otherness upon himself. *No Road* is a heteroglossic text that destabilises and contests colonial history and confronts it with what it represses—the intersubjective colonial encounter. However, Muecke is attempting to find new ways to write Australia and forge alternative forms of belonging. He inscribes his interpretations of the country and, as James Paull (1997) argues, he thereby constitutes (alternative) histories (146). However lightly Muecke travels across the surface of the country, he nonetheless generates a poetic history, or what could be called *becoming* postcolonial, which has transformational capacities.

In attempting to forge a sense of belonging Muecke acts to reaffirm his subjectivity. Muecke's methodology, in which he gathers and assembles textual remnants to construct a dialogic text that reworks ways of knowing the country, could also be understood as the generation of a place from which to speak. This textual site, in the hope of forging a dialogue across cultural difference, both unsettles and confirms his subjectivity. The act of constituting a heteroglossic text is an unmaking and re-making of ways of knowing the country. It is, however, an anti-colonial making of history, knowledge and interpretative practices that does not settle, but keeps moving. Postcolonial belonging and subjectivity are constituted through dialogic storytelling that is not accumulative or progressive, but rather invites participation and dialogue. Muecke suggests the possibility of generating a homeland through narrating everyday experiences of negotiating intersubjective, intertextual and cross-cultural relations, which result in a subject becoming other than what they are. In so doing, Muecke sets forth a vision in which Indigeneity operates as a transformational force in this country and he *sees* postcolonial Australia as highly culturally miscegenated.

As Muecke argues, the exposure of mainstream Australia to Indigenous knowledges affirms different forms of cultural life. This not only challenges Australian identity, but also strains at narrative forms

(*No Road* 228). Dominant narratives not only tell stories, they prevent stories being told. They prevent questions being asked that might lead to answers to contemporary problems. As Stuart Hall (1984) argues in an interview, ideologies, whether explicit or implicit, construct the framework of interpretation and understanding:

> narrative tells a story into which it is impossible to enter or introduce any questions at all. I think one is then aware in retrospect of the degree to which historical reconstruction wraps up or moves around the contradictory interpretations, which are always there when one deals with a historical event. (O'Hara 4)

Particular, singular events acquire historical significance by being imagined as conforming to a narrative model. The particularity of the event is abstracted at the cost of that which is in excess of the narrative frame (Fineman 74). Western historical narratives privilege causation over the contingent and the accidental. To write of the particular experiences of individual lives risks being ahistorical. However, to conform to narrative models risks marginalising and excluding alternative experiences and histories. If we continue to tell stories in the same way, to paraphrase Hall, those stories, or ways of telling stories, write the storyteller (O'Hara 17). What might be repressed in normative narrative forms is the experience of living in a colonised and contested country.

Muecke rightly asks, "what kind of story do you tell on the road if you don't want to write like an Imperial highway, on the road to further colonial expansion [. . .]?" (*No Road* 192). One could argue that in the face of such difficulties and restraints, the writer who desires to write Australia otherwise, is doomed either to be ahistorical or to romanticise otherness. Despite the problems of resuscitating the romantic imagination, which has the potential to efface difference by synthesising alterity into one's desires, the political urgency of contemporary Australian race relations requires risks. However, Muecke both takes risks and proceeds with caution, by juxtaposing the "literary" with the theoretical and self-reflective. In so doing, he limits his imperialising, romantic imagination. As Muecke writes in questioning his methodology:

> for the moment I was a tangential tourist, refusing to do "disciplined" research in favour of the interdisciplinary mode of enquiry. That seemed to call for a judicious mix of the anecdotal and banal backed up by the "solidity" of theory so that one can relativise the position of

> the theorist in relation to the so-called objects of research. But at the same time having to remain rigorously cynical and unenchanted by the "usual" tourist spots, an attitude typical of the "bourgeois" traveller. (*No Road* 32)

Muecke chooses a fictocritical style because contemporary intellectual engagement has not only failed to solve contemporary problems of race relations, but also has obscured them. Indigenous people have long played the role in the national psyche of "the absent people from the 'dead centre' " (*No Road* 227). Through the rise of the land rights movement, coupled with the official enquiries into black deaths in custody and the stolen generations, Aboriginal people were transformed, in the national imaginary, from objects of history, to subjects of history. Indigenous historical perspectives have denied the closed narratives of colonial history, challenging the narrative of benign settlement and the rightful political sovereignty of non-Indigenous people. Furthermore, the exposure of Aboriginal knowledges affirms different forms of cultural life, which might in turn reconfigure the social imaginary, and therefore the civic body. An uncertainty has infused the country. White authority is being undermined as Australians are reinterpreting their country and history.

Muecke answers the failures of contemporary politicians, writers and academics to respond to the challenges of contemporary cross-cultural engagement, by renovating "disciplinary textual spaces" (Kerr 119). *No Road* begins with the problematic of "what language can I use to *carry* this story?" (15). Muecke suggests that representations of Aboriginal people are utilised to fill a lack in non-Aboriginal Australia, that of the "*eros* to our *thanatos*" (*No Road* 15). This has resulted in Aboriginal people being deployed to play out a limiting and prescriptive role upon the stage of white Australia. Muecke deploys writing as a method of enquiry, a partial and provisional form of storytelling and textual vulnerability, in the hope of forging new social connections. Muecke affirms that:

> getting to know may mean leaving home and getting lost for a while, to admit that there may not be a road going anywhere that we all agree on, but that somewhere along the road is a local guide [. . .]. (*No Road* 130)

Muecke's writing acts, like the local custodians who guide him, as a guide for his readers. *No Road* interrupts the readers' interpretative process, unsettling them from normative ways of knowing the country, and opening up a site of uncertainty, which might induce new ways of thinking about Australia, and in so doing generate new cultural forms.

Making Stories Up

Muecke emphatically states that "[i]f Australia is to be changed, for example, by becoming a republic, then the kinds of stories we tell about Australia will have to be changed" (*No Road* 220). In response to the impossibility of speaking for the other, the ethical imperative of negotiating and respecting incommensurabilities (Kerr 120), and the need for Indigenous and non-Indigenous Australians to co-exist, Muecke proposes alternative forms of storytelling. As Heather Kerr (2001) argues, the other's voice is unrepresentable without synthesising it or recuperating it into a dominant narrative (120). However, one must not only "realise" the other, but also take account of the little histories or unrepresentable voices that unsettle and disrupt master narratives. Although Muecke's nomadic text runs the risk of essentialising, romanticising and synthesising the other into his imaginative gaze, his textual incoherence—shifting between the personal and the theoretical—sets limits on his poetic imagination. He is returned to speaking for him*self*—a self, who continually exposes his limitations. However, by accumulating fragments of little histories and unrepresentable voices Muecke composes an assemblage that articulates anti-narratives of Australia. In so doing, he proposes an alternative country in which to live with and be remade by difference.

No Road can profitably be read in terms of Deleuze and Guattari's notion of the nomadic text. To insist, as does Muecke, that getting to know might mean getting lost for a while and relying on local guides is to generate nomadic thinking. Universal authority is deferred to the local. New assemblages, moreover, are continually disbanded, to initiate new connections and prevent local knowledge becoming codified into normality. *No Road* is a nomadic text, an enunciative assemblage, which refuses disciplinary boundaries in the interest of privileging local knowledge and little histories. It incorporates what Leelha Gandhi (1998) calls historical non-players (173), whose speech acts fall outside of recorded historical consciousness. In attending to local knowledge Muecke forges new alliances in an attempt to negotiate the impasses of cultural differences. Each chapter of *No Road* operates as a *plateau*, a site where seemingly disparate theories, anecdotes, incommensurable cultural perspectives, experiences and sensations are assembled in an attempt to forge new connections. In short, what in *No Road* could be read as textual incoherence, I understand to be a site in which differences are assembled, not as a gesture of cognitive mastery, perpetuating Imperialism, but rather in an attempt to "realise" the other(ness), without synthesising otherness into the same. In the fragmentary style of the text, Muecke urges the reader to consider what might happen if we were to conceive of Australia as already full—"not lacking anything so that we have to look to others to complete our national psyche" (*No Road* 225).

Making Room for Anecdotes and Little Histories

How can white writers represent cross-cultural engagements that tell of reciprocity and exchange without falling into the trap of speaking for the other? In juxtaposing his commentary on the straight roads of the Nullarbor Plain, on which he set out as a young academic, with his rich and transformational friendship with Gloria, Muecke hints at an answer to the question he poses—"what language can I use to *carry* this story?" (*No Road* 15). Muecke's answer to this question is in the posing of it. It is the fragments of a story, in this case the anecdotal, which disrupt and exceed representative narratives as they open the narrative frame to "complicitous alternatives" (Fineman 74). Anecdotes introduce into the empty historical time of modernity the singularity of events. In so doing, they interrupt and challenge the type of historical narratives that purport, through abstracting from experiences, to represent historical truths. The anecdotal—"elements of a story"—reintroduces history's other, the particularity and singularity of events that cannot be contained within conventional narratives.

The anecdote ruptures historical and racial discourse as it privileges the *experiences* of history. Gloria relays to Muecke an incident in which she met a local Aboriginal man in Darwin. She is greatly charmed by the man but perplexed by his answer to a question she poses to him. He invites Gloria to his country and she asks, " 'Is there a road out there, is it a good road?,' " to which he responds, puzzled, " 'Road? No road . . . NO ROAD. Bitumen all the way. Bitumen aaall the way' " (*No Road* 18). In incorporating this "second hand" anecdote Muecke reveals that like him, Gloria also negotiates cultural differences with Indigenous people. Muecke suggests similarities between himself and Gloria without negating their differences. He incorporates Gloria's voice into his text by acknowledging her as the source of a story he shares with the reader. He addresses the story to his now dead friend. Gloria's anecdote, from which the title of the book is taken, is not only a technique for "realising" the other, but also a means whereby Muecke can introduce the voice of the other without assuming authority over it (Kerr 120). By borrowing the words of Gloria, Muecke dialogises his text, inferring that both his text and himself are composed from intertextual and intersubjective relationships.

There is no beginning, as such, to *No Road*; instead the reader is positioned, like Muecke, in the middle of an assemblage of thinking. Several times throughout the text the reader is introduced to writing projects that Muecke is setting out on, all of which involve him leaving Sydney and principally heading into "remote" Australia. Muecke frames the text to give the impression of candour. The anecdotal style and seeming conversational ease and meditative tone of the text give the impression that readers are privy to what would normally operate as the outside of the finished text, that is, the context of Muecke's writing, what motivates him both personally and professionally, and his influences and desires, in all their multiplicity and diversity. When he sets out to write, in collaboration with other artists, a book on the Bungle Bungles, he visits one of the traditional custodians of the country, Bonnie Edwards. He meets her with the expectation that she will share her stories and knowledge of the Bungle Bungles. Instead she entertains him with anecdotes and takes him camping with her family. Muecke speculates that Bonnie "cannot, and doesn't want to, tell stories of the Bungles. Or not yet, and in the meantime *gardiya*[1] talk is weaving the fabric which will recreate the site as a National Park" (1997: 144). Muecke suggests that dominant white narratives, which limit the terms of inhabiting and co-existence in Australia, are further territorialising the country.

His project of recording stories of the Bungle Bungles appears to be stalled or derailed by an absence of Indigenous knowledge. It is, however, this blocked way that forces him to listen and attend to Bonnie Edwards on her own terms. Muecke poses the question:

> With what voice do I speak, and why have I in this case sought witness in the voice of Bonnie Edwards, the voice supposedly without force? Why is it that I cannot simply write with an inherited authority, continuing to footnote the great European authors, dragging their old dreams from the cellar and packing them away again in the attic? (*No Road* 141)

Muecke inserts Bonnie's voice, a voice supposedly without force, as a means of exposing himself, and his non-Indigenous readers, to the limitations of ourselves and our powers of conception. The power of dominant white Australia is maintained by having the right to decide on the interpretative context and in so doing mainstream white Australia denies justice to many Aboriginal people. Muecke the cultural studies academic, with his ready tape recorder, has no place here. However, when camping Bonnie inserts him into her "social architecture" that is organised according to age and gender. Muecke is deterritorialised from his authority as white academic and positioned in accordance with Bonnie's cultural knowledge. Different social codes are in operation from those of the cosmopolitan academies. These alternative social codes slow down Muecke the cultural theorist. This deceleration loosens Muecke from his academic authority and opens him to accepting the authority of someone else's alternative knowledge.

Furthermore, by inserting this anecdote into his text Muecke takes up his own challenge that the "task of contemporary thought is to attribute a value to the strangeness of others, and to provide occasions for giving this value a force and a usefulness" (*No Road* 182). Muecke gives a value to Indigenous cultural knowledge by attempting to belong according to Bonnie's social codes and also by retelling this story and disseminating alternative cultural knowledge. Muecke writes that he thinks that culture is "a set of competing forces" and that it is productive (*No Road* 220). He argues that writers, in producing books, concepts and stories, create forms of subjectivity (*No Road* 221), since stories trace a path for readers to follow. Writing forges connections between seemingly disparate fragments, stories and cultural knowledge and in so doing reconfigures the way people perceive the world and their subjectivity. By including the story of how he was inserted into Bonnie's social architecture, Muecke suggests that Indigenous and non-Indigenous cultural knowledge are not in opposition to each other, but rather can and do co-exist.

The racial discourse that establishes uncrossable distance between Aboriginal and non-Aboriginal people ignores, at Australia's peril, the diverse possibilities of co-existence. *No Road* represents a diversity of anti-colonial forms of co-existence. In the section entitled "textual suburbs" Muecke reflects upon the time when he first began to write, wanting to learn about the medium of writers—language. He did a lot of study and went to lectures on linguistics: "They kept telling me that language is a system, a 'system of meaning' [. . .]. I learnt a lot about the infinite power of language to generate words" (*No Road* 20). However, in "keeping quiet for a bit" (*No Road* 22), and thinking about language, he comes to a different understanding:

> A language like English is like a group of textual suburbs [. . .]. In each suburb the language is like the architecture, like spaces it vibrates in [. . .]. There is no overall system, no capacity for infinite generation. We can sometimes find ourselves in a space where a word has never been used before, where that is just the right word to use in that time and place. Sometimes we travel to the edge of the city and the words run out at the same time as the houses. Then we might find ourselves in a culture and a community where words might have a completely different purpose to the one we imagine they have: the landscape changes colour, we begin to lose our grip (*No Road* 22-23).

Muecke's textual topography imaginatively takes the reader to places where "words might have a completely different purpose" (*No Road* 23). He situates the reader at a point of cross-cultural contact. At this site, someone else's place, Muecke privileges negotiation and co-existence.

The Power of the Word

If we can no longer assume that how we perceive the world exists in the world prior to discourse, then inserting alternative knowledge into a representational terrain potentially reconfigures interpretation. As Muecke insists in "Lonely Representations" (1992), if the

> subject is always partially constituted in advance by discourse, and there is never a general world or structure behind each utterance, but only the specific linguistic rituals that make each social occasion function, then one can argue that words are not used primarily for referral or representation, but that words are interventions [. . .]. While "things" are continually changing, and these changes provide the occasion for speech (things intervene in language), it is also the case that speech has the power to instantly transform things through,

> for eg, performative speech (judge sentences defendant). Words and things, in their mutual interventions, can antici pate each other, be retrospective, speed up or slow down their effects, but there is never a priority of the one over the other, or a strict causality; one is not the referent while the other is always representation [. . .].The chain of speech is like a chain of commands, instructions for living, not because language "tells us about the world," but because acts of speech are, for the most part, all one has to go on. (39)

Therefore, language is not so much a vehicle of communication, as of power. It is a means to make people act. As Muecke recognises while at Fitzroy Crossing, where the words of tourism do not belong, the locals act in ways that are different to tourists' expectations. To protect Aboriginal sites and to inform tourists of significant Aboriginal sites, the state has erected signs that read "*Site of Significance*." As Muecke insists:

> Significance is the wrong word, these sites are not full of meanings, cluttered with signs like a library. Ask the locals: *something there* they will say, it *moves*, there's a *power*. But if you put up a sign saying *Site of Power*, the authorities would laugh: mumbo jumbo [. . .]. But you have to ask yourself, what has that site been doing over the years, getting people to do things or producing meanings? (*No Road* 35)

The power to fix meaning, that is the context of interpretation, requires, as Derrida argues, a community of consensus (Caputo 1997). The state's tourism body is one community of consensus that determines that traditional knowledge is "mumbo jumbo," and another community, the local Indigenous community, recognises it as their truth. Of course the state has more power to determine the context of broader interpretations and the locals' interpretation is dismissed by mainstream Australia as pre-modern. But, as Muecke insists, there are places where the "words you have brought with you are radically im plausible" (*No Road* 35). Although the traditional custodians hold very little authority beyond Fitzroy Crossing, when at home they hold the power not only to unsettle the self-assured Western visitor's "truth," but also to realign visitors' interpretative practices. The visitor is reminded that this is contested country and there is a continual struggle over meaning.

To traverse the cultural differences that he experiences at Fitzroy Crossing, Muecke defers to local knowledge. In investing something of one's self in local knowledge one acts to help create new enunciative sites for marginalised knowledge. Marginalised people affect the powerful discourses of nation making and therefore partici pate in creatively remaking the world. By introducing these voices into his text Muecke establishes a dialogue with Aboriginal and non-Aboriginal histories. He cannot return from his foray across the "other side of the frontier" with Indigenous knowledge, but he can, in his storytelling, trace emergent, hybrid cultural forms, which are and have always been possible in colonial Australia.

Muecke tempers the desire to enfold otherness into an unrestrained romantic imagination by deferring to local authorities. When listening to a story on Aboriginal television,[2] Muecke ponders, "what gave one the right to follow" (*No Road* 197). The story tells of travellers coming to Alice Springs and only being able to enter through Honeymoon Gap escorted by an elder. The travellers must follow in the footsteps of the Elder: "each footprint on top of the other" (*No Road* 197). He goes on to write that there is:

> a lesson here for thinking about getting to know places, or texts—it's all in the approach. If you want the opinion of the Aboriginal custodians of sites, then you have to observe the protocols. In observing the rules, that is, the footsteps, you can get new insights into places and their meanings. (*No Road* 198)

Muecke suggests that forms of knowing can be experienced by following in the footsteps of local custodians, either literally or, in the case of texts, metaphorically, rather than mapping a site with knowledge from elsewhere.

Muecke exposes himself to a different way of knowing the Bungle Bungles by following in the "footsteps" of a local, Joy, a young Aboriginal woman, who tells Muecke that

> she likes to let her gaze rest on the empty space which other people leave behind. In such moments, it seems, she lets her body go, a body which has become responsive through intense multiple relationships of Aboriginal social life. She encourages, without judging it, the feeling which is growing in her and at this very moment lets herself be overcome by a sensation of liveliness and power. (*No Road* 109)

Joy's local knowledge acts as a guide for Muecke to disrupt his interpretative process and to be open to Indigenous ways of knowing. Muecke writes:

> "What would it be like if I wasn't here?" the post-tourist might ask, or "How can I lose myself in this place by following a track to the point of disappearance (instead of earnestly and quickly crunching around spectacular sites until they are gone)?" Instead of imagining myself "at

> one" with a place, a plodding spirituality, might I not just imagine I'm already gone—that much *will* be certain—and in this lightness lift ever so slightly off the ground so that objects are only faintly touched, real seeing is in the glimpse, sounds reduced to a whisper [. . .]? (*No Road* 135)

Muecke's reference to a "plodding spirituality" could be read as a reference to non-Indigenous people's desire to reaffirm their self-identity by imposing an imported knowledge upon a place. Hence the "plodding spirituality" is a recuperative gesture. Indigenous knowledge is reduced and limited to some*thing* similar to Western knowledge, which leaves the "tourist" untouched by difference and not subject to another's knowledge or ethics. Muecke perceives the Bungle Bungles through the prism of his understanding of local, Indigenous knowledge, in an attempt to offer Indigenous knowledge a broader cultural value. Furthermore, he advocates "faintly touch[ing]" as an anti-colonial gesture, as grasping at knowledge reduces it to an object and disavows knowledge as lived and always in process. Readers are offered a trace to follow that is a complex, dialogic path in which desire and writing have been realigned toward Indigeneity (Paull 147).

Muecke's speculation that "getting to know may mean leaving home and getting lost for a while" (*No Road* 130), paradoxically suggests that to *see* contemporary Australia one needs to lose sight of oneself and one's country. Muecke's juxtaposition of Bonnie Edward's light and entertaining anecdotes and her more serious cultural knowledge with his mediations on alternative understandings of Australia, suggests that his 'getting lost' is supported by taking a place in the local social network. The artistic project that he is setting out on (the book on the Bungle Bungles), is one in which he wants to imagine himself out of European enculturation. Arguably, this is a futile endeavour. However, although one cannot cleanse oneself of cultural knowledge, one can gain new insights and alternative perspectives by talking and listening to people hitherto designated as "other." Bonnie acts as a local guide, not in the sense that Muecke had initially wanted. Muecke is hoping that Bonnie will be able to share her traditional knowledge of her country. Instead Bonnie entertains him with anecdotes about shoplifters in her local store. Her generous and humorous storytelling sustains him in the comfort and care of friendship, a space in which he is safe not to know himself, and thereby safe to make his self available to knowing differently. In Bonnie's "safe house," in which she is the host, hospitality is extended according to a law that Muecke must attend to as a guest. The effect of Bonnie's storytelling is to slow Muecke down: his project disappears, only to reappear transformed, having found a new way. In slowing Muecke down, Bonnie is not a site for the collection of meanings, a utility from which whitefellas might procure "other" knowledge; rather she acts to reassert reciprocity into cross-cultural engagements. Muecke learns, or relearns, that knowledge and insight are not the accumulation of facts, but negotiating living together.

Muecke attempts to negotiate the impasse of cultural differences, not by driving along the straight roads and Imperial highways of Western knowledge, but by getting lost and being pulled into affective encounters with others and otherness. The textual topography of *No Road* opens up spaces between one text and another—one voice and another—in which in nobody (no body) owns the representational ground (99). In this third space, between identities, one is made aware that "I" is other-constructed, and thereby one has reciprocal responsibilities to the other. Furthermore, this space is the site of socialising forces—a shared space in which in order to travel across cultural differences one must forego a coherent, cohesive identity. The results of these affective encounters with others are new cultural formations and subjectivity. Muecke's answer to the question he poses—"what language can I use to *carry* this story?" (*No Road* 150)—is to reconfigure the representational terrain by acknowledging and accepting his place in a network of Indigenous rights and obligations.

Muecke ends *No Road* by playfully tracing cultural growth that is generated from a dialogue with cultural difference. In his re-telling of the story of Captain Cook's shoes, he suggests that the "postcolonial is, ideally, a way of thinking oneself out of imperial and Oedipal stories about Australia. And recognising Aboriginality will help forge a new postcolonial Australia" (*No Road* 237). In the story (perhaps fictional) of Captain Cook's shoes, which have been abandoned on the beach and become a local song, Muecke wonders about the wonders of cultural convergence and transformation. As he writes, "the anticolonial gesture is to chuck out those shoes and to create a song—a resonance—not to tolerate the intolerable, but to transform it into artful politics" (*No Road* 238). This is the path that *No Road* takes and Muecke encourages his readers to follow. Situated in *No Road*s plural and heterogeneous textual landscape, in which no one text or perspective dominates, both the writing subject, Muecke, and the reader's interpretative authority are continually blocked. As Caputo argues, there is no justice when the way is not blocked, when "we are just sailing along on automatic with cruise control and with our hands barely on the wheel" (*No Road* 135). Within Muecke's dialogic textual landscape, the reader is reassured that there is always a local guide, who leaves a friendly trace (*No Road* 197), if one is willing to be open to the other and learn to belong according to the ethics and laws of the locals. In so doing, Muecke remembers colonisation. Muecke recognises the country is overflowing with stories and generates a form of anti-colonial storytelling in which the white writer is at home with discomfort and dislocation. In so doing, he makes Australia different.

Endnotes

[1] Gardiya is Gooniyandi (Kimberly language group) for White person; see Thieberger (1994): 209.

[2] Muecke footnotes (*No Road* 249) that he was watching *Wedgetail Eagle Dreaming*, CAAMA, 1991, Arrente/English, Presented by Rosalie Riley, Narrated by Harold (Ross) Ellis.

Works Cited

Brewster, Anne. "Fictocriticism: Pedagogy and Practice." *Crossing Lines: Formations of Australian Culture*. Ed. Caroline Guerin et al. Adelaide: ASAL, 1996. 89-92.

——. "Fictocriticism: Undesciplined Writing." *Writing–Teaching, Teaching Writing*. Ed. Jan Hutchinson, and Graham Williams. Sydney: U of Technology, 1996. 29-32.

Caputo, John. *Deconstruction in a Nutshell: A Conversation with Jacques Derrida*. New York: Fordham UP, 1997.

Carter, Paul. "Crossing the Line: Space as Colonisation." *Crossing Lines: Formations of Australian Culture.* Ed. Caroline Guerin et al. Adelaide: ASAL, 1995. 1-12.

Dawson, Paul. "A Place for the Space Between: Fictocriticism and the University." *Westerly* 47 (2002): 139-151.

Deleuze, Gilles, and Felix Guattari. *A Thousand Plateaus: Capitalism and Schizophrenia.* Trans. Brian Massumi. Minneapolis: U of Minnesota P, 2000.

Fineman, Joel. *The Subjectivity Effect in Western Literary Tradition: Essays Toward the Release of Shakespeare's Will.* Cambridge: Mass. Institute of Technology P, 1991.

Gandhi, Leela. *Postcolonial Theory: A Critical Introduction.* St. Leonards, NSW: Allen & Unwin, 1998.

Healy, Chris, and Stephen Muecke. "Moving Around: An Interview." *Meanjin* 58.3 (1999): 174-91.

Kerr, Heather. "Sympathetic Topographies." *Parallax* 7.2 (2001): 107-126.

Muecke, Stephen. *No Road.* Fremantle: Fremantle Arts P, 1997.

——. "Lonely Representations: Aboriginality and Cultural Studies." *Power, Knowledge and Aborigines.* Ed. Bain Attwood and John Arnold. Melbourne: La Trobe UP, 1992. 32-44.

O'Hara, John. "The Narrative Construction of Reality: An Interview with Stuart Hall." *Southern Review* 17.1 (1984): 3-17.

Paull, James. Rev. of *No Road,* by Stephen Muecke. *New Literatures Review* 34 (Winter 1997): 138-151.

Probyn, Fiona. "A Poetics of Failure is No Bad Thing: Stephen Muecke and Margaret Somerville's White Writing." *Journal of Australian Studies* 75 (2002): 15-26.

Thieberger, Nick. *Macquarie Aboriginal Words.* Sydney: Macquarie Library, 1994.

The Politics of Diasporic Desire
A Study of Vijay Mishra's Key Works

Gunjeet Aurora

Vijay Mishra (b. 1945) needs no introduction in the field of post colonial criticism as he is one of the most eminent Post-colonial critics of recent times who is based in Australia. He has authored several books and essays in diverse areas in the field of post-colonial criticism. As Wimal Dissanayke (1994) says,

> Vijay Mishra belongs to that rare breed of literary scholars who are equally at home in English and Indian literatures. (*The Gothic Sublime* Backcover)

Himself being a part of the "Great Indian Diaspora," Mishra has a broad understanding of both the Eastern and Western cultures and stands in the enviable position of objectively analyzing both.

The corpus of his works extends from the Gothic to the Indian Sublime along with essays on Diaspora, films and a whole book on popular Indian cinema. He has applied post-colonial theories and the Indian tradition of philosophical thought to areas such as the Indian cinema and the new manifestations of the Diaspora through various cultural forms such as cinema and literature. Mishra's concept of "The Diasporic Imaginary" is of immense value in understanding the Indian Diaspora along with its cultural implications from both sides—the Diasporas mystique for the Indian society at home and the motherland's pull for the diasporic. Being a part of the diasporic community, his insights into this problematic area of identity and identification with any nationality are very original. Mishra's grandparents went to Fiji as indentured labourers. Mishra's childhood was spent there as he reminisces about his experiences in the preface to his book *Bollywood Cinema: The Temples of Desire* (2002) and in the essay "The Feudal Post-Colonial." He moved to New Zealand in 1964 for higher studies and after that shifted to Australia where he's been living ever since apart from two years that he worked in the University of Alberta, Canada. He asserts in his book *Bollywood Cinema* that despite his growing up in the colonies he "belongs racially and as Hindu, to India" (ix). So one can understand his preoccupation with Diaspora and India despite his being a third generation diasporic Indian. Moreover his theories are based on first hand experiences of Diaspora rather than a study of second hand accounts of this phenomenon and I think this lends greater credence to his theories.

The main body of his works consists of four main books and numerous articles on post-colonial criticism, Diaspora and film studies. Chronologically placed the books are: *The Dark Side of the Dream: Australian Literature and the Postcolonial Mind* (1991), *The Gothic Sublime* (1994), *Devotional Poetics and the Indian Sublime* (1998), *Bollywood Cinema: Temples of Desire* (2002). Apart from these, he has just released a book titled *The Diasporic Imaginary*(2007). An incomplete list of his seminal essays includes the following: "Towards a Theoretical Critique of Bombay Cinema" (1985), "David Shulman and the Laughter of South Indian Kings and Clowns" (1987), "The Centre Cannot Hold: Bailey, Indian Culture, and the Sublime" (1989), "The Great Indian Epic and Peter Brook" (1991), "Decentering History: Some Versions of Bombay Cinema" (1992), "The Diasporic Imaginary: Theorising the Indian Diaspora" (1996), "(B)Ordering Naipaul: Indenture History and Diasporic Poetics" (1996), "Diasporas and The Art of Impossible Mourning" (2001), "The Feudal Post-Colonial" (2001) and many others.

Although a cursory glance might indicate that all his works are in diverse areas, yet closer look shows that a common strand does run through them. This seemingly eclectic corpus of books and articles is bound by the concepts of diaspora, the sublime and Indian cinema. I would consider his essay "The Diasporic Imaginary: Theorising the Indian Diaspora" (1996) to be his seminal text in the area of Diaspora studies. In this essay he's discussed the concepts of "Border" and "Exclusivist" diasporas based on old and new capitalism, in relation to the modern and traditional Indian Diaspora. Taking James Clifford's (1994) definition of the diasporic, Mishra says the Diasporic Imaginary is any

> ethnic enclave in a nation-state that defines itself, consciously, unconsciously or because of the political self-interest of a racialised nation-state, as a group that lives in displacement. ("The Diasporic Imaginary" 423).

The diasporic imaginary is the self-defined image that the diasporic subjects construct for themselves whereby they would be as close as possible to the homeland as also expecting to be considered a part of the current nation-state. Mishra has based his theory on a study of various diaspora writers and filmmakers such as V. S. Nai paul, Bharati Mukherjee, Hanif Kureishi, and Mira Nair.

Mishra explores the overwhelming presence of diaspora in literature, films and music in contem porary times. The diasporic make their presence felt most vocally by appropriating these cultural forms for enunciating their hyphenated subjectivities. He traces the beginnings of the Indian diaspora starting with the movement of indentured labour from India to Fiji, West Indies etc. Mishra contends that the diasporic community is characterized by a hyphenation that causes a split in their identities and they are rendered as Fiji-Indian or American-Indian. They can never be any one identity because this hybridity is an integral part of their psyche, the defining feature that renders them as subjects of Diaspora. They can't relinquish the love and pull they feel for their motherland but at the same time they owe an allegiance to their new homes also. As a way of negotiating between the two they construct "imaginary homelands" for themselves whereby they live in the faint hope of being regarded in their spirit and values as Indians, yet at the same time in their everyday life as accepted citizens of their new nationalities.

A very positive im pact of the Diaspora can be seen in the multiculturalism it has brought in its wake seen most prominently in the vast popularity of fusion music forms such as those of Bhangra with Caribbean reggae and Black Hi p-Hop music. Mishra also discusses movies such as *My Beautiful Laundrette* (1985), based on Hanif Kureishi's story, as evocative of such a move beyond the stronghold of the motherland's values to a newer area where there are transgressions because it is no longer possible to keep living forever in the mini Indias typified in Nai paul's *A House for Mr. Biswas* (1969). Mishra asserts that the Diaspora is a "defining feature of the late modern world" ("The Diasporic Imaginary" 442). Diaspora affirms the com plexity of the postmodern nation-state with its amalgamation of multifarious ethnicities.

His other essays on Diaspora also embody the same ideas more or less. However one wishes Mishra had picked up some new exam ples at least. The other essays such as "Diaspora and the Art of Im possible Mourning" (2001) have the same exam ples as those in the "The Diasporic

Imaginary" giving a strong a sense of déjà vu. They seem to be a reworking of the same essay over and over again. One encounters this in his chapter on Indian cinema and diaspora also in *Bollywood Cinema: Tem ples of Desire* (2002). Mishra remains obsessively concerned with Nai paul and Srinivas Krishna's film *Masala* (1991). In "Diaspora and the Art of Im possible Mourning" Mishra also takes up the theories of Derrida and i ek along with an analysis of Indian films and literature (Nai paul once again) as also a discussion of the terms: mourning, specter, identity, "the Jews," and trauma in respect to Diaspora. However, in the "The Feudal Post-Colonial" (2001) he discusses the Fiji crisis by tracing the history of the revolt that took place in 2000 coup in view of the socio- political and cultural aspects that permeated it.

While the essays dwell mostly on the concept of diaspora, Mishra's books show a totally different concern. *The Dark Side of the Dream* (1992) written in collaboration with Bob Hodge focuses on the "Aboriginalism" of the aborigines in Australia. According to Graham Huggan (1993), the book is valuable in exposing the "pseudopostcolonialism" of contem porary Australian culture (134) but beyond that the book has received a lot of criticism since most people felt it to be rather shallow and unable to offer any concrete theorizations on the com plexities of an Australian culture still grappling with a disturbing past and a multicultural present. The dominant criticism leveled against the authors is that of raising the "ogre of Aboriginalism" without having made any first hand studies in the field of aboriginal studies (Tonkinson 311). There is an attem pt at deconstructing the Australian society and exposing the anthropologists who according to them aim at constructing such discourses about the aborigines that effectively seek to silence the voices of these mariginalised people. However within this also the authors also have been criticized for a rather "patronizing mystification" of the aborigine culture (Tonkinson 311). But despite this the book raises some rather pertinent and thought provoking questions.

His book *The Gothic Sublime* published in 1994 deals with western Gothic texts and analyses them from a postmodern perspective. According to Mishra the gothic represents our own doomed desire to pass beyond the hyppereal. The book is a theoretical reading of some of the key gothic texts by writers such as Mary Shelley (b. 1797 – d. 1851), William Godwin (b. 1756 – d. 1836), and Herman Melville (b. 1819 – d. 1891). The gothic is not just a thing of the past to be laughed or mocked at, but as Mishra affirms, very much a part of the post-modern scenario. As Rob Wilson (1994) remarks,

> The Gothic Sublime is a study of the gothic as a discourse/genre centered in the psychological tactics and "uncanny" thematics initiated in *The Castle of Otranto*, moving [. . .] into the tactics and thematics of the postmodern condition as influentially figured in theorists such as Lyotard, Jameson, Sedgwick, and Lacan. (*The Gothic Sublime* Backcover)

It can be said that the book marks the beginnings of Mishra's preoccupation with the category of the sublime, which further developed into a study of the Indian sublime in the book *Devotional Poetics and the Indian Sublime* published in 1998. Steven P. Hopkins (2000) in his review of the same called it "an ambitious, thoughtful, intellectually omnivorous book" (1076). The book studies the Hindu Brahman as the non-western sublime thereby shifting focus from the study of the sublime only in context of western texts, the book is interesting in that, although it focuses on Indian texts for the study of the sublime, yet it uses western theories of the sublime from Longinus (1st century AD) to Immanuel Kant (b. 1724 – d. 1804) along with Indian classics such as the *Gita* and the *Bhagvata Purana* to theorise it and therefore construct a theory of the Indian sublime. It also studies devotional or *bhakti* poetry by fusing together the classica *rasa* theorists with contem porary critics such as Stanley Fish (b. 1938), Jacques Derrida (b. 1930 – d. 2004), Slavoj i ek (b. 1949), and Paul de Man (b. 1919 – d. 1983).

It is a highly experimental book in that it is a coming together of both the western and eastern philosophies in one book although it also leads to a multi plication and overcrowding of themes at times as Hopkins points out (1076). There is John Donne (b. 1572 – d. 1631) and Kabir (b. 1440 – d. 1518), i ek and Alberuni and not as disjunct entities but with common ties of the concept of sublime and devotional poetics. According to Mishra, the Hindu Brahman represents the most fully developed of all sublimes. The sublime is that which can't be represented and it resists any attem pts at being totalized by reason or represented. It is, as Paul de Man says, a "purely inward experience consciousness" (qtd. in *Devotional Poetics and the Indian Sublime* 6). Mishra says that the Brahman is the sublime because although it is desired it can't be represented. Brahman is thus an "embodiment of negativity" (*Devotional Poetics and the Indian Sublime* 18). For Mishra, there is a certain negative em ptiness at the heart of devotional poetics also and it is around this em ptiness that the Hindu symbolic order revolves. For analyzing *bhakti* poetry, Mishra has made use of the classical *rasa* theory, which is the dominant hermeneutic mode of reading in Hindu culture. In the fourth chapter of the book, titled "Temple of,Fire: Plurality-with-Unity," Mishra takes up the theme of the Muslims as the "others." He gives a historical account of the way in which the Muslim identity got constructed (negatively) as the demonized other. This is a theme, which later refigures in his book on Bollywood called *Bollywood Cinema: Temples of Desire* with reference to the depiction of Muslims in vein of the stereotyped "others." In this chapter, however, Mishra takes up the *bhakti* poetry of Sufis and Kabir and argues that the sublime object of desire in all such poetry, Hindu or Muslim, is the unrepresentable-God.

From the mystical and otherworldly Mishra's incursion into the very materialistic and this-worldly world of Bollywood cinema might seem too abrupt, but it is not so. Apart from his personal relation with Bollywood cinema, which goes back to his Fiji days, as a critic also he has written several essays on Bollywood cinema before this book. It is this book *Bollywood Cinema: Temples of Desire* that I intend to lay my focus on in this paper. Within this book also, I will be dealing mainly with two essays—"After Ayodhya: The Sublime Object of Fundamentalism" (203-234) and "Bombay Cinema and Diasporic Desire" (235-270). In my opinion this book is a coming together of all his major theories so far. His theorizations on diaspora, the sublime and Indian cinema, all coalesce into this one text and more so in the two essays that I will be focusing upon (on Indian film theory and importance of Mishra's work, see Sarwal 2006).

The book is a chronological account in respect to the socio-cultural development and growth of Indian popular cinema called Bollywood from its nascent stage to the full-fledged glamour industry that it is today. Taking off from Chidanandan Das Gupta's (1981) categorization of cinema as "the temples of modern India," Mishra calls them the "Temples of Desire" (*Bollywood Cinema* 1). They give the audience what they want to see. Indian cinema is a "jadui nagri" (a magical place) where all that one desires gets transformed into colourful celluloid images. Places where the masses come to take darshan of their self-constructed gods and goddesses. The darshan givers are in a more powerful position than the darshan-takers. And these are the gods of fantasies, of glamour, of dreams fulfilled on the silver screen. The audience goes dutifully every Friday to see new gods come and bestow their darshan onto the masses. This holds frighteningly true for the devoted viewers of religious epics such as the *Ramayana*, *Mahabharata* and the more recent Jai Ma series etc., where people actually cover their heads and sit as though they were before the divine presences themselves. The weight and truth behind the seemingly amusing metaphor is overwhelming and quite daunting when we get down to actually considering the im pact that cinema has on "popular mass culture" as Ashis Nandy (1998) says.

The Indian psyche is dominated by the concept of dharma and Mishra in this book explains with textual analysis of classics such as *Achyut Kanya* (1936), *Mother India* (1957) down to modern films such as *Ram Lakhan* (1989), *Dilwale Dulhaniya Le Jayenge* (1995) etc. that ultimately it is the *dharmik* values that hold true. No matter how many transgressions they might make, these films can't go beyond the boundaries of *dharmik* princi ples thus retaining the sanctimonious character of the tem ples that they are. Mishra says that unlike the earlier expression of a "collective middle-class desires" onto the cinema, it is "now the aggressive desire of phantasmal self-projection" (*Bollywood Cinema* 1). The self, according to Mishra, is now more dominant than the whole. This is in contrast to Ashis Nandy's view of Indian popular cinema being a "slum's eye-view of politics" (2). For Nandy, the Indian cinema is anything but a tem ple. So while Mishra has taken it to ironically sublime heights, Nandy relegates it to lower classes of society and says that it is representative of their desires. He says that both the slums and Indian popular cinema stress upon the lower-middle-class sensibilities and on the self-made, informal theories on politics and society which they throw upon the bourgeoisie to shock them with their directness. The upper echelons of society might not like them but they can't forget their existence geographically as well as psychologically. The normal Bombay film (which is supposed to be "different" for every director or actor) is representative of the crude, lowbrow, vulgar mentality of India garbed in sophisticated designer clothes. He feels "Studying popular film is studying Indian modernity at its rawest, its crudities laid bare" (7).

As a corollary to this, I would like to add that modern slum India is the popular film in all its vulgarity, romanticized and glorified in reality. Nowhere do you see this more clearly than in the swaggering gait and latest "hero" haircuts that the young bus-conductors of DTC buses support or in the mannerism that the maids em ploy. This stratum of the Indian society lives out the Indian film. They are the real gods and goddesses of these "tem ples of desire." Nandy explains that this Indian slum is not necessarily absurd or vulgar; however, it is marred by a cloying sentimentality and fondness for over dramatization of life. For Nandy, even the upper classes are basically slum dwellers with more money. Nandy's metaphor for Indian cinema is radically different from Mishra's metaphor. I feel that maybe the reality lies somewhere between the two metaphors.

The Indian popular cinema does portray the desires and sensibilities of the lower middle classes but it is increasingly shifting towards a new category: that of the Indian diasporic. This is the new power category and it is their desires garbed once again in shades of the slum mentality that we see as the new branded, glamorous and picturesque tem ples set in the Swiss Alps or Australian landscape.

Moving beyond these two divergent views of the Indian cinema, I would like to discuss the book *Bollywood Cinema: Temples of Desire*. The book moves chronologically in discussing the beginnings of Indian popular cinema and moves into the present where it has become a powerful medium, at times silently com plicitous in carrying forward dangerous propaganda and in moving to areas beyond the motherland. Mishra has conjoined both the chronological and thematic aspects of different decades in a very appropriate manner. Moving from an exposition of the beginnings of Indian cinema, Mishra shows its continuities with older cultural forms such as those of the *Ramayana*, *Mahabharata* epics and also with the legacy of the Parsi theatre and the paintings of Ravi Verma (b. 1848 – d. 1906). Mishra then discusses its beginnings with Dadasaheb Phalke (b. 1870 – d. 1944) in 1913 and also makes a textual study of some key film texts such as *Achyut Kanya* (1936), *Aadmi* (1939), *Devdas* (1935 and 1955), as well as the other founding directors–Barua (b. 1903 – d. 1951), Rai (b. 1892 – d. 1940), Bose (b. 1897 – d. 1986), Shantaram (b. 1901 – d. 1990) etc.

Mishra also discusses melodrama as being an integral part of the Indian cinematic tradition. Since melodrama was supposed to be a theatrical performance replete with songs and dances, the Indian cinema is very true to the tradition that it follows. Mishra offers a very detailed account of one of the most popular movies in Indian cinema: *Mother India* (1957), which earned India a nomination in the best foreign film category in the 1958 Oscar Awards also. He has analyzed the film from the perspective of it being a primary text, which constructed the woman as the all-powerful mother of the nation. It analyses the way this film reinforced the already existing discourse of the woman as a sacrificing mother which is also echoed in the way that Hindu goddesses are see; as loving, sacrificing mothers yet wrathful angels against any kind of wrong be it by their own offspring. It also shows how Nargis attained an iconic status with this movie and how it was later appropriated by Indira Gandhi for political purposes. He further discusses the auteur theory with respect to two prominent directors Raj Kapoor (b. 1924 – d. 1988) and Guru Dutt (b. 1925 – d. 1964). The phenomenon of the super star that created a parallel text in the film is examined with respect to none other than the legendary Amitabh Bachan. However the above mentioned offer nothing really original or new in the field of film criticism as they have been dealt with in some measure or the other. It is in the last two chapters (203-269) of the book which deal with the problematic categories of fundamentalism and diaspora that Mishra scores over the others as these areas not really been theorized upon much.

These are more socio-cultural than textual in their nature and are concerned with analyzing the dynamics of change and power equations resonating within them. In "After Ayodhya: The Sublime Object of Fundamentalism" Mishra has taken up the assumption that "Hindu fundamentalism is symptomatic of an undertheorised silence or repression located at the very heart of national culture" (*Bollywood Cinema* 203). It is the repressed side of the Hindu psyche that is kept as such so as to maintain the façade of a united, secular nation with perfect communal harmony. For him, as for Gyan Pandey (1992) partition is the absent center around which the discourses of secularism and unity are constructed and it is this very centre that asserts itself whenever communal riots break out. An entire fractured and multiplicitous narrative has been subsumed under the grand narrative of a united India. Cinema is also seen as being complicitous in the construction of such metanarratives as can be seen in movies such as *Amar Akbar Anthony* (1977), which show that all the religious entities are basically part of the motherland and that there is perfect unison amidst the different sons of the motherland. It espouses the idea of "different beliefs yet one mother," which is a very idealistic way of ignoring the ground reality of communal unrest in the country. However this grand narrative got smashed to smithereens during the Babri Masjid demolition (1992) and the spate of senseless violence that came in its wake. Herein Mishra identifies two key issues, which need to be addressed: First, how was it that the discourse of fundamentalism came to centre on the figure of Rama rather than any other mythological figure? And second, what is the repressed aspect of the collective Indian psyche? Mishra proceeds to give a historical reasoning for the first problem and analyses the way it is the figure of Rama as the hero and saviour that has been invoked every time the Indian state or culture has faced any kind of crisis. The powerful sway that the Rama monomyth holds over the masses lies in its simple yet eternal opposition between the forces of good symbolized by Rama and the demonic forces of evil lead by Ravana. Mishra also feels it is important to analyze the conditions under which this monomyth has been repeatedly evoked. He discusses Sheldon Pollock's essay "Ramayana and Political Imagination in India" (1993) and says that the Rama myth gained prominence around the twelfth century with the rise of the temple cult when several temples dedicated to Rama including the Rama complex at Ramtekri were being built. It was around this time that the invasions from outside started and coincidentally one Yadav king who resisted these "melechhas" was also called Rama. The melechhas were later identified with the Muslims, thus leading to binarism between the Hindus and Muslims in Manichean terms as being good and evil respectively. It is this divide that has carried itself forward through the ages into contemporary India also.

Mishra's concern about the construction of such a history is valid because of its appropriation by extremist factions such as the VHP (Vishwa Hindu Parishad) and RSS (Rashtriya Swayam Sevak Sangh) as a historical justification for this othering of the Muslims. "The demon of partition" (*Bollywood Cinema* 208) exposed the myth of brotherhood and revealed this unconscious categorization of Muslims as the "others" lurking underneath. If the earlier temple destruction had demonized the Muslim community then partition was the supreme act of their "rakhshasisation" as it was the wrenching away of a part of the "Bharat Mata" by the melechhas. This is how partition and Muslims are still conceived of in India. Partition is the demon that continues to haunt the Indian psyche, it is the sublime that can't be represented simply because its horrors exceed the limits of imagination and yet this renders it all the more powerful; because it is the absent center that keeps getting displaced and orders events in contemporary scenario also. It is this legacy of the absent sublime that surfaced in Ayodhya with the demolition of the Babri Masjid. Around the end of the 1980s, the popularization of the serial

Ramayana (1986) came in the wake of Indira Gandhi's assassination (1984) and the terrorism in Punjab and Jammu and Kashmir. It was in a real life opposition between the forces of good and evil, that *Ramayana* made its stronghold in Indian popular culture. It was also at this time that the BJP chose to bring up the dormant center once more into action and to reclaim the repressed half—the Ram Janm Bhoomi—from the "others" (Muslims). The Babri Masjid issue rose with great fervour amongst the Indian masses as the center had always been there locked in some part of their psyche. Ayodhya, according to Mishra, has become a narrative about seizing the repressed self of Hindutva by reaffirming most vociferously "the decontaminated past" (*Bollywood Cinema* 212).

So, in a nation where religion is the most passionate of all obsessions, it is inevitable that Ayodhya has a major influence on the Indian cinema. Mishra contends that the Indian cinema has, at times, been complicitous consciously or unconsciously in presenting this repressed self. Mishra has analysed film texts such as *Ramayana*, *Ram Lakhan*, *Khalnayak* (1993), and *Krantiveer* (1994) to show the at times subliminal, and at times, the in-your-face brand of Hindu fundamentalism. While earlier in films such as *Ram Lakhan*, the Ram monomyth was at a subliminal level only, affirming with dharmik principles of Ram, in *Khalnayak*, it is more obvious as the fight between Ram (Jackie Shroff) and Bhola (the Khalnayak, Sanjay Dutt) also symbolizes the fight between good and evil. Later, in movies such as *Krantiveer* there is an appeal for a fight against the fundamentalist forces of India, which seek to destroy it. Mishra sees this as Indian cinema's attempts to make up for its own silent complicity in this "act." According to him, it is not the depiction of the myth per se, rather something in their own psyche that arouses the fundamental instincts of Hindus. The Ram monomyth has been shown in movies such as *Hum Saath Saath Hain* (1999), which is a direct adaptation of the *Ramayana* in contemporary times, although Mishra does not discuss this text, I feel it is a very important film in this context. It is not to say that the film advocates Hindu fundamentalism, however, it shows the immense hold that the Ram monomyth has over the Indian psyche even in the glamour world along with the general masses. Although cinema as an art form is not really in favour of endorsing this fundamentalism in explicit terms, however, the discourse that enters the narrative is extremist in its nature.

Where the representation of Muslims is concerned, Indian cinema has for the most part been silent in giving them the centrestage for enunciating their position and has most of the times stereotyped them into identifiable "others." Very few directors in Indian cinema such as M. S. Sathyu in *Garam Hawa* (1964) have been able to break this barrier. In recent times, movies such as *Bombay* (1995) or *Fiza* (1995) are seen as an attem pt on the part of Indian cinema to redeem itself by showing the Muslim side of the story. So Mishra sees Indian cinema as becoming aware of its responsibility in this whole discourse of fundamentalism. However, while reading the essay, I could not help but feel that the film texts he has chosen do not really augment his arguments, especially where the narrative of Partition is concerned. Since these movies do not really show any opposition between Hindus and Muslims as such so it is hard to find out the extremist ideologies within these texts unless one forces such a narrative in them. The com plicity of Indian cinema is there in the othering of Muslims, and I feel he should have dwelled on this more to put his point more clearly. Mishra has used a lot of secondary sources for these essays and has quoted people such as Gyan Pandey (1992), Rey Chow (1995), Urvashi Butalia (2000) and others to posit his case about the demon of Partition. He has made use of direct quotes as also the ideas given by these critics and writers.

If there is Hindu fundamentalism at one end of the spectrum, then on the other, there is global capitalism. The second essay that I intend to discuss "Bombay Cinema and Diasporic Desire," which depicts the phenomenon of global capitalism. In this essay, he shows mutual dependence of the diasporic and Indian cinema upon each other in contem porary times. Ever since the mid-90s, the category of the *pardesis* (NRIs) has come to be a very powerful figure in Indian cinema. The cult of the diaspora emerged in all its strength after (1990s) the phenomenal success of *Dilwale Dulhaniya Le Jayenge*, which Mishra has taken up for analysis in this regard. The diasporic have always fascinated the ones at home since they see a desirable space of wealth and luxury within this category. And it is this picture of good living, which is a blend of western lifestyle and eastern values that is projected onto the silver screen. Mishra has discussed two categories of such films: those made by actual filmmakers of the diaspora—such as Gurinder Chadha, Hanif Kureshi, Srinivas Krishna and many others—and those made by Indians—such as Karan Johar, Aditya Chopra and others For the diasporic, Indian cinema and cable TV have been crucial in linking them up to their homeland and in creating what Mishra calls an "imaginary solidarity" (*Bollywood Cinema* 237) across the linguistic and cultural differences that mark the Indian diaspora. Cut off from their homeland, the diasporic construct and imagine them through what they see on the screen. What Ashis Nandy calls the "slum's eye-view" gets transported into a global scenario as can well be seen in movies such as *Kabhi Khushi Kabhi Gham* (2001). Although Mishra doesn't take this film up, however, I feel it exemplifies the Indian home perspective of the diaspora most powerfully. A deconstruction of the entire film would show how the categories of Indians, diasporic and the "*goras*" are constructed. While the Indian diaspora is marked by multiculturalism as seen in movies such as *Bend it like Beckham* (2002), *Bhaji on the Beach* (1993), or *Masala*, it is still a very exclusivist diaspora that gets reflected in the Indian popular cinema.

The double consciousness, which is a major feature of diaspora, is removed in the cinematic representation of the diaspora wherein Indians are seen as espousing non-negotiable Indian values, which govern their lives even on foreign shores. Apart from the cultural aspect Mishra has also cited statistical evidence to show that the diaspora is a huge market for both Indian cinema and TV. Since most Indian films are doing better abroad than home, it is natural for filmmakers to target the diasporic subjects as their audiences rather than the masses at home. "The slum temples" have now been shifted to foreign lands, but there too, they are the temples of desire, because on the one hand, they arouse the diaspora's desire to be like the images they see on the screen and on the other, they represent the homeland's desire for an idyllic life of wealth and luxury in foreign lands. The diasporic make use of the Bombay cinema for showing the ambivalences and splits in their own consciousness. In his discussion of Srinivas Krishna's film *Masala* (1991), Mishra says that it is marked by kitsch and this kitschiness is central to the movie because it doesn't seek to show any identifiable representation of the diaspora. Along with this construction of the homeland by the diaspora, there's also the construction of the diaspora by the homeland which espouse the "*subah ka bhula, shyam ko lauta*" syndrome. In every such movie that comes out, one can witness western values holding sway over the protagonist or some other character that is later brought back into the folds of the native culture through a series of events or by the influence of another character who is a paragon of all the virtues that the homeland reveres. Very rarely do films of diaspora transgress the values of the native culture. *Purab aur Paschim* (1970) is a typical case of such a movie, while *Lamhe* (1991), also dealing with diaspora as the background transgresses certain values as it shows a love between a young girl and her mother's former lover. However, while a simple east versus west binarism became a hit, the other, which blurred the boundaries, did not. His analysis of five clips from the movies, *Dilwale Dulhaniya Le Jayenge* and *English Babu, Desi Mem* (1995), show various moments of transgressions, that the Indian cinema indulges in, in order to show that it belongs to the diaspora. However, ultimately, these are controlled transgressions, which are not allowed to grow up and, therefore, remain within the folds of the Indian dharmik values. The diaspora sees Indian films as providing them the rules according to which they comport themselves in the west because the Indian cinema shows them what is acceptable or unacceptable in the home country. *Dilwale Dulhaniya Le Jayenge* shows a hero who is brought up in London yet divorced from the Western culture and fully aware of his Indian values. The heroine too might be wearing minis, yet she is still the "*maryada bhari*" Indian girl. Unlike the many real-life cases of lovers running away to get married, in the face of family opposition, this ideal couple, though diasporic, decide for their parents' assent for marriage. No wonder Indians, home and abroad, relish such a display of Indian values, no matter how empty they might be in reality. It's actually nauseating at times to see the way Indian values are glorified in such movies especially in comparison to western values. Moreover there is a complete absence of any White characters in movies of diaspora and if at all they are present, it is only as stereotypes or as extras in the dance numbers. So instead of multiculturalism, what we see are mini-Indias in foreign lands constructed in purely essentialistic terms, rendering them more Indian than India itself. Mishra also talks about the seamier side of the diaspora where everything is not a grand Punjabi wedding, but one comprising fake marriages, unpleasant divorces, sometimes culminating in marital murders also. Such temples of reality are glossed over by Indian popular cinema, which continues to show only the glamorous, desirable side of the diaspora.

The need, according to Mishra, is to address the complicity of Indian cinema in both pandering to the diaspora and in constructing an imaginary diaspora for the diasporic themselves. He ends with the conclusion that Bollywood cinema can no longer do without a theory of diaspora because it is global and diasporic in its form now. Diaspora is a key influence on both the cultural and economic aspects of the Indian cinema. It is no longer "out there" but very much here in our homes. Mishra's work can be seen as an exercise in the diaspora's attempts to objectify Indian popular cinema and by it the Indian popular culture. He analyses the film texts using theories of diaspora and other post-colonial theories such as those of nationalism, fundamentalism and minority discourse. The film theories such as Auteur Theory that Mishra uses along with Darshan Theory show that there is no one Indian school of film criticism. We still depend on the western theories, but this may not be such a bad thing in the ultimate analysis because most of our films are still sorry imitations of Hollywood hits or even their B-class movies. He has also made use of his own idea of the diasporic imaginary and analysed the Indian cinema's new love for the diaspora according to this theory. Along with the historical background to the diaspora, we are given an overview of the cinema of the diaspora. The purpose behind Mishra's preoccupation with diaspora and Indian cinema can be seen as part of a project to problematise the category of the diaspora and to show it as a major player in the contemporary socio-cultural scenario of India. The essays written by him offer newer perspectives in analyzing Indian cinema and reveal the dynamics behind the changing face of media culture.

WORKS CITED

Aadmi. Dir. V. Shantaram. Prod. Prabhat Studio, 1939.

Achyut Kanya. Dir. Franz Osten. Prod. Bombay Talkies, 1936.

Amar Akbar Anthony. Dir. and Prod. Manmohan Desai. 1977.

Bend it like Beckham. Dir. Gurinder Chadha. Prod. Deepak Nayar and Gurinder Chadha. Helkon SK and Fox Searchlight Pictures, 2002.

Bhaji on the Beach. Dir. Gurinder Chadha. Prod. Nadine Marsh-Edwards. First Look Pictures, 1993.

Bombay. Dir. Mani Ratnam. Prod. S. Sriram and Mani Ratnam. Aalayam, 1995.

Butalia, Urvashi. "Community, State, and Gender: Some Reflections on the Partition of India." *Inventing Boundaries: Gender, Politics, and the Partition of India*. Ed. Musirul Hasan. New Delhi: Oxford UP, 2000. 178-207.

Chow, Rey. *Primitive Passions—Visuality, Sexuality, Ethnography and Contemporary Chinese Cinema*. New York: Columbia UP, 1995.

Clifford, James. "Diasporas." *Cultural Anthropology* 9.3 (1994): 302-338.

Das Gupta, Chidanandan. *Talking about Films*. Delhi: Orient Longman, 1981.

Devdas. Dir. and Prod. Bimal Roy. 1955.

Devdas. Dir. P. C. Barua. Prod. New Theatres, 1935.

Dilwale Dulhaniya Le Jayenge. Dir. Aditya Chopra. Prod. Yash Chopra. 1995.

English Babu, Desi Mem. Dir. and Prod. Praveen Nischol. 1995.

Fiza. Dir. Khalid Mohamed. Prod. Javed Siddiqi. 1995.

Garam Hawa. Dir. M. S. Sathyu. Prod. Absivani Isan Arya. 1964.

Hopkins, Stevens P. Rev. of *Devotional Poetics and the Indian Sublime*, by Vijay Mishra. *The Journal of Asian Studies* 59.4 (November 2000): 1076-1077.

Huggan, Graham. Rev. of *Dark Side of the Dream: Australian Literature and the Postcolonial Mind*, by Bob Hodge and Vijay Mishra. *Transition* 62 (1993): 130-135.

Hum Saath Saath Hain. Dir. Sooraj R. Barjatya. Prod. Ajit Kumar Barjatya, Kamal Kumar Barjatya, and Rajkumar Barjatya. Rajshri, 1999.

Kabhi Khushi Kabhi Ghami. Dir. Karan Johar. Prod. Yash Johar, Hiroo Johar, and Karan Johar. Yash Raj Films and Dharma Productions, 2001.

Khalnayak. Dir. and Prod. Subash Ghai. Mukta Arts, 1993.

Krantiveer. Dir. and Prod. Mehul Kumar. 1994.

Lamhe. Dir. And Prod. Yash Chopra. Yash Raj Films, 1991.

Masala. Dir. and Prod. Srinivas Krishna. 1991.

Mishra, Vijay. *The Diasporic Imaginary*. New York: Routledge, 2007.

——. *Bollywood Cinema: Temples of Desire*. London: Routledge, 2002.

——. "Diasporas and the Art of Im possible Mourning." *In Diaspora: Theories, Histories, Texts.* Ed. Makarand Paranjape. New Delhi: Indialog, 2001. 24-51.

——. "The Feudal Post-Colonial." *In Diaspora: Theories, Histories, Texts.* Ed. Makarand Paranjape. New Delhi: Indialog, 2001. 319-340.

——. *Devotional Poetics and the Indian Sublime.* Albany: State U of New York P, 1998.

——. "(B)Ordering Nai paul: Indenture History and Diasporic Poetics." *Diaspora: A Journal of Transnational Studies* 5.2 (1996): 189-237.

——. "The Diasporic Imaginary: Theorizing the Indian Diaspora" *Textual Practice* 10.3 (1996): 421-447.

——. *The Gothic Sublime.* Albany: State U of New York P, 1994.

——. "Decentering History: Some Versions of Bombay Cinema." *East-West Film Journal* 6.1(1992): 111-155.

——. "The Great Indian Epic and Peter Brook." *Peter Brook and "The Mahabharata."* Ed. David Williams. (1991): 195-205.

——. "The Centre Cannot Hold: Bailey, Indian Culture, and the Sublime." *South Asia* 12.1 (1989): 103-114.

——. "David Shulman and the Laughter of South Indian Kings and Clowns." *South Asia* 10.1 (1987): 83-88.

——. "Towards a Theoretical Critique of Bombay Cinema." *Screen* 26.3-4 (1985): 133-146.

Mishra, Vijay, and Bob Hodge. *Dark Side of the Dream: Australian Literature and the Postcolonial Mind.* Sydney: Allen & Unwin, 1992.

Mother India. Dir. and Prod. Mehboob Khan. 1957.

My Beautiful Laundrette. Dir. Stephen Frears. Prod. Tim Bevan and Sarah Radclyffe. Story. Hanif Kureishi. Mainline Pictures, 1985.

Nai paul, V. S. *A House for Mr. Biswas.* Harmondsworth : Penguin, 1969.

Nandy, Ashis. "Indian Popular Cinema as a Slum's Eye View of Politics." Introduction. *The Secret Politics of Our Desires: Innocence, Culpability and Indian Popular Cinema.* Ed. Ashis Nandy. New Delhi: Oxford UP, 1998. 1-18.

Pandey, Gyan. "In Defence of the Fragment: Writing about Hindu-Muslim Riots in India Today." Representations 37 (1992): 27-55.

Pollock, Sheldon. "Ramayana and Political Imagination in India." Journal of Asian Studies 52.2 (1993): 261-297.

Purab aur Paschim. Dir. and Prod. Manoj Kumar. 1970.

Ram Lakhan. Dir. Subash Ghai. Prod. Ashok Ghai. Mukta Arts, 1989.

Ramayana. Dir. and Prod. Ramananda Sagar. Doordarshan. 1986.

Rushdie, Salman. *The Imaginary Homelands.* London: Granta, 1991.

Sarwal, Amit. "Is there an Indian film Theory?" *English Studies, Indian Perspectives.* Ed. Makarand Paranjape, Amit Sarwal, and Aneeta Rajendran. New Delhi: Mantra, 2006. 472-486.

Tonkinson, Robert. "Postcolonialism and Its Discontents." Rev. of *Dark Side of the Dream: Australian Literature and the Postcolonial Mind*, by Bob Hodge and Vijay Mishra. *Pacific Affairs* 66. 2. (Summer 1993): 310-312.

Walpole, Horace. *The Castle of Otranto.* 1766. Ed. W. S. Lewis. New York: Oxford UP, 1996.

Wilson, Rob. *The Gothic Sublime.* 1994. 21 November 2004 <http://www.sunypress.edu/details.asp?id= 52831>.

Afterword
Reminiscences
Monsoon Semester, JNU, New Delhi, 1989

Richard Hosking

In 1989 I spent the monsoon semester at Jawaharlal Nehru University (JNU) in New Delhi; it was my second trip to India. In 1984 I had spent a very pleasant couple of months traipsing around India with my old teacher, friend and colleague Syd Harrex and his wife Jane. Syd had advised me to bring lots of ball-point pens with me on that first trip, so I had a top pocketful in various colours when I stepped off the Air India flight at Indira Ghandi Airport. I was very gratified when my taxi driver asked for a biro with the fare; I gave him three, in various colours. Syd greeted me at the door in Jor Bagh where we were staying with an open Foster's.

Growing up on South Australia's Eyre Peninsula, our home had what I now know to have been a trace, an echo, here and there, of India. Like many other Australian houses, on the mantelpiece there was the row of ebony elephants, with tiny ivory tusks. My grandfather Johannes Adolf Pahl (known as Jack) had stopped off at Bombay on his way back from France on the troopship *Argyllshire* in 1919, returning from the battlefields of France and the Somme; he must have bought the elephants there. During the Second World War while my father served in the Royal Australian Air Force, my mother lived for a while in a gardener's cottage beside a big house in Aspendale south of Melbourne. The house was owned by a Lady Hazlett, a widow who had lived in India—her husband had worked for a British oil company in what was then called Calcutta. After he died she had retired to Melbourne, Australia. She gave my mother various items: pieces of jewellery, a honey jar, cutlery, a lamp shade, rugs, draperies and screens, some of the homely detail in my South Australian childhood growing up in the outback. That's why my sister Pip's engagement ring featured an Indian diamond. There were also family stories; my mother still talks of one of Lady Hazlett's servants who, when preparing sandwiches for the memsahib's tiffin, was caught melting the butter in his mouth. Then later, when I married Sue, we accumulated one or two pieces of family paraphernalia that had belong to her great-great-father, a Lieutenant-Colonel in the British Army in Bengal during the Raj; his pith helmet, his leather gaiters and a .22 single shot rifle that weighed as much as a Lee-Enfield .303, officer issue for target practice.

At JNU I taught a course in Australian Literature to some two dozen students from all over India. I designed and taught a rather orthodox course, surveying what had emerged by the 1980s as the canon of Australian writing, including such writers as Marcus Clarke (b. 1846 - d. 1881), Henry Lawson (b. 1867 - d. 1922), Henry Handel Richardson (b. 1870 - d. 1946), Xavier Herbert (b. 1901 - d. 1984) and Patrick White (b. 1912 - d. 1990). We organised for multiple copies of the texts to be sent from Australia, with a supporting library of critical, historical and cultural materials to be placed in the library. At the time I thought that a conservatively-chosen reading list would make it easier for colleagues who might follow on afterwards. I now regret that decision, wishing instead I had put together a reading list based on the best *contemporary* Australian writing from the late 1980s. I might have taught a list of texts that had been written in the lead-up to the Australian Bicentennial the year before, which had created a flood of provocative, fascinating and stimulating books, a golden age of Australian writing. I might have taught Janette Turner Hospital's *Borderline* (1985), David Malouf's *12 Edmonstone Street* (1985), Mudrooroo's *Doctor Wooreddy's Prescription for Enduring the Ending of the World* (1983), Helen Garner's *The Children's Bach* (1984), Frank Moorhouse's *Room Service* (1987), Elizabeth Jolley's *The Well* (1986), Tim Winton's *That Eye, the Sky* (1986), Thea Astley's *It's Raining in Mango* (1987), Murray Bail's *Holden's Performance* (1988), Peter Carey's *Oscar and Lucinda* (1988), Tom Keneally's *The Playmaker* ((1987), Kate Grenville's *Joan Makes History* (1988) and Gerald Murnane's *Inland* (1988), all published in the 1980s. We might have read Murray Bail's edition *The Faber Book of Contemporary Australian Short Stories* (1988), Les Murray's *The New Oxford Book of Australian Verse* (1986) and Dale Spender's *The Penguin Anthology of Australian Women's Writing* (1988). Or I might have been really adventurous and required that the students read only 1990s creative nonfiction, those significant and resonating works: A. B. Facey's memoir-novel *A Fortunate Life* (1981); Robyn Davidson's travel book *Tracks* (1980); Stephen Muecke and Paddy Roe's *Reading the Country* (1984), one of the books that helped transform ideas about both country and Indigenous people; Robert Hughes' history of the convict system, *The Fatal Shore* (1986); Bruce Chatwin's controversial *The Songlines* (1987); Paul Carter's ideas about spatial history in *The Road to Botany Bay* (1987); Clive James' *Falling Towards England* (1985); Brian Matthews' influential experimental biography *Louisa* (1987); Sally Morgan's *My Place* (1987) and Ruby Langford's *Don't Take Your Love to Town* (1988).

As it turned out, my rather tame and conservative "tradlit" reading list meant there was at least one significant personal bonus for me; I was able to enjoy re-reading a number of classic texts, something I have never had the time to do since then. Sitting in a cane chair on the verandah at "The Residency" at 193 Golf Links, I read most of Patrick White's novels in the order in which they were written. My two favourites this time around were *Voss* (1957) and *Riders in the Chariot* (1961), offering as intense a reading experience as I can remember.

The first day of teaching, I caught an autorickshaw to work, arriving at 8.30 am as I would in Australia. Walking into what I discovered to be the temporary English Department building, I had to be careful where I put my sandalled feet; an enterprising family had made good use of the footpaths for drying dung. That kind of thing makes an impression on an Australian who comes from a gardening family; my father used to send the nearest child out into the street with a dust-pan when we heard the bread-man's or ice-man's or night-cart-man's horse passing in the country town where we lived in the Mallee. And digging under shearing sheds produced all the manure my father needed for his tomatoes and roses. I was much taken with the enterprise of the young women who had spread her cowshit patties out to dry. I watched her over the months to come patrolling the boundaries of her business empire.

I sat on the steps of the building and waited. In 1989 the department was occupying temporary buildings while renovations took place back at the main campus, so things were rather provisional. Allowances had to be made. Of course the place was busy, so I chatted with people, discovering that we could always talk about cricket. Some people assumed from my accent that I was British, which interested me. A boy brought sweet and milky tea; I watched a bullock pull an old rotary mower around the grounds, people coming and going. At eleven someone turned up to open the doors, and I was presented with some stationery and shown to my office.

It was the monsoon semester, with tremendous heat and unbelievable humidity, a combination rarely experienced by a southern Australian; this one had grown up on the Southern Ocean, looking south to the whaleroads of the Antarctic. From the start I dressed accordingly, in shorts and sandals, until one day I was asked by one of my students why I dressed like a *peón*, a workman or menial. I was surprised to hear what I assumed to be a Spanish word; only later I was told that the word is widely used in South and South East Asia. I remembered the Australian writer Helen Garner's short story "The Life of Art" (1985), where her character wonders why Australian men dress like little boys. I wore long pants thereafter.

In the absence of the usual critical and historical library sources that I might have expected back in Australia, I decided to prepare as many visual resources as possible. I took with me hundreds of slides of Australia, including art works as well as other images of the nation and as many films as I could gather. We would track over to the languages building where there was a slide projector—and an air-conditioned teaching space. Someone told me that the building had been donated to JNU by the Russian government. One week I showed a slide of Clifford Possum Tjapaltjarri's "Man's Love Story," a magnificently allegorical and metaphorical painting from Papunya in the western desert, completed in 1978. Drawing freely on an essay by Tim Johnson (1988), I spoke with what (in my ears at least) sounded like great authority about this painting. These days I know the difference between "speaking for" and "speaking about."

Some days the power would go off, but debates would proceed without a pause, twenty faces glistening in the forty degree gloom. These days we carry water bottles, but then we waited until the boy came with tea or limcas. After teaching we would often retire to the small shop by the main gate for another lime soda, and furious conversations resumed. Often young men would join us, wait for a break in the conversation and then ask me about some Australian *state* cricketer's

Sheffield Shield average. I found their cricket knowledge amazing. How did they know who was playing well for Kensington or St Kilda? I barely knew the names of the teams in the Indian national competition.

I befriended a Syrian postgraduate whose first words to me were "I am not a terrorist." I would go home with him for coffee and we would talk about politics, about what we were learning to call "theory" in the 1980s. I was intensely aware of how little I knew, how my horizons were so low. He introduced me to some Palestinian students who were also living in the same building; we would sit and drink coffee, talk politics and watch the buffaloes being fed or milked in the little courtyard below.

Most days in between classes I would sit on the balcony outside the departmental office, drink tea and chat. As the department was housed in a temporary building outside the main campus, most of my colleagues would only come in to teach, so I had to negotiate a number of on-going conversations that spread themselves over days and even weeks. I did my best to comment on a discussion about Australian Indigenous people, whom one colleague's father had insisted were Dravidians, he having published on the matter. My only contribution was to note that southern Indian villages seemed to be over-run with what we would call dingoes. Since then there has been some controversial DNA evidence that does indeed link Australian Indigenous people with a possible place of origin in South India (see Macaulay et al. 2005). Another discussion with the Professor of French involved the extent to which Michel Foucault's works had made an impression in Australia, but at least I was able to describe the famous model prison at Port Arthur in Tasmania and the Round House in Fremantle, Western Australia, with their famous panopticons. Someone else asked if I was Dennis Lillee, as I sported a moustache rather like the great bowler, but not quite as luxuriant or assertive as his. Mind you, he's much balder than I am now.

The students were a splendid group. There were passionate conversations and arguments, with a degree of intensity that surprised me, especially when some of the brilliant young women gave just as much as they got from the young men. Indian students were (and I assume remain) much more demonstrative and outgoing than their laconic and laid back Australian counterparts. One or two of the students seemed to find me hard to understand; they had trouble with my rather old-fashioned Australian irony: I'd smile when I was serious, while dead-pan meant I was joking. Most worked me out pretty smartly. There were some comments made about my Australian accent; they made me remember my first class at university, when our German-born professor asked me to read a paragraph, after which he declared to the class that "Rick has a characteristic Australian working-class accent." His remark surprised me; *he* was the one with the bloody accent.

Perhaps my vowels had been rounded off a little by the time I reached India. There was some discussion in a staff meeting about the matter, and Professor Meenakshi Mukherjee stopped all debate with the remark: "Rick's accent is a political weapon." In my ears, of course, all my colleagues, everyone around me at JNU, had accents.

In the late 1980s Professor Mukherjee was head of department; her reputation was (and remains) considerable and far-reaching. I had first met her during a visit she made to Australia, to Flinders University. During a seminar at JNU one day I made the rather solemn remark that the Australian visitor to India responds strongly to an overwhelming sense of India's history. Professor Mukherjee remarked that Indians travelling in Australia were equally aware that Australia seemed to be all geography. She recounted how she had walked from Flinders University in the southern suburbs of Adelaide to Blackwood in the foothills of the Mount Lofty Range; she described how she felt after she had encountered not one single individual on her walk of several miles. I wondered at the time how she might have responded to camping out in one of Australia's many deserts, sleeping with the dingoes, the starlight bright enough some nights to read by, and no obvious trace of human presence. I remembered her remark when, a few years later, I travelled to the World Heritage listed Lake Mungo with colleagues teaching Archaeology, where we saw the remarkable grave of a young Indigenous women buried some 40,000 years ago, her body decorated with red ochre from Bookartoo in the Flinders Ranges. We now think of Australia as a palimpsest, layered with history and story, and not just mere landscape.

I lived for six months in Golf Links, in "The Residency," in what we Australians would call a boarding house. The landlady was Mrs. S—, a convivial and caring woman. Arriving home late one night and having to rouse up the watchman, I discovered that every night we were locked in, and I wondered what might happen if there were a fire. Her husband was a retired Indian Civil Service public servant. I would sometimes have tea with him on the verandah in the early morning and we would discuss the events of the day: the Berlin Wall was about to come down, there were big changes afoot in the Soviet Union and Rajiv Gandhi had to face the polls later that year. The family owned a collection of vintage British cars, including a couple of MGs, but they could not be driven around the streets of Delhi as they might be scratched and defaced. Mr. S—— told me once that in some ways he regretted the departure of the British. Mrs. S— asked me not to hold the door open for the sweeper boy with all his buckets, because such a gesture might "confuse him." He was sharp and street-wise, and ran errands for me.

Most nights we would congregate on the roof and watch the local children flying kites and the sun go down over Golf Links. In 1989 there were army posts outside the houses where embassy staff from dozens of nations lived: the Bulgarian Cultural Centre was just across the road. Australia had no such cultural centre in India, then or now. One evening I arrived home from JNU and went up to the roof, where I found a young man with a flamboyant moustache resting an equally imposing machine gun on the parapet. I did the decent thing and offered him a gin and tonic, but he refused, very politely. It turned out that Prime Minister Rajiv Gandhi was due some time that evening to visit the house of a cabinet colleague who lived nearby. We sat and waited until an entourage of identical Ambassadors tore down the road at high speed. Once the vehicles had departed the young soldier also left, joining his fellow-soldiers in the park below the house where they waited for trucks to come to pick them up to take them back to barracks. I had not seen machine guns up close since living in Madrid in Spain in 1971, towards the end of General Franco's regime. In Australia in those more innocent times, the police did not even wear side-arms.

In my little suburban bank in Golf-Links there was always a guard with a double-barrelled 12-gauge shotgun. When I lined up to change 100 rupee notes into something smaller, he would usher me into the appropriate queue with the barrel of the gun. He had another flamboyant moustache (this one white), and after several visits he began to recognise me. He had been a soldier in the Indian Army. We would chat about this and that, usually about cricket. I remember one conversation about Nissan Patrols, which the Japanese car company had originally developed for the Indian Army; I drove one back in Australia, and found it reassuring to find so many in India, reminding me of home.

Cultural attaché Brett Martin was my contact at the Australian High Commission. He and his wife Mas helped me cope with being away from my family for such a period of time. One dinner party I sat beside an officer from the Indian Army and, as we chatted, I realised how little I knew about Indian military history. Travelling in to the city centre, I had often noticed the name "Gallipoli" on the India Gate war memorial on Rajpath, so I asked my dinner-companion about the Indian experience of Gallipoli, the campaign in Turkey in World War One at which the Australian nation had supposedly "come of age." He told me that while only 5,000 Indian soldiers had served there, their casualty figures were appalling.[1] This discovery intrigued and moved me. Dr. Peter Stanley, Principal Historian at the Australian War Memorial in Canberra, has observed that

> Just over 8,000 of the Australians died as a result of the campaign, a loss rate of about one-in-six. But 1,624 of the Indian combatants were killed, a loss rate of greater than one-in-two. This was the heaviest casualty rate of all the protagonists in the campaign: much heavier than the Turkish and British empire loss rates, grievous though they were.[2]

The next time I see the India Gate I'll reflect again on these figures.

Most evenings in the little park outside where I lived in Golf Links there would be an impromptu game of cricket. I used to wander over to umpire, to watch and, occasionally, to give the odd bit of advice about how to bowl in-swingers with a touch of the leg cutter. The servants' children did the fielding. My landlady's son would walk across from his house in full regalia: helmet, gloves, pads and neckerchief, practising his forward defensive stroke as he advanced. Starring with the bat, he expected me not to give him out unless the LBW was absolutely plum. I congratulated him once for a fine shot through the covers and into the brick fence; he told me that his coach was Bishen Bedi. I had seen the former captain of India bowl his left-arm spinners at Adelaide Oval during the Packer days and World Series Cricket, a decade or so before. Now and again a boy would ask me if I was Dennis Lillee; of course I said yes.

Colleagues at JNU advised me to seek out Faqir Chand's bookshop in Khan Market, where I would often go to buy books and chat about Indian writing. Faqir Chand told me his family had been bookbinders to the Moghuls, so I managed to get some battered editions bound while I was there. He would send the boy out and then serve milky cappuccino, and we would sit and talk. He sold me (among many other books) what was then the latest novel by Anita Desai, *Baumgartner's Bombay* (1987). In return I told him a story about going to R. K. Narayan's (b. 1906 - d. 2001) house in Mysore with my friend Syd Harrex, only to find that the great man was away in Chennai.

Like all visitors, I was fascinated with Indian variety and diversity, the exhilarating mix than can be overwhelming sometimes for those of us from more austere places. One day walking down to Khan Market I counted seven varieties of excrement, which remains a personal best: buffalo, cow, human, dog, monkey, elephant—and bear. The day the bear came to Golf Links, all the dogs for miles around began barking.

They got me in CP, Connaught Place, and it cost me 200 rupees. I was wandering around the circle there one morning, no particular place to go, passing the shop that sold solar topees, when at the traffic lights a considerate young man pointed out to me that something had crapped on my left shoe. He ushered me to one side of the footpath, and offered—for a small sum—to clean it for me. I removed the shoe, and the considerate young man gave me a sheet of the *Times of India* to stand on. Another considerate young man then came up to me, and we started chatting about Australia—he recognised the accent—and he told me at some length about his experiences studying in Melbourne. The first considerate young man then interrupted, pointing out to me that for some strange reason my shoelace and the lining from inside the shoe had inexplicably disappeared. Not to worry: a third considerate young man was right there with his shoe repair kit under his arm. By now quite a crowd of considerate onlookers had gathered. I stood there on what I like to remember these days when I tell the story as the cricket pages of the *Times of India* with news of another win to Australia until the shoe was restored to something like its former glory. I then lined up the young men, and asked them how much. The considerate young fellow with Melbourne experience did all the talking from there on: whatever I thought fair, he helpfully suggested. I gave them 200 rupees, but insisted that in return I might photograph the team. When I congratulated them on their wit and ingenuity, they all looked suitably modest.

Brett and Mas invited me to spend a weekend with their family at Mussorie, where Anita Desai was born and where the Australian Government maintains a "weekender." We drove there from Delhi, stopping on the way for a picnic in a forested area. A bloke on a bike appeared, but we had difficulty understanding him. There seemed to be something he wanted to tell us. Brett's Tamil cook was travelling with us; it took him a little time to work out that the man was warning us in Hindi that we were picnicking on a track that was used by elephants moving down to the river to drink. We gave him a six-pack of Foster's for his consideration.

We had hoped to arrange a meeting with the celebrated writer Ruskin Bond (b. 1934) in Mussorie, but it turned out that the weekend we were in his hill town he was in Delhi, so a much-antici pated meeting did not eventuate, to my regret. We did, however, find the grave of John Lang (b. 1817 - d. 1864), the first Australian-born writer of note; Bond had discovered the grave some years before in the old English camel's back cemetery. Lang is buried high on a ridge among the deodars, facing the snow-covered Srikanta peak and the Banderpunch massif, where today a family run their goats and drape their washing on the moss-covered headstones (see Bond 1972 and 1980). I have my photograph of Lang's grave on the wall before me.

I started my journey home to Australia with a flight from Delhi to Hyderabad, a flight I happened to share with the Dalai Lama. He was seated just a few seats away, and just about everyone on the plane came to acknowledge him, including the pilot. I was travelling to Mysore to attend one of the late Professor C. D . Narasimhaiah's celebrated conferences at his magical research centre Dhvanyaloka. When we landed in Hyderabad, I joined the Dalai Lama's entourage as we strolled across the tarmac to the terminal building; there were signs everywhere celebrating the great man and his role as a peacemaker.

After the conference I flew on to Singapore, where I joined the crowd waiting for the Qantas flight to Adelaide. Many of the Australian men were wearing shorts and what we Australians call thongs, which does not mean g-string. I was startled and disconcerted by the intensity and volume of their accents. I read *Baumgartner's Bombay* on the flight home, and knew I would be back to India.

Endnotes

[1] The Australian Commonwealth Government Department of Veterans Affairs has casualty figures at <http://www.dva.gov.au/commem/commac/studies/anzacsk/aday4.htm#cas>.

[2] Peter Stanley, "Australia, India and Gallipoli: A Study in Contrasting National Consequences," Unpublished paper. Dr. Stanley's figures are taken from *Statistics of the Military Effort of the British Empire During the Great War* (London: War Office, 1920). See also, Peter Stanley, *Quinn's Post, Anzac, Gallipoli* (Sydney: Allen & Unwin, 2005).

Works Cited

Astley, Thea. *It's Raining in Mango: Pictures from the Family Album.* Ringwood, Victoria: Viking, 1987.

Bail, Murray, ed. *The Faber Book of Contemporary Australian Short Stories.* London: Faber, 1988.

——. *Holden's Performance.* Ringwood, Victoria: Viking, 1988.

Bond, Ruskin. "Coda to Nancy Keesing." *Hemisphere* XXIV. 2 (1980): 89.

——. "Looking for John Lang's Grave." *Blackwood's Magazine* CCCXI (1972): 237-242.

Carey, Peter. *Oscar and Lucinda.* St. Lucia: U of Queensland P, 1988.

Carter, Paul. *The Road to Botany Bay: An Essay in Spatial History.* London: Faber & Faber, 1987.

Chatwin, Bruce. *The Songlines.* London: Vintage, 1987.

Davidson, Robyn. *Tracks.* London: Jonathan Cape, 1980.

Department of Veterans' Affairs, Australian Government. "The Galli poli Cam paign." 25 April 2007 <http://www.dva.gov.au/commem/commac/studies/anzacsk/aday4.htm#cas>.

Desai, Anita. *Baumgartner's Bombay.* 1987. London: William Heinemann, 1988.

Facey, A. B. *A Fortunate Life.* Perth: Fremantle Arts P, 1981.

Garner, Helen. "The Life of Art." The Australian Literary Magazine 6-7 July 1985: 1.

——. *The Children's Bach.* Melbourne: McPhee Gribble, 1984.

Grenville, Kate. *Joan Makes History.* St. Lucia: U of Queensland P, 1988

Hospital, Janette Turner. *Borderline.* Sydney: Hodder & Stoughton, 1985.

Hughes, Robert. *The Fatal Shore.* London: Collins Harvill, 1986

James, Clive. *Falling Towards England: Unreliable Memoirs II.* London: Jonathan Cape, 1985

Johnson, Tim. "Love and the Wind." *Creating Australia: 200 Years of Art 1788-1988.* Ed. Daniel Thomas. Adelaide: Art Gallery of South Australia, 1988. 222-223.

Jolley, Elizabeth. *The Well.* Ringwood, Victoria: Viking, 1986.

Keneally, Tom. *The Playmaker.* 1987. Sevenoaks, Kent: Sceptre, 1988.

Langford, Ruby. *Don't Take Your Love to Town.* Ringwood, Victoria: Penguin, 1988.

Macaulay, Vincent, et al. "Single, Rapid Coastal Settlement of Asia Revealed by Analysis of Com plete Mitochondrial Genomes." *Science* 308.5724 (13 May 2005): 1034-1036.

Malouf, David. *12 Edmonstone Street.* London: Chatto & Windus, 1985.

Matthews, Brian. *Louisa.* Melbourne: McPhee Gribble, 1987.

Moorhouse, Frank. *Room Service.* Ringwood, Victoria: Penguin, 1987.

Morgan, Sally. *My Place.* Fremantle, WA: Fremantle Arts Centre P, 1987.

Mudrooroo [Colin Johnson]. *Doctor Wooreddy's Prescription for Enduring the Ending of the World.* Melbourne: Hyland House, 1983.

Muecke, Stephen, Paddy Roe, and Tim Benterrak. *Reading the Country: Introduction to Nomadology.* Fremantle, WA: Fremantle Arts Centre P, 1984.

Murnane, Gerald. *Inland.* Richmond, Victoria: William Heinemann, 1988.

Murray, Les, ed. *The New Oxford Book of Australian Verse.* Melbourne: Oxford UP, 1986.

Spender, Dale, ed. *The Penguin Anthology of Australian Women's Writing.* Ringwood, Victoria: Penguin, 1988.

Stanley, Peter. "Australia, India and Gallipoli: A Study in Contrasting National Consequences." Unpublished paper.

——. *Quinn's Post, Anzac, Gallipoli.* Sydney: Allen & Unwin, 2005.

Statistics of the Military Effort of the British Empire During the Great War. London: War Office, 1920.

Thomas, Daniel, ed. *Creating Australia: 200 Years of Art 1788-1988.* Adelaide: Art Gallery of South Australia, 1988.

White, Patrick. *Riders in the Chariot.* London: Eyre & Spottiswoode, 1961.

——. *Voss.* London: Eyre & Spottiswoode, 1957.

Winton, Tim. *That Eye, the Sky.* Melbourne: McPhee Gribble, 1986.

CONTRIBUTORS

Alessandra Senzani is a pursuing PhD in Comparative Studies at Florida Atlantic University, Boca Raton, USA. Her research focuses on representations of ethnic and class identities and the role of humor in negotiating the discourses that define them. She has published articles on Italian-American literature and film and presented her work at international conferences.

Amit Sarwal is currently pursuing PhD at the Centre for English Studies, School of Language, Literature and Culture Studies, Jawaharlal Nehru University, New Delhi. From 2006-2007 he was also a Honorary Visiting Scholar at the School of Political and Social Inquiry, Monash University, Australia as an Endeavour Asia Award winner. His current area of study is South Asian Diasporic Short Stories from the Pacific. His areas of interest include Contemporary Australian Literature, Translation Studies and Indian Cinema: Theory and Practice on which he has published. He has co-edited *English Studies, Indian Perspectives* (2006) and *Australian Studies Now* (2007).

Aneeta Rajendran is a doctoral research scholar at the Centre for English Studies, School of Language, Literature and Culture Studies, Jawaharlal Nehru University, New Delhi. She is pursuing research on Indian Lesbian writing. She has co-edited *English Studies, Indian Perspectives* (2006).

Beverley Curran is Associate Professor in the Department of Creativity and Culture (Multicultural Studies) at Aichi Shukutoku University in Nagoya, Japan, where she teaches classes in linguistic, cultural, and media translation. She is currently working on a study of theatre translation theory and performance in contemporary Japan.

Carol Hetherington is currently employed as Content Manager of the database *AustLit: The Resource for Australian Literature* and as an editorial assistant for *Australian Literary Studies.* She has worked for many years as a research assistant and bibliographer with the English Department at the University of Queensland, and as a librarian in the Fryer Library of Australian Literature, University of Queensland. As well as the crime fiction of Arthur Upfield, she is interested in the American publication of Australian Literature.

Chandani Lokuge is the Director of Centre for Postcolonial Writing and Coordinator, Creative Writing, Faculty of Arts, Monash University, Australia. She is also the Commissioning Editor, *Oxford Classics Reissue Series* on Indian Women's Autobiography and Fiction, and Consulting Editor, *Empire On-Line* (London: Adam Matthew Publications). She is the author of *Turtle Nest: A Novel (2003), If the moon smiled: A Novel (2000), which was* shortlisted for *NSW Premier's Award* 2001 in the Best Book, and Community Relations categories, *Moth and Other Stories (1994).*

Dunya Lindsey is currently a doctoral research scholar in the School of English, Communications and Performance Studies at Monash University, Australia. She is a 2006 Norman McGann Summer Scholar at the National Library of Australia. She has published articles in national and international journals of repute. Her thesis examines Irish convict writings and their appropriation and re-writing in Australian historical fiction.

Gunjeet Aurora is a doctoral research scholar at the Centre for English Studies, School of Language, Literature and Culture Studies, Jawaharlal Nehru University, New Delhi. She is pursuing research on Literature produced during the Indian Emergency in 1975.

Igor Maver is Professor of English at the Department of English, Faculty of Arts, University of Ljubljana, Slovenia, EU, where he holds a personal Chair in Literatures in English. He teaches English medieval literature, Canadian literature, Australian literature, early 20th century American novel and William Shakespeare's Drama. He has attended, presented papers, and organized numerous national and international congresses and conferences, and also served on the executive boards of various international and Slovene associations. He has published almost two hundred scholarly articles in various books, conference proceedings and international journals. He is also the author of two monographs in English on Australian literature (1997 and 1999) and co-author of two books of essays (2000 and 2005). In 2006 he published a book of essays *Critics and Writers Speak: Revisioning Post-Colonial Studies.* He has a special research and teaching interest in the literatures in English, Post-colonial, Diasporic literatures, and American literature.

Isabelle Bénigno holds a DEA in Cultures and Civilisations of the Commonwealth from the University of Saint-Etienne. She has just com pleted her Doctoral thesis on the Representation of Aborigines in Australian literature. She is presently doing field work on multiculturalism and hybridity in postcolonial societies.

J. V. D'Cruz is an Adjunct Professor in Australia-Asia Relations at Monash Asia Institute, Monash University. He has researched and published widely in a number of areas, as series editor of multi-volume publications in the areas of Education and in the areas of Language, Linguistics and Literature; with some 16 authored and edited volumes to his credit in areas such as politics, philosophy, education and culture, and some 16 chapters in books. An expression of his current multi-disci plinary research can be found in a volume published in 2003 by Monash Asia Institute titled *Australia's Ambivalence Towards Asia: Politics, Neo/Post-colonialism, and Fact/Fiction.*

Jean-François Vernay holds a PhD from the Université Toulouse-Le Mirail, France. It wa his French-Australian background that led him to take a vested interest in Australian fiction. His doctoral thesis was on the works of Christopher J. Koch. As Founding Editor of *Correspondances Océaniennes,* a Nouméa-based postcolonial journal focussing on Oceanic cultures, he has been editing articles on postcolonial societies for five years, while regularly publishing articles in national and international refereed journals and collections. He is the author of a monograph entitled *Water From the Moon: Illusion and Reality in the Works of Australian Novelist Christopher Koch* (2006).

Jonathan Highfield is Associate Professor of English at Rhode Island School of Design. He has published articles in various national and international journals of repute. He is also the co-editor of *The State of the Art(s): African Studies and American Studies in Com parative Perspective* (2006).
Krishna Barua is Associate Professor in the Deparrtment of Humanities & Social Sciences, Indian Institute of Technology-Guwahati. Her PhD

on Patrick White (1986) was one of the pioneering works on Commonwealth Literature. She has published extensively on Australian Studies both in India and abroad. Her area of study includes Comparative Literature, Cultural Studies and Translation.

Lisa Slater is a Lecturer at the Koori Centre, University of Sydney. She has articles published in *Cultural Studies Review, Meanjin, Journal of Commonwealth Literature* and *Southerly.* Her latest research project is examining Indigenous Cultural Festivals as direct cultural-political responses to the unresolved issues of colonisation and as forces for democratic change.

Malathy Anandavalli works as Lecturer in English at Indira Gandhi National Open University (IGNOU), New Delhi. She was awarded MPhil by the University of Nottingham, UK. She is currently working for a PhD in Australian studies from Centre for English Studies, School of Language, Literature and Culture Studies, Jawaharlal Nehru University, New Delhi. Her interests include research into the relevance of Indian critical theory for contemporary discourse, D. H. Lawrence studies, Australian fiction, Indian fiction in English and ecocriticism.

Marilyne Brun is a PhD research scholar at Université Toulouse 2 – Le Mirail, France and The University of Melbourne, Australia. She is currently working on Brian Castro's novels and is interested in issues of national identity, deconstruction and hybridity. Her PhD thesis is entitled "Resisting Categorisation: Hybridity in Brian Castro's Novels."

Mark Mckenna teaches in the Political Science Program RSSS at Australian National University. He is the author of *The Captive Republic. A History of Republicanism in Australia 1788-1996* (1996). He is currently writing a book on the politics of Australian history.

Nicholas Birns teaches in the Department of Humanities at New School University, specializing in nineteenth- and twentieth-century literature. He is editor of *Antipodes* and Secretary-Treasurer of the Council of Editors of Learned Journals. He is the author of *Understanding Anthony Powell* (2004) and *Companion to Twentieth-Century Literature Since 1900* (2007).

Patrick West is a Senior Lecturer in Writing in the School of Arts at Griffith University. His research interests include Australian and New Zealand Literature, Feminist Psychoanalysis, Screen Studies and Adaptation. He is co-editor of the forthcoming *M/C Journal* issue "Adapt" and is working on a monograph on screen product and time. He has published articles in various national and international journals. He is also a widely published and awarded short story writer.

Phillip A. Ellis is an external student at the University of New England, Armidale. His interests include bibliographical research, and the study of contemporary poetics. He is currently engaged in working on bibliographies of Brennan and Les Murray, and a concordance of Brennan's poetry as well.

Reema Sarwal is pursuing a PhD on Contemporary Australian Fantasy Fiction at the Centre for English Studies, School of Language, Literature and Culture Studies, Jawaharlal Nehru University, New Delhi, India. From 2006-2007 she was also a Honorary Visiting Scholar at the School of English, Communication and Performance Studies, Monash University, Australia. Her areas of interest include Contemporary Australian Literature, Popular Fiction, Translation Studies and African Literature on which she has published. She is also working as an Annotator on *Routledge Annotated Bibliography of English Studies.*

Richard Nile is the foundation Professor of Australian Studies (since 2000) and the Director of the Australia Research Institute at Curtin University. His previous appointments have been as Deputy Head of the Menzies Centre at the University of London (1989-1992) and Director of the Australian Studies Centre at the University of Queensland (1993-2000, in addition to lecturing appointments at the Universities of New South Wales and Western Australia. The foundation Director of Australian Studies in Hungary (1990-1992), Richard Nile was the University of Copenhagen's 2007 Distinguished Visiting Professor of Australian Studies. He is currently working on a history of the novel in Australia.

Richard Hosking is a Senior Lecturer in English and Australian Studies at the Department of English, School of Humanities, Flinders University. His areas of expertise includes Australian literature, creative writing, contact history, South Australian studies, South Australia,

Australian studies, and writing. He is the co-editor of *Fatal Collisions: The South Australian Frontier and the Violence of Memory*, (2000), which won the Historical Society of South Australia John Tregenza Award for National Community History.

Salhia Ben-Messahel currently holds a position of Senior Lecturer of English at the Université Charles-de-Gaulle Lille 3, France. She is the author of *Mind The Country, Tim Winton's Fiction* (2006), the first book-length critical study of one of Australia's major authors. She is currently working on the publication of conference papers as a book on "intercultural issues" in areas ranging from literature, linguistics, culture, history and economics, with the University Press of Lille 3.

Sharyn Pearce is currently a Teaching Fellow in the Faculty of Creative Industries at the Queensland University of Technology in Brisbane. She has published extensively in Australian Studies and, most particularly, Children's/Youth Writing. She has contributed to a range of national and international journals. Her co-edited collection of scholarly essays, *Youth Cultures: Texts, Images and Identities* (2003) was an International Research Society for Children's Literature Honour Book in 2003. Her other books include *Shameless Scribblers: Australian Women's Journalism, 1885-1995* (1997) and *Strange Journeys: the Works of Gary Crew* (1998).

William Steele is an Honorary Research Associate with the Monash Asia Institute, Monash University. He has completed Masters degrees in German linguistics and taxation studies and teaches and researches in the Department of Communication, Languages and Cultural Studies, Victoria University. He is the co-author of *Australia's Ambivalence Towards Asia: Politics, Neo/Post-colonialism, and Fact/Fiction* (2003).

INDEX